Hume's Philosophic

Hume's Philosophical Politics

DUNCAN FORBES

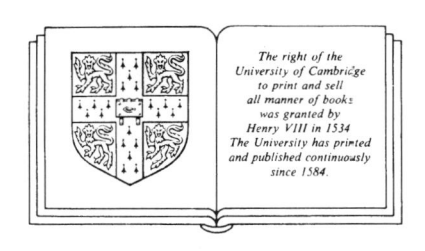

CAMBRIDGE UNIVERSITY PRESS

CAMBRIDGE
LONDON   NEW YORK   NEW ROCHELLE
MELBOURNE   SYDNEY

CAMBRIDGE UNIVERSITY PRESS
Cambridge, New York, Melbourne, Madrid, Cape Town, Singapore,
São Paulo, Delhi, Dubai, Tokyo

Cambridge University Press
The Edinburgh Building, Cambridge CB2 8RU, UK

Published in the United States of America by Cambridge University Press, New York

www.cambridge.org
Information on this title: www.cambridge.org/9780521319973

© Cambridge University Press 1975

This publication is in copyright. Subject to statutory exception
and to the provisions of relevant collective licensing agreements,
no reproduction of any part may take place without the written
permission of Cambridge University Press.

First published 1975
Reprinted 1978
First paperback edition 1985
Re-issued in this digitally printed version 2010

A catalogue record for this publication is available from the British Library

Library of Congress Catalogue Card Number: 75–9282

ISBN 978-0-521-20754-6 Hardback
ISBN 978-0-521-31997-3 Paperback

Cambridge University Press has no responsibility for the persistence or
accuracy of URLs for external or third-party internet websites referred to in
this publication, and does not guarantee that any content on such websites is,
or will remain, accurate or appropriate.

Contents

Introductory Preface		vii
Abbreviations		xiii

I. The Foundations of Politics

1	The experimental method in morals: the natural law forerunners	3
2	A modern theory of Natural Law	59
3	Political obligation for 'moderate men'	91
4	Social experience and the uniformity of human nature	102

II. Philosophical Politics

5	Scientific and vulgar Whiggism	125
6	Applied philosophy, genuine and false: Hume and the Court and Country parties in 1741–2	193
7	The primacy of political institutions	224

III. Philosophical History

8	*The History of England*: philosophical history as establishment history	233
	(i) Ancient constitutionalism: Rapin, Bolingbroke, the government journalists, Lyttleton, Blackstone, Guthrie, Hurd	233
	(ii) The philosophical revision of ancient constitutionalism	260
9	The limits of philosophical history	308
Appendix		324
Bibliography		327
Index		329

Introductory Preface

[handwritten annotation: Political intentions & the historical context]

This is not an exposition, analysis and critique of Hume's political philosophy as such. That is why it is not called 'Hume's Political Philosophy'. Nor is it a comprehensive and exhaustive study of every aspect of Hume's political science as such. That is why I abandoned the title originally chosen: 'Hume's Science of Politics', reluctantly, as 'science of politics' was contemporary usage, because for one thing, Hume's science of politics included economics; that was a very large and important part of it indeed, and full-scale, serious study of that should be left to economists, just as full-scale serious study of his political philosophy, which would involve Hume's ethics, an extremely controversial subject, is best left to philosophers. 'Hume's Philosophical Politics', however, describes what I have tried to do better than any other title I can think of. It is presumed to have a slightly archaic, essentially eighteenth-century sound, for this is <u>a study of Hume's thinking on politics in the light of his political intentions and the historical context:</u> the emphasis is on *historical*.

This is not where political theorists who write about past thinkers are inclined to put the emphasis; they are not primarily historians, and they probably have little inkling of the enormous hinterland which is beyond their horizon. This no doubt explains the enviable ease and confidence with which they handle their predecessors (Hume has been handled less than some in this way because he is not usually considered to belong to the first league of great political thinkers, and until quite recently there was a notable dearth of full-scale studies of this aspect of his thought).

This anti-historical attitude, if that is not too strong a word for what is really an indifference to and failure to appreciate the sheer thickness and complexity of the texture of the past – it is a question of degree, may be a good thing in its own sphere, but this is not the place to make out such a case. On the contrary the historian proper, who has his own task and peculiar sensibility, may even venture, and risk a snub, to suggest the paradox that a past thinker cannot be made relevant, or be seen as 'alive and frondent for us', to use Carlyle's expression, unless the historical minutiæ, that, as such, are wholly irrelevant, are made most thoroughly one's own and properly understood in all their detail and bearings, as far as this is possible. Obviously if a past political thinker is to be made relevant to us, all sorts of adjustments have to be made, and allowances for the times he lived in, and the special needs of the times as he saw them. But how can one make the adjustments and allowances adequately unless one knows very precisely and comprehensively what to adjust and allow for? And reading even quite a lot of modern historians and textbooks will not necessarily give one that ability: indeed, if one confines oneself to the most modern ones, one may be led most seriously astray. Historians of ideas have to do their own history, and the fact that so many of them do not, is why other professional historians call their subject 'marshy'.[1]

The principles of warfare, it seems, remain much the same; but if one is to learn from the study of an old battle or campaign, one must recreate its every detail with the utmost care and precision, no matter that the uniform, weapons, formations and tactics are wholly outmoded and 'irrelevant'. Failure to account for any of these 'irrelevant' matters may make a useless nonsense of the whole. How many 'historians' of political thought are in love with their subjects in the way in which even a novelist like C. S. Forrester, for example, was in love with the ships and naval tactics of the Napoleonic era? Do we make ourselves equally expert in the spars and rigging and scientific manuals of the old controversies, so that we could, as it were, sail any of those old ships with equal skill ourselves? Most of us would probably be sunk by the lightest pamphleteer.

Leaving aside the political theorists who do their history in the manner of a military expert re-fighting the battle of Waterloo on a flat and featureless table – and perhaps one can get something out of that, but just what is for others to determine – those who make a more genuinely historical effort, perhaps in order to win the relevance which is denied them otherwise, face formidable difficulties of interpretation. Hume is terrible campaign country, rugged, broken, cross-grained, complex, remorseless in its demands. One has to fight every inch of the way, and can never feel really secure. No interpretation ever seems to get going before it is pulled up almost immediately by some difficulty. The more of his writings one takes into account, the less confident one feels

[1] See, for instance, Sir Herbert Butterfield's Preface to *Man on his Past*.

that one can ever break through. This is the 'general impression' that one ought to get; but one will not get it by trying 'to get a general impression'. And this perhaps is the ultimate mystery of Hume's 'scepticism', which the devotees eventually attain to.

That the precision of his language does not match the precision of his thinking is a common complaint, but Hume is uniquely difficult to interpret because no other thinker probably covers so much ground and says so much with such economy. Since one cannot be sure at any given moment just what he is saying, it is necessary to cast the net as widely as possible, and this is one reason for carefully studying all the variants in the different editions. But then because significant juxtaposition is part of our art and because in Hume there are not only so many different pieces that can and must be moved about in the process of interpretation, but so many different contexts, one is open to the danger of linking things together that really belong apart, using A to explain B when it does not really do so. No other thinker is such a challenge to one's intellectual honesty; and if an interpretation can be too clever,[1] it cannot be too honest, and it is much easier to be clever than honest in the history of ideas. It is one of the hazards of the trade. That is why I have deployed much quotation and reference, giving variants and dates, so that the reader can keep some sort of check on what is being demonstrated.

I have also deployed, and at some length, a great deal that does not belong to Hume's philosophical politics, some of it in Hume himself. This is in order to help define what is 'philosophical' in Hume's politics, by contrasting it with what is not. Generalized abridgement does not do this adequately. And if it looks like a mere display of learning, one might ponder an aspect of Hume's scepticism that is not much remarked on, because for most people Hume means a gadfly intelligence rather than a stock of learning:[2] viz: that if increasing knowledge is accompanied by increasing awareness of ignorance, and of the meaning of ignorance, then a display of learning can be also the sign – and the greater the learning, the larger the sign – that one knows that one does not know. Vulgar criticism of 'mere' learning is apt to forget this. It is also another aspect of a more truly historical approach to the history of political thought: an attempt to counter the tendency to rely

---

[1] *L'interpretazione non deve essere troppo intelligente.* Franco Amerio on Croce in *Introduzione allo Studio di G. B. Vico* (1947).

[2] But see, for example, the essay on the *Populousness of Ancient Nations*; and how many philosophers today could write a History of England, or part of one? The example of R. G. Collingwood shows that the question is not unfair.

INTRODUCTORY PREFACE

almost exclusively on internal lines of communication in the interpretation of a given thinker, which in Hume's case usually means trying to connect everything to his philosophy, as though he lived in a cocoon of his own spinning. One can display great ingenuity in this, but the question is: who is displaying the ingenuity? A historical interpretation will be more open-ended, generally more untidy, more tentative, with fewer tracks leading so obviously from A to B, from *this* in the philosophy (that is, the philosophy of the *Treatise* and *Enquiries*, which, incidentally, it is easy to generalize about with more verve than understanding) to *that* in the *Essays* or the *History*.

This does not mean that Hume's philosophical politics has to be presented as a formless mess. Viewed as an attempt to give the established, Hanoverian, regime a proper intellectual foundation, it falls fairly naturally into three main phases, which overlap only because Hume thought that the first part of his programme had been a failure, and had to be presented again in a different form. The *Treatise of Human Nature* was broken up and scattered about in essays, one of which (*Origin of Government*) was written as late as 1774. Otherwise the sequence is roughly chronological: a theory of political obligation; a science of politics; and a *History of England*: all three parts of a programme of political education for changed circumstances and new opportunities.

The term 'philosophical' changes its meaning, as will appear. It is a key eighteenth-century word, with many meanings and shades of meaning. In Hume it spreads out from an original sharp focus in a theory of association of ideas to attitudes less strictly defined, but the idea of philosophical politics provides an essential continuity in Hume's thought, which will be stressed in order to challenge and modify the commonly accepted notion that there was a significant development in a conservative direction. This is another reason why I have been free with variants and dates, not in order to dwell on change, but on the contrary to make the point as fairly as possible that in spite of it there was an essential continuity. The reader can see that if I put together and treat as one things that are twenty years apart, I am doing it consciously.

There is no standard edition of all Hume's works. I have used Selby-Bigge for the *Treatise*, *Enquiries* and *A Dialogue*. My edition of the *Essays* is an Edinburgh edition in two volumes of 1800. This has been collated with the Green and Grose edition of the *Essays*, and also, because Green and Grose do not have all the variants, with the editions published as revised and corrected by Hume himself. I have also used Rotwein's edition of Hume's *Writings on Economics*, and other editions at different times. But all references to the *Essays* are to the Oxford University Press edition of 1963: *Essays, Moral, Political and Literary*, because this is the most complete of the easily available editions. It has a number of important variants in the form of notes, though they are not dated, and it is not explained what they are. It does not have *A Dialogue*. Wherever possible I have tried to give an easily traceable reference without referring to the pages of this edition, but it is not possible to do this very often. It is true that most of the essays are not very long, but they are very full and they seem long when one wants to check a reference in a hurry. As for the *History of England*, I have explained my procedure with respect to it in an Appendix. With the exception of Hume's letters, I have modernized the spelling, use of capitals etc of the old texts, but not absolutely consistently, and I have quoted from translations of Grotius, Pufendorf and the other theorists of Natural Law, giving the sort of references which can be checked easily enough with the originals, if anyone wishes to do so. These translations are contemporary, but that is an advantage.

Some years ago I wrote a general study of the eighteenth-century Scottish thinkers, which began with Hume, the idea being to bring out the differences between Hume and the others, and between the others themselves, and this was done, and the whole thing given some sort of thematic unity, by showing how the idea of social progress meant different things in all of them, when it was seen in the light of their respective systems, the differences being at times a matter of subtle nuance. I called this 'The Progress of Society': that seemed to be the central and characteristic idea of the Scottish Enlightenment. Some of this had already formed part of a Special Subject at Cambridge on the Scottish Englightenment – though in fact I was not allowed to call it that, because in those days the Scottish Enlightenment was still a somewhat backwoods kind of affair: it had to be 'Hume, Smith and the Scottish Enlightenment'.

'The Progress of Society' will, I hope, see the light of day, though not in its original form, because for one thing, the Hume section has been removed and made to stand on its own feet. Something of this interpretation of Hume has appeared very briefly already, without the necessary apparatus and references, and under different conditions, in a review article of Giarrizzo's *David Hume, politico e storico* in the *Historical Journal* (1963), and in

INTRODUCTORY PREFACE

my Introduction to the *Pelican Classics* edition of the first (1754) volume of Hume's *History: the History of Great Britain, Volume One, containing the reigns of James I and Charles I*. I do not agree with Giarrizzo's interpretation, but I found it extremely helpful at a critical stage of my own campaign. The reader will see that I owe debts all round, especially to the philosophers. And, of course, to the staffs of libraries and other institutions, especially the National Library of Scotland, Edinburgh University Library, the Signet Library, New College Library, the Central Public Library, the Register House, the Speculative Society, the Royal Society – all of Edinburgh, the Bodleian, the University Library and the Library of King's College, Cambridge.

NOTE ON THE 1978 PRINTING

I have taken the opportunity provided by a reprinting to correct as many misprints and minor errors as I have been able to find. But I have not been able to rectify other mistakes that I have become conscious of, as, for example, that the so-called letter to Dr Cheyne was quite likely written to Arbuthnot, as Mossner has argued, or that the *Craftsman* had ceased by 1740 to be an opposition journal, or that my reference to Domat is not helpful as it stands. The reader can decide how important such things are, and will no doubt discover other weaknesses of this sort that I have missed.

D.F.

Abbreviations

Treatise	Hume's *Treatise of Human Nature*. ed. Selby-Bigge.
Enquiry or *Enquiry concerning Morals*	Hume's *Enquiry concerning the Principles of Morals*. ed. Selby-Bigge. 2nd ed, Oxford, 1902.
Letters	*The Letters of David Hume*. ed. J. Y. T. Greig. 2 Vols, Oxford, 1932.
New Letters	*New Letters of David Hume*. ed. R. Klibansky and E. C. Mossner, Oxford, 1954.
Essays	*Essays Moral, Political and Literary* by David Hume (O.U.P. 1963). Any page reference number after the title of an essay refers to this edition.
History	Hume's *History of England*, London, 1808–10, 10 Vols.
Pelican Classics	Hume's *History of Great Britain containing the reigns of James I and Charles I*. (Pelican classics, 1970, ed. Duncan Forbes.)

I The Foundations of Politics

I
The experimental method in morals: the Natural Law forerunners

One of the more important and characteristic aspects of the rehabilitation of Hume's philosophy in the twentieth century has been the recognition of the importance of the sub-title of the *Treatise of Human Nature*: 'being an attempt to introduce the experimental method of reasoning into moral subjects'. The 'Newtonian' aspect of Hume's science of man has by now long been taken for granted, and has become one of the many fossils in the history of ideas, firmly embedded in the pages of text books and general histories, and accepted uncritically by the commentators: until recently no one has tried to investigate thoroughly what it means. There was nothing very original in the programme of the now only too well-known subtitle as such – after all, the argument from design was regarded as precisely that – and it was in fact the basis of the Natural Law theory which Hume is so often said to have destroyed. The fact is brought home by a useful coincidence.

In the year after the publication of the first two volumes of the *Treatise*, the year of the publication of Part III (1740), George Turnbull produced his *Principles of Moral Philosophy, An Enquiry into the wise and good government of the Moral World*, in which his aim was to 'vindicate' human nature, 'by reducing the more remarkable appearances in the human system' to 'general laws', treating them as questions of fact or natural history, in which hypotheses assumed at random and by caprice, or not sufficiently confirmed by experience, are never to be built upon (*Principles*, ii, iv). Moral philosophy, like natural philosophy, is not just a system of facts discovered by experiment and observation, but a mixture of experiments with reasonings from experiments – anything else is 'mere' hypothesis (19, 20, 22). The reader is referred to the *Principia* and Cotes' Preface. Next year appeared Turnbull's annotated translation of one of the standard text-books of natural jurisprudence – Heineccius' *Methodical System of Universal Law* – and appended to it, a discourse by Turnbull on the nature and origin of moral and civil laws, 'in which they are deduced by an analysis of the human mind in the experimental way, from our internal principles and dispositions'. In the Preface to the *Methodical System*, the discourse is described as 'an attempt to introduce the experimental way of reasoning into morals, or to deduce human duties from internal principles and dispositions in the human mind': its object was to derive natural law, those laws of natural and universal obligation which in all well-regulated states constitute the sum and substance of what is called the civil laws (*Methodical System*, II, 322), from the frame and constitution of man and the connexions of things relative to him and his actions, which are a natural law to man, as unalterable as the laws of motion and gravity, which limit, fix or settle the effects of his behaviour and conduct, and which are laws to us in the same sense that the laws of motion are laws to human arts for the attainment of their ends, and all connexions of nature of whatever kind can only be learned from experience; this is too evident to be insisted on (247–53, 293). 'We reason from fact or experiment, and what we have maintained can only be refuted by shewing our analysis of the human mind not to be fact' (304). 'For we ought, as in physicks, so in morals, to reason from the real state, frame, constitution or circumstances of things' (150).

In spite of the claim made on his behalf by James McCosh, in *The Scottish Philosophy* (1875), that he was the first metaphysician of the Scottish, or indeed of any school, to announce unambiguously and categorically that we ought to proceed in the method of induction in investigating the human mind (99), Turnbull does not seem to have regarded his programme as especially original or even exclusively post-Newtonian, or post-Baconian. For in the Preface to his translation of Heineccius, having announced his intention of applying the experimental way of reasoning to moral subjects, he forthwith appeals to Cicero, who in his excellent treatise of laws told us long ago that this was the only valid method in ethics and jurisprudence. Cicero calls them laws of nature, because the obligation to them is founded in human nature; mankind are pointed and prompted to fulfil them by natural dispositions or principles in their minds (225). How an enquiry into human nature or natural philosophy ought to be carried on, we learn from Cicero *de Finibus*...(*Principles*, 10n).

McCosh says that in following this method, Turnbull claims to be superior to Pufendorf, Grotius and the older jurists (*op. cit.* 100), but this remark must be qualified, because it applies only in political philosophy, where it is certainly important. Turnbull insists that the only solid basis to build on here, as in physics, is induction from experiments, which means history and the instruction it affords as to the natural effects of various constitutions in different situations. (Domat he recommends as an excellent author: *Methodical System*, II, 312.) Turnbull is anxious to supplement and correct the views of Heineccius and the older jurists, particularly with respect to the rights and duties of magistrates and subjects, by taking into account the natural causes of government and their necessary operations and effects, 'a consideration of great moment overlooked by Grotius, Pufendorf and all the moral-system writers I have seen' (222): 'here, as well as in the moral world, effects may be with certainty inferred from their causes', that is, in the 'science of politics', and to be convinced of this, says Turnbull, one need only look into the political reasonings of any good writer on politics, Aristotle, Polybius or 'our own Harrington' (*Principles*, 201), for everything in moral or corporeal nature must have its natural course, its natural rise, progress and variations. And as to know the one is to be a natural philosopher, so to know the other is to be a moral philosopher or politician (*Methodical System*, II, 119). And indeed Turnbull's use of the experimental method to improve the political science of Grotius, Pufendorf and Heineccius consists almost wholly in the uncritical acceptance and application of the thesis, or rather 'laws', concerning the balance of property and power of Harrington, 'who reasons from natural causes in these matters as natural philosophers do about phenomena commonly called natural ones' (*id*, cf. 82), and who, Turnbull suggests elsewhere, was a Newtonian before Newton, in so far as he managed to reduce several great phenomena in the moral world to a few very simple laws or principles, even if he did not compare these with the laws of the material world – but natural philosophy has much improved since his time. (*Principles of Moral and Christian Philosophy*, i.e. Vol. II of *Principles*, London, 1741, Preface.)

This insistent appeal to 'our' Harrington, 'our excellent politician' (*Methodical System*, I, 295), is a criticism of the too exclusive use of the 'a priori' method of the 'older jurists' – Turnbull for example says that if they had attended more to the 'natural causes' of 'empire' or civil government, they would not have debated its origin so much (*id*, II, 145) – but the method of the older jurists was equally 'experimental', in so far as 'a priori' in this context means prior to experience of the observed effects, not prior to experience of the facts of human nature given to observation,[1] and

[1] Thus Kames, for example, arguing that property is founded in the Law of Nature, derives it 'a posteriori' from the growth of population, the need for industry etc,

in so far as the application of experimental method to morals meant, to use Turnbull's words, 'deducing human duties from the internal principles and dispositions in the human mind', this is what not just Cicero, but the whole school of modern natural law from Grotius onwards, to which Heineccius belonged, had done. The foundations of the science of jurisprudence were empirically established and confirmed in so far as the first principles of natural law were said to be certain obvious and undeniable facts of human nature which anyone could ascertain and confirm for himself by introspection and observation. This was what Grotius meant, or a large part of what he meant, when he said, arguing against Carneades as representative of those who altogether denied the existence of natural law, that the proof of it from man's social nature would have 'a degree of validity' even if God did not exist (*De Jure Belli ac Pacis*, Prolegomena § 11).[1] That is, even if one were to grant Carneades and his like the truth of such an absurd (and wicked) hypothesis, their denial of any such thing as justice and natural law would not square with the facts of human nature. As Barbeyrac pointed out in his note on this paragraph, Grotius' assertion is to be admitted only in the sense that the maxims of the law of nature are not merely arbitrary rules but are founded on the nature of things in the very constitution of man, from which certain relations result between such and such actions and the state of a reasonable and sociable creature. 'For the very nature of man, which even if we had no lack of anything, would lead us into the mutual relations of society, is the mother of the law of nature' (*De Jure*, Prolegomena, § 16). And Pufendorf began the main part of his book on the Law of Nature, after the preliminary definitions, by showing that man is an animal so made that he cannot live without society and therefore without law (Book II, Chap. 1: 'It is not agreeable to the nature of man that he should live without law'),[2] later pointing out that this is what is meant by saying that the law of nature is 'the dictate of right reason', viz: that 'the

---

but says that it is also founded 'a priori' in the nature of man and consequently in the original or 'abstract' laws of nature. *Essays upon several subjects in Law*, (Edinburgh, 1732), 100–1.

[1] I am quoting from the translation of the Prolegomena by F. H. Kelsey (The Liberal Arts Press, 1957), and the 1738 (London) edition of *The Rights of War and Peace*, with Barbeyrac's notes.

[2] Cf. Hume, *Enquiry concerning Morals*, Section 4, § 3. 'Human nature cannot, by any means, subsist without the association of individuals: and that association never could have place were no regard paid to the laws of equity and justice. Disorder, confusion, the war of all against all are the necessary consequences of such a licentious conduct.' I am using Basil Kennett's edition of *The Law of Nature and of Nations* of 1703 (Oxford).

understanding of man is endued with such a power as to be able from the contemplation of human condition, to discover a necessity of living agreeably to this law; as likewise to find out some principle by which the precepts of it may be clearly and solidly demonstrated'. This is what the Scriptures mean when they say that it is written in the hearts of men: not that the general principles of natural law are innate, because not everybody can apprehend 'the artificial method of demonstrating these natural precepts', and most men come to learn and observe them by custom and use in society ('the common course and tenour of living'), and to that extent they may be said to have a sociological origin in so far as Pufendorf explains how the ability to distinguish right and wrong is 'owing in a great measure to exercise and use', and is learnt like a language (see the *Whole Duty of Man according to the Law of Nature*, 55): from their earliest years children see certain things approved and disapproved and their minds become 'so fixed and disposed by daily practice and by the whole series of common life, that few of them so much as doubt whether they may not proceed by other methods'. But the principles of natural law or 'dictates of right reason' can be seen to be true principles which agree with 'the nature of things well observed and examined', when deduced by correct rules of reasoning from accurate observation. The phrase in *Romans* 11.15 means that, and is 'certainly figurative' (*Law of Nature*, Book II, Ch. III, XIII). And this presumably is what Locke meant by it.[1]

To the young Hume, who thought he had found the 'experimental' clue to the science of man and all the moral sciences,

---

[1] *The Second Treatise of Government* (Ed. P. Laslett), 292-3. It is not, as Laslett says in his note, the most conspicuous instance of Locke's willingness to take advantage of the belief in innate ideas and innate practical principles excoriated in Bk I of the *Essay concerning Human Understanding*. Cf. Hans Aarsleff in *John Locke: Problems and Perspectives* (Ed. J. W. Yolton, Cambridge, 1969), esp. pp. 129-31. Aarsleff does not mention Pufendorf in this connection, but Pufendorf was, of course, a standard author, recommended by Locke (*On Education*, § 186). It is worth noting that Viscount Stair, in his *Institutions of the Law of Scotland*, does hold what Yolton in *John Locke and the Way of Ideas* calls the 'naive' form of the doctrine. Stair's *Institutions*, 2nd ed. 1693. pp. 2-3: Like those instincts by which animals know what is necessary for their preservation, 'so the first principles of this natural law are known to men without reasoning or experience, without art, industry or education, and so are known to men everywhere...though they keep no communion or intercourse together, which is an unanswerable demonstration of the being of this law of nature. It is said to be written in the hearts of men, because law useth to be written on pillars or tables for certainty of conservation: so this law is written by the finger of God upon man's heart, there to remain for ever...With these common principles with which God hath sent men into the world, he gave them also reason', that they might be able to deduce his law in more particular cases.

including politics and criticism, in the principle of association of ideas, and was accordingly anxious to stress the novelty of his approach to the science of man, this grounding of natural law in human nature must have seemed rudimentary, scarcely an experimental science of man at all. Book III of the *Treatise*, in which the first version of Hume's political philosophy is to be found, was not designed to stand alone; together with the books on the Understanding and the Passions (for a study of the comparatively neglected Book II and its connexion with Book III, see P. S. Ardal, *Passion and Value in Hume's Treatise* (1966)) it is part of an attempt at a unified Newtonian system of the moral sciences with association as the ultimate explanatory principle.

In the Introduction to the *Treatise*, Hume says that 'some late philosophers in England' (the footnote refers to Locke, Shaftesbury, Mandeville, Hutchinson (*sic*), Butler etc.) have 'begun to put the science of man on a new footing'; that it is not surprising that it has taken 'above a whole century' for the experimental philosophy to be applied to moral subjects since the space of time between the 'late philosophers' and Bacon is 'nearly equal' to that between the origins of these sciences in Thales and the time of Socrates respectively. This is rather typically imprecise, but the implication seems to be that the putting of the science of man on its 'solid foundation' of 'experience and observation' is a fairly recent event. Hume's 'foundation' for 'a compleat system of the sciences', 'the only one upon which they can stand with any security', is 'almost entirely new'. (*Treatise*, xx . . . this surely is not meant to refer simply to his use of the principle of association.) The natural law writers are not included among the pioneers of the application of experimental method to moral subjects, presumably because at this time Hume's thinking was dominated by the importance of the science of man in its narrower, exclusively psychological sense; the writers he mentions – a mixed bag otherwise, and why for that matter does he not mention Hobbes?[1] – could all be regarded as having 'begun' a rather more intensive study of the human mind, and in addition they were all 'English', belonging to a land of liberty in which such speculation can flourish – a point Hume was anxious to make. So he does not mention the very acute psychology of Malebranche, which he must have known. (In the *Inquiry concerning the Principles of Morals*

---

[1] Dugald Stewart thought that Hobbes' writings on psychology were the only part of his works that could still be read with any interest: they had, he thought, plainly been studied with the utmost care by Locke and Hume. Dugald Stewart, *Collected Works*, I, 81.

he professed to regard Malebranche as having started the 'abstract theory of morals' afterwards adopted by Cudworth, Clarke and the ethical rationalists, (197n), a system that 'never will be reconciled with true philosophy'.)[1] And why not even Descartes, described by Dugald Stewart as the father of the experimental philosophy of the human mind? (*op. cit.* I, 113).

In the famous letter to Dr Cheyne, which is dated 1734, Hume made it clear that he did not agree with the view that the classical moralists had grounded their moral philosophy on a properly philosophical or Newtonian study of human nature. Having described his physical symptoms, he goes on to tell 'how my mind stood all this time... I began to consider seriously how I should proceed in my Philosophical Enquiries. I found that the moral Philosophy transmitted to us by Antiquity, labor'd under the same Inconvenience that has been found in their natural Philosophy, of being entirely Hypothetical, and depending more upon Invention than Experience. Every one consulted his Fancy in erecting schemes of Virtue and of Happiness, without regarding human Nature upon which every moral Conclusion must depend. This therefore I resolved to make my principal Study, and the Source from which I wou'd derive every Truth in Criticism as well as Morality' (*Letters*, I, 16).[2]

For an example of what Hume meant by deriving natural law from the principles of human nature, one can turn to the *Treatise* Book III, Part I, Section III, 'Of the rules which determine property', in which he applies his 'singular method of reasoning', (510n) in order to show the important role played by what he calls the 'imagination' (which for Hume means the principle or regular activity of the association of ideas), in determining the main rules

---

[1] The importance of Malebranche for Hume's philosophy is well enough known to those who do not take the narrow Locke–Berkeley–Hume approach to it. See, for example, C. W. Hendel, *Studies in the Philosophy of David Hume* (1925), 49 *et seq*, 82 *et seq*, R. W. Church, *Hume's theory of the Understanding* (1935, 80, 94–5, 171–2, 211). In a letter of August, 1737, Hume tells one of his friends to read 'le Recherche de la Verite de Pere Malebranche' [sic] (followed by Berkeley and Bayle) as a way of 'entering into' the *Treatise of Human Nature* 'more easily'. (Quoted in I. S. Ross, *Lord Kames and the Scotland of his Day* [Oxford, 1972], 76: it is not in *Letters* or *New Letters*.) A copy of *De la Récherche de la Vérité* with Hume's book-plate is in Edinburgh University Library. See the catalogue of the exhibition 'Benefactors of the Library in Five Centuries' (1963), item 132. There is more in this book that reminds one of Hume than most of the commentators, who are primarily concerned with causation, seem to realize, especially Malebranche's emphasis on men's psychological dependence on one another.

[2] Contrast Turnbull: 'no sooner had I conceived this idea of moral researches [i.e. following the Newtonian method] than I began to look carefully into the better ancients... to know their opinion of human nature', especially Plato. *Principles*, iii.

of natural jurisprudence as to the allocation of goods, viz: present possession, occupation, prescription, accession and succession. Since motives of public interest are also involved for most of the rules which determine property, and 'since no questions in philosophy [= natural philosophy] are more difficult, than when a number of causes present themselves for the same phenomenon, to determine which is the principal and predominant', Hume, though he suspects that 'these rules are principally fixed by the imagination', is going to explain their causes and leave it to the reader to decide whether public utility or the workings of the 'imagination' is the most important (504n). The principle of human nature involved is that very crucial one in Hume's philosophy, which makes a rigidly mechanistic interpretation of the principle of association inadequate: the tendency to generalize beyond the fragmentary and discontinuous evidence provided by the senses, to close the gaps in experience, which Price calls the 'inertia of the imagination':[1] the natural propensity of the mind to join two closely related objects still more closely by adding another relation: '... the mind has a natural propensity to join relations, especially resembling ones, and finds a kind of fitness and uniformity in such an union. From this propensity are derived these laws of nature, *that upon the first formation of society, property always follows the present possession*; and afterwards, *that it arises from first or from long possession*' (509n).[2]

[1] H. H. Price, *Hume's Theory of the External World* (1940).
[2] Cf. 504n: 'Since, therefore, we can feign a new relation and even an absurd one, in order to complete any union, [Hume says that the inclination is so strong as often to make us run into errors in order to complete the union], 'twill easily be imagined, that if there be any relations which depend on the mind, 'twill readily conjoin them to any preceding relation, and unite, by a new bond, such objects as have already an union in the fancy. Thus for instance we never fail in our arrangement of bodies, to place those which are *resembling* in *contiguity* to each other, or at least in *correspondent* points of view; because we feel a satisfaction in joining the relation of contiguity to that of resemblance, or the resemblance of situation to that of qualities'. What Price called the 'inertia of the imagination', or something similar, is to be found in Malebranche, *De la Recherche*. See Bk. III, Part II, Chapter x, for example. '...l'attention fatigue beaucoup l'esprit...l'esprit suppose donc des ressemblances imaginaires où il ne remarque pas les différences positives et réelles; les idées de ressemblance lui étant plus présentes, plus familières et plus simples que les autres...Les hommes s'imaginent donc que les choses de différente nature sont de même nature; et que toutes les choses de même espèce ne diffèrent presque point les unes des autres. Ils jugent que les choses inégales sont égales; que celles qui sont inconstantes sont constantes; et que celles qui sont sans ordre et sans proportion sont tres-ordonnées et tres-proportionneés. En un mot ils croyent souvent que des choses différentes en nature, en qualité, en étendue, en dureé et en proportion sont semblables en toutes ces choses...' Cf. Chapter XI: 'Cette facilité que l'esprit trouve à imaginer et à supposer des ressemblances partout où il ne reconnait pas

THE EXPERIMENTAL METHOD IN MORALS

Without any very prolonged examination of Hume's demonstration, which is detailed, with examples from Roman law and the civilians, and as usual extremely condensed, and also unique in the *Treatise* for the length of its footnotes – the chapter is nearly all footnotes, possibly due to Hume's belief, later expressed to Kames, that law and literature do not go together – one can see how he tries to show that the rules of natural jurisprudence concerning property are the 'effect of the relations of ideas and of the smooth transition of the imagination' (510n). Like a good experimental philosopher, Hume considers cases which seem to contradict his 'hypothesis'; he explains, for example, why, when the imagination passes more easily from little to great than from great to little, small objects become accessions to great ones, as the **Orkneys**, Hebrides and Isle of Man to Great Britain, and not vice versa, i.e. why authority over the former does not naturally imply any title to the latter. (If a great and a small object are related together and a person is strongly related to the great object, he will likewise be strongly related to both the objects considered together, because he is related to the most considerable part. But if he is only related to the small object, he will not be strongly related to both considered together, since his relation is only with the most trivial part, which is not apt to strike us in any great degree when we consider the whole. The objection is thus easily solved by a more careful consideration of the working of the 'imagination'.) The reason why it is 'the general opinion of philosophers and civilians' that the sea cannot be the property of any nation is that it is impossible to 'form any such distinct relation with it as may be the foundation of property'; 'friths and bays' on the other hand can be; not that they have any bond or union with the land any more than the Pacific Ocean would have, 'but having an union in the fancy, and being at the same time *inferior*, they are of course regarded as an accession'. Big rivers, like the Rhine or the Danube cannot, like small ones, belong to relatively small proprietors; they can be the property of the relatively much larger countries through which they flow. A portion of river bank dislodged does not become any one's property till it unites with the land, and till trees and plants have spread their roots into both – before that, 'the imagination does not sufficiently join them' (511n). The distinction in Roman law between 'confusion' and 'commixtion' is explained on the same principle; Hume quotes from the

visiblement de différences jette aussi la plupart des hommes dans les erreurs très dangereuses en matière de morale.'

11

"inertia of the imagination"
(Price)

THE FOUNDATIONS OF POLITICS

Institutes of Justinian (512n). Trebonian's decision of the dispute between Proculus and Sabinus as to the problem of who owns the ship made from the wood which is not the property of the shipbuilder, 'plainly depends upon the fancy' (513n).

As to succession, one of the natural causes is the fact that the dead person's children 'naturally present themselves to the mind; and being already connected to those possessions by means of the deceased parent, we are apt to connect them still farther by the relation of property' (512–13). Succession depends 'in a great measure' on the 'imagination', and Hume adds an example in which it does so entirely, because the public interest is not in the least concerned in the outcome (513n).[1]

Hume uses the same method in his account of political obligation in general and the right of resistance to oppressive government. Government is founded in the interest of the governed, and when the interest ceases, the natural obligation ceases also. But our moral obligation might be expected not to, owing to the inertia of the imagination, the fact 'which we have frequently taken notice of', that 'men are mightily addicted to general rules', and tend to carry their maxims beyond the reasons which first induced them to accept them. According to this principle of human nature, therefore, should not men be morally bound to accept and obey tyrannical rulers, against their own and the public interest? But further inquiry shows that although we seldom make any exception to general rules, we do if the exception has itself the quality of a general rule and is founded on numerous and common instances. And this is the case with unjust rulers. We expect men

[1] Kames used Hume's theory to explain succession in general and the rules of feudal succession in his *Essays upon several subjects concerning British Antiquities*, written in 1745 and published in 1747. Succession or descent, he said, depends mostly on remote principles of the imagination, showing, in a multitude of instances, how much we are governed by feelings, which, abstractly considered, appear to be of the weakest sort. That is why there are no universal rules of succession, although we are apt to think that they are now settled without fear of change. So no doubt did our ancestors, for "tis a common mistake, from any short specimen, to infer a constant uniformity' (123–4). There is a strong propensity in our nature to act by general rules, without regard to the variation of circumstances (141). (To change the law of entails was one of Kames' great objects of 'improvement'.) For an example of Kames' application of the 'law in our nature, that the connection among objects is ever to be considered to be in proportion to the facility of the transition of our ideas from the one to the other', see 152, 148 *et seq*: we more readily contemplate a future than a past object, our fancy 'flows along the stream of time', the mind finds a difficulty in mounting from inferior to superior objects etc. This explains Hume's remark in his letter to Kames about the *Essays on British Antiquities*: 'You do me the honour to borrow some principles from a certain book: but I wish they be not esteemed too subtle and abstruse' (*Letters*, I, 108).

12

to be unjust, because it is in order to get security against this that government is established: we change the situation, but not the nature of the men who are to be our magistrates, making it their immediate interest to rule justly. But from our experience of the irregularity of human nature we often expect them to neglect even their immediate interest and to be transported by their passions into all the excesses of cruelty and ambition. We therefore conclude that 'we may resist the more violent effects of supreme power, without any crime or injustice'; and the doctrine of passive obedience is seen to be unphilosophical. And the 'a priori' demonstration is confirmed 'a posteriori', because such resistance has never in fact been condemned by 'the general practice and principle of mankind' (550–2).

In Section x Hume applies the same technique to the rules or principles involved in the question of the legitimacy of particular governments: viz, long possession, present possession, conquest, succession and positive laws. The effect of custom, than which 'nothing turns the imagination more strongly to any object' (556), on which the title of long possession is grounded, depends on the length of time involved: 'one thinks he acquires a right to a horse, or a suit of clothes, in a very short time'; since in considering a kingdom the mind embraces a much longer duration, the right to a kingdom needs proportionately more time, because a small duration makes less of an impression or influence on our sentiments': 'a century is scarce sufficient to establish any new government, or remove all scruples in the minds of the subjects concerning it'. Also a shorter period of time will suffice to give an established ruler a title to any additional power he may usurp: the Kings of France have not been absolute for more than two reigns, 'yet nothing will appear more extravagant to Frenchmen than to talk of their liberties. If we consider what has been said concerning *accession*, we shall easily account for this phenomenon' (557).

The second source of all public authority, present possession, rests on the ease with which the mind joins the idea of the right to authority, which is 'nothing but the constant possession of authority maintained by the laws of society and the interests of mankind', with the present possession, 'according to the principles above mentioned'. In the case of private property these principles do not prevail, because they are counter-balanced by 'very strong considerations of interest'; all restitution would be prevented and every violence authorized and protected. In the case of public authority the same considerations of interest are opposed by a contrary interest: the preservation of peace, so that here the principles do prevail, that is, considerations of interest cancel each other, leaving the working of the imagination in possession of the field (557).

The right of conquest resembles that of present possession, but has a superior force owing to the notions of glory and honour ascribed to conquerors as opposed to the feelings of hatred for usurpers. Men naturally favour those they love and are more apt to ascribe a right to successful violence between one sovereign and another than to the successful rebel (558–9).

As for Succession, public interest is obviously involved, but here too 'there concur some principles of the imagination' to any one who considers the matter impartially. The royal authority seems to be connected with the heir even in his father's lifetime, and still more after his death, 'by the natural transition of the thought', so that 'nothing is more natural than to complete this union by a new relation', i.e. to give him the authority which seems to belong to him. 'To confirm this we may weigh the following phenomena, which are pretty curious in their kind'; the preference for members of the family of the late king in elective monarchies, so that in some, one of them is chosen to succeed, in others they are expressly excluded 'by a refinement in politics' which makes people sensible of their propensity and jealous of their liberty and the elective principle. These contrary phenomena proceed from the same principle. Cyrus who claimed the throne above his elder brother, because he was born after his father's accession, would never have made use of such a pretext were it not for the 'qualities of the imagination above mentioned, by which we are naturally inclined to unite by a new relation whatever objects we find already united' (559–60).

These examples are sufficient to show in what direction and how much further and more analytically than his predecessors Hume was concerned in the *Treatise* to carry the derivation of rights and duties from the principles of human nature. In particular one can see how much more sophisticated is Hume's derivation of prescription from human nature than that of his friend Kames, who had argued against the majority of natural law writers that prescription was not a matter of statute and municipal law exclusively, but belonged to natural law because it was grounded immediately on human nature (*Essays upon several subjects in Law* (1732), 100–9). Kames' argument rests on a peculiar affection for property which is said to be part of the constitution of the human mind, which becomes more pronounced with the progress of society, the growth of population and need for industry. When a man loses a prized possession, and when eventually his affection for it cools and vanishes and he 'loses entirely the consciousness of property', the connection between the man and the object is as thoroughly dissolved as if he had derelinquished it by the most positive act. The affection and consciousness upon which his property is founded ceases, and property ceases of consequence, and this holds *a fortiori* for his heirs. This is the natural basis of prescription, and compared with Hume's, it is a relatively simple analysis. What is more, Kames brings in final causes and providence, a Deity who has wisely implanted the affection for property in our natures, because man is an indigent being etc., – a penchant for which he later became notorious. Providence foresaw the need for appropriation and fitted us with affections and faculties leading to that end.

What particularly excited Hume's interest was the psychological ground of natural law in the working of the 'imagination'. But it is well known how Hume's early enthusiasm for a new system of the moral sciences based on the principle of association waned, and how the latter is recessive in the republication of his philosophy in the *Enquiries*, so that, for example, he retreated from the suggestive and original analysis of sympathy in the *Treatise* to the classical 'humanity' or 'fellow-feeling' of the *Enquiry* as the 'origin of morals'. In the first edition of the *Enquiry concerning the Principles of Morals* the long footnotes tracing the rules of property to the working of the imagination have disappeared. Instead of psychological analysis Hume points briefly to the reasonings of lawyers who have recourse to the slightest analogies (depending on 'very slight connexions of the imagination') where guidance from obvious utility is lacking (Section III, Part II, § 157). In the edition of 1753/4 the argument of the footnotes in the *Treatise* appears, in an abbreviated form, in one footnote in an appendix, which eventually became Appendix III. Also in the *Enquiry*, Hume makes a point of claiming that the writers on the law of nature, whatever principles they set out with, are really in agreement with his hypothesis, which derives justice from utility, a concession 'extorted in opposition to systems' (§ 156).

In some ways the general trend of Hume's thought helped to narrow the distance: his 'logic'[1] served to confirm the beliefs of

---

[1] Cf. W. Duncan, *The Elements of Logick* (1748): 'Logic may be justly stiled the history of the human mind in as much as it traces the progress of our knowledge from our first and simple perceptions' (4).

the vulgar consciousness and dish the philosophers who tried to explain them rationally, while the application of experimental method to moral subjects was very soon seen to be an impossibility, at least in any sense more properly scientific and Newtonian than the procedures of Hutcheson, Pufendorf or for that matter Cicero.[1] Even in the *Treatise*, Hume's experimental method, considered purely as method, as one can see from the examples given earlier, did not really attempt to – it could not – keep up with the stricter usage of the word which set in between Galileo, who used 'thought experiments', and Newton and Boyle.[2] As Dugald Stewart said, Hume had no very correct idea of the manner in which the experimental mode of reasoning ought to be applied to moral subjects (*Collected Works*, I, 456). It was not his more elaborate involvement in psychology, on the originality and importance of which he initially prided himself, which made his science of man more genuinely empirical.

It is being assumed here that anyone who asserts that Hume destroyed the foundations of natural law, which was once, and may still be, quite a common saying, knows precisely where he stands: either insisting that any theory of natural law must have a supernatural foundation, that otherwise it is impossible or meaningless, or employing quasi-historical rhetoric for some purpose which has nothing to do with the attempt to discover 'how it really was', because for that, it is not a very helpful generalization. Natural law theory was not one of Hume's targets, except in so far as it shared the abstract rationalism of those who derived morality from eternal fitnesses and unfitnesses, supposing all right to be founded on certain *rapports* or relations, a theory which Montesquieu 'sets out with' (*Enquiry*, 197n). But the natural jurisprudence taught in the Scottish universities was not like this: it was moralists like Cudworth, Samuel Clarke and Wollaston who bore the brunt of Hume's criticism. They correspond to the philosophers of Book I of the *Treatise* who are shown as straining rational explanation to breaking point in trying to resolve the difficulties of the reflective consciousness by the use of reason, instead of methodizing and correcting the beliefs of the vulgar consciousness;[3] and Grotius had described the principles of natural law as almost as evident as the things which we perceive

[1] See James Noxon, *Hume's Philosophical Development* (1973).
[2] In his *Elements of Logick*, Duncan says that perception or thinking and volition or willing, are what every man 'experiments in himself' (23). 'We also experiment in ourselves thinking and volition' (35).
[3] Cf. *Treatise*, 569: 'the practice of the world goes farther in teaching us the degrees of

by the external senses, which do not err if the organs of perception are properly formed (*De Jure*, Prolegomena § 39), and Pufendorf had said that the truth of its first principle is clear to us from daily experience (*Law of Nature*, Book II, Ch. III, § XIV, 108), and its general and most useful points so plain and clear that at first sight they force the assent (*Whole Duty*, 55). Natural law at least could be methodized and corrected; nothing positive could be done with the 'subtle' philosophy of the rationalists.

It is the well-known thesis of Norman Kemp Smith that Hume wrote the *Treatise* backwards, beginning with morals. Since natural jurisprudence played such an important role in morals, especially in Scotland, where the impression produced by Grotius and Pufendorf was especially remarkable (Dugald Stewart, *Collected Works*, 1, 26-7, 93),[1] perhaps one can make one more contribution to the problem of 'Hume's intentions' by suggesting that the two main currents of advanced speculation in Scotland at that time: natural law teaching and Newtonian or Baconian experimental science came together, and allied to Hume's religious scepticism, produced his famous 'new scene of thought', and one aspect of this was a modern theory of natural law. Keeping in reserve for the moment the religious scepticism which made Hume's experimental method more Newtonian, more truly experimental, in theory at least, from a modern point of view, than that of the Newtonians, it is worth looking at the route to his thought provided by Grotius and his successors, which is not one of the more familiar routes, no doubt because it is the driest and dustiest and the most completely forgotten, except for specialists, and perhaps because Hume is so often thought to have turned his back on it so completely. But no threads are ever cleanly snapped in the history of ideas, and it would be very strange if there were no significant links or affinities between Hume and the natural law writers of the school of Grotius and Pufendorf, systems which, as Dugald Stewart said, with revealing exaggeration and emphasis, for a hundred and fifty years engrossed all the learned industry of the most enlightened part of Europe and were destined to prepare the way for that never to be forgotten change in the literary taste of the eighteenth century, which has turned the spirit of philosophical inquiry from frivolous and abstruse speculations to the

our duty, than the most subtle philosophy, which was ever yet invented.' Cf. *Enquiry*, Section I, § 134, Section IX, § 217.

[1] Dugald Stewart criticized natural law with great severity and said that it was now useless, but he also said that it constituted the first rudiments of pure ethics and of liberal politics taught in modern times, grafted on to the parent stock of Roman law.

business and affairs of men (*op. cit.*, 26–7 – part of this is a quotation from William Robertson).¹

As has been seen, for Grotius natural law is derived from and proved by the undeniable fact that man is a social being. This he calls deriving or proving it *a priori*, 'from the very nature of the thing', meaning its agreement or necessary relation of fitness or unfitness with a reasonable and sociable nature, i.e., with certain fundamental conceptions which no one can deny without doing violence to himself, which are 'reinforced' by considerations of expediency, because to obey the natural law is in man's best interests. (This is not the doctrine of 'relations' criticized by Hume as incompatible with true philosophy, which as far as he knew, originated with Malebranche.) In addition to 'these essential traits planted in man', Grotius availed himself of the testimony of philosophers, historians, poets and orators when in universal agreement, and of what has generally been believed by all, or at least the most civilized nations – and this he called *a posteriori* and regarded as the more popular method, less subtle and abstract than the first (*De Jure*, Prolegomena, § 40, Book I, Ch. 1, § XII). This was the approach which Grotius seems to have been usually regarded as having made peculiarly his own: he was to be much criticized for relying so heavily on his massive mobilization of authorities. At the same time he was criticized for holding a theory of the inherent rightness or wrongness of the actions which were the object of natural law, which Pufendorf regarded as a circular argument (*Law of Nature*, Book II, Ch. III, § IV, 95).²

According to Cumberland (the edition of his *Treatise of the Laws of Nature* referred to is the translation by John Maxwell, London, 1727), the laws of nature, which are 'the foundation of all moral and civil knowledge' (*op. cit.*, 10) could be deduced in two ways: either 'from the manifest effects which flow from them', or 'from the causes whence they themselves arise'. He described the first as

---

1 What follows is a brief sketch of a few of the more important of these systems from a particular point of view. I know of no thorough, comprehensive, historical study of them. This route to Hume has the additional advantage of avoiding serious entanglement in the political philosophies of either Hobbes or Locke, discussion of which would inevitably become discussion of the views of x, y and z as to how they ought to be interpreted.

2 The criticism does not seem to be just. Perhaps confusion was caused by the tendency noted by Rachael Kydd for Grotius and other seventeenth-century moralists to refer to moral propositions as necessarily true and eternal even when derived entirely from the nature and condition of man (R. M. Kydd, *Reason and Conduct in Hume's Treatise*, [Oxford, 1946], 8–15).

that of Grotius: it was valid, because given the likeness of human nature, it was not impossible to say from the study of a few nations what all agree in. He however was going to use the second method, because the first is unable to show that the conclusions of reason in moral matters are laws, laws of God (12–14) and consequently cannot account for moral obligation, which is unintelligible without respect to a law (328). The obligation of a law is discovered by its sanction by rewards and punishments (229), and Cumberland will show that these are inherent in the nature of things, and we come at our knowledge of that empirically (1) more confusedly by obvious experience and daily observation, and (2) more distinctly by contemplation and philosophical enquiries founded upon experiments cautiously made (54). His procedure is that of natural philosophy, whose business is to discover and demonstrate the causes and effects of sensible phenomena (200). The human mind functioning properly is acting according to the maxims of the law of nature, this is the 'cause'. The 'effect' is what is necessarily produced thereby: the common good, 'the greatest end of human actions...by this means, moral and political questions are converted into terms in use among natural philosophers: whether these efficient causes can produce this effect or no?' After we have determined to act, the connexion between our actions and all the effects thence depending is necessarily and plainly natural and therefore capable of demonstration (196–7).

From the observed facts of human nature one can demonstrate the necessary connexion between virtue and happiness, vice and misery, and show that all virtue is comprehended under obedience to the maxim of actively promoting to the best of one's ability the good of all rational beings; the sanctions, the happiness and misery connected with this, show that it is not simply a precept of prudence, but a law which obliges and which presupposes a lawgiver; 'laws being nothing but practical propositions, with rewards and punishments annexed, promulg'd by competent authority' (14). Not that natural law obliges simply because it is the creation of the divine lawgiver, which could not be demonstrated 'philosophically' or empirically, but because it is 'sufficiently promulg'd', i.e. men can see its necessity for their well being in the nature of things, as well as the fact that it is 'promulg'd' by God, without which it would not be morally binding.[1] Knowledge of

---

[1] '...moral obligation may be thus universally and properly defined. Obligation is that act of a legislator, by which he declares, that actions conformable to his law are necessary to those for whom the law is made. An action is then understood to be necessary to a rational agent when it is certainly one of the causes necessarily

God is the ultimate ground of moral obligation (225): Cumberland makes this quite clear. But the first cause is the 'last discovered' (272), because 'we come not at the knowledge of God by immediate intuition of his perfections, but from his effects first known by Sense and Experience, nor can we safely ascribe to him attributes which from other considerations we do not sufficiently comprehend' – a remark which came home to roost in Hume. We must first know what justice is and whence it is (empirically) derived, before we can distinctly know that justice is to be attributed to God (15).

The starting point, officially, is the nature of man: the fact that he is so made that he can only be happy or even survive in active pursuit of the common good: this includes doing God's will, or 'cultivating the friendship of God and man'. Happiness is necessarily connected with the most full and constant exercise of all our powers about the best and greatest objects and effects which are adequate and proportionable to them, hence men endowed with these faculties are naturally bound under penalty of forfeiting their happiness to employ or exercise them about the noblest objects in nature, God, and man, his image (23). This is not an empty 'Ought' or sheer *Sollen*. Care of the common good is found in some measure everywhere among men (27), their more powerful inclinations, jointly considered, are carried towards that which we daily see procured thereby: the preservation and further perfection of the whole, just as the natural functions of the body are adapted to preserve life and propagate the species (28); Europe, with all its disadvantages and want of advantages, would be much worse off if its states only consulted their own interest (352). And it is supported by the 'general principles of mechanical philosophy' (118), and the study of the 'inward frame' of animals. Hobbes is refuted by the facts: his fiction that good and evil are changeable is inconsistent with the necessary and immutable causes, which he everywhere asserts, of the being and preservation of man (62). Only by peaceable association are blood, spirits, brain and nerves preserved in a sound condition, and what applies to animals in this context applies *a fortiori* to men, because what is peculiar to

required to that happiness which he naturally, and consequently necessarily, desires' (233). 'The Legislator obliges us by the law sufficiently promulg'd, and he sufficiently promulges it when he discovers to our minds that the prosecution of the common good is the cause necessarily requisite to that happiness which every one necessarily desires' (234). The intrinsic force of the arguments which the Legislator uses to enforce universal benevolence is, 'in my opinion, all that is meant by the obligation of laws' (246). Here, as in the laws of civil states, the obligation of the Law is discovered from its sanction by rewards and punishments (229).

human bodies makes them more disposed than animals to society; the brain is bigger, the circulation brisker etc (112 *et seq*).

Knowledge of the law of nature and its author is thus grounded in philosophy or 'natural science' – a phrase which Cumberland uses (58); it can be confirmed by truly scientific procedure, and most of the scientific men of his day would have agreed. Epicurus denied Providence because his knowledge of nature was superficial (263).

Cumberland's account of natural law 'builds upon no hypothesis' such as that of Hobbes: that the earth produced the bulk of mankind full-grown, like mushrooms. It does not *suppose* men born either in or out of civil society, thus by-passing the controversy with Hobbes, nor does it *suppose* a relation between all men born of the same common parents. Its first principles would have been as intelligible to our first parents (27) as they are to all nations unacquainted with the Scriptures (18). Cumberland says that he has abstained from theological questions, and endeavoured to prove the laws of nature only from 'that reason we find ourselves at present possessed of, and from experience' (34), in other words, the experimental method of reasoning applied to morals.

Cumberland did not use Grotius' '*a posteriori*' procedure, but he did not regard it as invalid. Pufendorf rejected the attempt to find the law of nature in the consent of all mankind in general or on the agreement of all, or at least the most polished, nations (*Law of Nature*, Book II, Ch. III, § VII, 97). We cannot properly know the manners and customs of all nations; and if we confine ourselves to the most civilized, what nation is going to own the title of barbarous? And what nation could set itself up as the standard for all? (*id.*, 98). Innocence and integrity may be found sooner in the less highly polished nations. Besides, the actual laws and customs and manners of nations are of infinite variety, and mere use and custom puts on the face and semblance of natural reason. Nor can natural law be derived directly from knowledge of God, although God is of course its author, because it is presumptuous to assume that divine and human justice coincide (Book II, Ch. III, § V, 95–6). And what makes a science of morals possible is not as some think that there are actions which are inherently good or bad necessarily so in the very nature of things; moral entities, unlike physical entities, cannot be called necessary in an absolute sense because they are 'imposed', that is not created but superadded to created things by intelligent beings for the regulation of men's lives. But those, the chief part of them, which are made necessary by the very nature of man, cannot be said to be unsettled and uncertain: to this extent morals can be a science (Book I, Ch. II, §§ V, VI, 12–13). And the most direct route to the discovery of the law of nature seemed to Pufendorf to be the 'accurate contemplation of our natural condition and propensions' (Book II, Ch. III, § XIV, 107) beginning with self-love, not because each particular man ought in every respect to prefer himself to all others or to measure all things by his own private advantage, but because by nature man is sooner sensible of the love he bears towards himself, perceiving his existence sooner than that of others (*id*, 108), and 'regularly speaking', self-love is so strong as to supersede any inclination which a man may have for another – whatever a man does for another, he never forgets himself – together with man's 'wonderful impotency and natural indigence' by himself, and his consequent need for the aid and comfort of his fellows. Given these elementary facts, 'it is an easy matter to discover the foundation of natural law'. Man is an animal extremely desirous of his own preservation, of himself exposed to many wants, needing his fellows, at the same time malicious, easily provoked and prone to mischief, an animal more corrupt, with more wants, more variety, and stronger and more insatiable passions than any other so that the restraint of law is absolutely necessary (Book II, Ch. I, §§ VI, VII, 77–8). Such a creature, in order to survive and prosper, must be social: the fundamental law therefore is sociability; all the other rules can be deduced from this. 'Every man ought as far as in him lies to promote and preserve a peaceful sociableness with others...' (Book II, Ch. III, § XV, 108). Appealing to reason and experience against Hobbes, Pufendorf argued that the fundamental law of nature was not due to any covenant or agreement between men but sprang from human nature itself, and obliged independently of any human pact or covenant (*Whole Duty*, 45–52). In Pufendorf, said his English translators, were to be found 'philosophical deductions from the nature of men and reasons of things', whereas Grotius had chosen to insist rather on authorities taken from the historians, civilians and canonists.

On the foundations thus empirically laid down, leaving out what Hume regarded as incompatible with genuine experimental method, and making allowances where necessary for the need to take into account the authority of the Scriptures, we get, prima facie at least, a reasonably naturalistic account of society and its rules and institutions. In Cumberland's words, 'as physicians suppose the parts of animals already formed, so moral philosophers suppose societies already established' (307), which did not prevent them speculating about the origin of society, though on another level of discourse, and though Cumberland himself spent less time on this than most writers on natural law. Property, contracts and promises, civil society or government are seen as human inventions which appear as and when required to meet the needs of a social animal, and man had never been anything else.

In Book II of *De Jure Belli ac Pacis* Grotius gives an account of the origin of property – how men departed from the ancient community of property, first of moveable then immoveable things – based on what we learn from the Sacred History and agreeable to what philosophers and poets have spoken of the original community of goods and of the divisions which followed. God at the creation, and again after the deluge, gave to mankind in general a dominion over things of this inferior world – what the natural law writers called negative communion – which would have lasted if men had retained their primitive simplicity, as is proved by some American peoples, or lived together in perfect friendship. However, they applied themselves to various arts, that is, to the knowledge of things which may be used either well or ill, as symbolized by the Tree of the Knowledge of Good and Evil, first agriculture, and the feeding of cattle; a division of labour which, as exercised by the first brothers, gave rise to diversity of inclinations, leading to jealousy and crime. Good men being insensibly corrupted by bad, there followed an age of violence (a kind of gigantic life) and then one of hedonism. But as the Tower of Babel shows, what most tended to disunite men was ambition: thereafter the land was divided among various nations, but there was still a community among neighbours, not of cattle, but of pastures, until the growth of population forced a division of these among families. Social progress, the desire for a more agreeable manner of life, the need for industry and the division of labour, the defect of equity and love which resulted and which made any sort of equality in goods or labour impossible, destroyed the ancient community and introduced private property. But since property could not have derived from a mere internal act of the mind, because no one could possibly have guessed what others designed to appropriate in order to abstain from it, and several might have had a mind to the same thing at the same time, it must have resulted from a certain compact or agreement, either expressly, by a division, or tacitly, by seizure (*De Jure*, Book II, Ch. II, § II).

Cumberland does not present a detailed 'historical' account of this sort. Human nature, he says, suggests certain rules of life in the same manner as it suggests the skill of numbering, which is much assisted by industry and artificial characters, but these helps too we owe to nature... whatever assistance we may procure from art, the whole effect is to be ascribed rather to nature than to art. Just as after the art of cookery has fitted meat for nourishment, no one will deny that we are nourished by the power of nature – otherwise life itself were not natural (*op. cit.*, 97). At first glance, this looks similar to Hume's rules concerning property, which are the work of a naturally inventive species, and that is why he is prepared to call them natural laws. 'Nothing is more vigilant and inventive than our passions, and nothing is more obvious than the convention for the observance of these rules' (*Treatise*, 484, 526). The context of Cumberland's remarks is also the introduction of private property. Men, he argues, need the use of things if they are to survive, and the labour of others, which implies exclusive use, and possession, of the thing or service for the time being, and this applies to everybody and is seen to be in the interest of everybody – hence the right of occupancy. The will or benevolence conformable to this conclusion is as truly Justice as that which gives everyone his rights later in civil society (64–5, 314). That necessary limitation of the use of one thing to one man for the time it benefits any person is a 'natural division', and from this 'natural division of things' and its necessity to the preservation of all, is derived that primitive right to things by first occupancy. And for Cumberland, the 'whole essence, force and efficacy' of property (as opposed to occupancy) is contained in the continued limitation of things and labour, and consists in the realization that what is necessary to-day, in the interests of the individual and society, will, so long as circumstances remain the same, continue to be necessary tomorrow and always. If the same thing can promote the end for several days or years, the same reason which gave a right to them the first day will give a right while things continue as they were (314). Property is thus a relation of cause and effect,[1] which is Hume's definition.[2] Cumber-

[1] For nothing is more evident than that the future use of things or of human labour has the same relation to future life or health, which the present enjoyment has to present life: there is in both the relation of a necessary cause (66).

[2] 'We are said to be in possession of any thing... when we are so situated with respect to it, as to have it in our power to use it... this relation, then, is a species of cause and effect; and as property is nothing but a stable possession, derived from the rules of justice... 'tis to be considered as the same species of relation' (*Treatise*, 506). Cumberland was a standard author.

land also said that men's strongest passions are those which concern property in things and human services, 'than which nothing moves men more strongly', and that the whole matter of the laws of nature consists in settling and defending a distinction of property. The context is the connexion between the laws of nature and man's physical and mental health, the need to observe the former in the interest of the latter. '...from the very structure of our body we are continually admonished of the necessity of governing our affections with a strict hand because all the virtues and the whole obedience we owe to the law of nature are contained in the government of those passions which are employed in settling and securing every man's property' (153). He goes on to say that there is a necessary connexion between knowledge of the laws of nature and the inclination to observe them, and life in the human family: because man's care to support and govern his family is greater than in the animals (because their venereal inclinations are not uninterrupted), knowledge of the law of nature is necessarily presupposed; for no provision can be made for a family without settling and preserving some division of things and mutual services for that purpose (156).

The division of things which establishes property as opposed to limited occupancy is made by consent, but of the making of this division Cumberland 'will not say much, because we all find it ready to our hands in a manner plainly sufficient to procure the best end'. It was made necessary by disputes and by the sloth of those who neglected to cultivate the common fields. Once settled, and Cumberland seems to envisage this as a gradual process (the rights will be 'gradually settled' to each particular man, family, city and state, 322) the same reason which gave rise to it demands its inviolable maintenance, because any attempt at a new division would lead to so wide a difference of opinion among so many that all would be reduced to a state of war. Therefore a desire of innovation in things pertaining to property is unjust, and Cumberland does not only highly approve, with Grotius, of the saying of Thucydides, that 'it is just for everyone to preserve that form of government in the state which has been handed down to him', but thinks that it should be extended to private property, and asserts that it is just to preserve inviolably the ancient division or dominion over things and persons, both among different nations and in particular states (323). Disputes must be settled by arbitration, and if the parties cannot agree on an umpire, the matter should be decided by chance, rather than by war in which both

THE FOUNDATIONS OF POLITICS

parties may perish. 'I mention this by the way in order to show the reason why we ought to acquiesce in some methods of disposing of things and employments which partake more of chance than of rational choice', such as besides casting lots, primogeniture and first occupancy (322).

The agreement to establish property gives rise to justice, in the sense of a will to preserve property so distributed to each. A property in things is supposed before there is any room for keeping faith; a dominion over things being established, particular persons have somewhat of their own to give or promise, absolutely or upon condition (324). The agreement to establish property cannot therefore involve men giving promises to each other, because promises and contracts are only made possible by it. It is obvious, Cumberland said, that beneficence towards others, the obligation and faith of compacts, gratitude, temperance, frugality, modesty, natural affection cannot be clearly explained unless a division of property, by which what is ours may be distinguished from what is anothers, be first established or supposed, and that the same general law by which this division is made and preserved obliges men to the exercise of all these virtues and to all others contained in them, or which may be deduced from them (325). It is also the foundation of civil authority or government, an equal division of things being inconsistent with civil dominion (325).

Anyone acquainted with Hume's theory of the origin of justice cannot fail to be reminded of certain characteristic features of it when reading Cumberland's account: the rules concerning property bridle men's most powerful passions; they establish 'justice' and are as natural as counting; they do not arise as the result of men giving promises to each other, but from a sense of common interest; they are necessary to the existence of the human family; there is nothing very rational about primogeniture and first occupancy, because a desire of innovation or a new division would lead to endless dispute (on the 'rational' level) and is dangerous and unjust.

Hume is sometimes given credit for not thinking in terms of a 'convention' to establish property, although he uses the word; that is, for having thought in terms of something much less artificial and deliberate, a slow process, not a single event. Such a view however does not seem to have been a peculiarly Humian innovation or improvement on natural law theory. Hume himself, explaining in the *Enquiry concerning the Principles of Morals* what he means by a 'convention' to establish property, viz, not a promise, which he says is the most usual sense of the word (it cannot be a

26

promise for a variety of reasons which make it impossible for promises to precede the convention) but an agreement between two or more people to do something, or simply the doing of it, which one knows the other person or every one else involved will too, in the common interest, like pulling the oars of a boat or using words or gold and silver as a means of communication and exchange, expressly says that his view of the origin of property and therefore of justice in this way is substantially the same as that of Grotius, and he quotes the passage from *De Jure Belli ac Pacis*, or part of it, referred to earlier, to make his point (*Enquiry*, 306–7). The notion of language as a tacit convention was part of natural law teaching. Hutcheson, for example, says that 'without presupposing any old covenant or formal express agreement, the very use of signs in certain circumstances may plainly contain the nature of a tacit convention, and he who exhibits them is justly understood to covenant with the other to communicate his sentiments, according to that interpretation of these signs which is either natural or customary' (*A Short Introduction to Moral Philosophy*, 187).[1]

Grotius and Pufendorf had been criticized by later writers, Barbeyrac and Hutcheson for example, and, implicitly at least, Locke (*Second Treatise*, § 25: 'without any express compact'), for thinking of the origin of property in terms of a compact or convention – such a convention was not necessary because the right to property was grounded in human nature. Blackstone thought the dispute scholastic (*Commentaries*, II (1766), 8), but what Grotius and Pufendorf wanted to stress was that property in its very nature implies agreement between men, (See Grotius, *De Jure*, Book II, Ch. I, § II, 5; Pufendorf, *Law of Nature*, Book IV, Ch. IV, §§ V, VI, 321–2) and Hume, as usual on the side of any theory that stresses the social context of human 'inventions', found himself in agreement.[2]

---

[1] Cf. Pufendorf, *Law of Nature*, Book IV, Ch. I, § V, 278. As all signs except those which we call natural denote some determinate thing by virtue of human imposition, so this imposition is attended with a certain agreement, consent or compact, tacit or express; from the force of which there arises a necessity of applying such a sign to such a particular thing, and to none else. The like covenant must be supposed in relation to all those things which we use for signs.

[2] Heineccius traces it to necessity, meaning by that not only extreme need, but even such as makes it impossible to live conveniently and agreeably. The divine law that all things should be in common admits of exceptions in cases of 'necessity' (*Methodical Sytem*, I, 172). Turnbull in his remarks on this chapter refers the reader to Locke, and says that the substance of his teaching on property is to be found in Quintilian: *quod omnibus nascitur, industriae praemium est* – what is common to all by nature is the purchase, the reward of industry, and is justly appropriated by it.

Pufendorf makes it clear that the covenant to establish property is to be regarded as a gradual development made necessary by developing social needs and particularly the growth of population and the need for industry. Men left the original negative communion and by covenant settled distinct properties, not at the same time and by any single act, but by successive stages according as either the condition of things or the number and genius of men seemed to require (322). Property is not expressly commanded by the law of nature, but the law of nature can also mean that sound reason advises the reception and settlement of such a thing among men from the general consideration of a social life; property was gradually introduced as it appeared requisite to the common peace (*id* § XIV, 331). It is made necessary by the niggardliness of nature (322) producing quarrels and hostilities, and the fact that many things need human labour to fit them for use. It was highly conducive then to the common peace that immediately upon the multiplication of mankind properties should be appointed in moveable things...(322). The compact which accompanies the origin of property in Grotius and Pufendorf is no more incompatible with an account in terms of social evolution than is Hume's 'convention'.

Apart from the fact that Hume's account reads more naturalistically because it is wholly secular and streamlined – there was no need to attempt to square it with the Sacred History or enter into learned dispute as to the nature of God's grant to Adam etc – what seems to be truly original in Hume's use of the 'convention' and the slow development implicit therein is the realization that it is an agreement which involves having an eye to the whole plan or purpose envisaged by the rules concerning property, even when in particular instances an action might seem to contradict that purpose, as for example, when a good poor man has to pay his debt to a bad rich man even if it involves ruin for himself and his family. Hume is well aware that this is a highly sophisticated point of view, only possible at an advanced stage of social progress (see, e.g. *Enquiry into Morals*, 274n).

But for none of these thinkers is the idea of social evolution at the centre of attention; nowhere is it dwelt on or elaborated for its own sake. However it is not a forced or distorted interpretation which points out how, for the natural law writers, as for Hume, government or 'civil society' is a purely human expedient which emerges with the development of society to meet human needs, psychological and material, and not as their contract theory of government prima facie seems to suggest, or used to, something wholly artificial, unrealistic and unhistorical. Cumberland says that the foundation of government is a matter of common and obvious experience; its necessity as means to an end is easily learned from the common experience of all in those things which respect the care of a family or building a house, or the production of any other effect to which the different services of several persons are required, where we perceive that all our labour is bestowed in vain, except some command and others obey (348). In his account of the origin of government, and in that of Pufendorf, a patriarchal orientation and content lacking in Hume, nevertheless ensures a continuity in the whole story: something aboriginal in the family is gradually enlarged and extended to meet new needs. Thus for Cumberland, the first example of order and government is that between husband and wife, in which the husband is naturally superior and the family is the first regular society and civil state (350). Hume makes nothing of parental government.

Pufendorf is probably best known to students of political theory in general for his elaborate account of the way in which governments were originally instituted: the well-known two covenants and decree. It is meant as an analysis of what is involved or implicit in any form of established government: 'let us conceive in our mind a multitude of men all free and equal etc'; and it belongs to the chapter dealing with the 'inward structure and constitution of civil states'. His account, he says, is not pure arbitrary fiction; although the historical origin of most governments is in fact unknown, we can trace out by the disquisitions of reason the origin of some things not committed to the monuments of time and history.[1] Given civil states as we find them, and given man's freedom and equality, these agreements or covenants must, tacitly at least, have passed in the institution of commonwealths.

Pufendorf was especially anxious to point out that man's natural desire for society, which he champions against Hobbes, does not explain the origin of civil society or government, because this receives adequate satisfaction in the primary societies. Aristotle's arguments prove man to be naturally a sociable, but not naturally a

---

[1] For Cumberland's theoretical or conjectural history of the origin of government, see *op. cit.*, 33. It is to be distinguished, he insists, from the question of their actual formation, which is wholly a matter of fact, depending on free agents, and therefore not demonstrable from principles of reason. In fact, he says, it is notorious from the most authentic histories, that most of the governments now in being have been set up by force (359). (Hume says 'almost all' in the famous passage in his *Original Contract* essay.)

political, animal. No creature in fact is more fierce and unruly or liable to more failings which lead to the disturbance of society: men's endless thirst after things superfluous, their ambition, quick resentment of injuries and eager desire for revenge, the variety of opinions as to the best way of living . . . (*Law of Nature*, Book VII, Ch. I, § IV, 134). Civil subjection runs counter to men's natural tendencies and drives: their natural inclination to be subject to no one, to do what they want, to consult their own advantage in everything: few men are naturally good subjects, putting the public welfare first (*Whole Duty*, 283). In Pufendorf, human nature does not change, as it does in Grotius, becoming vicious with the invention of arts and loss of primitive simplicity and innocence: his psychological account of the origin of government stresses man's malice and the need for security, especially of life, in a Hobbesian manner which offended a Whiggish commentator like Gershom Carmichael. The truth of the saying that man is a political animal, says Pufendorf, is not that we are all fitted by nature to be good citizens, but that some at least can be educated and disciplined 'to acquit themselves well under that character', and that since men have increased and multiplied, civil societies are absolutely necessary to their safety (*Law of Nature*, Book VII, Ch. I, § IV, 135). With the growth of population men have to find a remedy in themselves for their own weak and unruly natures; and the origin of government is therefore not solely or principally economic necessity, or even the prospect of living better – opulence is the result of living in cities, not in commonwealths (*id.*, § VI, 136) – but the need for security against mutual injuries. This is seconded by those who find the origin of government in fear, meaning by that only a wary provision against future evils (*id.*, § VII, 36). For fear is not purely negative, as if it meant simply flight; it is the natural effect of fear to find out remedies against itself (*id.*, 137). And although the advantages of living peaceably and sociably with others are obvious, most men do not act by rational motives, and are 'wholly intent upon the present... and are commonly moved by these objects which thrust themselves upon their senses while those of a higher and nobler nature are too refined for their affections and too remote for their desires'. One is reminded of Hume's psychological foundation of government, and also of the essential difference, because Pufendorf is thinking of Divine punishment (*id.*, § XI, 140). In addition men are such that they do not willingly co-operate in a single design, but have to be compelled, because of the variety of opinions as to what is most expedient for the common end, and a sluggish coldness in business (Book VII, Ch. II, § V, 144).

Pufendorf emphasized man's original depravity and the 'almost infinite miseries of the state of nature' (Book VII, Ch. VIII § 1, 218; *Whole Duty*, 253-4) in order to drive home the necessity for strict obedience to established government: government is necessary for any decent social life - which finds an echo in Hume, though without the corresponding theory of sovereignty. It is the state which makes civilized life possible at all: another Hobbesian bias which called for Whig glossing later, as when Carmichael agreed with Barbeyrac that Pufendorf had exaggerated the contrast between the evils of the state of nature and the benefits of civil society as such, claiming that bad government could be as bad as anything in the state of nature (S. Puffendorfii, *De Officio Hominis et Civis juxta legem naturalem*, supplemented with observations by Gershom Carmichael, Edinburgh, 1724, 318).

Heineccius' account of the establishment of civil government - 'these larger societies, which we call states or republics' - (*Methodical System*, Book II, Ch. VI) follows that of Pufendorf. There is 'almost no nation so barbarous' as to be without some semblance of a civil state (85). Men are not compelled to it by want of necessaries; in *Genesis* 4, 17 there is an account of something like civil society when the world could not have been so populous as to give rise to a want of necessaries; there has been much greater indigence in civil societies as the result of 'luxury and wantonness'; and nothing hinders commerce taking place where there is no government (86). Nor is there anything to prevent men improving their reason and refining their manners in a state of nature; Abraham, Isaac and Jacob were free from all barbarity and 'polite', and the arts and sciences can be cultivated to a great degree of perfection without government. Nor is it for the sake of justice; this can be dispensed by the heads of separate families (87). The true cause of the founding of 'civil society or political states' is the 'strength and violence of wicked men', the association of several heads of families in order to oppress others. Since a large society cannot but be 'unequal and rectoreal', these bands of robbers would have to choose a leader and prescribe a certain form of government to him. The result would be other such associations for purposes of defence. The just heads of families would join together under a common head on certain conditions; in such a state of affairs there would have been no republics (90). This is the 'most natural account of the rise of civil government if we attend to the reason and nature of things'; ancient history sets it beyond all doubt. 'For that is found in the sacred writings' (89). And who can doubt that civil states were originally formed as the result of violence, since this has so often happened later? Hertius has shown by instances brought from universal history that the most potent kingdoms took their rise from oppression and robbery.

Thus those who say that the origin of government was fear and force (Bodin, Hobbes); those who say it was the need for security of property (Cicero, *De Officiis* Book II, Ch. XXI); those who say it was due to the 'imbecility' of segregate families (Grotius), all in effect agree (90). Bands of robbers may in time become lawful states; lawful states degenerate into bands of robbers; in both the end is the same: the security of their members (91). But since there can be no society without consent, civil states are constituted by an intervening contract: civil states, like other societies, are constituted, or augmented, either by voluntary consent or by forced consent (94).

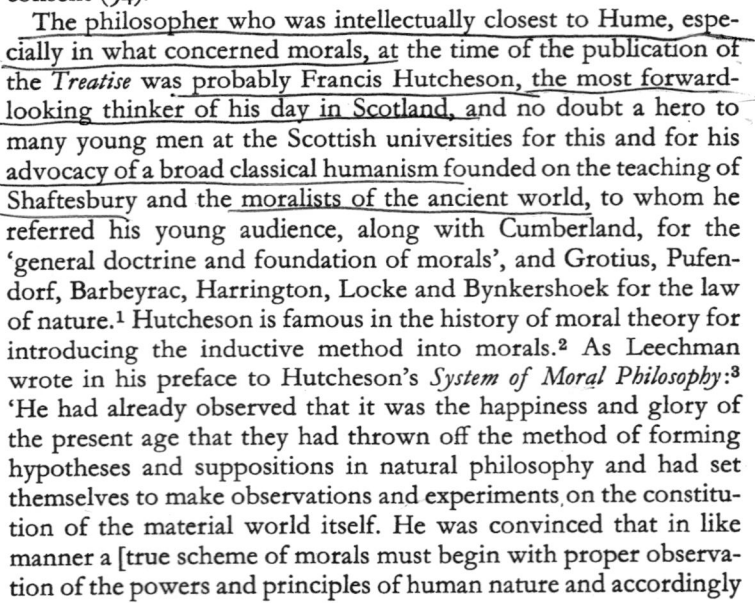

The philosopher who was intellectually closest to Hume, especially in what concerned morals, at the time of the publication of the *Treatise* was probably Francis Hutcheson, the most forward-looking thinker of his day in Scotland, and no doubt a hero to many young men at the Scottish universities for this and for his advocacy of a broad classical humanism founded on the teaching of Shaftesbury and the moralists of the ancient world, to whom he referred his young audience, along with Cumberland, for the 'general doctrine and foundation of morals', and Grotius, Pufendorf, Barbeyrac, Harrington, Locke and Bynkershoek for the law of nature.[1] Hutcheson is famous in the history of moral theory for introducing the inductive method into morals.[2] As Leechman wrote in his preface to Hutcheson's *System of Moral Philosophy*:[3] 'He had already observed that it was the happiness and glory of the present age that they had thrown off the method of forming hypotheses and suppositions in natural philosophy and had set themselves to make observations and experiments on the constitution of the material world itself. He was convinced that in like manner a [true scheme of morals must begin with proper observation of the powers and principles of human nature and accordingly

---

[1] *A Short Introduction to Moral Philosophy*, vii–viii.
[2] D. Daiches Raphael, *The Moral Sense* (1947), 15. W. T. Blackstone, *Francis Hutcheson and Contemporary Ethical Theory* (University of Georgia Press, 1965), vii.
[3] Leechman was Hutcheson's disciple, successor at Glasgow, and 'continuator'; it was probably through Leechman, who was tutor to one of Hume's closest friends, that Hume got in touch with Hutcheson.

we should] inquire into our internal structure as a constitution or system composed of various parts, to observe the office and end of each part...He thought there was ground to hope, that from a more strict philosophical inquiry into the various natural principles or natural dispositions of mankind, in the same way that we enquire into the structure of a plant or the solar system, a more exact theory of morals may be formed...' (Francis Hutcheson, *A System of Moral Philosophy*, I, xiv–xv). As has been seen, this programme is an elaboration of the tradition Hutcheson was conscious of being heir to, thrown into relief by the contrast with his philosophical opponents, the ethical rationalists, and made more self-conscious and aware by the achievement and method of Newton. As one historian of the law of nature in Scotland has noticed, almost two-thirds of Hutcheson's *System of Moral Philosophy* is in fact jurisprudence.[1]

A system of moral philosophy, then, begins with a description of 'the constitution of human nature and its powers'; and the maxims or rules of conduct 'discoverable from the constitution of nature without any aids of supernatural revelation', are called laws of nature (*System*, I, i), which are 'moral determinations of the heart and the conclusions of right reason from those determinations' (I, 268) – they are discovered by our reason observing the natures of things (*Short Introduction*, 105); the laws of nature are inferences we make, by reflecting upon our inward constitution, and by reasoning upon human affairs, concerning that conduct which our hearts naturally must approve as tending either to the general good or to that of individuals consistently with it. These inferences we express in general precepts: they are discovered to us sometimes immediately, sometimes by induction, when we see what conduct ordinarily tends to good (*System*, I, 119). Moral philosophy is derived from the structure of our nature, which is more immediately known[2] (*Short Introduction*, 1) and from this source flow all the rights and obligations of the various 'states' of man, 'natural' and 'adventitious'. (The natural law writers were primarily concerned with these 'states': a 'state' being defined by Pufendorf as 'a field for moral persons to exist in', analogous to space in the physical world (*Law of Nature*, Book I, Ch. I, § VI, 3) and by Hutcheson as 'some permanent condition one is placed in, as it includes a series of rights and obligations' (*Short Introduction*, 130).)

[1] W. G. Miller, *The Law of Nature and Nations in Scotland*, Edinburgh, 1896, 12.
[2] Hutcheson's views as to the nature of this structure changed in some important respects, particularly with regard to the 'moral sense', under the influence of Bishop Butler, but this is not relevant here.

The several rights of mankind, Hutcheson says, are first made known by the natural feelings of men's hearts; that is, our automatic approval of everything judged to be of advantage and which does not hurt others. They are derived from the very structure of our nature; from our desires and appetites and the moral sense, previous to any consideration of law and command (*id*, 110–11). Private rights, as they immediately and principally regard the benefit of the individual, are pointed out by the senses and appetites. To discover them, we should attend first to the several natural appetites, and then to the general interest of society (*id*, 132). They are intimated to us in the constitution of our nature – the heart approves the pursuit of all private gratifications which are consistent with wider interests and do not contract the mind too much within itself (*System*, I, 285). The sense of everyone's heart shows that each one has these perfect rights, to life, to unblemished character, to liberty etc. They are confirmed by considerations of common utility and our more extensive affections (*Short Introduction*, 133–4).

As for private property, since like all rights this is derived from human nature, from powerful feelings morally approved by all, we need not have recourse to any original compact or agreement to explain it, as in Grotius and Pufendorf, nor as in Filmer to any grant or decree to our first parents (*id*, 149, *System*, I, 331). Nevertheless, knowledge of this right is something men 'attain' to. At first, men would have no notion of a right to appropriate things but would probably consume them as their appetites and instincts dictated, like the animals, without any notions of right and wrong. When they 'attained' to the knowledge of a wise and good God, the creator of all these curious forms, and to the notions of right, they would soon discover that it was the will of God that they should use the inanimate products of the earth for their support and more comfortable subsistence and that they had a right thus to use them (*System*, I, 309–10). Hutcheson goes on to put into the mouths of what are presumably primitive men a somewhat sophisticated argument as to the right to consume inanimate things, for example: to things inanimate, all states are alike, and no diminution or increase of happiness is occasioned by any changes which befall them. He says that a new created pair would not need a revelation to teach them their right; they would need one to teach them how to use it: they would be in jeopardy if uninstructed as to what was fit to eat and in the arts of shelter and provision for the future. Instruction in the use of inferior animals would be still more necessary and the right to use them not so obvious, and yet reason would pretty soon teach one the right of mankind in this matter. A rational being with notions of right and wrong, and, owing to the growth of population, in need of the labour and other use of creatures so much inferior in dignity, and conscious of his powers to make such creatures subservient to his support and happiness, would readily presume upon his right, and a little reflection would confirm his presumption: men have superior senses and powers of enjoyment and suffering, sublimer pleasures, and are therefore the supreme part of the animal kingdom (*System*, I, 311–12); human domination over the animals makes the tameable kind happier etc. (314). Hutcheson says that animals have their rights not to be maltreated, even though they have no notion of right and wrong, but nor do children (314). He discusses at some length the question of the right to use animals for food: its tendency to the general good of the whole system shows that men have this right, and men might discover the right, when they feel the need, and yet it is so opposite to the natural compassion of the human heart that one cannot think that an express grant of it by revelation was superfluous. The point, he adds, is little debated in 'these Northern nations', and yet it is known that many sects and nations have denied men this right, and 'some great names among ourselves' have alleged that we would have no such right without revelation or an express grant from God (316).

The right of one man to exclude others from the use and enjoyment of a thing begins with first occupancy: the first impulses of nature toward supporting ourselves, and those dear to us, point out this right of the first occupant to such things as are fit for present use. Men who have attained to moral notions are led by their natural appetites and desires to take such things as lie in common with full persuasion of their right, and must easily see the inhumanity and injustice of wantonly violating it (*Short Introduction*, 140. *System*, I, 317–18). Thus is established the first rule of property that 'things fit for present use the first occupier should enjoy undisturbed'. The accident of first occupation may be a trifling difference, but a trifle may determine the right to one side when there is no consideration to weigh against it on the other. Further rules of property become necessary with the multiplication of mankind and the need for greater industry: as the world is at present, the subsistence of our species requires universal laborious industry. Nature has given to all men some ingenuity and active powers and a disposition to exert them, and each man has not only selfish desires toward his own happines but some tender generous affections in the several relations of life. From these strong feelings in our hearts we discover the right of property that each has in the fruits of his own labour: that is, we must approve the securing them to him, where no public interest requires the contrary, and this right is further confirmed by considerations of social utility (*System*, 318–20) – without private property there is no other motive to labour than the general affection to his kind, commonly much weaker than the narrower affections to friends and relations (*id*, 321). Thus both the immediate feelings of our hearts and the consideration of the general interest suggest the law of nature that each should have the free use and disposal of what he has acquired by his own labour (322). And in order to understand the natural grounds of property more fully we may observe that men are naturally solicitous about their own future interests as well as their present interests, and a large part of those things which yield the greatest and most lasting use require a long previous course of labour to make them useful: flocks, herds, gardens, arable grounds, pastures (324–5).

The grounds of property are thus to be sought in human nature, the strong feelings in our hearts, the resentment we feel when we see our right violated by others, the disapprobation we feel even if we are not personally involved, of such avarice and selfishness as breaks through all regard to the peace of society and all humanity to our fellows for the sake of a little private gain (339), and which 'every good spectator' instantly condemns, without thinking of the distant effects upon society (254), together with considerations of the general interest of society (that universal diligence is necessary). The latter would not hold if a wise political constitution could compel all to labour and ensure equitable distribution according to the indigence or merit of the citizens. But the other factors – the natural sense of liberty and the tender affections – would still be present, and could not be catered for: the necessary constant vigilance and nice discernment of merit is not to be expected. What magistrate can judge of the delicate ties of friendship by which a fine spirit may be so attached to another as to bear all toils for him with joy? The inconveniences arising from private property are not so great as those which must ensue upon community, and most of them may be prevented by a censorial power and proper laws about education, testaments and succession (*System*, I, 323).

It should be noted that according to Hutcheson property is one of the more special laws of nature which are derived from the fundamental precepts, and although a 'perfect right' (one which can be enforced), it is not absolute. The fundamental precept of promoting the good of all is the ground of all the exceptions from the more special laws (*System*, I, 120). As the laws of nature comprehend not merely the original moral determinations of the mind, but also the practical conclusions made by the reasoning of men as to what tends to the public good, they cannot be perfect, as the reasoning of even the most ingenious is not perfect. Superior beings might see a rule of conduct conducive to public good which no human could ever have discovered to be useful. In so far as the precepts of natural law are conclusions from observation of what sort of conduct is ordinarily useful to society, singular cases may happen in which departing from the ordinary rule may be more for the general interest than following it (*id.*, 273). Therefore the various natural rules of property not only admit of exceptions in cases of compelling necessity, but may justly be altered and limited under civil policy, as the good of the state requires. Property can never be so extensive as to prevent or frustrate the diligence of mankind (326, 329).

From the fact that the labour of each man cannot provide him with all his needs, Hutcheson derives the rights of commerce, and of alienating our goods, also the rights from promises and contracts,[1] which become necessary with the growth of population and division of labour (*Short Introduction*, 154). As commerce is an absolute necessity in life, so are contracts and the maintaining of faith in them; even if all men were as just and good as one could desire, contracts would still be necessary because without them no man could depend on the assistance of others. Therefore the rights founded on contracts are of the perfect sort, to be pursued even by force. But their necessity to life in society is not the ground of the obligation to keep promises. This rests on (is 'first suggested by') 'some more immediate principles in our nature' or 'social constitution', such as our ability to communicate our sentiments, designs and inclinations to others, our proneness to do so by a natural openness of mind, so that dissimulation and disguise are plainly artificial effects of design and reflection, and a natural approbation of this disposition, and still more of truthfulness, with a natural dislike and disapprobation of sullen taciturnity and still more of falsehood and deceit, and other aspects of our 'social

---

[1] *An Inquiry into the Original of our Ideas of Beauty and Virtue*, 2nd edition, London, 1726, 287.

nature', including an immediate sense of the beauty of keeping faith: these parts of our constitution more immediately suggest our obligation to faith in contracts and the moral turpitude of violating them (*Short Introduction*, 167-8, *System*, II, 2-3.)

Since if all men were faithful in the discharge of their duties, associations other than the state would provide all the affluence and happiness that men require, the need for government must be due, if not exclusively to human wickedness, because many of the evils of 'anarchy' are not the result of wickedness but may be due to different opinions among just men as to what is right, or the mistaken ideas of those who are too positive under the secret influence of self-interest, or the obstinacy of the ignorant,[1] at any rate to a mixture of 'depravity' and 'weakness' or 'imperfection'. This does not mean that we can call civil society unnatural or contrary to nature. Man is 'fitted by nature for civil polity' in so far as being by nature a creature of reason and sagacity and forethought, he can see what is necessary or very conducive to obtain what he naturally desires. This is what the ancients meant by calling man a political animal by nature; they did not mean that he desires a state of civil subjection or a political union as immediately as he desires the free society of others in natural liberty, from immediate instincts (*Short Introduction*, 266, *System*, II, 212-13).[2]

Hobbes and Pufendorf exaggerate both the burdens of civil society and the evils of anarchy: it is not true that the worst state is better than anarchy at its best. In a state of anarchy there may be much happiness and innocence of manners, zeal for mutual defence and for preserving justice, and even considerable improvements in arts: this is better than a despotic government. But on the whole civil society is preferable to anarchy, especially as the latter is suitable only to the simple manners of a primitive social state. ' 'Tis enough on this subject that all the advantages desirable or that could be hoped for in a state of anarchy are more effectually obtained and secured by a good plan of polity.' Hutcheson virtually says that

---

[1] *System*, II, 213-14. Hutcheson points out how difficult it is for the more ingenious who invent useful contrivances to satisfy the stupid and prejudiced about the expediency of them: " 'Tis well known how hard it is to make the vulgar quit their own customs for such as are far better in agriculture or mechanick arts.'

[2] Turnbull's argument is more purely Aristotelian. Glossing Heineccius' account of the origin of government, he says that although men can arrive at great opulence and politeness in segregate families living independently of one another, yet they can achieve a perfection and happiness in a rightly constituted state which is not otherwise attainable, and this is an end for which they are clearly designed by nature (and the Author of Nature). See Heineccius, *Methodical System*: Turnbull's remarks on Book II, Ch. 6.

given the fact of social progress, and therefore corruption, government is essential (*System*, II, 214-15, 219); given the prevalence of injustice, avarice and ambition, civil power is the obvious remedy, 'such a one as must strike the senses of the most inconsiderate', because men united, even if the majority or everyone is corrupt, are not likely to enact unjust laws – each will be ashamed of his own dishonesty and will live in dread of receiving injuries from others, unless all are restrained by equal laws (*System*, II, 215, *Short Introduction*, 268). He seems curiously anxious to make the case against anarchy. Even in the worst plans of government, he says, many evils are prevented and justice maintained, and the people protected from injuries: indeed instances where the civil power is useful far outnumber those in which it is abused, which would make one hesitate in allowing that the imperfect and foolish plans of power which have appeared in the world have on the whole done more mischief than good, and occasioned more evils than would have ensued from as long a continuance of anarchy. We tend to take the blessings of civil society for granted – we are not much struck with the good it does in a general protection and administration of justice, whereas every perversion deeply affects our minds and is long remembered with indignation (*System*, II, 219). On the other hand, this should not prevent men, when opportunity offers with fair hopes of success, from attempting 'even by such violence as may occasion some temporary anarchy', to obtain such amendments of a foolish concerted plan of polity as may be necessary to prevent the perversion of it, and procure such good as overbalances the temporary inconveniences occasioned by violent change (*id*, 220).

Given the pressing need for government, what probably happened was that the 'wiser and more sagacious', observing the inconveniences of a state of anarchy, fell upon this as the only remedy: that a large number of men should covenant with each other about entering into a firm society, to be regulated by the counsel of the wiser few, in all matters relating to the safety and advantage either of individuals or of the whole body. And discerning the many conveniences to ensue upon such a project, explained it to others and persuaded them to put it in execution (*Short Introduction*, 268-9). This is the more likely because there is 'something in our nature which more immediately recommends civil power to us', that is, recognition of superior wisdom. 'Tis highly probable that not only dread of injuries, but eminent virtues and our natural high approbation of them, have engaged men at first to form civil societies' (*id*, 267). Many men being united in society, the superior goodness, prudence or courage of some would naturally procure them superior esteem and confidence; controversies would arise; the mischief of deciding them by violence would soon appear. They would soon see the danger of divided counsels either about improving their condition or common defence. The most esteemed would be chosen arbitrators of their controversies, and directors of the whole body in matters of common interest; and as their prudence suggested, laws and political institutions would be established. The rest, finding the sweets of good order, safety and laws, would have a veneration for the society and its governors and constitution (*System*, I, 34–5). It is unlikely therefore ('scarce credible') that 'a rude and incautious multitude', full of admiration of the shining virtues of some more eminent characters, took the three formal steps described by Pufendorf: the contract of each with all, the decree establishing the government and the contract between governors and people. But in every just constitution of power, no matter what the form of government, something was originally done which plainly included the whole force of these three transactions; where power is just, there is something equivalent to these deeds; even in founding a democracy there is always some deed equivalent to all these three, since the end known and professed by all sides in the constitution of power was the common good of the whole body.[1] Hutcheson refers the reader to Carmichael's notes on Pufendorf, but Pufendorf had made this point himself (*Short Introduction*, 274, *System*, II, 227).

What actually made men unite to form the political union is of minor importance. It may have been force, though this seems unlikely. However 'we are inquiring into the just and wise motives to enter into civil polity, and the ways it can be justly constituted, and not into points of history about facts' (*System*, II, 223–5). The 'main use' of civil polity is the settling of controversies; this is revealed by the question of how controversies should be settled in natural liberty, which also shows the first steps toward civil government. The dangerous consequences to be apprehended from the immoderate passion of men, who are more moved by present prospect of gain than deterred by any moral principles or

[1] If a people dreading injuries from each other, or from some foreign force, agree by one deed to constitute some just and brave man their monarch, they certainly also agree with each other to unite into one body to be governed by him. And he implicitly engages for a faithful execution of his power for the purpose given, and the people expressly engage for obedience.

distant prospects of future evils (*System*, II, 214–15), in defence and prosecution of their rights by violence have probably been among the first motives which excited men to contrive civil government and arm magistrates and judges with sufficient power to enforce their sentences (*System*, II, 146–7).

But submission to civil power, and the notion of a just power or right of governing is 'intimated' to us by the structure or constitution of human nature, from the power over his children with which nature has invested the parent as manifestly tending to their good, and also from the dependence, known to all by constant experience, of the greater part of the practical sagacity and wisdom of the generality on the 'discoveries and instructions' of a few, who have had greater penetration and sagacity – hence the notion of just power or a right of governing is among the most common and familiar with mankind; hence also the notion of law is obvious to all. These notions are prior to the notion of the just power of God and the notion of his laws (*Short Introduction*, 102–3).

Hutcheson and the other thinkers who have been considered claimed to have established a science of law and morality without the aid of revelation, grounded on human nature and the 'nature of things' given to reason and experience. This has led to the description sometimes found in general histories and even more specialized studies, of the modern school of natural law of Grotius and his followers, as wholly secular, entirely independent of theology and without theological foundations, or more carefully, that any such foundation had disappeared by the eighteenth century.[1] Modern natural law had always been non-denominational, independent of any form of specifically or exclusively Christian theology – this was one of its vital functions – and this for contemporary orthodoxies was equivalent to non-theological, no doubt, but one must be careful to avoid what perhaps one can call the fallacy of premature secularization which has oversimplified the interpretation of so many thinkers of the seventeenth and

---

[1] See, for example, A. H. Campbell, *The Structure of Stair's Institutions* (Glasgow, 1954) 27. 'By the 18th century the theological foundation as a foundation in any real sense had completely disappeared.' Peter Stein in his article 'Law and Society in Eighteenth-century Scottish thought' in *Scotland in the Age of Improvement* (Edinburgh, 1970) contrasts Stair with the continental natural lawyers for whom 'a rational theory of law could be independent of theological assumptions. Although the obligation to obey natural law might come from God, yet the whole contents of natural law could be ascertained by logical deduction from man's nature as a rational being' (148–9). This is true, provided 'man's nature as a rational being' includes knowledge of God and the duties that flow therefrom.

eighteenth centuries. Natural law was derived 'empirically' from the nature of things, but, as Cumberland said, the nature of things does not only signify this lower world, but also its creator and supreme governor (*op. cit.*, 191). Morality was the daughter of religion (Barbeyrac);[1] the laws of nature, whether physical or moral, were laws of God, said Turnbull; if by laws the appointments of some supreme Being be not meant, they are words without any meaning. (Turnbull's Discourse appended to his edition of Heineccius, *op. cit.*, II, 253.) Natural theology was the indispensable ground of natural law; and these systems of natural law are 'independent' of theology only in so far as that is presupposed, and proof, including 'experimental' proof of the existence and attributes of God, taken for granted. 'The just opinions concerning God are taught in natural theology and metaphysics...We take these principles as granted in treating of morals' (Hutcheson, *Short Introduction*, 68).[2]

If natural jurisprudence really had been divorced from theology, there would not have been all the trouble and misunderstanding caused by the problem of moral obligation, nor the controversy over Grotius' notorious definition. As Pufendorf said, the rules are plainly useful; to make them laws which oblige, as doctors' orders do not, one must presuppose a God who governs all things by his providence, who has enjoined us mortals to observe the dictates of our reason as laws, for law presupposes a superior (*Whole Duty*, 52, *Law of Nature*, Book II, Ch. 3, §§ XIX–XX, 112 *et seq.*). According to Barbeyrac, Grotius does in fact do so.[3] As was seen earlier, it was in order to show that the laws of nature oblige that Cumberland adopted the method of discovering them 'from the cause to the effect', because by this method we arrive at last at their first Author or efficient cause: although it is discovered last, the obligation of the laws of nature takes its first rise from the discovery of the will of God. This means that they do not

---

[1] Pufendorf's *Le Droit de la Nature*, trs. J. Barbeyrac (Amsterdam, 1734). Barbeyrac says in his Preface: 'il est certain que la morale est la fille de la religion, qu'elle marche d'un pas égal avec elle et que la perfection de celle-ci est la mesure de la perfection de celle-là' (xxii).

[2] '...the whole enquiry into rules of moral conduct, may be called an enquiry into the natural laws of God concerning our conduct...It is not properly the business of such an enquiry to prove the being of a God...It supposes that done and proceeds...to deduce general rules or laws of conduct'. Turnbull (Heineccius, *Methodical System*, I, 17).

[3] Pufendorf's *Le Droit de la Nature*, trs. Barbeyrac, 199n. '...il semble meme que [Grotius] ait aussi reconnu avec Pufendorf que cette nécessité [the necessary relation between a good action and a reasonable and sociable nature] n'est pas une nécessité absolument indépendante de la volonté divine...'

oblige simply because they are God's will. And Cumberland was anxious also to remove the purely negative associations or stigma of the punishments and sanctions which show these rules to be laws. It is punishment to be deprived of one's highest possible happiness: this is the sanction which reason discovers in the nature of things. And a sanction is properly regarded as the deprivation of a good, rather than the infliction of an evil: the force of law is from reward as much as punishment. Thus although the laws of nature are laws with sanctions, laws properly defined, the appeal is not so much to self-interest in the shape of fear of punishment as to love of life.[1]

Barbeyrac, on the other hand, in a long note criticizing Grotius' assumption that we can be obliged without being answerable to any one, argued that moral obligation can proceed only from the will of God; that reason's discovery of the fitness or utility of actions cannot in itself oblige: it cannot show why we should not prefer the more powerful contrary inclinations of our passions, where satisfaction is present and certain; it can show that this is imprudent, but not that it is a violation of a duty or obligation, 'properly so called'. And reason, considered as independent of the Being who endowed us with it, is nothing but ourselves, and a man cannot impose a necessary obligation on himself. As Seneca said, no man owes anything to himself, the word can take place only between two. Barbeyrac therefore concluded that no matter how conformable the maxims of reason may be to the nature of things and the constitution of our being, they are by no means obligatory till the same reason has discovered the author of the existence and nature of things, whose will gives those maxims the force of a law and imposes an indispensable necessity on us of conforming to them (Grotius, *The Rights of War and Peace* with Barbeyrac's notes, 10–11n).

Heineccius agreed. Since the law of nature comes from God as the Supreme Legislator, an atheist, doing a good action by his good disposition and through the guidance of reason, because he knows it to be good in itself and advantageous also, cannot on that account be said to act justly, that is, conformably to the law of nature considered as such. Much less can it be said that there would still be a law of nature if there were no God, or if God did not take care of human affairs – as Grotius had asserted. They cut

---

[1] What moves men to act is really a positive good, the procuring or continuing whereof is hoped for from the removal of the contrary causes. Privations and negations do not move the will of man (*op. cit.*, 259).

the nerves, so to speak, of the law of nature who conceive or define it independently of all regard to God, and thus feign a law to themselves without a lawgiver. All who have philosophized about it with accuracy as well as religiously have acknowledged that it proceeds from God, and that if the divine existence be denied there remains no difference between just and unjust. And he reinforces his remarks with a quotation from *De Natura Deorum*: Cicero was a much quoted authority in this context (*Methodical System*, I, 10). Heineccius concluded that 'internal obligation' was uncertain, and could not be described as a rule, without 'external obligation'.

Turnbull regarded Heineccius' position as illogical; because God's command to do or forbear an action can only be inferred, as Heineccius himself asserts, from the intrinsic goodness or badness of the action, we cannot be more certain about the external than the internal obligation. Turnbull accordingly puts forward a kind of pre-established harmony: our internal obligation, that is our duty as reason discovers it from the nature of things, is at the same time our external obligation, God's laws concerning our conduct (*id.*, I, 16–17).

Cleghorn, who got the chair of Moral Philosophy at Edinburgh that Hume did not, objecting that Heineccius seems to ascribe almost nothing to the benevolent principle, reason or conscience, told his class that the trouble was that most of the natural law moralists were civilians who were led to consider morals as having their ground and obligation from law, and thought of obligation in terms of positive law and therefore of the appointment of God, whereas 'simple ethics...has a different genius'. Its obligation is drawn from the internal nature of the mind which is found ultimately to determine to such actions and conduct as coincide with that which flows from the will of God, yet independently of this view these obligations from the nature of the mind are binding in some degree though heightened by this coincidence.[1] Cleghorn recommended Hutcheson's 'compend', and what he said is a brief resumé of Hutcheson's views on obligation, and they have the same defensive vagueness. In the *Short Introduction*, Hutcheson says that the notion of rights, and therefore of obligation, arises from the moral sense naturally and previous to any consideration of law or command, but that when we have ascended to the notion of a divine natural law our definition

---

[1] Taken down by a student in April 1747. *The heads of Professor Cleghorn's Lectures*, Edinburgh University Library, MS. p. 343.

of moral qualities may be abridged by referring them to a law (111), and shortly after goes on to say that obligation has two senses: (1) approval or condemnation by the inward sense or conscience, which is previous to any thought of the injunction of a law; (2) obligation is sometimes taken for a motive of interest superior to all motives on the other side, such as must arise from the laws of an omnipotent being. This latter meaning seems chiefly intended in those metaphorical definitions of great authors who would have all obligation to arise from the law of a superior. A note refers to Pufendorf and Barbeyrac's note on Grotius. In the *Inquiry into the Original of our Ideas of Beauty and Virtue*, in a chapter deducing some complex ideas, including obligation, from the moral sense, he maintains that we can have a sense of obligation abstracting from the laws of a superior, whether we take obligation to mean the internal sense or instinct toward benevolence which influences our actions and makes us uneasy without any thought of a sanction, or whether we mean by it a motive from self-interest, as for example, the realization that a constant course of benevolent actions is probably the best means of promoting the natural good of every individual as proved by Cumberland and Pufendorf, and all this without relation to a law (268). But he goes on to say that a law with sanctions given by a superior Being of sufficient power to make us happy or miserable is needed if our moral sense is supposed weakened and the selfish passions grown strong, to counter those apparent motives of interest, to calm our passions, and give room to the recovery of the moral sense, or at least for a just view of our interest (269). If pressed hard by the orthodox, Hutcheson could always fall back on this 'weakness' as man's normal state and the need for the sanctions. According to Leechman, Hutcheson asserts that we are laid under a real internal obligation to promote the good of mankind, but Leechman hastens to point out that Hutcheson did not mean, as some have maintained, that all other obligations from the consideration of the will of God were superseded (*System*, 1, xvii).

But even if Hutcheson had dispensed entirely with the 'external obligation', his system is not independent of natural theology, and one cannot make it independent without destroying its whole structure, and this is true of all these thinkers: the conscience or inward sense or reason cannot be divorced from the system of the God-governed universe, which is an inseparable whole. The question of moral obligation in Hutcheson brings out what is really implied in the 'experimental' approach to human nature: its

45

object is to discover God's purpose for man by examining the several powers or faculties of human nature as constituting a 'system', that is, a hierarchy, or microcosm. Human nature would be a chaos, said Hutcheson, unless we can discover some connexion or order in the various senses and governing principles; it is the main business of moral philosophy to show how all these parts are to be ranged in order (*Short Introduction*, 34). Only what is approved by the highest governing principle, the moral sense, reason or conscience, is truly natural, 'though every event, disposition or action incident to men may in a certain sense be called natural, yet such conduct alone as is approved by this divine faculty, which is plainly destined to command the rest, can be properly called agreeable to or suited to our nature' (*id*, 24). As Leechman wrote, applying the experimental method to morals meant inquiring into our internal structure as a constitution or system composed of various parts, to observe the office or end of each part, with the natural subordination of these parts to one another, and from thence to conclude what is the design of the whole; and what is the course of action for which it appears to be intended by its great Author (*System*, I, xiv). This is what is meant by a more strict philosophical enquiry into the various natural principles or dispositions of mankind. Hutcheson attempted to 'unfold the several principles of the human mind as a moral constitution'. It was in this sense that human nature was his 'favourite study', a profoundly pious sense with final causes written into the 'experimental' method as a matter of course. '...'tis plain that this structure of our nature exhibits clear evidence of the will of God and nature about our conduct' (*Short Introduction*, 102). Observation of human nature, 'these several powers, dispositions or determinations as universally found in mankind' (*System*, I, 36), for example the natural propensity to action and to society, the ardour to excel in anything that is praised by others, the sense of sympathy, the sense of honour and shame, shows that man is so designed as to find his supreme end and happiness in actively promoting the good of the whole system of which his reason tells him he is a part. Such conduct ensures the harmony of the two 'calm determinations of the soul': (1) towards one's own perfection and happiness of the highest kind, (2) the calm determination to desire the greatest happiness of the greatest possible system of sensitive beings, abstracting from any connection with our private enjoyment (*System*, I, Ch. III). And reason shows that the maxims of conduct discovered by reflection on our constitution are divine laws, required of us by God (*Short Introduction*, 35). They can be reduced to the two fundamental general laws: to honour and obey God, and promote the common good of all (*id.*, 109).

Turnbull's application of the experimental way of reasoning to moral subjects turns out to be similar to that of Hutcheson, the thinker from whom, he says in the Preface to his *Principles of Moral Philosophy*, he has 'borrowed most'. Stressing the harmony of his account of our nature and duties with the Scripture doctrine, Turnbull says that the two great commands which revelation tells us are the whole of human duty, of religion and virtue, love to God and love to mankind, are the very laws which our constitution prescribes, clearly pointed out by nature (Turnbull's Discourse appended to Heineccius, *Methodical System*, II, 318). Men are 'framed by nature' for social exercises (*id.*, 275). The mind of man is made for exercise; exercise is its natural pleasure; it is of a restless temper and must be employed, this is shown by the strange amusements invented for their relief by men of leisure (269–70). And men are social, bound together by mutual wants, unable singly to attain to any goods internal or external, obliged to mutual aid, and finding no pleasure without participation or communication (273, *et seq.*). They are dependent on one another both in general and also in so far as inequality of property is caused by the natural superiority of some who constitute a 'natural aristocracy', and for other reasons, and men are furnished by nature with the affections such dependencies require: the auctoritas patrum and verecundia plebis of Roman history (*id.*, 282–6). Such truths are matter of observation and experience; the 'connexions of things relative to man' are analogous to physical laws of nature, and, as seen already, all connexions of nature, moral and physical, can only be learned by experience, this is 'too evident to be insisted on' (253). But Turnbull insists that a truly 'philosophical' or scientific enquiry into human nature, as into any part of nature, means studying it as a whole, 'from all the parts taken together, as they are united, and by that union constitute a particular frame or constitution. The final cause of a constitution can only be inferred from such a complex view of it', that is, the end for which it was so framed or the intention of its Author in so constituting it. The end of our frame can only be inferred from the nature of our frame, but no part of this frame can be left out in the consideration (Heineccius, *Methodical System*, I, 122). Thus the experimental method gives the lie to the selfish system of ethics, according to which self-interest engrosses the whole of our nature and makes the sole principle of action – this is the context of the remarks just quoted. In order to judge of a constitution, he says in the *Discourse*, we must consider all its parts as they mutually respect one another and by these mutual respects make a whole. Thus we judge of all other constitutions or structures, natural or artificial. And thus likewise ought we to judge of the fabric of the human mind (299). This is why Butler's Sermons are the best introduction to moral philosophy (*Methodical System*, I, 122); this is why Turnbull appeals to Cicero as an exemplar of the experimental method in morals. How an enquiry into human nature or natural philosophy ought to be carried on he says, in the *Principles of Moral Philosophy*, we learn from Cicero *De Finibus*: all the speakers in it agree that the natural end for which man is made can only be inferred from the consideration of his natural faculties and dispositions as they make one whole (*Principles*, 10n). This is 'naturally' a kind of self-regulating mechanism: the mind of man is so constructed, for example, that natural sociability does not degenerate into 'clannishness': pity and sympathy for those in distress is a 'security' in our constitution against the degeneracy of family attachments into too narrow and confined a benevolence (*Discourse*, 289–90); resentment and compassion check each other so that each is socially beneficial and not harmful (295). But this natural mechanism or harmonious functioning of our 'frame' or 'constitution', which is its 'nature', implies the presidence or empire of reason, producing order within and without the mind (313), which is variously called, according to different points of view, prudence, virtue, self-love and self-command (263), and which is indeed the whole of virtue, human excellence or duty. So that if the first and second 'particular' laws of nature are the law of industry and the law of sociality, the 'first law of nature with regard to our conduct' is to maintain reason in our mind as our governing principle (262), and education should therefore aim to produce the love and patience of thinking, to establish the deliberative disposition and temper (264).

As in the teaching of Shafesbury and the Stoics, human nature is a 'system' or 'moral constitution' because it is an inseparable part of the whole system of rational beings, which includes God. A science of law and morality independent of revelation meant one based on principles of human nature which include an ability to recognize and acknowledge God's government of the kingdom of rational beings which is as common to the human species as living in society, the use of speech or the sexual instinct (Hutcheson, *System*, I, 36). And the senses and feelings and propensities from which rights and obligations and justice are derived are dispositions and determinations that have been, or are capable of being, approved by reason or conscience, which means that they have been commanded by God: they are propensities which are seen by reason to make for the good of the whole system, or at least do nothing to hurt it. They are derived from our 'social constitution' in that sense, that is, our membership of the community of rational beings as such.

In the light of our membership of this great society, the primary impressions of nature, our most immediate natural feelings and propensities, are seen to be commands of God, and the latter are prior therefore to the instincts which are superadded by God to assist his and nature's intentions. As Grotius, appealing to the authority of Cicero, said: the impressions which come after the first impressions of nature ought to be the rule of our action. After the instinct of self-preservation, follows the knowledge of the conformity of things with Reason, which is a faculty more excellent than the body. The first impressions of nature recommend us to right reason. Yet that should be dearer to us than the natural instinct (*De Jure*, Book I, Ch. II, § I, 1-2).

Among the rules of life which Cumberland said that human nature suggests in the same manner as it suggests the skill of numbering was the necessary acknowledgement by all that the good of all rational beings is greater than the good of any part, and that in promoting the former one is promoting also the good of individuals. This, like the skill in numbering, is improved by helps which we also owe to nature, but it is natural in a sense in which it is not natural in Hume: viz, part of man's initial mental equipment, and not the product of social evolution (Cumberland, *op. cit.*, 97). When Cumberland says that the usefulness of private property was suggested by nature, he means that it is obvious to all that no one can promote the common good unless he preserves his life, health and strength by the use of things: private property is derived from self-preservation only as that is recognized to be necessary for the good, or at least not to the detriment of the whole system of rational beings, which includes God; there is no right of self-preservation, and therefore no right to property, apart from this. Every man has a right to preserve his own life and limbs because those are his most certain means of serving God and man, in which consists the common good: it cannot be known that a man has a right to preserve himself unless it be known that this will contribute to the common good, or at least is consistent with it (64–5). Since the right to property can only be deduced from the care of the common good (in the widest sense) – and the distribution and settling of property with a view to the common good is a 'command' (325) – it 'manifestly follows that the dominion of God over all things is preserved unviolated'; therefore no one can have a right over others which will licence him to take from the innocent their necessaries (68). And since property does not mean simply material possessions, but includes life and reputation, life itself is to be parted with for a greater good; salvation of a man's soul, the common good of men, the glory of God, take precedence over preservation of one's life (77).

Pufendorf said that although self-preservation is a strong instinct, it is also a duty: we should rather imagine that the force of instinct was superadded to the dictate of reason (*Law of Nature*, Book II, Ch. IV, § 16, 136). Self-love appears to be the official empirical starting point, but since the self is not isolated but is an inseparable part of the whole system, and we do not live only to ourselves, but to God and human society, self-love is a duty not merely to preserve one's being but to improve oneself in every way, the better to fulfil God's laws and the laws of society. It includes duties concerning culture of the mind and of the body: correct opinions about religion, accurate self-knowledge, control of the passions, as well as procuring goods for ourselves and others. All these duties are obligatory: therefore self-preservation is a law; the powerful instinct is superadded. Pufendorf starts with the facts of human nature, but man is endowed with reason, unlike the animals, and is able to see that he is not single but part of a whole created by God to whom and to whose laws he owes obedience. In this context self-preservation does not mean what it means for the animals; it means self-control and self-culture in order to be able to obey God's law and live for society. This is what Pufendorf means by saying that man has a 'sociable nature', and man's right to self-preservation and all his rights and obligations are derived from this 'sociable nature', i.e. man's ability to see that he is not made to live for himself alone but for God and society. Man therefore has duties towards himself, or as Hutcheson put it, Mankind as a system has rights upon each individual (*System*, II, 105, *Short Introduction*, 235). Pufendorf considers these first, beginning with the individual's duties to God, and then lists his duties towards others; it is from the former that there spring men's obligations to men as such. Sociability is in the first place a command of God, and Pufendorf explains, by sociableness is not meant a bare readiness or propension to join in particular societies, no matter what our intentions. Sociableness is not ethically neutral; what is meant is a disposition of one man towards all others as shall suppose him united to them by benevolence, peace and charity, and so, as it were, by a silent and secret obligation (*Law of Nature*, Book II, Ch. III, § 15, 108).

The command of God is prior to the human propensity, though it is from the existence of the latter that one proves the former 'experimentally'. The procedure was regarded as compatible with the experimental method because one could, from experience, prove the existence of God and his laws, and God's benevolence towards his creatures.

There are therefore two senses, both 'empirical', in which man is a social animal. When Hutcheson and the natural law theorists stressed the fact that man was a social being they had in mind his membership of the 'one great society' (*Short Introduction*, 235: 'from the common bond of all with all, by which mankind are constituted by nature one great society'), of all rational beings as such, a society which included God,[1] as well as the empirical social animal with his desires and needs, material and psychological, for society (as set out for example in Hutcheson, *System*, I, 34). The law of nature, said Grotius, comprised alike that which relates to the social life of man and that which is called so in a larger sense, proceeding as it does from the essential traits implanted in man (*De Jure*, Prolegomena, § 12). The social life of man thus has a lower and a higher, or a more confined and a more extended meaning, and man has always been social in both senses.

This seems to have been overlooked or was somehow unacceptable to those, notably Samuel Cocceius, who criticized the attempt to derive natural law from the principle of sociability. Heineccius agreed with Cocceius. This principle, he argued, with which Grotius, Pufendorf and several ancients were 'wonderfully pleased', could not be 'the true, evident and adequate principle of the law of nature', because it could not account for those of our duties, to God and to ourselves, which would take place 'even though men lived solitary and without society in the world'. (Heineccius, *Methodical System*, I, 50). If the obligation to these duties holds good independently of all social relations between men, the duties cannot be derived from the necessity to be sociable.

[1] Cf. Cumberland. By 'rationals' he understands God as well as man, on the authority of Cicero (*op. cit.*, 42). True ethics instructs us to enter into and to keep up the most enlarged society with God and all men (306). Barbeyrac and Grotius also quote *De Legibus*, I, vii.

Those who live in the state of nature are no less bound than we who have put ourselves into adventitious states, to love and obey God, to love, preserve and protect themselves, to render every one his own. This is the chief argument by which Heineccius exploded that first principle of sociality, laid down by Pufendorf, who derived the law of nature from our obligation to sociality, to which men are compelled by necessity itself. But man would be under obligation to perform duties to God and to himself, though he were not united by ties with other men, and every man lived apart and independently (*id.*, II, 5–6). For sociability, Heineccius substituted love as the first principle of natural law, and as has been seen, Turnbull made sociability into the second particular natural law, the first law of nature being to maintain reason as our governing principle.

Pufendorf does derive the first principle of natural law from man's need to be sociable (*Law of Nature*, Book II, Ch. III, § XV, 108); but there is also the 'society' of men *qua* rational creatures. In particular, the criticism of Cocceius and Heineccius does not consider carefully enough Pufendorf's description of the state of nature, which is complex and makes fine distinctions which call for careful reading. There is no need to sort out the whole matter here:[1] all one needs to notice is that even if men are thought of as being in a state of absolute independence of one another, 'abstracting from all the rules and institutions, whether of human invention or of the suggestion and revelation of heaven' (*id*, Book II, Ch. II, § 1, 79) – an absolute unqualified state of nature which as applying to all men at once has never in fact existed, but always qualified or in part (*id*, § IV, 84–5), this would not be a state of war, as in Hobbes, because it is not the natural state of a mere animal, but of an animal 'whose noblest and chiefest part is reason', able to discern the dictates of natural law (*id*, § IV, 89). 'We have been so cautious as to attribute no such natural liberty to man, as shall exempt from the obligation of natural law, or of divine commands' (*id*, § IV, 85). In the imaginary, absolute state of nature men are still under obligation to obey God's commands, and have duties towards God, themselves and other men. What Cocceius and Heineccius overlooked is that there is a necessity to sociality not only compelled by earthly needs, but by God's will (*id.*, § XX, 114): Pufendorf's absolute state of nature is a transcendental society of 'rationals' linked together by common obe-

---

[1] See Hans Medick, *Naturzustand und Naturgeschichte der bürgerlichen Gesellschaft* (Göttingen, 1973), Ch. III, 'Das Naturzustandstheorem bei Pufendorf'.

dience to God and his law, and therefore by the obligations of their common rational humanity as such, but by nothing else.

This 'imaginary' state, that is, the absolute as opposed to the qualified state of nature, has been seen as the perfect, negative *Gegenbild* of civilization: as such it has the role mentioned already of emphasizing the need for absolute government;[1] but in one crucial respect it cannot be the perfect negative of civilization if the obligation incumbent on rational humanity as such is always present. This is not subject to historical development: Pufendorf says that the 'strange barbarity' found in most of the ancient nations, who lived by and for robbery, and who regarded it as a profession, was due to 'corrupted manners' blinding the dictates of sound reason: some men even then were able to see that this state of affairs was unnatural (*Law of Nature*, Book II, Ch. 2, § X, 90).

The first principle of sociality in Pufendorf, therefore, does not seem to be exclusively derived from social necessity in the sense and at the level criticized by Cocceius and Heineccius, in so far as men, regarded hypothetically as independent in every other way, are still able to recognize each other as rational creatures. '...the very being a man is a state, obliging to certain duties, and giving a title to certain rights' (*id*, Book I, Ch. I, § VII, 3). It is a state imposed by God himself. In an imaginary absolute state of nature men would still recognize the rights and obligations of humanity as such, or Justice in the broadest sense.[2] According to Cumberland, Hobbes had held that justice and injustice are none of the faculties either of the body or of the mind; if they were, they might be in a man alone in the world, as well as his senses and passions; they are qualities that relate to men in society, not solitude. This is false if understood of a society formed by human compact...the propension or will to give every one his own, in which the nature of justice consists, both may and ought to be in a man in solitude. Were there but one man in the world, he might be disposed to allow others, whenever they should be created, equal rights to those claimed by himself. Nor is there any reason why such an inclination should not be called natural, though it could

---

[1] Hans Medick, *op. cit.*, 49.
[2] cf. Cumberland, *op. cit.*: the words 'of a rational agent' (in his definition of natural law) are indefinite, he says, and therefore applicable to any man whomsoever, for example to the first man yet alone, and then the common good would be whatsoever would be acceptable to God and him, though the laws of nature speak, as civil laws usually do, to many at once (195). For Pufendorf on justice, see *Law of Nature*, Book I, Ch VII. What is particularly under fire in these thinkers is Hobbes' notion of justice as simply the keeping of contracts.

not produce external acts, in a man existing single. Hobbes himself would not deny man's propension to propagate his species to be natural, though he were supposed alone, as Adam before Eve (*op. cit.*, 89).

There is Justice which is prior to justice, because it is prior to society, as opposed to Society. What Cumberland called universal justice is nothing else than a constant will agreeing with that wisdom which designs the best and greatest end, the common good (366), or a will to obey the law of nature (352) – temperance being justice towards ourselves, employed in taking care of the body in order to the common good; liberality is a species of justice, including alms-giving and hospitality, so are the virtues of common conversation, doing good to others by a use of voluntary signs subservient to the common good, so is modesty etc (332–6). This was the sense, as Hutcheson pointed out, in which justice was the cardinal virtue of the ancients, defined as the habit of constantly regarding the common interest, and in subservience to it giving and performing to every man what is his due; under which are included all the kind dispositions by which a friendly intercourse is maintained among men, or which leads us to contribute anything to the common interest, such as friendliness, courtesy, gratitude, liberality, fidelity, love of our country, veracity etc and principally piety towards God (*Short Introduction*, 64). Elsewhere Hutcheson says that piety towards God is the highest branch of justice (*id.*, 96). This universal justice is prior to that justice which in Cumberland's words, 'almost wholly consists' in 'the making contracts, in the distribution, conveyance and preservation of rights' (59), or the will to preserve property so distributed to each (324), what Pufendorf calls 'strict justice', which requires some antecedent pact (*Law of Nature*, Book III, Ch. IV, § I, 200), and what Heineccius, commenting on Leibniz's definition of justice as the love of a wise man, calls the lowest degree of love, rendering a man his due in the sense of not hurting him and leaving him in the undisturbed possession of what he owns – rendering a man more than his due being beneficence or love of humanity, a higher degree of love (*Methodical System*, I, 53–5).

Justice, as giving every one his own, implies faithfulness, which Cicero called the foundation of justice (Grotius, *De Jure*, Book II, Ch. XI, § 1,5, Cicero, *De Officiis* I, VII) and is antecedent to the introduction of property, and promises and contracts. The obligation to perform promises, as Grotius said, arises 'from this society founded on reason and speech' (*De Jure*, Book III, Ch. XIX,

§ 1, 3), i.e. the universal society of rational beings; to perform promises is a duty arising from the nature of immutable justice which, as it is in God, so it is in some measure common to all such as have the use of reason. A promise is called by the Hebrews a bond or chain, and is compared to a vow (*id.*, Book II, Ch. XI, § 4, 1). Grotius also said that natural law is not only concerned with things that do not depend on human will, but with many things consequent to some act of that will. For example, property as now in use was introduced by man's will, and being once admitted, the law of nature informs us that it is wicked to steal (*De Jure*, Book I, Ch. I, § X, 4). Pufendorf quotes this passage to illustrate the distinction between 'absolute' and 'hypothetical or conditional' laws of nature. The former oblige men in all states and conditions independently of any human settlement or institution, the latter presuppose 'some public forms and civil methods of living to have been already constituted' – hence the division of man's state and rights and duties into 'natural' and 'adventitious'. Men are not obliged to institute private property, but once they have done so, natural law informs us that it is wrong to take the goods of another without his consent (*Law of Nature*, Book II, Ch. III, § XXIV, 120). Pufendorf says expressly that the laws of nature do not arise from the agreement of men. The first precept of natural law: to exercise peace towards all men, as such, is instituted and established by bare nature, without the intervention of any human deed, and depends solely on that obligation of natural law by which men are bound as they are reasonable creatures (*id*, Book II, Ch. II, § XI, 90). This precept includes in itself all the others, so that for instance when with the development of society and social needs men found it necessary to agree to institute private property, 'and it was gradually introduced as it appeared requisite', the precept of nature about abstaining from what is another's then 'first began to exert its force'. 'Before this time it lay concealed (as it were virtually or potentially) in that general precept which enjoins us to stand to our covenants and not injure the right of our neighbour. Nor is it any absurdity to affirm that the obligation we lie under not to invade the goods of others is coeval with human race, and yet the distinction of meum and tuum was afterwards ordained' (Book IV, Ch. IV, § XIV, 332).

Before looking at Hume's application of experimental method in relation to these systems, two more things need to be noticed about Hutcheson's ethics: (1) that for Hutcheson the science of human nature was not pure theory, not what Hume called moral 'anatomy' or 'mental geography'. 'Laying the foundations of morality' in human nature for Hutcheson was at the same time the art of getting people to act virtuously. It was the task of the moralist to promote virtue; to give reasons why men should act virtuously; to demonstrate that it was in their best interests to do so and in accordance with their nature, which meant 'not the ordinary condition of mankind...but the condition our nature can be raised to by due culture...and the principles which may and ought to operate when by attention we present to our minds the objects or representations fit to excite them' (*System*, I, 77). The 'calm principles' have to be 'confirmed by frequent meditation' in order that we obtain 'true liberty and self-command'. False associations of ideas have to be corrected (*id.*, 102 *et seq.*). Hence the crucial educational role of the moralist, especially towards those who are able and have the opportunity to form, and act on, more extensive views (*id.*, 241, *et seq.*). The description of man's powers and faculties is also prescription, and as a result, as one critic has pointed out, Hutcheson often confuses giving moral reasons for an action with giving a causal analysis of an action.[1] It is well known how Hutcheson made it his task to 'preach' morality, and the tradition this established in the Scottish universities. (2) For this reason, belief in God has an important part to play in Hutcheson's ethics – whether or not men can arrive at moral notions independently of God and revelation – in so far as so much of his ethics is concerned with 'exciting' reasons, geared to motivate men to the pursuit of the common good.[2] Piety 'excites to and confirms' all the other virtues (*System* II, 317: the virtues most necessary to a state, after piety, which excites to and confirms all the rest, are sobriety, industry, justice and fortitude). But belief in God is necessary not only because the moralist is primarily concerned with practice – and in this context Hutcheson can appeal to man's self-interest: piety towards God, the highest branch of justice, secures men his favour (*Short Introduction*, 96). That Hutcheson's system does not hold together without belief in God can be shown by one final consideration.

It was Hutcheson's object to show that virtue and interest, rightly considered, are connected and not opposed, because the highest and most lasting happiness is what is approved by the moral sense, that is, such dispositions as tend most to the general good. But given the transient nature of human affairs, of which

---

[1] W. T. Blackstone, *Francis Hutcheson and Contemporary Ethical Theory*, 1–2.
[2] See Blackstone, *op. cit.*, especially 51–2.

Hutcheson showed himself fully aware, the wider one's sympathy and the more extensive one's benevolent feelings and actions, the greater is the chance and indeed likelihood, of disappointment and unhappiness, unless one can hope for an eternal city of God.[1] Accordingly we find Hutcheson saying that the soul should be inured to a generous contempt of worldly things, which we can acquire by meditation on the fleeting, unstable, corruptible state of all mortal things, which must speedily perish and be swallowed up in the boundless ocean of eternity (*Short Introduction*, 83-4), and the *System of Moral Philosophy* has, as a 'Conclusion', a solemn panorama of the necessary decay and dissolution of every body politic, even the greatest empires – here we have no continuing cities – and a final sentence in capital letters: 'So let us look for one that hath a solid foundation, eternal in the heavens, whose builder and maker is God.'

Historians seeking the origins of the eighteenth century Enlightenment and 'modern' thought have been prone to the sort of premature secularization, noticed earlier in connexion with the modern school of natural law, which the *philosophes* themselves started, when for instance they refashioned Pierre Bayle in their own image and in the process seriously distorted his thought. Plenty of examples could be produced: the secular interpretation of Butler's ethics by modern philosophers, for instance.[2] Hutcheson has often been seen as the father of the Scottish Enlightenment and as the first to formulate the principle of the greatest happiness of the greatest number, but there are aspects of his teaching that are very far removed from what is usually regarded as most characteristic or typical of the Enlightenment, and as for Utilitarianism, the best way probably to get to the heart and centre of Bentham's science of morals, properly understood, is to regard it as a full-scale offensive against Hutcheson's ethic of benevolence.

[1] Cf. *Short Introduction*, Book I, Ch. 2, § VI. Hutcheson says that there is 'plainly no other refuge from these evils', that is, sympathetic pain at the misfortunes of others, no 'other foundation for tranquillity or stable joy to a kind heart, but a constant regard to the Deity and his wisdom and goodness governing this world...'

[2] See P. Allan Carlsson: *Butler's Ethics* (The Hague, 1964). His thesis is that Butler's ethics cannot be formulated in non-theological language or be properly understood apart from his theistic metaphysics. J. S. Spink in *French Freethought from Gassendi to Voltaire* (1960) says that Bayle remained a Christian writer; his criticism though pushed as far as any non-Christian could have pushed it, did not take him outside the Christian orbit. Readers of the *Dictionnary* were not to know that he always looked on unbelievers as 'them' and not 'us' (285). See also W. Rex, *Essays on Pierre Bayle and Religious Controversy* (1965), for more detail. Rex concludes that when all has been said, the mystery of Bayle's faith or lack of it remains.

For Hutcheson taught that God is the supreme objective good, without which we can have no real happiness, and his system is firmly anchored to that. In spite of Berkeley's attack, his is a profoundly religious system.

2
A modern theory of Natural Law

In the letter to Dr Cheyne in which Hume refers to his 'new scene of thought' (March or April, 1734), his complaint of the moral philosophy of Antiquity as 'entirely hypothetical, and depending more on invention than experience', is followed shortly afterwards by the remark that 'most of the philosophers who have gone before us, have been overthrown by the greatness of their genius, and that little more is required to make a man succeed in this study than to throw off all prejudices either for his own opinions or for this of others. At least this is all I have to depend on for the truth of my reasonings...' (*Letters*, I, 16). Some might be tempted to say that this goes quite a long way to explain the illness Hume is describing; especially when read in conjunction with what we know about his crisis of faith as a young man. In itself, 'throwing off all prejudices' looks innocent enough; it acquires special significance in the light of Hume's thought as a whole, when one remembers too that the immediate context is a science of morals. It is not surprising that Hume makes no mention in the letter of his religious doubts; Cheyne, though a fellow-countryman in a foreign land, was a complete stranger and also a Newtonian in the full sense, author of *Philosophical Principles of Natural Religion* (1705).

Hume's object was to give morals a sure basis in experimental philosophy, that is, a 'science of man' based on experience and observation. This in itself was not a 'new scene of thought'; what was really and radically new, apart from the attempt to apply the principle of association consistently, was what set Hume apart from the Newtonians: the discovery that a genuine experimental philosophy ruled out final causes and involved a conscious separation or bracketing off of the natural from the supernatural.

In a letter to Hutcheson (September 1739) Hume wrote, 'I cannot agree to your sense of *Natural*. Tis founded on final Causes; which is a Consideration, that appears to me pretty uncertain and unphilosophical. For pray, what is the End of Man? Is he created for Happiness or for Virtue? For this Life or the next? For himself or his Maker? Your Definition of *Natural* depends upon solving these Questions, which are endless and quite wide of my Purpose. I have never call'd Justice unnatural, but only artificial' (*Letters*, 1, 33). A few months later, in March 1740, he wrote to Hutcheson that 'If Morality were determined by Reason, that is the same to all rational Beings. But nothing but Experience can assure us that the Sentiments are the same. What Experience have we with regard to superior Beings?' 'I wish from my heart', he wrote, 'I coud avoid concluding, that since Morality, according to your opinion as well as mine, is determin'd merely by Sentiment, it regards only human Nature and human life. This has been often urg'd against you, and the Consequences are very momentous' (*Letters*, 1, 40). He was a moral 'anatomist', he told Hutcheson, not a 'painter' (*id.*, 32-3). His task, as he said in the *Abstract*,[1] was to 'anatomize human nature in a regular manner', to analyse and dissect, not to recommend virtue and moral excellence by depicting its beauty, the beauty of a system governed by reason, itself part of a larger system governed by God. This sort of hypothetical reasoning was out of place in experimental philosophy. The recommending of virtue, the task of the moral 'painter', was important; it was not to be confused with the experimental philosophy of the 'metaphysician' or 'anatomist'. The 'metaphysician' could give advice to the 'painter': their roles were distinct. 'I imagine it impossible to conjoin these two views'. From Hutcheson's point of view this would have meant reducing the task of the moralist to mere exhortation: the descriptive content, the hierarchical system of the mental faculties and powers, was not 'philosophical'.

This presumably is part of the background of Hume's complaint about 'every system of morality' he has 'hitherto met with', in the so-called is/ought passage in the *Treatise*, which has generated so much discussion in this century (*Treatise*, 469). Hutcheson's 'social constitution' of man, like that of Pufendorf, for example, includes the moral imperative among the facts of human nature. One starts, officially, with the facts, an empirical account of self-preservation, sociability, the sex instinct etc., only to discover that in the light of the system as a whole, governed by reason, they are laws, duties, commands of God, prior to the mere facts given to observation. The change is, as Hume says, imperceptible. The whole procedure was 'empirical' because the whole system, and the existence of God who rules it, could be proved 'empirically'. Newton himself had no doubts about that.

[1] *An Abstract of a Treatise of Human Nature* (ed. J. M. Keynes and P. Sraffa, 1938).

A MODERN THEORY OF NATURAL LAW

But this is what Hume had come to doubt, and that is all that need be said here, without going any further into precisely when and how, or raising the whole question of what exactly Hume's religious belief, or lack of it, amounted to.[1] What is clear is that for Hume the unquestioned alliance of Christianity and/or natural religion and the experimental method would not do: a properly conceived experimental method ruled out of any science of man and morals what he came to describe as the 'religious hypothesis'. Not that this term by itself gives one any guidance as to his meaning or attitude, as might at first sight seem to be the case, if one equates 'hypothesis' with philosophical romance. This was perhaps the 'popular' meaning of 'hypothesis', based on what Newton had said, not done, as used for example by Leechman in presenting Hutcheson's *System* to the public, or for that matter by Hume, who described himself in the *Abstract* as talking 'with contempt of hypotheses' (many other examples could be amassed). But 'hypothesis' had different meanings in eighteenth century usage, as in Newton himself, as Cohen and other scholars have shown,[2] so that one finds the same thinker scorning and yet using hypotheses almost in the same breath. Hume does this, as any reader of the *Treatise* and *Enquiries* cannot fail to notice. For Newton, as all the commentators agree, the existence of a God, who in Koyré's words was 'an eminently active and present

---

[1] The tendency to prematurely secularize the thought of allegedly 'modern' thinkers has been referred to already. There is also the danger of going too far in the opposite direction, making out, for instance, that Hume was really a convinced Christian, perhaps of a proto-Existentialist variety. Nevertheless, given Hume's Scottish background, and the fact that at the time of his intellectual coming-of-age intellectuals in Britain were in the grip, above all, of the Deistic controversy, it seems quite plausible in discussing 'Hume's intentions' to regard religion as the starting-point or grit-in-the-oyster. No one, at any rate, can deny his life-long concern with every aspect of it: philosophical, ethical, psychological, sociological and historical. Perhaps the fullest and most suggestive reconstruction of Hume's intentions from this point of view is C. W. Hendel's, *Studies in the Philosophy of David Hume* (1925), one of the most enjoyable of the many enjoyable books about Hume's philosophy: 'it seems that Hume's studious career opened with searchings into the religious beliefs of the time. Hume could not confirm himself in the faith of the Christian...' (14). Hendel points to the crucial importance of Hume's discovery, via Bayle's *Dictionary*, of Strato's atheism; the idea that order is in matter from the beginning. This 'naturalism' was what made Hume's mind restless and prevented him from finding any enduring satisfaction in the reasonings of other philosophers to establish the existence of the God of religion (30). Hume caught a glimpse of a very real alternative: order coming into things without the deliberate construction of some mind (99). If this was so, he did not carry this insight into social philosophy, in so far as he still subscribed to the classical idea of the Legislator creating social order out of chaos (see below, Pt. III, Ch. 9).

[2] I. B. Cohen, *Franklin and Newton* (Philadelphia 1956), A. Koyré, *Newtonian Studies* (London 1965).

being' (*op. cit*, 21), was in no sense a hypothesis – it was an absolute certainty verified and verifiable by experience 'from the appearance of things'. But even those who were convinced of that might use 'religious hypothesis' in a wholly inoffensive sense to mean something whose certainty is for the moment suspended while discussion proceeds towards it – a truth temporarily open for discussion. In *An Inquiry concerning Virtue*, Shaftesbury although he says that the perfection and height of virtue must be owing to the belief in God (*Characteristics*, II, 76), nevertheless talks of the 'hypothesis of theism' 'being supposed false', and 'the hypothesis of theism being real not imaginary' (Cf. 69: 'any hypothesis of theism; 73: according to the hypothesis of those who exclude a general mind'). And if Shaftesbury was suspect, one can turn to James Balfour of Pilrig (*A Delineation of the Nature and Obligation of Morality with reflections on Hume's Inquiry concerning the Principles of Morals*, Edinburgh, 1753), who says that in reasoning about morality one must have a religious system or an atheistical one: we must at least tacitly adopt 'one of the above contrary hypotheses', and in such a competition every phenomenon of nature will allow us to give the preference to religion (31–2). 'But let us for a moment suppose it doubtful which of the two hypotheses is the truest...' then for reasons too obvious to be mentioned we must choose what now becomes 'the religious principle' (36). 'Hypothesis' could thus be used in this context in a perfectly innocuous way, and as used by Hume must be regarded as part of the smokescreen which has made it so difficult to penetrate to his real meaning, especially in the *Dialogues concerning Natural Religion*, though modern scholarship moves fairly consistently in the negative direction, though in various ways.[1]

Religious 'hypothesis' in the 'good' sense would fit what Hume says about natural religion in the Introduction to the *Treatise* – a strange remark that does not seem to have caused any stir – that it is dependent on the science of man, and given a thorough knowledge of that is capable of improvement. ''Tis impossible to tell what changes and improvements we might make in these sciences ...' i.e. Mathematics, Natural Philosophy and Natural Religion (*Treatise*, xix). Perhaps the latter is susceptible only of 'change' and

---

[1] I find the interpretation of A. Jeffner (*Butler and Hume on Religion*, Stockholm, 1966) even more convincing than that of Norman Kemp Smith (in his Introduction to the *Dialogues*). According to Jeffner, no one, not even Philo the sceptic, is meant to represent Hume in the *Dialogues*: *all* the arguments are destroyed, and all three positions are untenable (192–209). This tallies with the conclusion of the *Natural History of Religion*: 'the whole is a riddle, an enigma, an inexplicable mystery'.

not 'improvement'; perhaps he really did believe at the time that his philosophy ('the author's principles concerning causes and effects') did not damage in any way 'the solid arguments for natural religion', as he asserted in *Letter from a Gentleman* of 1745 (24), even though the latter was part of his campaign to get the chair of moral philosophy at Edinburgh; in view of his remarks to Hutcheson previously quoted it is not easy to see how natural religion was going to be 'improved' by the science of man, unless improvement consisted in reducing it to the sort of 'philosophical' as opposed to 'popular' religion described later by Hume, which is harmless but also wholly ineffectual and lacking in any truly religious content. Perhaps this is a tongue-in-cheek remark, an example, the first, of Humian irony: perhaps it means that natural religion would be improved by the elimination of revealed (the section of the *Treatise* which Hume cut out before publication, for prudential reasons, what he described to Kames as its nobler parts).

At the very least experimental philosophy meant the temporary bracketing off of the religious hypothesis, and therefore what Colin Maclaurin in his *Account of Sir Isaac Newton's Philosophical Discoveries* (1748) called 'learning from observation and experience the true constitution of things' as opposed to supposing and imagining systems, not inquiring (4–5), in Hume meant something not found in the Newtonians; the elimination of final causes, and those 'purposes of a higher kind' to which, said Maclaurin, natural philosophy was subservient. (Natural philosophy was 'chiefly' to be valued as it laid a sure foundation for natural religion and moral philosophy etc. (3).) This really was a new scene of thought, and even if by that expression Hume meant his discovery of the principle of association, as some think, that narrower prospect of novelty presupposes the broader one, in so far as the whole notion of a mental mechanism implies the rejection of the 'mere' hypothesis of human nature as a structured system or value hierarchy. And this does not mean that one must think of Hume's psychology as 'mechanistic' and 'atomistic'; such an interpretation misses some notable aspects of it. The revision of the older view does not affect the issue however: Hume's science of human nature is still incompatible with any such idea of human nature as is proved 'experimentally' by Hutcheson; and whatever the role of reason may be in Hume's philosophy, to mention another controversial matter, it is not the reason which presides over a 'system' or 'constitution'. Hume does not range the powers and faculties and passions in a pyramid: he really is doing for the human mind something like what the scientific revolution of the previous century had done for the universe, and this is the positive aspect of his much abused, because allegedly 'mechanical', idea of mind.

Given the generally prevailing notion of 'experimental' method,[1] Hume's new scene of thought was almost in the nature of the crazy hunch of a man who refuses to accept 'the true constitution of things', and this is the importance of his crisis of faith, because otherwise his empiricism would surely have been the empiricism which included natural religion without question. The crucial thing is not the 'Newtonianism' which has become a cliché, but the conjunction or coincidence of experimental philosophy and religious scepticism.[2] In the light of contemporary empiricism, Hume was not a Newtonian or experimental philosopher; in questioning and refusing to accept the *a posteriori* proof of natural religion, he was flying in the face of experience: he was falling short of the proper limits of experience, not refusing to go beyond its bounds.

His application of experimental method was also a risky venture, only possible in 'a land of toleration and liberty' (*Treatise*, Introduction, xxi), 'where liberty, at least of philosophy, is so highly valu'd and esteem'd' (*Letter from a Gentleman*, concluding sentence. And one should remember the quotation from Tacitus which comes immediately below the sub-title of the *Treatise of Human Nature*.) There are remarks in the *Essays* which suggest that Hume thought the times were, or were becoming, suitable for a science of morals and politics and 'criticism',[3] independent of theology in a sense in which for the natural law writers they were not, in so far as one of their leading characteristics, in Britain, at

---

[1] The alliance of experimental natural science and theology is too well known to call for extensive sign-posting. See, e.g. R. S. Westfall: *Science and Religion in 17th century England*, R. H. Hurlbutt: *Hume, Newton and the Design Argument*, James Noxon: *Hume's Philosophical Development*.

[2] Empiricism, as Hume understood it, precluded theological presuppositions as well as *a priori* method, though the critique of theological assumptions in ethics is less familiar (M. S. Kuypers, *Studies in the 18th Century Background of Hume's Empiricism* (1930) 97, 99). I do not agree that the critique of theological assumptions was as 'outspoken' as that of *a priori* method. This aspect of Hume's Newtonianism has been thoroughly explored by Noxon, *op. cit.*

[3] 'criticism' did not mean exclusively literary criticism. Cf. Hutcheson *System*, II, 147 n. 'As there are no rules of interpretation peculiar to contracts or laws which do not hold equally about any other sort of speech or writing, it seems better to leave them entirely to the art of criticism, which may have laws and contracts as a part of its object.'

any rate, was an almost total indifference to religion, a belief which was shared by leading churchmen, such as Warburton and Berkeley. Thus in the essay *Whether the British Government inclines more to Absolute Monarchy or to a Republic*, Hume wrote: 'Most people, in this island, have divested themselves of all superstitious reverence to names and authority: the clergy have entirely lost [1741-8, thereafter 'much lost'] their credit: their pretensions and doctrines have been ridiculed; and even religion can scarcely support itself in the world.' And to the essay *Of National Characters* was added in 1753-4 the remark that the people of Britain 'are now settled into the most cool indifference with regard to religious matters that is to be found in any nation of the world'. If this means that Hume thought that opinion was moving into a secular phase (and he was still waiting on his death bed, if one can believe the reports),[1] he was nevertheless careful to keep his study of the foundations of politics and his examination of the religious hypothesis in two separate compartments. Whether he did this consciously and with set purpose or not, the fact is undeniable that in the *Treatise* we have a political philosophy in which there is no mention of God, an unbroken, and for the historian at any rate, though the fact may simply be taken for granted by a modern reader, uncanny silence with respect to anything to do with religion, natural or revealed.[2]

Hume's political philosophy is wholly and unambiguously secular.[3] And because this is so, and because the scrutiny of the

---

[1] Cf. Adam Smith's report of the excuses Hume thought up to get Charon to delay the boat. 'If I live a few years longer, I may have the satisfaction of seeing the downfall of some of the prevailing systems of superstition. But Charon would then lose all temper and decency. "You loitering rogue, that will not happen these many hundred years".' *Letters*, II (Appendix I), 451, Mossner's *Life*, 600-1.

[2] There is no use of Scripture or mention of it. In the Section on Justice in the *Enquiry concerning Morals*, there is mention of the 'supreme Creator' (191), but the context, the 'absolute' state of nature, only spotlights the wholly gratuitous nature of the reference. The unbroken silence in the account of justice and political obligation in the *Treatise* is all the more striking when one turns to the *Original Contract* essay, and finds Hume beginning with the remark that no one who admits a general providence will ever deny that the Deity is the ultimate author of all government, and filling his paragraph with references to that beneficent Being, that omniscient Being, the Divine Superintendent, and the intention of Providence. No doubt by then Hume thought that he had better do a bit of bowing down in the house of Rimmon.

[3] The contrast with the political philosophy of Locke will strike anyone who has followed the more recent commentaries on it, those of Polin, Dunn and others who in different ways have stressed the crucial importance of natural religion, or in the final analysis even Christianity. See, for instance, *John Locke, Problems and Perspectives* (ed. J. W. Yolton), pp. 93n., 105-7, 214. The argument of the *Second Treatise* is grounded on the fact that the fundamental law of nature concerning the

religious hypothesis is kept separate, it is easy to overlook the fact that Hume's political philosophy is not complete without it, in so far as it was designed to take the place of the contract theory which rested on the religious hypothesis in the final analysis.

Hume's target in the ethical part of his philosophy was the system of the ethical rationalists: they had been under heavy fire for some time, from Hutcheson and others, and in orthodox religious circles they were not above suspicion either. But demolition of the ethics of Cudworth, Clarke and Wollaston did not affect the ground of what Hume called the 'fashionable system' of politics, viz: the contract theory of political obligation. And Hume did not, in fact, directly confront the ethical systems in the standard books of natural law, or the notion that the precepts of natural law are the laws of God, even if they do not oblige simply and solely for that reason.

Hume's critique of the contract theory of political obligation is sufficiently well known: what is not so well known is the fact that without his critique of the religious hypothesis he has only scotched the snake, not killed it. Hume argues, in the *Treatise*, that on the first formation of government there could be no other obligation except the promise contained in the original contract, and to that extent he agrees with the contractarians, but when government has upheld the interests of society for some time, that becomes the ground of the obligation to obey. Political obligation detaches itself from the obligation to perform promises and carries an obligation of its own, independently of promises and contracts, because it is government which now upholds contracts and ensures that promises are performed. The two interests, that of performing promises and that of obeying the magistrate, are distinct, but the latter is superior because without it, the former is impossible; it is government that makes promises possible at all and enforces them.

If anyone wonders why Hume's apparently simple and devastating argument had so little effect, the answer presumably is that it would not by itself convince a believer in the truths of natural

---

preservation of mankind, 'that general rule which nature teaches all things', as Locke calls it in the *First Treatise*, § 56, is a declaration of the will of God (§ 135). Natural law is not an innate idea, but Locke makes no show of experimental philosophy in deriving it from the condition of man as given to observation, though this no doubt was not called for in the *Second Treatise*. But since Locke did not use this powerful weapon of experimental philosophy, as others had done, the question remains: was he avoiding the use of it, or was he taking a short cut? The answer to the question depends on how empirical one regards Locke's philosophy as a whole. Presumably Hume regarded Locke as applying the experimental method to the science of man in the narrower sense of psychology, and no further, or not much.

religion who was not going to admit that the two interests, in keeping promises and obeying government, are qualitatively the same. The contract theory which Hume attacked rested on some supernatural sanction; for the contractarians, the promise, unlike government, was not just one more invention in the interests of society, that is, human society in the 'lower' or 'narrower' sense, which for Hume is its only meaning. The obligation to keep faith, according to the 'fashionable system', would hold even if there were no such thing as society in Hume's sense at all. Therefore political obedience rests on the promise, because the promise carries the higher, and ultimately divine, sanction; it was not on the same plane of experience as government, and carried a higher authority and superior moral sanction.

As Hume said:

'Tis reasonable for those philosophers, who assert justice to be a natural virtue, and antecedent to human conventions, to resolve all civil allegiance into the obligation of a promise, and assert that 'tis our consent alone, which binds us to any submission to magistracy. For as all government is plainly an invention of men, and the origin of most governments is known in history, 'tis necessary to mount higher, in order to find the source of our political duties, if we wou'd assert them to have any *natural* obligation of morality. These philosophers, therefore, quickly observe, that society is as ancient as the human species, and those three fundamental laws of nature [concerning the stability of property etc] as ancient as society: so that taking advantage of the antiquity and obscure origin of these laws, they first deny them to be artificial and voluntary inventions of men, and then seek to engraft on them those other duties, which are more plainly artificial. But being once undeceived in this particular, and having found that *natural* as well as *civil* justice, derives its origin from human conventions, we shall quickly perceive, how fruitless it is to resolve the one into the other, and seek, in the laws of nature, a stronger foundation for our political duties than interest, and human conventions; while the laws themselves are built on the very same foundation. On which ever side we turn this subject, we shall find, that these two kinds of duty are exactly on the same footing and have the same source both of their *first invention* and *moral obligation*. They are contrived to remedy like inconveniences, and acquire their moral sanction from their remedying those inconveniences (*Treatise*, Book III, Part II, Section VIII, 542–3).

'On which ever side we turn this subject' only applies if read in conjunction with the *Dialogues on Natural Religion*, or those parts of the *Treatise* which Hume excised, or Sections X and XI of the *Enquiry concerning Human Understanding*. Hume was committed to a purely historical, that is conjectural-historical, account of the origin and development of justice, and this was as close as he got to an explicit rejection of the religious ground of political obligation. But, as Hume could not quite bring himself to say in the passage quoted, for the natural law writers and contract theorists government was a purely human invention in the interests of society, but the obligation to keep faith was a superior obligation, so that government and political obligation must rest on the latter. Only if one accepted Hume's secularization of politics, operating solely on the 'lower' plane of social experience, could one accept his demolition of the contract theory, and agree that Grotius and Pufendorf, in order 'to be consistent' should derive justice exclusively from social utility. (*Letters*, I, 33: Hume to Hutcheson, September, 1739. '*Atque ipsa utilitas justi prope mater et æqui*. Says one of the best moralists of antiquity [Horace]. Grotius and Pufendorf, to be consistent, must assert the same.') It is disingenuous of Hume to say, in the *Enquiry concerning the Principles of Morals* (195), that whatever principles the natural law writers set out with, they always 'assign as the ultimate reason for every rule which they establish, the convenience and necessities of mankind', and to regard this as a concession extorted in opposition to systems. The 'ultimate reason', established and confirmed by 'experimental' philosophy, for them was God.

What Hume put before his contemporaries therefore was an exclusively secular because exclusively empirical (or the other way round) version of the fundamental principles of natural law, an attempt to lay the foundations of a science of morality and law in a science of man which had no need of the religious hypothesis, or for that matter of the atheistic hypothesis of Hobbes,[1] which had thrown off 'all prejudices', and was 'consistent', as Grotius and Pufendorf were not. Being exclusively empirical and secular is what made Hume's account 'consistent', and what distinguishes it from the 'empirical' theory of natural law of Hutcheson and the authors recommended by Hutcheson: Pufendorf, Locke – if or in so far as Locke's is or was meant to be an 'empirical' theory of natural law – and the rest. It meant pruning the idea of justice of its universal or superior meaning, as also the idea of society as the society of rational beings as such, for whom justice means promoting the good of the whole and giving every one his due in

---

[1] 'Hobbes's politics are fitted only to promote tyranny, and his ethics to encourage licentiousness. Though an enemy to religion, he partakes nothing of the spirit of scepticism; but is as positive and dogmatical as if human reason, and his reason in particular, could attain a thorough conviction in these subjects.' *History*, VIII, 412.

the light of it. Justice could not be defined as giving every one his due until what was everyone's due had been established and defined by 'convention': the 'convention' therefore came first and could not be explained in terms of justice: it explained the notion of justice, not vice versa. So justice was what Hume called an 'artificial' virtue.

An empirical account of justice must seek its ground in human nature: this is what Hutcheson and Pufendorf and the natural law theorists had in their various ways done. Hume could find no immediate relation between justice – or any of the 'artificial' political virtues – and any natural inclination or propensity of human nature given to observation and experience. There was in human nature no such thing as love of humanity as such. The moral imperative to promote the good of the whole system of rational agents, the classical definition of justice as *suum cuique tribuere* had no empirical foundation. There is no natural motive to the performance of acts of justice: no simple original instinct for justice, like hunger, thirst, resentment, love of life, attachment to offspring, because there is no simple original instinct for property which is the object of justice (*Enquiry concerning Morals*, 201). 'We may as well expect to discover, in the body, new senses, which had before escaped the observation of mankind.' For Hutcheson and the natural law writers, the natural motive to acts of justice in the final analysis, allegedly as natural as any of those mentioned by Hume, is piety, and the whole range of natural motives comprised under that. Hume does not mention them in his account of justice: but explained later, in the Introduction to the *Natural History of Religion*, that there is no primary religious sentiment or natural motive to piety: 'the first religious principle must be secondary'.

Hume argues that for an act to be moral, there has to be a motive considered good independently of the sense of the virtue of the action, and his difficulty was to find one in the case of justice, because there is no natural inclination to be just. Analysis of justice showed that the passion involved was contrary to just action and socially destructive, in itself: it pointed the wrong way. Justice and hence human society was possible because the socially destructive passion was redirected by the understanding; reason acting obliquely on the passion, as always in Hume's account of the relation between reason and the passions. Since man was a creature of understanding and passion, society must be as old as the species; only abstraction for the sake of exposition could separate them; that is (1) the passions and the understanding and

THE FOUNDATIONS OF POLITICS

(2) man and society (*Treatise*, Book III, Part II, Section II, 493). This philosophical, experimental separation gives one the imaginary or 'supposed' state of nature, 'which never had and never could have any reality', which Hume variously describes as 'that savage condition which precedes society' (*Treatise*, 493), 'that savage and solitary condition, infinitely worse than the worst situation that can possibly be supposed in society' (497), that 'imaginary state which preceded society' (501), 'men in their savage and solitary condition' (502), and 'that wretched and savage condition which is commonly represented as the state of nature' (534). All these references are to something entirely fictitious: in fact, Pufendorf's absolute state of nature, except that in Hume it is a wholly amoral state and really is the negative *Gegenbild*[1] of civilized society.

Therefore to describe justice as 'artificial' did not mean that it was an arbitrary invention in the Hobbesian style: it was an invention of a naturally inventive species, and from that point of view 'natural': the spontaneous product of life in society, and like that, as old as the species. Therefore Hume was prepared to call the rules of justice 'natural laws', since they are as old and as universal as society and the human species, but prior to government and positive law.

Using the state of nature as a useful analytical tool, which is all it possibly can be, one can see that although the rule for the stability of property is so obvious and simple that every parent in order to preserve peace among his children, must establish it (493), it is not simply the product of the understanding realizing its necessity for such an animal as man, who without society, is worse off than any animal – this knowledge men in their 'wild, uncultivated state' cannot attain, 'by study and reflection alone', but is inconceivable without the pressure of another necessity, 'which having a present and more obvious remedy may justly be regarded as the first and original principle of human society' (486). According to Hume, 'the natural appetite betwixt the sexes' in human beings necessarily gives rise to the family, and life in the family demands elementary rules of meum and tuum. As men cannot foresee the advantages of something of which they have had no experience, the family is man's first social tutor: 'in a little time, custom and habit operating on the tender minds of the children makes them sensible of the advantages which they may reap from

---

[1] For this aspect of Hume's 'wild, uncultivated state', see especially 485, the § beginning "Tis by society alone that he is able to supply his defects', where Hume refers to the division of labour.

society as well as fashions them by degrees for it...' (486) The extension of the rule about stability of possessions beyond the family is due to a sense of common interest or 'agreement' or 'convention', and this is something which becomes more firmly established as the rules are more strictly and universally observed and the advantages become more obvious: the first rudiments of justice must every day be improved, as the society enlarges (493). This is what Hume means when he says in the 'convention' paragraph, that the rule concerning stability of possession 'arises gradually and requires force by a slow progression...' (490). A gradual development is envisaged. In using the fictitious device of the state of nature to explain the origin of the rule concerning present possession, in which men are viewed as entering into a convention in order to remedy the disadvantages of that state, Hume says that he is only supposing 'those reflections to be formed at once, which in fact, arise insensibly and by degrees' (503). What is involved is the realization that the rule must 'extend to the whole society and be inflexible either by spite or favour' (502), and this can only be the result of the progress of civilization. In the essay on the *Rise and Progress of the Arts and Sciences*, Hume says that all general laws are attended with inconveniences, when applied to particular cases; and it requires great penetration and experience to see that these inconveniences are fewer than what result from full discretionary powers in the magistrate (*Essays*, 116). But the fundamental rules of justice themselves are aboriginal: the interest which all men have in the upholding of society and observation of the rules of justice is 'palpable and evident, even to the most rude and uncultivated of human race; and 'tis almost impossible for any one, who has had experience of society, to be mistaken in this particular' (*Treatise*, 534).

Hume has sometimes been given credit for being more sociologically realistic in his political philosophy than the natural law writers and contractarians, either in a rather general sort of way which leaves much to be explained,[1] or else, more specifically, for the wrong reasons – as though he did away with or had no use for the sociological absurdity of the 'state of nature' except as a methodological device, because he knew that men had been social from the first, owing to the aboriginal existence of the family – the implication being that his 'opponents' did not. But this is to

[1] As, for example, by John Laird: 'from the genetic point of view, he showed himself to have a much firmer grasp of social realities than either Hobbes or Locke had had'. He went a very long way towards recognizing the implications of a *developing* social sense. *Hume's Philosophy of Human Nature*, (1932), 232.

mistake the nature of the social realism of Hume's account of justice and society, to give him credit for the wrong reason. One suspects that behind these mistaken notions there lurks the assumption that in contractarian theory, the social contract creates society, that prior to that no social state had existed.[1] This mistake may be due to the fact that these writers often use 'society' as a shortened form of 'civil society', and it is 'civil society' or government, regular political authority and subordination in the state, that is created by the social contract, not society as such. The state of nature before the contract was a social state: any wholly non-social state or absolute unmodified state of nature, applying to all men at once, could only be, as in Hume, a fictional device. Pufendorf said that one must assume that Hobbes meant his state of nature to be taken in that way (*Law of Nature*, Book II, Ch. II, § VII), as an imaginary state, and Pufendorf used it himself, and one of the purposes of Pufendorf's use of it was carried over into Hume's picture of the contrast between the miserable condition of men without the advantages of social union, the division of labour etc., and civilized society, in which the state makes possible a more commodious way of life. But as Hutcheson said, that the state of solitude was unnatural was 'abundantly explained' by almost all authors upon the law of nature (*Systems*, I, 288), and Dugald Stewart, expounding the leading ideas of the systems of natural jurisprudence, said that one of the objects was to lay down those rules of justice which would be binding on men 'living in a social state, without any positive institutions; or (as it is generally called by writers on the subject) living together in a *state of nature*', (*Works*, I, 173). They thought of the state of nature as consisting of very large family units, with dependents and servants, almost small clans,[2] and it is the heads of these families who establish

---

[1] Sir William Temple thought that this was what contract theory implied. He was searching for some 'natural authority' as a more likely origin of government than 'any contracts: though these be given us by the great writers concerning politics and laws'. This principle of contract, he says, seems calculated for the account given by some of the old poets of the original of man, whom they raise out of the ground by great numbers at a time in perfect stature and strength. Whereas if we deduce the several races of mankind in the several parts of the world from generation, we must imagine the first numbers of them to assemble not as so many single heads, but as so many heads of families whom they represent in the framing any compact...and consequently who have already an authority over such numbers as their families are composed of. *Essay upon the Original and Nature of Government* (1672). *Works of Sir William Temple* (1750), I, 99–100.

[2] Cf. Heineccius: '...we can never say that Abraham, for example, lived in a solitary state, who besides a wife and a hand-maid, and many children by both, had such a numerous retinue of servants that he could bring into the field three hundred and eighty servants born in his family, Gen. XIV, 13'. *Methodical System*, II, 88.

regular civil government, or 'civil society', when the growth of population and developing social needs makes it essential.

Hume's account of 'the state of society without government' is similar, except that between the family and civil society he interposes a 'conjunction of many families' in a tribe, with 'the American tribes' in mind, and uses this to drive home the point that 'the state of society without government is one of the most natural states of men, and must subsist with the conjunction of many families, and long after the first generation'. Nothing but the increase of riches and possessions could oblige men to quit it, and given the primitive nature of the prevailing social conditions, 'many years must elapse' before this could become dangerous to the enjoyment of peace and concord (*Treatise*, 541). So that Hume's primitive state of society without government is more of a genuine social state than the state of nature of Locke and Pufendorf, let alone Hobbes, in so far as for Locke especially, it can be so uncomfortable and so short-lived as to appear more like an argument for government than a possible human state.[1] The point Hume is making is a factual, anthropological one, because he too regarded this state as exceedingly primitive and government as alone what makes possible any sort of civilized existence.[2] But when Hume

---

[1] As for example, without going into the matter of Locke's state of nature any further, when he says that mankind, notwithstanding all the privileges of the state of nature, 'being but in an ill condition, while they remain in it, are quickly driven into society [i.e. civil society]. Hence it comes to pass that we seldom find any number of men live any time together in this state'. *Second Treatise*, § 127. Hume's remarks do seem like a reply to this. They seem to be contradicted by what he says in the second paragraph of the *Original Contract* essay, where Hume says that as it is impossible for the human race to subsist, at least in any comfortable or secure state, without the protection of government, this institution must have been intended by that beneficent Being who means the good of all his creatures 'and as it has universally, in fact, taken place in all countries and all ages' etc.

[2] M. Seliger, *The Liberal Politics of John Locke* (1968), 90. For Locke government is 'the vital pre-requisite of social life'. If Locke means civilized or decent social life, he is in agreement with Hume. Otherwise the question becomes the difficult one as to what constitutes 'government' in primitive peoples (there is a point beyond which it becomes rather useless to press questions about which we have so much more knowledge and awareness and sophistication. One creates a shimmer of suppositions and forced interpretations). In the *Enquiry concerning Morals*, the tribal stage between the family and civil society is absent (192. The context makes it clear that the 'one society' into which the 'several families unite together', is civil society). Hume is not interested in the stages of social evolution, but in proving the ground of justice to be utility. Also the family as the original social unit appears here as an axiom, and belongs to logic rather than sociology: the war of all against all can hardly be called a *state*: 'men are necessarily born in a family-society at least; and are trained up by their parents to some rule of conduct and behaviour' (190). In the *Treatise*, 'we not only observe that men *always* seek society, but can also explain the principles on which this natural propensity is founded', viz: the sex-instinct (Book II, Part III, Section I, 402).

says that man's 'very first state and situation may justly be esteemed social' (*Treatise*, 493), he is thinking of the sex instinct and the family, and the remark is wholly in line with natural law theory: the stress falls on 'justly' and implies agreement with a tradition of social theory against the eccentrics of the 'selfish system', ancient or modern.

Moreover recent commentaries on Locke have been inclined to stress the natural continuity between the state of nature and civil society in the *Second Treatise*, so that the transition from the 'political society' of the family to that of the state appears as smooth, and lacking the rational contrivance and artificiality which contractarian thinkers in general and Locke in particular have so often been accused of: contract and consent belong, it is pointed out, to two different levels of discussion.[1]

[1] M. Seliger, *op. cit.*, 88–9, 221–3. G. S. Schochet 'The family and the origin of the state in Locke's political philosophy' in *John Locke: Problems and Perspectives* (ed. Yolton). Also Hans Aarsleff in *ditto*, especially 108n. Cf. Sterne, *Tristram Shandy*, chapter 31; the foundation of 'political or civil government' is laid in the first conjunction of male and female etc. Blackstone says that 'when society is once formed, government results of course, as necessary to preserve and keep that society in order'. What keeps men together is their sense of weakness and imperfection: this is the 'natural foundation as well as the cement of society', and this is what is meant by the original contract of society, not some meeting of individuals, motivated by reason and a sense of their wants and weaknesses, in order to elect a governor. Such a state of nature, in which men are 'unconnected with other individuals', could never have existed: man is incapable of living alone, 'as is demonstrated by the writers on the subject' (Blackstone singles out Pufendorf, with Barbeyrac's commentary), and moreover 'this notion of an actually existing unconnected state of nature' is plainly contradicted by the revealed accounts of the primitive origin of mankind and their preservation for two thousand years: both of which were effected by the means of single families. 'These formed the first society among themselves' (*Commentaries*, I, 43–8). Shaftesbury envisages a natural social evolution based on man's necessitous state compared with all other creatures, and the need for 'union and strict society' between the sexes, to preserve and nurse their growing offspring. 'Where, therefore, should he break off from this society, if once begun? For that it began thus, as early as generation, and grew into a household and economy is plain. Must not this have grown soon into a tribe? and this tribe into a nation? Or though it remained a tribe only; was not this still a society for mutual defence and common interest? In short, if generation be natural, if natural affection, and the care and nurture of the off-spring be natural, things standing as they do with man...it follows that society must also be natural to him, and that out of society and community he never did, nor ever can subsist' (*The Moralists* in *Characteristics*, II, 318–19). Shaftesbury is not especially interested in the origin of government, as such; the point he is anxious to make, against Hobbes, is that man is naturally a creature of society, and this includes civil society. His natural state is either any state in which he happens to find himself, and he must have 'endured many changes', or, if there must be only one, that in which nature is 'perfect and her growth complete' (*id.*, 316). In the *Essay on the Freedom of Wit and Humour*, Shaftesbury similarly traces the origin of 'civil government and society' to the social instinct, the 'herding principle' or 'associating inclination', as seen in the family 'gradually forming' a 'clan or tribe' and a 'public', and cannot understand

Hume does not subscribe to the idea of the family as a 'political society' provided by the patriarchalism of Cumberland, Pufendorf, Locke, Temple and others.[1] Although 'the parents govern by virtue of their superior strength and wisdom' and are at the same time restrained in the use of their authority by the affection they bear towards their children (*Treatise*, 486), Hume deliberately rejected the continuity between family and civil society thereby provided, finding it instead in a society's experience of wartime leadership, which instructs men in the advantages of government. 'This reason I take to be more natural than the common one derived from patriarchal government, or the authority of a father...' (*Treatise*, 541).[2] Observers have noted the sociological realism of this account of the origin of government; the suggestion of 'conflict sociology' in the famous saying that 'camps are the true mothers of cities'. Hume says that the weakness in human nature which leads men to forget the real but more remote interest they have in obeying the rules of justice in favour of nearer objects which strike more forcibly on the imagination, only becomes dangerous to society with the increase in wealth and material possessions. When this happens and government becomes necessary to uphold justice, men have already experienced its advantages in time of war, when the most valuable of all possesions, life itself, is at stake, and discipline and authority are essential. So the remedy

why the 'wit òf man' should make civil government and society 'appear a kind of invention and creature of art' (*Characteristics*, I, 110-11). The social contract is superfluous, and the Hobbesian state of nature a travesty or 'transformation' of human nature – such a condition cannot properly be called a state – its only possible use is to warn of the horrors of anarchy and make men better citizens (II, 312, 319).

Hoadly was anxious to demonstrate, against Filmer, that, although the fact, if it is true, that men had always been under civil government, does not prove that there is any right to government, 'properly so called', without the consent of the society which is to be governed, nevertheless there had been a space of time, from the creation to the deluge, when there was no civil government, and quotes Hooker to this effect. See the *Works of Benjamin Hoadly* (1773), II, 254, *et seq.* Cain did not fear trial, but that all men would be armed against him: no plainer proof of a state of things without civil government. It is also proved by the prodigious increase of wickedness in the whole period up to the deluge etc.

[1] Cumberland describes the family as the first regular society, the first civil state, and paternal power as the copy and origin of civil (and ecclesiastical) power (*op. cit.*, 350). Cf. T. Rutherforth, *Institutes of Natural Law* (1754). It is probable that the first civil societies were nothing else but so many distinct families with their respective parent at the head of each of them; this does not mean that these 'first rudiments of civil society' were from the beginning kept together by the same ties as at present. The fact that civil society is as old as mankind is no objection to civil societies being formed by consent, tacit or express (II, 27–8).

[2] In his last essay on the *Origin of Government*, the family is the 'society' man is compelled to maintain: in his further progress, he is 'engaged to establish political society' to administer justice.

is at hand, and the origin of government is to be sought in conflict, not within, but between societies.

But the realism of this account is immediately marred and the principle of economy offended[1] by the appearance of an original contract, which is less realistic than that of the contractarians in so far as it is presented simply as an historical (or conjectural-historical)[2] actuality; at least it has no other function in Hume, because it is immediately destroyed as the ground of political obligation after the first formation of government. Not only in the *Treatise*, but also in the essay on the *Original Contract*, Hume is at pains to demonstrate that all men being nearly equal in bodily force and mental powers, there must, on the first establishment of government, have been a contract: men must have given promises and been obliged by them. Material possessions are not mentioned in this context, but if it is the growth of wealth inside a society that makes government necessary, it is not easy to see how the sort of equality Hume refers to would not have been overborne by the sort of inequality Adam Smith had in mind when he traced the origin of government to the need of the rich to defend themselves from the poor: the contract is not, as in Pufendorf, a symbol of man's moral equality: it must be exclusively 'historical', but it is not realistic. It falls between two stools, and in Adam Smith and the other leading Scottish social theorists it disappears altogether, as it does in Hume's last essay, on the *Origin of Government*, written in 1774. Here the continuity between war and the 'casual' and 'imperfect' institution of regular government is unbroken. The long continuance of war in a savage state of society enures the people to submission; the leader in war becomes the arbiter of differences even in peace, and gradually, by a mixture of force and consent, establishes his authority; the hereditary principle is established, and with the progress of improvement the crucial step is taken: the magistrate acquires a revenue.[3]

[1] For Hume's application of the principle of economy, see below.
[2] In *Tristes Tropiques*, Lévi-Strauss vindicates the contractarian account of the origin of government against critics like Hume, claiming to have seen something like it actually taking place. But Hume does not criticize the 'historical' aspect of the doctrine where the origin of government as such is concerned. (Violence of course is the origin of most of the governments of recorded history.) Still it is difficult to see how Hume's contract tallies with the rest of his account of the origin of government: if Lévi-Strauss is right, Hume gets away with it more by good luck than good management, and any anthropologist who agrees with Lévi-Strauss would not use the word 'marred'.
[3] Hume's 'late' theory of the origin of government can be seen not only in the *Origin of Government* essay, but also in additions to the *Original Contract* essay, dating from the editions of 1770 and 1777. Hume had written in the *Contract* essay (first

From Hume's point of view, that is from the point of view of experimental philosophy proper, the break in continuity in natural law theory caused by departure from the experimental method comes not between the state of nature and civil society, i.e. between society and government, but between society and the origin of justice, because in natural law theory the fact that society is as old as the species does not explain the origin and nature of justice, unless the phrase applies also to another dimension, the 'society' of men *qua* rational beings, or the 'society' of rational beings which includes God and men, whose existence for Hume cannot be established empirically. The experimental method proper cannot endorse what it must regard as a two-dimensional approach, found in its most proto-Kantian form perhaps in Pufendorf, for whom there is something like a transcendental society of men who are morally obliged (though not wholly, because God's will is also necessary) as rational agents as such,[1] so that they would be able to recognize and be morally obliged by the law of nature and the principle of sociality even in a condition where there are no actual empirical social bonds or connexions at all. As Locke says: 'Truth and keeping of faith belongs to men, as men, and not as members of society', and the context shows that by 'society' he does not

---

published in 1748), that we trace the original contract 'plainly in the nature of man and in the equality which we find in all the individuals of that species' (*Essays*, 454). In 1770 was added 'or something approaching equality', which is no real change. The next paragraph was added in the 1777 edition. Having just written (in the 1748 edition) that because of men's equality nothing but their own consent could have given rise to government at first, he added this paragraph, pointing out that 'even this consent was long very imperfect, and could not be the basis of a regular administration'. The chieftain who had probably acquired his influence in war, ruled more by persuasion than command: 'no compact or agreement, it is evident, was expressly formed for general submission, an idea far beyond the comprehension of savages'; the particular exertions of authority, their frequent repetition, and their obvious utility gradually produced a voluntary and therefore precarious acquiescence in the people. This paragraph was presumably inserted to bring the *Original Contract* essay into line with the *Origin of Government*. But the 'consent' of the people in the *Origin of Government* is not the 'consent' of the *Treatise* and the (1748) unpatched *Original Contract* essay. It is the 'consent' won by the war leader. 'The persons who first attain this distinction by the consent, tacit or express, of the people' must be endowed with superior qualities to win it (*Essays*, 37). It is compatible with the account of government as arising 'casually', and probably as the result of war.

[1] See Hans Welzel, *Die Naturrechtslehre Samuel Pufendorfs* (Berlin, 1958), esp. 47, 53. As Polin says, for Locke society in the largest sense is in principle a moral obligation, and therefore an option for the free, reasonable man, not simply a datum of experience. Raymond Polin: *La Politique Morale de John Locke* (Paris, 1960), see p. 135: 'La sociabilité à laquelle Dieu a destiné l'individu humain n'est donc pas le produit d'un développement essentiel, mais l'oeuvre aléatoire et hypothétique d'une liberté humaine affronté à une obligation raisonnable...La sociabilité doit donc être définie, en termes lockiens, comme une obligation.'

here mean 'civil society', but has Pufendorf's absolute state of nature in mind.[1]

Hume uses the absolute state of nature (purely imaginary in so far as it is considered as applying to all men at once)[2] to demonstrate the precise opposite: viz. the 'artificial', exclusively social nature of the virtue of justice; where the social bonds are wholly absent, as in a siege or shipwreck, justice is wholly absent also, because it has no social utility. So that justice is simply and solely a human device in the interests of society, and society cannot mean anything other than men dependent on each other; a 'society' of men as such, qua rational creatures, autonomous ethical units, is a contradiction in terms. Wherever men meet for social intercourse of any sort, rules emerge of necessity, 'they cannot even pass each other on the road without rules' – the lighter machine yields to the heavier, pedestrians keep to the right ('the right-hand entitles a man to the wall') etc – war has its laws and 'even that sportive kind of war carried on among wrestlers, boxers, cudgel-players, gladiators, is regulated by fixed principles' (*Enquiry concerning Morals*, conclusion of Section IV). The rules of justice are no different.

When Hume was accused of the Hobbesian heresy of maintaining that promises were not binding independent of society, he replied that independent of society there would be no such things as promises, so the question simply did not arise (*Letter from a Gentleman*, 32). If men 'in some primitive unconnected state', should somehow come to the knowledge of those things we call contracts and promises, 'this knowledge would have laid them under no such actual obligation, if not placed in such circumstances as give rise to these contracts'. (This is clumsy writing for Hume, but the *Letter* was 'so hastily composed that I scarce had time to revise it' – quoted in the Editor's Introduction, xviii.) What he could not say was that the really decisive parting of the ways was the rejection of the religious hypothesis as the ground of political philosophy. The result was an exclusively sociological idea of

---

[1] *Second Treatise*, § 14. 'The promises and bargains for truck etc between two men [on a desert island] or between a Swiss and an Indian, in the woods of America, are binding to them, though they are perfectly in a state of nature, in reference to one another. For truth and keeping of faith etc'.

[2] Hume's fictitious state of nature is different from Pufendorf's, in so far as Hume is considering men not merely in abstraction from all dependence on one another (a state which could never have applied to all men at once) but as creatures of passion only, and as such 'incapacitated for society' (*Treatise*, 493). This for Pufendorf would have been a pointless experiment: in his imaginary, absolute state of nature men are still rational.

society and its rules, empirical in the modern sense: *all* the bonds between men are forged in society in what Grotius called the 'lesser' sense.

And the virtue of justice, the moral obligation to obey the rules, only emerges after the rules themselves have been established, and is posterior to the natural interest men have in keeping them, and is not, like the rules, or at least the fundamental one concerning stability of possessions, aboriginal and as old as the human species. Hume considers the two questions (a) concerning the origin of justice and (b) concerning the morality connected with justice separately, and cannot deal with (b) until he has explained (a), and this he finds in the sex-instinct, which is the original cause of justice and society. It is a basic physical necessity and no more – not, as in Pufendorf, a physical necessity superadded to a 'superior' moral imperative[1] – which gives rise automatically to the family and the need for the rule concerning stability of possession, which is 'established' by the parents.[2] The moral obligation comes on the scene when the interest involved in obeying the rules ceases to be immediately obvious; sympathy is then brought in to explain why men feel pleased or displeased with actions in which their immediate self-interest is not involved, and approve or disapprove accordingly, so that the virtue of justice is the result of the enlargement of society to the point where this happens. 'On the first formation of society', interest is a sufficient motive. 'But when society has become numerous, and has increased to a tribe or nation, this interest is more remote; nor do men so readily perceive that disorder and confusion follow upon every breach of these rules, as in a more narrow and contracted society' (*Treatise*, 499).

This is the most significant aspect of Hume's notion of social

---

[1] Pufendorf, *Law of Nature*, Book VI, Ch. I, §§ 2–3. To those who object that we do not need a law of nature when the instinct is so powerful, Pufendorf replies that the very power of the instinct argues a special care in Nature to have the law observed with the utmost strictness, as the immediate cause of the safety and welfare of mankind. Although the instinct has not in itself the force of an obligation, 'Yet it many times happens that we may, by some superior engagement, be obliged to undertake a performance which bare instinct before inclined us to.' One is tempted to say that this is not arguing from 'is' to 'ought', but from 'ought' to 'is', except that the original 'ought' is the command of God whose existence is certain. Cf. also, for example, the considerations on the nature of law in *Cato's Letters*: the law of nature *obliges* us to defend ourselves (6th edition, 1755, II, 69).

[2] Cumberland, who finds the origin of private property in the distinction of meum and tuum in the family, and the fact that the sexual instinct is uninterrupted in man, as opposed to the animals, does not do so wholly and so to speak in one dimension. Cumberland says that the facts of life in the human family necessarily 'supposes the knowledge of the Law of Nature', *op. cit.*, 156.

evolution vis-à-vis the natural law writers: to this extent justice and morality have a social evolution. But it comes out under the pressure of Hume's ratiocination, so to speak, and is not a theme in its own right; nor is it anything like so radical as the evolutionary ideas to be found in Vico or Rousseau or Monboddo. (What apparent intimations there are are really too vague to allow one to say that human intelligence and reason and notions of morality are not aboriginal but only develop with the development of society, and Hume takes it for granted that the family is as ancient as the species.) Still, the virtue of justice is a matter of social progress – 'that virtue, as it is now understood, would never have been dreamed of among rude and savage men' (*Treatise*, 488).[1]

Hume's emphasis on man's social interdependence is wholly in the tradition of the Natural Law writers and their classical progenitors, focussed more sharply in him as in them by the need to refute Hobbes and the 'selfish system' (which for Hume included Locke. See Appendix II to the *Inquiry concerning Morals*, 296). When he defined politics as the science which considers 'men as united in society, and dependent on each other' (*Treatise*, Introduction, xix), he was using a formula straight out of the school.[2] The difference is subterranean; a whole dimension has been removed. This can be illustrated by another useful coincidence.

Shortly after Hume's literary début, in the *Treatise* and the first *Essays*, there died, in January 1743 not far from Hume's home at Ninewells, at the age of 37, a philosopher, William Dudgeon, about whom little is known apart from his published writings (published in one volume in 1765 as *The Philosophical Works of Mr William Dudgeon*), but who has aroused some interest because of his advanced deistic views, which got him into trouble with the Kirk, and because with his farm so close to Ninewells, he must have been known to Hume. McCosh, who miscalls him 'David'

---

[1] Though strictly speaking, in its immediate context, this quotation really belongs to analysis rather than anthropology. The difficulty of distinguishing the two in a thinker like Hume is notorious.
  Man is a creature of passion and understanding, and Hume is considering him as the former only by a process of abstraction which is allowed to moral as to natural philosophers. As such, he is incapacitated for society (493). Interpretation would be easier if Hume did not call this his 'uncultivated' nature, and talk of 'rude and savage men', because that is anthropological discourse.

[2] Cf. Turnbull, *Principles of Moral Philosophy*. 'We are formed and made for society, and dependent one upon another' (176), 'social and reciprocally dependent' (202), or Turnbull in Heineccius, *Methodical System*, I, 200: 'Every man stands in need of man; in that sense all men are equal; all men are dependent one upon another...'

(probably a slip of the pen due to the fact that he is dealt with immediately before Hume) has a short section on him in *The Scottish Philosophy*, pointing out how, among other things, he anticipates Hume's doctrine of necessity, but mentioning also what is especially relevant here: his notion of justice as meaningless without reference to society. The relevant passage comes from a pamphlet first published in 1734, which belongs to the enormous literature of the Deistic controversy, in which Dudgeon says that '...the words just, unjust, desert etc are necessarily relative to society, and...it is nonsense to use them but with respect to men placed in a society'. To drink drunk when alone is to injure oneself, but it cannot be called unjust because the action has no influence on others; it might be wise to punish the man for his own good, and happiness, but it would be no act of justice. But once place this man in society and he is justly punishable for the same action from quite other reasons, to wit, the good and preservation of society and discouragement of others, and differently for the same crime in different societies, according as their different interests require (Dudgeon, *Philosophical Works*, 129–30). This brief passage stands alone; the argument is not followed up or enlarged or repeated. In fact Dudgeon seems to take it for granted that justice is a social utility, wholly relative to particular human societies, and can have no transcendental ground, which was one of the charges brought against Hume.[1]

Equally striking however is the difference between Dudgeon's idea of justice and that of Hume: the former is a stage in a closely knit argument whose whole trend is deeply and sincerely religious, and Dudgeon claimed, truly Christian (155). He thought that it was belief in hell that caused all the differences between religious sects: to remove this fear of eternal torment was to remove at once all contentions about articles of belief and all the evils of organized religion (156). This was the object of all his philosophizing. His writings do not show any interest in social and political philosophy as such. It led him to a consideration of God's justice, and this is the context of the remarks quoted above. They are immediately followed by the contention that it is therefore absurd ('hence appears the absurdity...') to think of God's justice as an attribute distinct from his wisdom and goodness. The usual idea of God's justice, he argues, does not involve the idea of a society: hence the

---

[1] 'Dudgeon fa cosi saltare esplicitamente...ogni fondazione trascendente della giustizia.' G. Carabelli: *Hume e la retorica dell'ideologia* (Firenze, 1972), 201. Carabelli's is the fullest exposition and discussion of Dudgeon's writings known to me.

wholly false idea of divine punishment as retrospective only. In fact it is not punishment at all, but simply the expression of a wrathful being who resents vice as a personal injury and is prevailed upon by the sufferings of another to pass an act of pardon for a few, which otherwise he would not have been inclined to do (132). Such doctrine is the necessary result of failure to grasp the social meaning of guilt, merit, justice, mercy and punishment.

There is, for Dudgeon, essentially no distinction between human and divine justice: in both it is the use of the properest ways to bring about the happiness of society by rewards and punishments (131). Society in fact has a transcendental meaning, which for Dudgeon is the crucial thing. That the other world will be a society, he says, is 'hardly denied or doubted by any reasonable man' (139). We are creatures plainly designed for improvement in knowledge and goodness, and this can only be brought about by mutual intercourse: if in the next world there were no society, there would be no possibility of further progress there, and improvement in this world would be pointless and inconsistent with our notion of divine wisdom. And if the next world is a society, although we will not have the same senses and objects of gratification as in this world, nevertheless senses of some kind, 'both public and private' there must be; there must be the inequalities and differences, 'the particular capacities, inclinations, appetites and particular ties and interests and subordination of creatures' which are necessary to that action, intercourse and improvement in which the happiness of a rational creature consists, so that there will be imperfections and mistakes and therefore rewards and punishments in proportion, 'for a society without laws and sanctions is an absurdity' (141–2). Thus the next world will see a continuation of the discipline necessary for progress in this one, not a manifestation of God's wrath or resentment. Dudgeon is arguing from the obvious fact of the social utility and relativity of justice on earth to a transcendental society and justice. As rewards and punishments are adjusted to suit the different needs of different earthly societies, so they will be in the next world, because God's justice cannot be divorced from his wisdom. Looking at his writings as a whole, one sees that the important thing for Dudgeon is to use the doctrine of moral necessity (which has not been mentioned here) to cleanse men's minds of fear and guilt in the interests of genuine virtue and religious belief – the only end consistent with the goodness of God of annexing punishment to vice is to make us wiser and better (84) – and his argument, depending on the analogy between human and divine justice, is what Hume regarded as impossible. Thus however arresting and outside the mainstream of natural law theory the passage first quoted may be, it is only by a very considerable surgical operation, which would leave very little of Dudgeon's thought, that one can approximate his notion of society and justice to that of Hume.

Hume's one-dimensional account of the social origin and nature of justice can be regarded as a ruthless application of Newton's 'chief rule of philosophizing',[1] 'explaining all effects from the simplest and fewest causes' (*Treatise*, Introduction, xxi); the philosophical as opposed to non-philosophical love of simplicity, 'which has been the source of much false reasoning in philosophy' (*Enquiry concerning Morals*, 298); the principle of parsimony or economy of causes, a crucial aspect of the experimental method applied to morals, much stressed by all the 'Newtonians', and used on all sides as a weapon of controversy, as for example by Hume, to refute the 'selfish system' of ethics: disinterested benevolence is a simpler and more obvious 'cause' than the self-love hypothesis (*Enquiry concerning Morals*, Appendix II, 299, 301). Commentators have noticed this and other aspects of Hume's use of the principle of economy: for example, Hutcheson's moral sense, which leads to a proliferation of other 'senses', is seen as an unnecessary hypothesis.[2] But Hume's criticism of contract theory as a theory of political obligation in general can be regarded as an example: when justice and society have only the one level of meaning the contract theory is redundant. Hume accepts the conclusion of the contractarians, that government is established in the interests of the governed and therefore our submission to it admits of exceptions, but does not need to 'take such a compass in establishing

---

[1] *Enquiry concerning Morals*, conclusion of Section III. This as Noxon points out, is the only published reference to Newton's text (*op. cit.* 71). Rule I says: '*We are to admit no more causes of natural things than such as are both true and sufficient to explain their appearances*. To this purpose the philosophers say that Nature does nothing in vain, and more is in vain when less will serve; for Nature is pleased with simplicity, and affects not the pomp of superfluous causes.'

[2] A. Leroy, *David Hume* (Paris, 1953), 213, 215 ('la méthode expérimentale refuse d'accepter la solution paresseuse, qui multiplie outre nécessité le nombre des principes primitifs') 217. In *La Critique et la religion chez David Hume* (1929), Leroy points out how Hume's use of the principle of economy as a purely logical principle differs from the metaphysical principle, as seen, e.g. in Leibniz (206-7). D. G. C. Macnabb (*David Hume, his Theory of Knowledge and Morality*, 1951) shows how Hume simplifies his account of human nature in certain respects as between the *Treatise* and the *Enquiry concerning Morals*: 'the simpler account, he says, is to be preferred' (190). John Laird, *op. cit.*, 189, 282. Hume, on the passions, like a 'skilful naturalist' used the principle of parsimony. Cf. 238.

our political duties' (*Treatise*, 550). As has been seen, he only hints at the surgical operation that makes this possible. As it renders superfluous also the idea of a 'negative community' (i.e. God's granting all things in common to men) prior to the institution of property: though Hume uses the phrase (*Treatise*, 495... 'men have been obliged to separate themselves from the community, and to distinguish betwixt their own goods and those of others'), it can have no real meaning for him.[1]

Presumably also a great deal more of the traditional apparatus of natural jurisprudence, such as the division of rights and duties into 'natural' and 'adventitious', becomes unnecessary. This however can only be conjectured, because Hume did not construct a system of natural jurisprudence, as he might have done if he had become what at one time he wanted and tried to be, a professor of moral philosophy at Edinburgh or Glasgow.[2] As it is, his work in ethics does not belong to this genre, as so much of Hutcheson's does, and his political philosophy, as we have it in the *Treatise* and the *Enquiry*, is a section of an argument about the nature of moral judgements, and is therefore inevitably less bulky, because it covers far less ground than the standard works of the natural law writers. Nevertheless it is surely not unreasonable to assume that Hume was also consciously and of set purpose applying the principle of parsimony to prevailing theories of natural law, and from this point of view, the experimental method in morals meant not only greater 'consistency', presupposing, as seen, secularization, but greater simplicity, of the correct 'philosophical' sort. Or perhaps one ought to say that the secularization of natural law has this automatic result of excluding certain traditional topics and features. For example, the executive power of the law of nature, which everyone surrenders on the establishment of government in order that it may be exercised on their behalf, which is crucial in Locke, simply disappears. What is not needed, is not there: in a

---

[1] Also Hume's account of occupation is simpler than Locke's. See his critique of 'some philosophers', who 'account for the right of occupation by saying that every one has a property in his own labour' etc. *Treatise*, 505n. Among other criticisms Hume says that it 'accounts for the matter by means of *accession*, which is taking a needless circuit'.

[2] Robert Garioch's poem on the new David Hume tower at Edinburgh University reminds us wittily that Hume did *not* get a chair there (*The Big Music and Other Poems*, 1971). What sort of lectures would Hume have given? It is difficult to imagine him 'covering the ground' and systematically and in exhaustive detail deducing rights and duties from first principles whose ultimate foundations he regarded as questionable, while at the same time he was rapidly losing his early enthusiasm for a 'Newtonian' psychology. To suggest that his lectures would have been something like Smith's raises a number of questions.

primitive society in which possessions are few and of no great value, there is nothing to quarrel seriously about, and men are not naturally quarrelsome and pugnacious, as they are in the psychology of Adam Ferguson. The first rudiments of government do not arise from quarrels among men of the same society, but among those of different societies; this sort of conflict is endemic in a primitive state of society though it is not clear why, and if the state of nature before government is established is uncomfortable, it is because it is materially wretched and primitive, not because of the absence of a common judge to enforce the rules, and it can and will exist so long as such primitive conditions prevail.

The whole apparatus of theology, natural and revealed, with the ramifications of the former in what was for Hume a pseudo-psychology or hierarchical system of human nature, was no longer required. Hume had no need of that hypothesis. By-passing the whole question raised by the writings of Hobbes and Mandeville, as to the goodness or wickedness of human nature, as irrelevant to the question of the origin of society (*Treatise*, 492), Hume singled out one passion alone as socially destructive, if unchecked. 'This avidity alone, of acquiring goods and possessions for ourselves and our nearest friends is insatiable, perpetual, universal and directly destructive of society... So that upon the whole, we are to esteem the difficulties in the establishment of society, to be greater or less, according to those we encounter in regulating and restraining this passion' (*id.*). All the others, vanity, pity and love, envy and revenge, are either relatively harmless and easily restrained, or may, like vanity, even be esteemed a 'social passion and a bond of union among men' (presumably an echo of Mandeville). No hierarchical structure of the human constitution, no moral sense, as in Hutcheson, no elaborate account of human depravity, as in Pufendorf, is needed to explain justice. All that is needed is a passion which 'restrains itself'. ('Whether the passion of self-interest be esteemed vicious or virtuous, 'tis all a case; since itself alone restrains it...' (492).) It is all very simple and obvious. Indeed, in the *Enquiry concerning Morals*, Hume does not need a psychology at all, in order to explain the nature of justice: all that must be granted is that men are usually found in a medium between extremes, neither wholly benevolent, nor wholly selfish, neither lacking everything, nor, as in the golden age of the poets, lacking nothing: in all these extremes, the rules of justice would be useless: here Hume has simplified his own simplification still further, and in the process lessened the impact of the 'economic interpretation' which is so striking a feature of the earlier account in the *Treatise*.

In the *Treatise*, the Newtonian principle of parsimony reinforces the economic bias of Hume's account of political obligation: 'justice' is technically a set of absolutely basic rules concerning property without which society is impossible and which government is set up to maintain, made necessary by a single passion: to acquire goods for oneself and those dearest to one, which satisfies itself indirectly in this way. Although Hume talks of an insatiable and destructive 'avidity...of acquiring goods and possessions', and 'the love of gain' (491-2), it is not simply an acquisitive instinct, because it is also described as a 'noble...affection' which must be 'acknowledged to the honour of human nature': it is a limited or 'confined generosity' (495), where the emphasis is on 'generosity' rather than on 'confined'; in fact it can be seen as self-preservation, or a need to provide for oneself and family, which necessarily produces 'an opposition of passions and a consequent opposition of interests', given the fact that material goods are not unlimited and unlike other kinds of goods can be advantageously ravished from us (487). But self-preservation, so vital in the natural law systems and in Locke, is either forgotten or taken for granted, and indeed Hume talks in such a way as to make it difficult to include self-preservation under 'property', as in the traditional manner ('talks' rather than 'argues'). And later on, in Hume's account of the origin of government, it does make a fleeting appearance, where Hume says that 'in a foreign war the most considerable of all goods, life and limbs, are at stake' (540). But there is nothing earlier to suggest that 'property' includes 'life and limbs'. It seems that Hume has simply ignored it, carried away by a dominating concern with the economic aspect of society which one sees again in his account of the promise. The promise, wholly secularized, any element of the oath[1] completely removed, becomes an invention, a feigned act of will, in the commercial interest of society: in its very nature conditional ('Your corn is ripe to-day; mine will be so to-morrow', 520), necessary to the division of labour and exchange of goods and services, the

[1] Cf. e.g. Grotius above (Book II, Ch. XI, § IV, 3). In *The Alliance between Church and State* (1736), Warburton says that the 'sanction of an oath' is 'the great fundamental cement of civil society'. The Oath was the sanction to everyone's word universally employed in all conventions. This followed from the fact that civil society was made necessary by everyone's 'equality of power', and could only have rested originally on everyone's will, free consent and promise to obey. The promise by itself could not be a sufficient obligation (3rd edition, 1748, 38-9).

transactions of self-interested commerce (Book III, Part II, Section V).[1]

Hume's political philosophy as expounded in the *Treatise*, because the striking economic orientation seen in the *Treatise* is not found in the *Enquiry*, seems to reflect, in its elemental character, stripped down to bare essentials, in the predicament which is its starting point: scarcity of material goods together with a clannishness which unchecked is fatal to society, and in the definition of liberty as essentially the security of the individual under the rule of law, which is 'justice' in its broader sense, the Scotland of the early eighteenth century, with its vivid memories of the poverty and insecurity of the recent past and great hopes for the future. Hume belonged to the class of lairds who were the leaders of 'improvement', (his close friend, Henry Home, later Lord Kames, was perhaps the greatest and most energetic of them) and who believed that what Scotland needed above all was the direction of energies into secular and economic channels.

It is an unquestioned assumption of Hume's social and political theory that the good life is dependent on economic progress, because the good life is the busy, occupied life and happiness depends on industry and 'that quick march of the spirits which takes a man from himself'.[2] The clearest statement of this belief is to be found in the essay on *Luxury* of 1752, called after 1760 *Of Refinement in the Arts*, in which Hume argues that 'the ages of refinement are both the happiest and most virtuous',[3] and presents a contrast: on the one hand, savagery, isolation, idleness, ignorance, vice; on the other, industry, sociableness, humanity, knowledge, good morals, which mirrors the contrast between Highlands and Lowlands in eighteenth-century Scotland and Hume's typical Lowland view of it.[4] This is Hume at his least sceptical: he had none of the doubts and misgivings which Adam Smith and all the other leading thinkers of the Scottish Enlightenment had

---

[1] See Laird, *Hume's Philosophy of Human Nature*, 230.

[2] From the essay on *Refinement in the Arts*. For an excellent account of Hume's economic psychology, see E. Rotwein's Introduction to his *David Hume: Writings on Economics* (1955).

[3] 'In times when industry and the arts flourish, men are kept in perpetual occupation and enjoy as their reward, the occupation itself, as well as those pleasures which are the fruit of their labour. The mind acquires new vigour; enlarges its powers and faculties... Banish those arts from society, you deprive men both of action and of pleasure...' (*Essays*, 277).

[4] James I's plan for the Irish was 'to reconcile that turbulent people to the authority of laws, and introducing art and industry among them to cure them of that sloth and barbarism to which they had ever been subject'. (*History*, VII, 371).

about the all-round benefits of commercial civilization. The progress of civilization is improvement on all fronts: the 'mechanical' and the 'liberal' arts advance together; 'nor can one be carried to perfection, without being accompanied, in some degree, with the other...the minds of men being once roused from their lethargy, turn themselves on all sides and carry improvements into every art and science' (278). Industry, knowledge and humanity are indissolubly linked together and 'from experience as well as reason' are found to be peculiar to the more polished ages. Moreover, these advantages are not attended with any proportionable disadvantages (278). The more refinement, the less excess of every sort. Knowledge in the arts of government gives rise to mildness and moderation: this humanity is 'the chief characteristic which distinguishes a civilized age from times of barbarism and ignorance. Factions are then less inveterate, revolutions less tragical, authority less severe and seditions less frequent. Even foreign wars abate of their cruelty...' But in this increase of the arts and commerce and humanity, there is no danger to the state. Men do not become enervated either in mind or body, or lose their martial spirit; there is no less courage, and there is more discipline; less ferocity, but a greater sense of honour (280-1). And in the essay *Of Commerce*, Hume argues that in the natural course of things, that is, taking human nature as it is and complying with 'the common bent of mankind', without the violence done to human nature by the policy of the ancient republics, which was only possible in the very special circumstances of a public spirit and *amor patriae* unnaturally heightened by perpetual war, industry and commerce increase the power of the state as well as the happiness of its subjects; there is no conflict between the two.

Thus economic progress brings happiness and the good life, without any diminution of the power and defensive ability of the state. And in Hume's political philosophy, government is there to secure the conditions of economic progress in an advancing society, to provide that security and that rule of law (= liberty) without which progress is precarious or impossible.

This economic orientation can, and has been, criticized as an 'impoverishment' of political philosophy: property and rights are thought of solely in economic terms; natural law no longer calls for the maintenance of personal rights, as in the earlier natural law doctrines.[1] In making this criticism one should remember once

---

[1] Frederick Watkins: Introduction to *Hume: Theory of Politics* (1951), xvi. Cf. P. Larkin, *Property in the 18th Century, with Special Reference to England and Locke* (1930):

again that Hume's political philosophy has limited terms of reference, because what we are given is part of a larger argument. Personal rights are not listed and discussed, but that does not necessarily mean that they are excluded from a modern theory of natural law as envisaged by Hume. All right is derived from the convention to establish property: that is equivalent to saying that it is of social derivation and is prior to government. This is all we are told, but there was no need for Hume to go any further at that juncture. As has been seen, the most considerable of all goods is 'life and limbs'. A more telling criticism of Hume's attempt to derive the principles of natural law exclusively from human nature is that it results in a notion of justice that is self-contradictory: there is a clash between the two senses of 'interest' involved: (1) that which establishes the rules in order to satisfy itself indirectly, and (2) the interest everyone has in seeing that the rules are inflexibly observed, no exception being made, in principle, for the poor man in debt to the millionaire, even if this offends our immediate feelings of equity. It is difficult to see how interest in the first sense is served by the poor man having to repay his debt, if that results in starvation or hardship for himself and his dependents; and such men might form the majority of a given society, as every eighteenth-century schoolboy knew from his Livy. Such a society would, on Hume's definition of justice, be 'just', that is, in the 'interest' of all; nor is there anything in Hume to guarantee that such a state of affairs cannot come to pass. It seems that the clash between the two senses of 'interest' cannot be resolved, because there is no appeal to anything else: not to reason, because Hume insists that reason has nothing to do with the actual distribution of property; who is to possess what? is left to contingency and the 'imagination', and not, as notably in Hutcheson, to a natural law in which God's ultimate dominion over all things remains intact and the rules of property 'may justly be altered and limited under civil polity, as the good of the state requires' (*System*, I, 329). The experimental method proper thus seems to lead to a theory of justice which is deadlocked in hopeless self-contradiction.[1]

Hume's views 'afford, perhaps, the best illustration of a social philosophy shorn of all enthusiasm save that for wealth production' (98). In the *Original Contract* essay, Hume talks of 'justice, or a regard to the property of others', and distinguishes it from 'fidelity or the observance of promises'. Further on he calls 'abstinence from the properties of others', 'private justice' (*Essays*, 466, 468).

[1] For a full discussion of Hume's dilemma, see Silvana Castignone, *Giustizia e bene commune in David Hume* (Milano, 1964). Cf. Larkin: Since for Hume the 'laws of

(*Footnote on p. 89 continued*)

society' are synonymous with the 'laws of justice', and justice is a human contrivance, it would seem to follow that if the State sanctioned a system of property rights which prevented a considerable section of its members from satisfying their minimal needs, one could not according to that view, find fault with it. The view of property which Hume favoured was one which obscured its social aspect (*op. cit.*, 100-1). The contrast in this respect between Hume and Stair and the Scottish institutional writers of the eighteenth century, for whom the owner of property was 'theoretically almost a trustee of his property on behalf of the community', is brought out by Peter Stein in 'Law and Society in Eighteenth-century Scottish thought' in *Scotland in the Age of Improvement*.

3
Political obligation for 'moderate men'

If one tries to understand Hume's political philosophy as a response to the needs of his age and society, as he saw them, certain aspects of it emerge which were long obscured by the fame of the critique of the contract theory, which was the official Whig theory, by his alleged, or at least over-emphasized 'Tory' political sympathies, and by the view of his philosophy generally, which held sway for so long, as essentially negative and critical. The positive side, the application of experimental philosophy to morals, shows us not a demolition of natural law or the 'fashionable system of politics',[1] but an attempt to give them new foundations, designed for a new, secular age, an empirical, scientific, post-revolutionary age in which the challenges and opportunities, the needs and drives of men were predominantly economic, and the old conflicts and loyalties, political, religious and dynastic, outmoded and irrelevant. The appeal was to Shaftesbury's 'men of moderation',[2] for whom politics was above all the science of men united in society and dependent on one another. This science was modern in style, suited to the circumstances and interests of a modern, commercial society, informed by the new scientific method and the predominantly secular outlook. In some respects indeed the ruthless application of experimental method to moral subjects was dangerously avant-garde – Hume's friends seem always to have realized this better than Hume himself – yet it was at the same time a post-revolutionary, establishment political philosophy: its object was to give the established regime, the Revolution Settlement, the Hanoverian succession, the respectable intellectual foundation which, in the 'fashionable system' it had not got, for as Hume said on more than one occasion, government is founded on opinion, not on force (*First Principles of Government, Essays*, 29, *History*, VIII,

---

[1] *Treatise*, 542. The contract 'has become the foundation of our fashionable system of politics'. Shaftesbury called compact 'the fashionable language of our modern philosophy', *Characteristics*, I, 109.
[2] *Characteristics*, I, 115. 'Men of moderation' were men who were too secure of their temper and who possessed themselves too well 'to be in danger of entering warmly into any cause, or engaging deeply with any side or faction'.

143, IX, 513: 'the great security for allegiance being merely opinion').

Contemporary political theory, of both Whigs and Tories, was out-of-date and backward-looking. Each of the rival systems, Contract and Passive Obedience, contained a kernel of truth, liberty and authority respectively, but exaggerated and distorted by party passion, and the result of both popular and hasty workmanship. (See the two essays on the *Original Contract* and on *Passive Obedience*, especially the opening paragraphs. Hume never seems to have realized, or refused to allow, that these systems had any pedigree, or European or classical ancestry. Both of them he regarded, or professed to regard, as British, parochial and recent.)[1] Since the belief in divine right and passive obedience had been undermined by a 'sudden and sensible change in the opinions of men within these last fifty years, by the progress of learning and liberty' (*Essays*, 51), and was an absurdity nullified by the practice of the Tories themselves in 1688, it was contract theory that bore the brunt of Hume's criticism. Its reasoning was faulty and its doctrine contradicted by the test of experience. The contract theorists 'intended to establish a principle which is perfectly just and reasonable' (*Treatise*, 549): that since government is set up in the interests of the governed, our submission to it must admit of exceptions, but, insisted Hume, since resistance was an extreme remedy that put everything in jeopardy, it could be justified only in cases of 'egregious' tyranny, like that of Nero. (*Treatise*, Book III, Part II, Section IX: the examples, Dionysius, Nero, Philip II (of Spain) are more useful than the rather vague phraseology: 'the more flagrant instances of tyranny and oppression', 'grievous tyranny and oppression', 'whenever the interest ceases in any great degree, and in a considerable number of instances', etc. Hume is more precise in the *Passive Obedience* essay, 'the last refuge in desperate cases, when the public is in the highest danger from violence and tyranny'.) Hume is stricter than Hutcheson, in so far as for Hutcheson resistance is not merely a last resort: he allows such violence 'as may occasion some temporary anarchy' where there is the hope of successfully altering a 'foolishly concerted plan of polity' for the better, or preventing it from getting worse (*System*, II, 220).[2] Hume also wished that Hutcheson's condemnation of

---

[1] In the *Original Contract* essay he was surprised to find the doctrine being used in France (by the legitimate princes protesting against provisions in the will of Louis XIV) (*Essays*, 471n).

[2] In the essay on *Passive Obedience* (1748), Hume 'confessed' that he would 'always incline to their side, who draw the bond of allegiance the closest possible'. In the edition of 1770, this was changed to 'very close' (*Essays*, 475).

Locke's theory of consent had been 'more express', it 'being the received one'.[1]

On the other hand in the essay on *Passive Obedience*, Hume finds two excuses for 'that party among us who have, with so much industry, propagated the maxims of resistance...which it must be confessed, are in general so pernicious, and so destructive of civil society', in that (1) they had to insist on the extraordinary exceptions which their opponents played down or excluded altogether, and (2) 'perhaps' the 'better reason', owing to the peculiar nature of the British constitution, where resistance 'must, of course, become more frequent than in less complex forms of government, because the prince is both limited and at the same time, in his person, above the laws. He is more likely to be tempted to abuse his powers, and in such a case there must be a remedy, which is the extraordinary one of resistance 'when affairs come to that extremity, that the constitution can be defended by it alone'. It will be noticed that in his second 'excuse', Hume uses the present tense, and is not talking history, as in the first. Nevertheless one gets the impression that Hume's stress on the exceptional nature of resistance to established government in *Treatise* Book III, Part II, Section X and in the second § of the Passive Obedience essay – government is entirely useless without an exact obedience etc. – is an implicit criticism of the 'fashionable system', as well as being directed against the Jacobites, because that is in itself and as such an insurrection-inviting theory. The resumé in the first § of the Original Contract essay suggests as much.[2]

What commentators watching Hume demolish the foundations of the 'fashionable system' in contract theory are likely to forget, is that this critique, and in particular Hume's doctrine of resistance, bears down not only on Whig theory but on Jacobite practice: one might say that it bears down on Whig theory because of the possibility of Jacobite practice, or at least, the actuality

---

[1] *Letters*, 1, 48. (Hume to Hutcheson, January, 1743.) The reference is to Hutcheson's *Philosophiae Moralis Institutio Compendiaria* (Glasgow, 1742), 266, line 18 *et seq.* Hutcheson says that those who made the original contract stipulated protection and all the other advantages of a civilized life not only for themselves, but for their posterity, who are therefore bound, whether they consent or not, to perform everything which could reasonably be demanded of them for such important benefits received. (Technically they are bound by an obligation *quasi ex contractu*.) Hume says this 'implies' a condemnation of Locke.

[2] 'The other party, by founding government altogether on the consent of the people, suppose that there is a kind of *original contract*, by which the subjects have reserved ('tacitly reserved' as from 1777) the power of resisting their sovereign, whenever they find themselves aggrieved by that authority with which they have, for certain purposes, voluntarily entrusted him.'

of the malcontent conscience. The relevant background is not 1689, but 1715, 1719 and 1745, and in this perspective Hume is to be seen as the honest friend of the Whigs and the established regime, the sort of friend who does not hesitate to point out faults and weaknesses. How serious a menace the Jacobites were or were thought to be need not come into question: the fact is that there was in Hume's words a 'very considerable' minority who believed that they had no moral obligation to recognize the Hanoverians as their legitimate rulers, indeed a moral obligation not to.[1] This considerable minority, Hume argued in a section of the essay on the *Parties of Great Britain* which was, for obvious reasons, withdrawn in the first edition of the essays to be published after the '45, was to be mostly found in England, because in Scotland 'the Jacobite party is almost entirely vanished from among us'. This 'sudden and visible alteration in this part of Britain' was due (1) to the clear-cut division between Presbyterian Whigs and Episcopalian Jacobites, so that Jacobitism in Scotland was more violent, and violent things do not last, and (2) the fact that Scotland lacked 'that middling rank of men' which is so numerous in England, both in cities and in the country, and which consists of men who, unlike the 'slaving poor', have curiosity and knowledge enough to form principles, but who, unlike 'gentlemen', have not enough to form true ones or correct any prejudices they may have imbibed. That is why Tory principles prevail most among the middling rank in England. (Hume's change of view about the middling rank is one of the most clear and indisputable and significant changes in his political and social theory.) This brief foray into the sociology of parties, which was also, at least until the autumn of 1745, good pro-Scottish propaganda, always badly needed south of the Border (it was not long since the Porteous affair), enhanced the importance of the Jacobites, if anything. When Hume writes, in the *Treatise* (554) that 'we ought always to weigh the advantages which we reap from authority against the disadvantages; and by this means we shall become more scrupulous of putting in practice the doctrine of resistance' etc., or 'no maxim is more conformable, both to prudence and to morals, than to submit quietly to the government which we find establish'd in the country where we happen to live, without enquiring too curiously into its origin and first establishment' (558), it is difficult to believe that he is not

---

[1] Some of Hume's close friends were Jacobites. See Mossner's *Life*, 180–2. Kames professed Jacobite principles until some time in the early 1730s. See I. S. Ross, *Lord Kames and the Scotland of his Day*, 44–5, and W. C. Lehmann, *Henry Home, Lord Kames and the Scottish Enlightenment* (1971).

appealing to the 'malcontents'; an appeal which at the end of the essay on the *Protestant Succession*, written in 1748 but not published until 1752, is repeated quite openly. In the *Treatise* he tells the Jacobites in effect that their scruples are not only inexpedient, but immoral. This was in accordance with the teaching of Grotius and the natural law writers: Hume says that any one who denies the right of the present possessor 'absolutely' and on moral grounds, 'would be justly thought to maintain a very extravagant paradox, and to shock the common sense and judgement of mankind' (558), but Hume grounds this right, as has been seen, on the 'imagination'. The question as to the legitimacy or otherwise of particular governments and forms of government (by no means, in 1740, a merely academic question) differs from the problem of political obligation and submission to government as such, in that it is not determined by any considerations of interest. As for the distribution of private property (who is to possess what?), so here: the question is determined not by rational consideration of the general interest but by more 'frivolous' considerations: the commonly accepted rules – long possession, present possession, conquest, succession, positive laws – are to a great extent the work of the 'imagination'. This is because men differ in their private interests and in their notion of what is best for the public interest, which becomes the source of endless dissensions. 'The same interest, therefore, which causes us to submit to magistracy, makes us renounce itself in the choice of our magistrates, and binds us down to a certain form of government, and to particular persons, without allowing us to aspire to the utmost perfection in either.' If men were to regulate their conduct in this question of allegiance to particular governments by their views of interest, the result would be endless confusion, and government would be rendered largely ineffectual (*Treatise*, 555).

An appeal to history completes the discomfiture of the Jacobites: it teaches us to regard the contest between the various titles to government as 'incapable of any decision in most cases, and entirely subordinate to the interests of peace and liberty'. 'Whoever considers the history of the several nations of the world, their revolutions, conquests, increase and diminution, the manner in which their particular governments are established, and the successive right transmitted from one person to another, will soon learn to treat very lightly all disputes concerning the rights of princes, and will be convinced that a strict adherence to any general rules, and the rigid loyalty to particular persons and families, on which

THE FOUNDATIONS OF POLITICS

some people set so high a value, are virtues that hold less of reason than of bigotry and superstition' (562).

'Entirely subordinate to the interests of peace and liberty' (which for Hume are virtually the same thing: viz the maintenance of the rules of justice); Whig theory and the conscientious scruples of Jacobites are both condemned by a political philosophy fashioned to meet the needs of forward-looking 'moderate men' in a modern progressive society.

But there was, it seems, a somewhat embarassing price to be paid. Precisely because they met the needs of moderate men of both parties or of none, these experimentally established, modern principles were not able to justify resistance to James II and the revolution of 1688, except retrospectively. From Hume's account of the foundations of society, could James II be said to have threatened them? These foundations are established without the aid of religion; they are entirely secular, so that religion is not involved in any way. The object of government is to maintain 'peace and liberty', 'Justice', security and property. The form of government is indifferent, provided it carries out its basic task; obedience to particular governments, as seen, rests on such things as long possession, present possession etc., not on the answer to such questions as: is this the best form of government? does it best promote freedom and welfare? The common rule therefore requires submission; resistance can be justified only in cases of 'egregious' tyranny. To describe James II as a Nero was simply bad rhetoric: Hume scorns to do so. And the fact that James II was aiming at absolute government does not in itself, on Hume's general principles, justify resistance. Absolute government is a perfectly legitimate form of government; it answers the end of society as well as any other.[1] What James attempted was successfully achieved in France. 'The kings of France have not been possessed of absolute power for above two reigns; and yet nothing will appear more extravagant to Frenchmen than to talk of their liberties.' And even if James II was a tyrant like Nero, on what grounds can one justify the exclusion of his innocent and rightful heir?

There was only one way in which Hume could, on his own general principles, justify the revolution of 1688, and this is put forward at the end of the Section in Book III of the *Treatise* (Section X) which deals with the 'objects of allegiance', where he says that the title of the Prince of Orange may have been dis-

[1] See below.

96

putable in 1688, but time and custom have given those princes who succeeded on the same title sufficient authority. 'Time and custom give authority to all forms of government, and all successions of princes; and that power, which at first was founded only on injustice and violence, becomes in time legal and obligatory'. Hume wanted to avoid giving unnecessary offence to either party: and to raise the question of the rights and wrongs of 1688 was only to unnecessarily exacerbate the animosities which he wanted to allay. And the same argument was used in the essay on the *Protestant Succession*: 'the settlement in the House of Hanover has actually taken place'; and long possession must have given it a title 'in the apprehension of a great part of the nation', independent of present possession, so that a revolution now would not end the dispute about a contested title. Publication of this essay, written in 1748, was delayed till 1752, because it was thought to be a bit too cool and sceptical. In the *Treatise*, too, Hume seems to have regarded this line of reasoning as rather bold; at any rate, he put forward a justification of the Revolution which was bound to contradict his general principles. Englishmen, he says, will naturally want to hear how we apply our principles to 'that famous *revolution*'. Resistance is justified in extreme cases, but it is impossible for the laws, or even philosophy, to lay down precisely and particularly when such resistance is justified. Even in a limited monarchy it will not be prudent to do so. But not only do the people retain their right of resistance in such mixed governments, but the cases of rightful resistance will be more frequent than in arbitrary governments; resistance will be justified whenever the chief magistrate 'Would encroach on the other parts of the constitution and extend his power beyond the legal bounds...For besides that nothing is more essential to public interest than the preservation of public liberty', every single part of a mixed constitution must be deemed to have a right of self-defence to maintain its 'ancient bounds' against encroachment. Hume is here falling back on a part of the Whig canon which stemmed ultimately from Grotius, (*De Jure*, Book I, Ch. IV, § 13) a passage which was quoted by Sidney in *Discourses concerning Government* (*Works*, London, 1772, 256), by Stanhope in the Sacheverell Trial,[1] and Richard Steele in his Preface to the *Crisis* (January, 1714), quotes Stanhope citing 'this memorable passage from Grotius'.[2]

[1] *An Impartial Account* [of the Trial of Dr Sacheverell], (London, 1710), 107.
[2] *Tracts and Pamphlets* by Richard Steele (ed. Rae Blanchard. Johns Hopkins Press, 1944) 135. 'If the King hath one part of the Supreme Power and the other part is in

It is a gross absurdity, says Hume, to suppose in any government a right without a remedy, or allow that the supreme power is shared with the people without allowing that it is lawful for them to defend their share against every invader. 'Those therefore who would seem to respect our free government, and yet deny the right of resistance, have renounced all pretensions to common sense...' (*Treatise*, 564).

But can Hume make use of this piece of Whig lore consistently with his view expressed earlier (555) that our allegiance to particular governments, as opposed to government as such, is not based on considerations of interest, whether public or private, at all, which means that the question of the advantages or disadvantages of a particular type of government, mixed or absolute, is not relevant, provided the object of government in general is maintained? This is the sort of consideration we expressly renounce when we bind ourselves to a particular magistrate or form of magistracy. Thus the 'common sense' Hume refers to in this context cannot be the common sense which approves of resistance as the last resort, when government is seen not to function *qua* government (that is, maintaining the rules of 'justice'), not *qua* a particular type of government, and which is a property even of the high monarchical party, however much some of them may profess a strict doctrine of passive obedience. In the case of a mixed monarchy, the last resort, 'egregious' tyranny, have a meaning different to that in the general theory.

In the very next paragraph however (564), Hume says that it is not his present purpose to show that what he has just said about the right of resistance in mixed governments is 'applicable to the late *revolution*; and that all the rights and privileges, which ought to be sacred to a free nation, were at that time threatened with the utmost danger'. (It would not matter if they were, according to Hume's own general principles.) He will leave this 'controverted subject, if it really admits of controversy', and 'indulge...in some philosophical reflections which naturally arise from that important event'. By this he means the application of the experimental science of human nature, showing how the right of the regime established by the revolution can be traced to the working of the 'imagination', and thereby by-pass all the legal complexities involved in the

---

the Senate or People when such a king shall invade that part that doth not belong to him, it shall be lawful to oppose a just force to him, because his power doth not extend so far...it is impossible for any to have a share of the supreme power and not likewise a right to defend that share.' T. Rutherforth, *Institutes of Natural Law*, quotes the same passage (II, 426).

question of the exclusion of James II's innocent heir.[1] Our approval of this 'is founded on a very singular quality of our thought and imagination'. It does not seem reasonable to exclude an heir who bears no blame for his father's actions, but 'when the public good is so great and so evident as to justify' the deposition of the father, 'the mind naturally runs on with any train of action which it has begun', and the 'ancient bounds of the laws being once transgressed with approbation, we are not apt to be so strict in confining ourselves precisely within their limits... As the slightest properties of the imagination have an effect on the judgements of the people, it shows the wisdom of the laws and of the parliament to take advantage of such properties, and to choose the magistrates either in or out of a line, according as the vulgar will most naturally attribute authority and right to them' (565-6). (In Hume's account in the *History* (IX, 513-14) of the conferences between the Lords and the Commons anent the settlement of the succession, this justification by psychology is still present, though in attenuated form, as part of the argument which the managers of the Commons might have used to combat the Lords' contention that the next heir by lineal succession could not rightfully be excluded.)[2] This argument rests on the assumption that James did justly forfeit his right, or at least that the 'vulgar' thought so. But it was not everyone's mind that worked in this way, because we are next told that the accession of the Prince of Orange to the

[1] This, according to the doctrine of Grotius, was not legal, in so far as for Grotius the immediate heir of a kingdom in lineal succession has possession of it in law, if not in fact, as soon as he is born, and his father's abdication cannot disinherit him, though it does so in the case of simple succession. Rutherforth argued at length that this Grotius is not true to his own principles: that an abdication dissolves a monarchical constitution altogether, that a man cannot have an heir as opposed to a successor until he is dead, that there is no difference between the two types of succession, etc. There is no need to go into all the legal subtleties. See T. Rutherforth, *Institutes of Natural Law*, II, 635-62. For Hutcheson's opinion, see *System of Moral Philosophy*, II, 302-4, *Short Introduction*, 314-15. Forfeiture which applies to descendants may be contrary to humanity in the case of private inheritances, but the regal office is a public trust. Those in remainder have only a legal claim, 'from the old deed or law', and the true intent of it is presumed to exclude all descendants, and sometimes the whole family, of such as forfeited. The intention of the old laws is clear enough in countries where all inheritances were anciently held as fiefs. Prudence may dictate that the Crown be transferred to a member of the royal family, but this is left to the prudence of the nation. A forfeiture is a *legal* bar to the claims of all descendants, and in the case of the royal office there is no argument from humanity.

[2] 'They might have said, that the great security for allegiance being merely opinion, any scheme of settlement should be adopted, in which it was most probable the people would acquiesce... that the recent use of one extraordinary remedy reconciled the people to the practice of another, and more familiarised their minds to such licences, than if the government had run on in its usual tenor...'.

throne at first gave occasion to many disputes, but time and custom give authority to all forms of government etc.

In all this twisting and turning, the plain fact seems to be that although Hume can defend, quite unambiguously and consistently with his general principles, the present establishment, he cannot unambiguously and consistently defend those who brought it about. At the end of the essay on *Passive Obedience*, the caution and hesitation of the treatment of the revolution of 1688 in the *Treatise*, are absent. It seems that they are no longer required; now that 'animosities are ceased', the truth may now be spoken that the reign of James II constituted 'such enormous tyranny as may justly provoke rebellion' (for this is what Hume says, in effect).[1] But this form of words merely covers Hume's difficulty. James II was not a Nero or Domitian. In the *History* (IX, 488) Hume says that it is 'indeed singular, that a prince whose chief blame consisted in imprudences and misguided principles, should be exposed, from religious antipathy, to such treatment as even Nero, Domitian or the most enormous tyrants that have disgraced the records of history, never met with from their friends and family'. The only thing wanting to make him an excellent sovereign was a due regard to the religion and constitution of his country; because this was lacking, the people were justified in their resistance (*History*, IX, 500). James' religion is a new consideration: his conduct, says Hume, serves to show how dangerous it is to allow any prince 'infected with the catholic superstitition, to wear the crown of these kingdoms' (X, 501). This is not catered for in Hume's theory of political obligation. Religion apart, it is clear that resistance to James II can be justified only on the special mixed monarchy theory – this is what the 'enormous tyranny' of the *Passive Obedience* essay amounts to: Hume says that in a constitution like that of England, resistance will be more frequent because the king is likely to break through the limits imposed on his authority. But this clashes with Hume's general doctrine of resistance: his insistence that any infringement of the bond of allegiance must be 'the last refuge in desperate cases, when the public is in the highest danger, from violence and tyranny' (*Passive Obedience*, 475). In such cases, what constitutes the exception to the general rule of obedience will be so obvious and undisputed as to remove all doubt: that is why there is no need to theorize about resistance; a general

[1] And in the *Original Contract* essay, Hume says that we blame the Jacobites for adhering to a family which forfeited all title to authority 'from the moment the new settlement took place' (*Essays*, 466).

doctrine is uncalled-for and dangerous, and it is impossible to be precise, so that theoretical disputes are meaningless, and resistance cannot be written into any law (*Passive Obedience*, 475–6, *History*, VIII, 143–4, X, 105–6, X, 144–5). This is to say that resistance is justified when and because it is automatic. But can it be automatic in a mixed monarchy in a way that is different, because not so obviously a question of life and death for everybody? The 'extremity' here is when the constitution cannot be defended in any other way (*Passive Obedience*, 477). This surely clashes with Hume's psychology of the force and relative lack of force with which things contiguous and remote respectively affect the imagination, as used to explain the origin of government: what is an 'extremity' for some (those in authority or some of them) will not be an 'extremity' for all; that is in accordance with the psychological explanation of the need for government. His general, 'Nero', theory of resistance on the other hand, is in accord with his psychology. The tyranny of a Nero is very much more contiguous than the 'imprudences and misguided principles' of a James II, who in many ways would have made an excellent king. Hume's ambivalence is carried on into his account of who made the revolution. In the *Original Contract* essay it is said to be a tiny minority who decided the matter (459), those presumably for whom James II's conduct (religion apart) was an 'extremity': the majority however willingly, 'acquiesed'. In the *History* (IX, 515) Hume deliberately contradicts what he had written in the *Original Contract* essay. 'It happens unluckily for those who maintain an original contract between the magistrate and people, that great revolutions of government, and new settlements of civil constitutions, are commonly conducted with such violence, tumult and disorder, that the public voice can scarcely ever be heard, and that the opinions of the citizens are at that time less attended to than even in the common course of administration. The present transactions in England, [1689] it must be confessed, are a singular exception to this observation.' From being a proof of it in the *Original Contract* essay, the revolution has become an exception to it: 'a great and civilized nation deliberately vindicating its established privileges' (*History*, III, 297).[1]

[1] Blackstone thought it best to consider the revolutionary settlement 'upon the solid footing of authority' rather 'than to reason in its favour from its justice, moderation and expedience', because that might imply a right of dissenting or revolting from it in case we should think it unjust, oppressive or inexpedient. Our ancestors having in fact decided the question, it is now 'become our duty at this distance of time to acquiesce' (*Commentaries* (1765), I, 205).

4
Social experience and the uniformity of human nature

A science of man necessarily presupposes some idea of an unchanging human nature. Hume's notion of it has been much criticized, especially by historians. Presented in a somewhat oversimplified version, it has been denounced as typical of the mechanistic, uniformitarian, unhistorical side of the thought of the eighteenth century. Adopted in a still further abridged form in general histories it became a caricature, which was nevertheless held up to view as a basic presupposition of the Enlightenment.[1]

J. B. Black's chapter on Hume in *The Art of History* (1926) has been very influential. In this, Black says that Hume's idea of a science of man demands the supposition that men's motives are qualitatively the same in all times and places, with the result that 'history is simply a repeating decimal. The great drama is transacted on a flat and uniform level: each age or group working up into forms that are already familiar the common stock of attributes.' But, says Black, it does not follow that because the springs of human nature are always the same, human nature is therefore unchangeable. Hume lays himself open to the same criticism as Voltaire. There is no parity between the conduct of a Greek or Roman and that of an Englishman or Frenchman. 'The quality of their acts is different, even although the qualities with which they are endowed are the same. But Hume could not see this', because of his 'false and mechanical psychology' (98). This, says Black, is why Hume's *History of England* is 'almost entirely a political narra-

---

[1] By no means all commentators accept this criticism of Hume, but some of them ignore the whole question, or merely touch it in passing, or point to features of his thought that make it appear dubious, without pushing the attack home. We have the criticism, more or less fully and forcefully expounded, and we have those who do not appear to accept it, but on the whole the two sides do not seem to meet. It is to be hoped therefore that this chapter is not flogging a dead horse. But I am not sure that the horse was ever properly flogged; the criticism of Hume's idea of the uniformity of human nature has had very powerful backing and wide dissemination; and anyway, the question has repercussions that go beyond Hume. Literary historians have long since rid themselves of the idea that eighteenth-century critics, even in the 1730s and earlier, were unable to appreciate the need to enter sympathetically into the mind of past ages. See, e.g. R. Wellek, *The Rise of English Literary History* (1941), 52 *et seq.*

tive, lacking background and explanatory principles' (86). Hume does not prepare the stage for the action with any account of geographical situation, national character, economic development etc., because 'he was dominated, as indeed were all the 18th century *philosophes*, by the belief that human nature was uniformly the same at all times and places. Why trouble to differentiate, why call in the aid of "materialist" interpretations, if there were no differences worth considering?'[1] The same line of criticism is seen in R. G. Collingwood and Meinecke.[2]

The *locus classicus* of this alleged weakness is a passage in Section VIII of the *Enquiry concerning Human Understanding* where occur the much-quoted words: 'Mankind are so much the same, in all times and places, that history informs us of nothing new or strange in this particular. Its chief use is only to discover the constant and universal principles of human nature' etc., and this famous passage will have to be examined later in the context from which it is usually torn. Taken out of its context, it gives what looks like absolutely conclusive support to a line of criticism which unfortunately ignores some very crucial and characteristic features of Hume's science of man.

[1] A. Cobban quotes Black on Hume. 'The historical writing of the Enlightenment also suffered from the inadequacy of 18th century psychological theories.' *In Search of Humanity* (1960), 109.

[2] Just as the ancient historians conceived the Roman character as a thing that had never really come into existence, but had always existed and had always been the same, so the eighteenth-century historians assumed that human nature had existed ever since the creation of the world exactly as it existed among themselves. Even so sceptical a thinker as Hume accepts the assumption. He had no suspicion that the human nature he was describing and taking as a norm was that of an eighteenth-century gentleman and that the very same enterprise, if undertaken at a widely different time might yield widely different results. He always assumes that *our* reasoning faculty, *our* tastes and sentiments, etc, are something perfectly uniform and invariable, underlying and conditioning all historical changes. He never suggests that human nature itself may be altered. His attack on the idea of spiritual substance should have demolished this conception of human nature as something solid, and permanent and uniform, but it did not, because Hume simply substituted unchanging psychological principles just as unchanging as any substance. He lacked a 'historical conception of mind'. R. G. Collingwood in *The Idea of History* (Oxford, 1946), 82-3. Meinecke says much the same sort of thing: although Hume is in a number of ways a precursor of *Historismus*, his delight in the 'variety of mankind' is superficial and naive, because his *Erkenntnissmittel fur die Geschichte* was *eine Psychologie alles Typischen in der menschlichen Natur*; he applies to the past a ready-made general psychology which prevents him from attaining a view of the essential individuality and uniqueness of historical phenomena, so that in spite of his anti-rationalist philosophy, he remained a man of the Enlightenment, dominated by the presuppositions of Natural Law and the belief in an immutable, eternal Reason: his historical writing *im Banne des naturrechtlichen Denkens stecken...durch das alte... Grundvorteil dass die menschliche Natur sich zu allen Zeiten gleiche*. Friedrich Meinecke, *Die Entstehung des Historismus* (München und Berlin, 1936), Vol. I, 209-15.

The term 'science of man' is Hume's, and he uses it in two senses. In its narrower sense it means psychology, the investigation of the workings of the human mind, the 'capital and centre' of all the other sciences, which are all more or less dependent on it. This accordingly, is the first phase of Hume's operations. Then, 'from this station, we may extend our conquests over all those sciences which more intimately concern human life', that is, every aspect of human, social activity 'which it can anyway import us to be acquainted with' (*Treatise*, Introduction, xx). There may or may not be a conscious analogy with Newton's method of analysis and synthesis as described in the final Query of the *Opticks* and by Newtonians like Colin Maclaurin (*Account of Sir Isaac Newton*, 8–9), but Hume's science of man consists similarly of two phases. The principles of human nature are established 'from experiments and observations by induction' (*Opticks*) and are then applied to the concrete phenomena of man in society in which the general principles are modified by a variety of circumstances.[1] Hume clearly set out with some such two-fold process in mind, and it seems perfectly legitimate to suggest that what is wrong with the usual criticism of Hume's notion of the uniformity of human nature is that it assumes that there is only one phase, the first, and that consequently Hume confuses general psychology with history, human nature in the abstract with human nature in society. Thus what Collingwood thinks is Hume's 'unhistorical' conception of mind is really only its analytic phase. But if in reality man is made what he is only in society, Hume's appreciation of the variety of mankind can hardly be described as superficial: the fact that he was not primarily interested in that as an end in itself, or the study of the past 'for its own sake', does not alter the case.

This second, social phase of Hume's science of man is liable to be played down or ignored by excessive or exclusive emphasis on the 'individualistic' 'atomistic', 'mechanistic' side of his thought – which is there. Obviously there is an important sense in which

[1] Cf. E. Rotwein (1955). 'When undertaking the *Treatise*, it is apparent then that Hume had in mind a twofold process. In the first and what may be termed the analytical phase of his inquiry, he would distil from all human experience those qualities and relations which seemed to be common to mankind as a whole, the underlying structure of all human behaviour. This is considered in Books I and II of the *Treatise*...and forms the body of his "principles of human nature", or as he sometimes called it his "science of man". The second part of the process – the synthetic phase – would then consist of the application of these principles to the various realms of experience for the purpose of organising their complicated relations into general uniformities...' Introduction to *David Hume, Writings on Economics*, xx–xxi.

Hume's political philosophy is 'individualistic', and its premises the same as those of the contractarians,[1] and this appears starkly enough if one adopts an Idealist perspective – the nation is a 'collection of individuals' and so on. But there are other aspects of his thought, including technical aspects of his philosophy, which pull in another direction, and when added together, with considerable force. As has been seen, the emphasis on man as 'the creature of the universe, who has the most ardent desire of society, and is fitted for it by the most advantages', (*Treatise*, Book II, Section V, 363) which was inherited from the natural law thinkers, was given new power in 'a secularist like Hume, who had more than a Baconian "savour of the nature of things"' (Laird, *op. cit*, 188–9). This does not in itself of course affect the question of the 'individualism' in the final analysis of his or any other political philosophy: but that is not in question here and belongs to a different sort of discourse. What is in question is whether one can subscribe to an unqualified statement, like that of Gough, in his book on the Social Contract, that Hume 'accepts the idea that the free individual is the natural unit'. Hume's awareness of man's social interdependence is so striking a feature of his thought, in the *Treatise* especially, that it would be nearer the mark to say that for him society is the 'natural unit'. Not only is man so peculiarly helpless by himself, his needs so many compared with other animals and his ability to satisfy them so feeble that 'it is by society alone that he is able to supply his defects' (*Treatise*, 485), not only are men knit together in a system of mutual interdependence (the division of labour etc. necessary to overcome their natural weakness and satisfy their ever increasing needs) so closely that an entirely independent action by any one of them is virtually inconceivable (*Enquiry concerning Human Understanding*, 89),[2] so that, as in Hegel's 'system of needs', their 'freedom' is in truth 'necessity', but given what Hume has to say about sympathy, that 'very powerful principle in human nature', it is difficult to see how an individual can ever become conscious of himself at all apart from society – sympathy, as expounded in the *Treatise*, being not a feeling belonging to the individual but the means of communication between men: 'it brings the thoughts and feelings and activities of different persons into unison, before they ever understand the

---

[1] See, e.g. J. W. Gough, *The Social Contract* (1936), 174.
[2] 'The mutual dependence of men is so great in all societies that scarce any action is entirely complete in itself, or is performed without some reference to the actions of others, which are requisite to make it answer fully the intention of the agent.'

grounds of their community with each other' (C. W. Hendel, *op. cit.*, 264). If we cannot observe the self as an object of perception, we nevertheless know it as real through intercourse with others, 'who define it for us by their own living presence'. Sympathy is then a phase of our own self-consciousness (*id.*, 269). Our individuality is not 'given', but is a product of social experience. However inadequate Hume's doctrine of sympathy may be from the ethical point of view,[1] it is the high-watermark of his sociological imagination: it means that what, without it, seems to be a mechanical collection of individuals, is in fact also 'a moral and spiritual unity, based upon the mutual influence of individuals, and possessing an individuality of its own'.[2] Men are psychologically, as well as materially, interdependent.

Hume's doctrine of sympathy and his use of it to explain group character in nations and smaller societies is a well known feature of his thought,[3] except, apparently, where it is needed to correct an oversimplified view of his idea of the uniformity of human nature. Even Meinecke, to whose theme of the origin and development of *Historismus* it would seem to be especially relevant, has nothing to say about sympathy in his chapter on Hume. And yet it plays a crucial role in his ethics and he refers to it repeatedly and in striking phrases. 'So close and intimate is the correspondence of human souls, that no sooner any person approaches me than he diffuses on me all his opinions, and draws along my judgement in a greater or less degree' (*Treatise*, 592). 'In general we may remark, that the minds of men are mirrors to one another...' (365). In themselves, apart from the thoughts and sentiments of others, the passions have no force, 'the soul or animating principle of them all is sympathy' (363); even opposition presupposes a degree of sympathy, which accounts for the 'commotion' which it produces in one's feelings – so powerful is the principle of sympathy that it 'often takes place under the appearance of its contrary' (593). Even if one ignores the *Treatise*, remembering that the doctrine of sympathy, as expounded there, was in some ways a casualty of Hume's later retreat from Newtonian psychology,[4] there is

[1] See Philip Mercer, *Sympathy and Ethics*, (Oxford, 1972).
[2] G. R. Morrow, 'The significance of the doctrine of sympathy in Hume and Adam Smith', *Philosophical Review*, Vol. 32 (1923), 68.
[3] *Treatise*, Book II, 316-17. 'To this principle we ought to ascribe the great uniformity we may observe in the humours and turn of thinking of those of the same nation, and 'tis much more probable that this resemblance arises from sympathy, than from any influence of the soil and climate...' a remark which is followed up in the essay on *National Characters*.
[4] It is the psychological mechanism that is the casualty, not the social emphasis.

enough left over to cast a large question mark against the usual critique of Hume's belief in an unchanging human nature.

What is relevant in this connection is Hume's insistence – the source is probably Malebranche – that men need the approval of others. A man's consciousness of his own worth, which Hume calls 'pride' or 'self-value', depends on this. 'Men always consider the sentiments of others in their judgement of themselves' (303);[1] they seek the good opinion of others, 'in order to fix and confirm their favourable opinion of themselves', for the same reason that a beauty surveys herself in the looking-glass (*A Dissertation on the Passions*, Section II, § 10); a proper degree of this 'love of fame' is a basic necessity of human existence, as well as being inseparable from virtue (*Enquiry into Morals*, 265). And most men have a tendency to over-value, rather than under-value themselves, Aristotle notwithstanding (*id.*, 264). (All this applies to normal men. Men like Diogenes and Pascal are pathological cases, the victims of philosophical enthusiasm and religious superstition respectively. Their way of life and standard of conduct are 'artificial'; 'they are in a different element from the rest of mankind; and the natural principles of their mind play not with the same regularity, as if left to themselves'. The science of man is not concerned with such 'experiments in a vacuum' [See *A Dialogue*, conclusion]. Strictly-speaking, there is no question of a vacuum, as Hegel pointed out with special reference to Diogenes; unless one is to regard such enthusiasts as literally mad.)

Now utility is crucial in men's moral sentiments and judgements: as Hume says in *A Dialogue* (*Enquiries* 336)[2] men judge an action or personal quality good in so far as it is good for something. By sympathy men are able to share each other's feelings: their thoughts and actions are largely determined by the prevailing opinions and standards of the group. 'Our opinions of all kinds are strongly affected by society and sympathy' (*Dissertation on the Passions*, Section II, § 10). Men seek approval and will for the most part fashion themselves and behave in such a way as to win it; they will act and feel and judge in accordance with the prevailing norms of their society. In so far as social circumstances differ, different views of utility prevail in different societies: what is generally approved or disapproved will be different. 'Particular

---

[1] Cf. 276. 'This constant habit of surveying ourselves, as it were, in reflection, keeps alive all the sentiments of right and wrong...'

[2] This reference is to Selby-Bigge's edition of the two *Enquiries*. He includes *A Dialogue* in this volume. All references to *A Dialogue* are to this edition.

customs and manners alter the usefulness of qualities: they also alter their merit' (*Enquiry concerning Morals*, 241). 'Man is a very variable being, and susceptible of many different opinions, principles and rules of conduct. What may be true while he adheres to one way of thinking will be found false when he has embraced an opposite set of manners and opinions' (*Of Commerce*, § 4). It must follow that the quality of men's motives and actions will be different in different ages and societies. 'The motives of men in the mass' cannot be 'quantitatively and qualitatively the same for all times and all countries', and Hume's view of the variety of mankind can hardly be described as naive and superficial, because it is grounded on the realization that men's ways of thinking and feeling are to a great extent moulded by those of the group to which they belong; so that human nature far from being rigid and invariable is in fact socially plastic and variable. And this is not altered by the consideration that since men cannot exist without society and some basic social rules, there must be some fundamental features which are the common property of man in society and therefore of human nature in general, nor by the fact that the passions as such remain the same everywhere and at all times – no historian or traveller is going to discover any passion of which we have no experience. No one quarrels with Hume's conception of the uniformity of human nature in this last sense, of course; what the critics accuse him of asserting or assuming is that the pattern of behaviour is everywhere the same; that the same stimuli produce the same passions, so that the quality of human actions is always the same. But the uniformity of human nature in Hume does not mean this: it does not mean that there is 'parity of conduct' between Greeks, Romans, Frenchmen and Englishmen.

Hume's position does not in fact seem to be very different from that of Marx, for obvious reasons one of the most radical critics of the idea of an unchanging human nature, when he said (in the *Grundrisse*) that hunger is hunger, but the hunger that tears raw meat with nails and fingers is a different sort of hunger to that which satisfies itself with the use of knife and fork on cooked food. Similarly Hume might have said, and did say in effect, that pride is pride, for example, but the pride and honour of an Athenian is a different sort of pride and honour to that of a Frenchman who satisfies it in the duel, duelling being unknown in ancient Greece. And the pride of an American Indian will differ from both. Again, a society which for reasons of social utility sets a high value on the military virtues will generate a different pattern of behaviour to one which values the commercial virtue of honesty. And the *same* virtue of courage is different among warlike or peaceful nations (*A Dialogue*, 337).

Hume is quite explicit on this point: that the same objects will not arouse the same passions, nor the same passions produce the same actions, in different societies. Men will feel insulted by quite different things, and seek satisfaction in different ways (*A Dialogue*, 326–7). The modern Frenchman does not feel a sense of shame in being made a cuckold, and the utmost disgrace and misery will not lead him to commit suicide. Contrast the Greeks and Romans. Love is love, but the 'Greek loves' are a very different kind of love to that of modern France.

These examples are taken from the essay (*A Dialogue*) in which Hume comes to grips with the problem of the variety of morals, and is concerned to show that in spite of all these differences in ways of thinking and feeling, the ground of moral judgements is always the same, viz utility. It is because views of utility differ that there are differences in what is approved and disapproved: nevertheless the principles on which men reason in morals are always the same. But these principles, though they are universal, being grounded on universal principles of human nature, are at the same time socially plastic. Men always and everywhere value certain qualities, love, friendship, honour, courage etc., because and in so far as they promote social solidarity, but views of what makes for social solidarity differ in different circumstances, so that these primary sentiments of morals will take different forms, and the quality of actions and general pattern of behaviour will vary.

The *Enquiry concerning the Principles of Morals*, which incidentally Hume regarded as his best book, does not contradict what has been said so far. The inspiration of Hume's ethics has in this work become more 'classical' than in the *Treatise*: sympathy, the source of morality and moral judgements, now means fellow-feeling, humanity – what moves men to praise or blame is what touches their common humanity. The *Enquiry* may appear to have shed the sociological relativism implicit in the more original and suggestive version of sympathy expounded in the *Treatise*.

Hume talks of mankind and the species feeling this or that, as though all men felt and thought like a civilized eighteenth-century gentleman inspired by Cicero and the models of classical antiquity. There is very little reference to differences in moral sentiment as between different societies. But this after all is not the point of the *Enquiry* and in any case Hume's thought in spite of the use of 'we', 'all men', 'mankind' etc. is not really uniformitarian. A great deal of what Hume describes in this work as universally approved qualities does not apply to primitive uncivilized peoples – who for example do not condemn theft or cattle-lifting, indeed regard it as a virtue. Hume is well aware of this,[1] but does not feel called upon to keep making a distinction that is obvious and not necessary to his argument. He is not concerned here with the variety of morals or the natural history of morality or the sociology of morality: what he is seeking is the ultimate ground of morality in human nature. He is for the most part describing the attitude of reasonable, humane and civilized men, and if the examples he gives (of qualities or actions approved and disapproved) are often quite obviously drawn from the experience of the European upper classes of the eighteenth century, they are only illustrations, concrete examples to illustrate his main thesis. He is not saying that all men approve or disapprove the same things which 'we' approve but that the original principles of human nature which give rise to approval or disapproval of no matter what are similar. That is Hume's main point in the *Enquiry*, and in making it he is committed only to the view that fellow feeling of a sort, no matter how feeble, is common to all men, no matter how uncivilized: that no man is without some tiny spark, at least, of concern for others; no man is hermetically sealed in his own selfishness. Grant that, and you have found the source, in human nature, of all moral distinctions. Obviously this is a very general and therefore very flexible principle or ground of morality, capable of very considerable modifications. It can accommodate, for example, the homosexuality of the Greeks, which we might consider repugnant and unnatural, but which was approved by the Greeks because they thought it promoted friendship and social solidarity. And the Greeks were a highly civilized, 'polished' people. And Hume says that as an active principle, promoting morally approved action, social sympathy or fellow-feeling or humanity is mobilized by the particular interests of the particular community to which we belong. It is the same in all men, but will take different forms and produce qualitatively different kinds of action in different communities.

So that the *Enquiry*, which appears to be putting forward a uniformitarian view of human behaviour, is not really doing so. Not of course that Hume's position is any kind of ethical relativism. Views of utility differ, but with the progress of society they be-

[1] How could an eighteenth-century Lowland Scotsman possibly fail to be?

come more enlightened. What was once regarded as socially beneficial is with more experience seen to be not so, thus tyrannicide is condemned in the light of fuller experience of its dangers and uselessness. And the Greeks recommended homosexuality, which is 'blameable', 'absurdly' as the source of friendship and social solidarity. But if certain manners and customs and institutions (e.g. polygamy and divorce) are condemned in the light of social utility, it is not without an attempt to understand them in the light of prevailing circumstances and prevailing notions of utility. As Hume says in *A Dialogue*, 'There are no manners so innocent or reasonable but may be rendered odious or ridiculous, if measured by a standard unknown to the persons' (330).

When in the essay on *National Characters* Hume talks about 'ingredients of human nature' that are 'variously mixed' in different societies, and that 'nature' does not always produce them 'in like proportions', he is using language which does not do justice to those aspects of his thought which reveal a greater sociological realism and insight, and which is bound to draw the fire of critics who approach him with preconceived notions of the 'mechanistic' mode of thinking typical of his age, and who do not make allowances for his notorious looseness of expression. But Hume at his best does not think of the principles of human nature as so many differently coloured pieces of paper in nature's kaleidoscope, and regard the pattern of behaviour of a society as a 'mixture' of 'ingredients' which are always the same, but as a socially conditioned modification of principles of human nature, which in themselves are abstractions from the concrete variety of human, social experience. It is not that there is more or less courage in different types of society as there is more or less fruit in different puddings: as has been seen, it is a different sort of courage, and Hume says so expressly.

Faced with the variety of mankind, the infinite diversity of manners and morals, what does the science of man do? It 'traces matters a little higher' (*A Dialogue*), that is, traces them back to the underlying general principles of human nature as such. The Rhine flows North, the Rhone South, but both have their source in the same mountain and obey the same law of gravity, though they flow through very different landscapes. The historian, one might say, explores downstream, the scientist of man works upstream to those more general and abstract principles of human nature which are constant. Tracing matters a little higher one can see that the Greeks esteemed homosexual love for the same reason that modern Frenchmen condone breaches of the marriage vow.

Thus sympathy and imitation are principles of general psychology which explain the variety of national characters, in conjunction with other factors, historical accidents, for example.

The historian is like the visitor to 'Fourli' in *A Dialogue*, who has to adjust himself to strange ways of thinking. Clearly it is not a simple matter to understand the motives of men in different ages and countries, if their manners and ways of thought are very different from our own, simply by applying what we know about human nature in our own society. Hume shows that he is aware of this when he says that the heroic virtues of the ancients appear just as incredible and unnatural to us as our more humane manners would have appeared to them, our whole way of life and cast of thought and feeling is so different (*Enquiry concerning Morals*, 256–7). The historian makes his report to the social scientist or psychologist, who 'traces matters a little higher', concerned as he is with the behaviour of man in society as such. And surely the two activities are not necessarily mutually exclusive?[1]

It is because human nature is variable that the science of man has to proceed with caution in fixing 'general truths' which will

[1] Clyde Kluckhohn has some helpful things to say in this connection. 'Anthropology – along with psychology and psychiatry – is building a model of 'raw' human nature, a general conception of man... The anthropologist's special contribution is that of documenting empirically the constants and the variants in the human record. The constants presumably reflect our common humanity...the variants mirror cultural differences, for cultures in their uniqueness represent precipitates of the accidents of history...' that 'human nature is in some sense the same throughout space and time' is a postulate demanded by all anthropological field work, but 'this does not signify...as common sense tends to assume, that similar stimuli will regularly produce similar responses'. He quotes Robert Redfield saying that 'one must get beyond the culture [the strangeness of which is at first so striking] to those elements in the behaviour of the people which are, after all, the same as one's own. For as one comes to understand people who live by institutions and values different from one's own, at the same time one comes to see that these people are, nevertheless, like one's own people', and 'to be able to find out what it is that a Zuni Indian is ashamed of, one must know what it is to be ashamed'. Although anthropologists commonly make assertions to the effect that 'human nature is infinitely malleable', or speak of 'the refutation of human nature' as an achievement of their science, they in fact recognize its existence every day. All (normal) men and women have the same human nature, but this does not mean that all groups have the same culture, but there will be 'a generalized framework that underlies the more apparent and striking facts of cultural relativity' – in Kluckhohn's words. A culture is unique in its concrete totality, like a human being, but cultures, though distinct, are yet similar and comparable. The anthropologist can see how a 'universal nature is molded by varying cultures', indeed a universal nature is 'an essential pre-condition of our being able to study each other'. See Clyde Kluckhohn in *The Human Meaning of the Social Sciences*, (ed. D. Lerner (Meridian Books), New York, 1959), 273–82. The institution of the potlatch among the Kwakiatul Indians is well known: to us a very peculiar method of

hold good 'to the latest posterity'. It is not merely that the science of politics is young, but 'we even want sufficient materials upon which we can reason. It is not fully known, what degree of refinement, either in virtue or vice, human nature is susceptible of; nor what may be expected of mankind from any great revolution in their education, customs or principles' (Essay on *Civil Liberty*, 1st §).

Bearing in mind all the aspects of Hume's thought that seem to contradict the notion that he regarded human nature 'substantialistically' as rigid and unchanging, what is one to make of the famous passage, mentioned earlier, in the *Enquiry concerning Human Understanding*, which has always been interpreted as the most dogmatic and unequivocal statement of the 'typical' eighteenth-century belief in the uniformity of human nature.[1]

The whole passage is as follows:

As to the first circumstance, the constant and regular conjunction of similar events, we may possibly satisfy ourselves by the following considerations. It is universally acknowledged that there is a great uniformity among the actions of men, in all nations and ages, and that human nature still remains the same, in its principles and operations. The same motives always produce the same actions. The same events follow from the same causes. Ambition, avarice, self-love, vanity, friendship, generosity, public spirit: these passions, mixed in various degrees, and distributed through society, have been, from the beginning of the world, and still are, the source of all the actions and enterprises, which have ever been observed among mankind. Would you know the sentiments, inclinations, and course of life of the Greeks and Romans? Study well the temper and actions of the French and English: You cannot be much mistaken in transferring to the former *most* of the observations which you have made with regard to the latter. Mankind are so much the same, in all times and places, that history informs us of nothing new or strange in this particular. Its chief use is only to discover the constant and universal principles of human nature, by showing men in all varieties of circumstances and situations, and furnishing us with materials from which we may form our observations

---

acquiring the social prestige which all men seek. Hume did not know about that, but the 'Greek loves' was an equally peculiar manifestation of friendship. (There are one or two references to this subject in Hume's *Early Memoranda*. Cf. also *Letters*, I, 152.)

[1] This passage, or part of it, has been quoted *ad nauseam* as illustrating the lack of historical sense etc of the eighteenth-century Enlightenment. For Carl Becker, for example, it is the 'sum and substance' of the matter, that is, of the 'new history' which was to provide the (pseudo-) empirical foundations in human nature of the 'heavenly city', which were in fact pre-existing values never to be called in question, (*Heavenly City of the 18th century Philosophers*, (1932), 95).

and become acquainted with the regular springs of human action and behaviour. Those records of wars, intrigues, factions and revolutions, are so many collections of experiments, by which the politician or moral philosopher fixes the principles of his science, in the same manner as the physician or natural philosopher becomes acquainted with the nature of plants, minerals, and other external objects, by the experiments which he forms concerning them. Nor are the earth, water, and other elements, examined by Aristotle, and Hippocrates, more like to those which at present lie under our observation than the men described by Polybius and Tacitus are to those who now govern the world. (*Enquiry concerning Human Understanding*, Part I, Section VIII, 83–4.)

If this is taken as the essentially 'unhistorical' manifesto of the science of man, if it means that there are no differences in the manner and ways of thinking of Greeks, Romans, Frenchmen and Englishmen, then it plainly contradicts a great deal of what Hume says and implies elsewhere. After all, in *A Dialogue*, Hume goes out of his way to stress the contrast in manners and ways of thinking between Greeks and Romans and Frenchmen and Englishmen: 'in many things, particularly in morals...diametrically opposite to ours' (324). This appreciation of contrast and difference in 'manners' is generally written off by the critics of Hume's 'uniformitarianism' as superficial; on the other hand, one can (as one should) accept it as much more than that, and then see a fundamental contradiction in Hume's thought between two things that cannot be reconciled, or at least are not reconciled by Hume. This is the thesis of George Vlachos in his *Essai sur la Politique de Hume* (1955). Unlike the unqualified 'uniformitarian' critics, Vlachos is aware of those elements in Hume's thought which point in the direction of *Historismus* and make this interpretation much too simple: the socially plastic human nature which together with the play of 'chance', make each nation something unique and incomparable. But he also sees things in Hume which seem to pull the other way: for example, the sort of science of politics envisaged in the essay with that title which is concerned to establish maxims of universal validity 'as general and as certain...on most occasions as any which the mathematical sciences can afford us',[1] and which are 'invariable by the humour or education either of subject or sovereign'.

[1] This is from the *Essays Moral and Political* of 1741, 31. According to Hume's philosophy they cannot be as certain as the truths of mathematics. Remembering this, no doubt, in later editions, as from 1748, Hume inserted an 'almost', and in 1777 we find also a 'sometimes'. These changes are not all in the Green and Grose edition of the *Essays*.

SOCIAL EXPERIENCE AND HUMAN NATURE

Accordingly, his thesis is that Hume's appeal to experience splits down the seam, and this is the prime source of confusion in his thought: on the one hand there is the principle of the uniformity of human nature, based on an essentially individualistic, analytical psychology which naturally leads to the view that there are in fact no real differences between people in different societies and history is a psychological monochrome; on the other, the 'sociological relativism' that cannot be squared with it. According to Vlachos, the sociological relativism leads Hume to a dead end – his 'suspicion' in the essay on *Civil Liberty* that the world is still too young to fix lasting truths in politics is crucial – and Hume falls back on a purely formal 'political geometry' concerned with forms of government independent of the social background and other conditioning factors. So he interprets the famous passage in the *Enquiry* in the usual way, and uses it in support of his argument.[1]

But should it be interpreted in this way? It occurs in the chapter of the *Enquiry* which deals with Liberty and Necessity – and it does not occur in the similar chapter in the *Treatise*. Hume is arguing that the dispute between freedom and necessity is purely verbal; however freedom be defined it cannot be defined so as to exclude necessity, because that would be to exclude causation and no event is uncaused. In making this point he appeals to men's behaviour in society: everyone acknowledges the doctrine of necessity in their whole practice and reasoning; if men really believed in a freedom which excluded necessity, life in society would be impossible. The behaviour of lunatics is free and unpredictable, but they are not described as 'free'. In accordance with their experience of it men get accustomed to a regularity of behaviour and act according to their expectations. Society rests on our expectations of a certain constancy in human behaviour. This applies universally. In any society there is a pattern of expectation based on past experience. Men expect their fellows to behave in a certain way and this as a general principle applies to any society. This is Hume's point, and it means that the uniformity of human nature is not a dogmatic presupposition, asserted *a priori* for which Hume offers no proof that is founded on experience, and to which

[1] ' "*Voulez-vous connaitre les sentiments, les inclinations et la vie des Grecs et des Romains? Etudiez le tempérament et la conduite des Francais et des Anglais d'aujourd'hui!*" Dans la lutte qui, dans la pensée de Hume, s'est engagée entre la raison et l'histoire, entre la psychologie universelle et la sociologie concrète, entre l'esprit géométrique et le relativisme historique, c'est la tendance rationaliste qui semble l'avoir emporté définitivement' (232). Elsewhere Vlachos quotes the passage in the essay on *National Characters* which deals with imitation and the formation of group character, and says that it is a far cry from the passage in the *Enquiry* (131).

therefore he has no right.[1] It is something which in any society men come to believe in the way in which, according to Hume, they come to hold any belief in matters of fact and existence.

It does not mean that the actual pattern of expectation is everywhere the same, as Hume points out, though in the examples of regular behaviour which he gives it is not necessary for him to explain that they might not apply in other circumstances. This would complicate the argument unnecessarily. Thus he says that a manufacturer hires labourers on the expectation that they will work for him, a man carries his goods to market and offers them at a reasonable price on the expectation that he will find purchasers. There was no need for Hume to point out that this will not apply to primitive societies where there is virtually no division of labour and no markets. If you invite an old friend to dinner you do not expect him to hold his hand in the fire until it is consumed. Given the circumstances, this applies 'universally' in ancient Athens or modern London. But in certain circumstances a man may do just that; every schoolboy knew the story of Scaevola. In a society in which tests of courage and endurance are highly esteemed, such an action would not be totally unexpected: as Hume said, the courage of the patriots of the ancient world, though almost unbelievable *to us*, is by no means supernatural; and the fortitude of the American Indians was much commented on in the eighteenth century. A certain pattern of expectation having been established, the onlooker is not surprised. Such examples confirm the principle of necessity. So there are local patterns of expected and predictable behaviour, of uniformity, as well as the general principle of the uniformity of human behaviour as such. Allowances have to be made 'for the diversity of characters, prejudices and opinions' and the force of education, custom and example. But in spite of the variety of such experiments, men everywhere, in any society, acknowledge the principle of the uniformity of human behaviour as such and act on it. The local uniformities prove the general principle of uniformity.

That this is so, that there are local uniformities and more general uniformities and no necessary conflict between the two, is shown in the account of Liberty and Necessity in the *Treatise*. There are patterns of behaviour characteristic of the sexes, of different age-groups, social classes and nations, all equally 'necessary', and at

---

[1] As B. M. Laing argues, *David Hume* (1932), 163. On his own philosophical principles the belief ought to be regarded as one not proved or even capable of proof but continually verified by observations from experience. This is just what it is.

the same time there are principles of human nature that apply universally. The existence of local patterns of behaviour proves the general principle of uniformity. Instead of the notorious paragraph in the *Enquiry*, which taken by itself is so open to misunderstanding and an interpretation which clashes with Hume's sociological relativism, Hume says in the *Treatise* that 'a very slight and general view of the common course of human affairs' will suffice to prove that 'our actions have a constant union with our motives, temper and circumstances... Whether we consider mankind according to the difference of sexes, ages, governments, conditions, or methods of education; the same uniformity and regular operation of natural principles are discernible'. Are the products of Guienne and Champagne 'more regularly different' than the sentiments, actions and passions of the two sexes? Can one expect philosophical reasoning in a four-year-old? Can one expect 'two young savages of different sexes' not to copulate? or the sentiments, actions and manners of a day-labourer to be similar to those of a man of quality? 'There is a general course of nature in human actions as well as in the operations of the sun and the climate. There are also characters peculiar to different nations and particular persons, as well as common to mankind' (*Treatise*, Book II, Part III, Section I, 401–3).

These remarks surely show that Hume's 'sociological relativism' is not incompatible with his belief in the uniform principles of human nature; and the exposition of the thesis in the *Enquiry* is not an improvement, because it is liable to give, and has done, a wrong impression.

You cannot be much mistaken, Hume says in the unfortunate passage in the *Enquiry*, in transferring '*most*' (the italics are Hume's) of your observations concerning the temper and actions of your contemporaries to the ancient Greeks and Romans. But the context of the passage, Hume's doctrine of 'necessity', shows that the 'most' is to be taken so absolutely literally that it cannot offend the historical-minded. It would refer for instance to one's expectation that men will leave rooms by the door and not by the window; or to use the examples of uniformity Hume gives in the *Treatise*, to the fact that young men and women can be expected to mate and look after their families, babies will not be expected to reason like grown men etc. History can inform us of 'nothing new or strange' about that greater, submerged part of the iceberg of daily living, about which indeed history can inform us of nothing at all. Its 'chief use' is to provide the material by the study of which we can arrive at some general conclusions about the 'regular springs of human action and behaviour' by showing men in all varieties of circumstances and situations.

(Incidentally it might be argued that Hume's insistence on the fundamental similarity of the ancients and the moderns was a useful *historical* corrective of the very common view of them as super-human, in some ways unnaturally, i.e. supernaturally, virtuous.)

The ordinary man, observing the workings of ambition, avarice, self-love, vanity, friendship, generosity and public spirit in his contemporaries will not be 'much' mistaken in assuming that the Greeks and Romans were similarly motivated, and transferring 'most' of what he has observed to them; this does not mean that he has the knowledge of them that the historian acquires when he visits 'Fourli' and discovers the peculiar form taken by friendship among the Greeks, for instance.

In certain fundamental respects, therefore, Greeks, Romans, Frenchmen and Englishmen are alike in their 'ways of thinking'. In other respects, while the English flatter themselves that they resemble the Romans, the French draw the parallel between themselves and the polite Greeks (*A Dialogue*, 333), and it is worth noting that Hume himself does not clearly endorse these views. Even so, he says, what enormous differences in the manners and customs and morality of people who are 'supposed to be the most similar in their national character of any in ancient and modern times'. Their 'ways of thinking, in many things' are 'diametrically opposite to ours' (*id.*, 324). 'What wide difference, therefore,... must be found between civilized nations and barbarians, or between nations whose characters have little in common?' Even though they both rise in the same mountain and obey the same law of gravity (the universal principles of human nature), the Rhine and the Rhone flow in opposite directions (333).

'The same motives always produce the same actions: the same events follow from the same causes.' But Hume does not say that the same objects always give rise to the same motives, or that the same stimuli produce the same passions. It is a vague sentence, and can only mean that one can expect a generous man, for example, to behave in some ways and not in others; he will not be expected to act maliciously.

It is not necessary therefore to regard Hume's science of man as nullified by an appeal to two incompatible types of experience: an 'individualistic', uniformitarian psychology on the one hand, and his view of human nature as socially conditioned and plastic on the other. The universal principles are to be regarded as abstractions from the concrete variety of human (= social) experience; Hume's 'general psychology' is concerned with the function and mechanism, not the content of mind, which is various and supplied by social and historical circumstances.

The science of man in its widest sense is concerned with the whole range of human experience and is an attempt to reduce as much of it as possible to general principles or laws. This can be done with more success in some fields than in others; some branches of the science of man are more certain than others. That there are many kinds and degrees of certainty is perhaps the central message of Hume's philosophy: it was thus that he was able to give the science of man its rightful place in the sun, as no less certain, and even more useful, than the physical sciences. Psychology, or the science of man in its narrowest sense, Hume thinks is about as certain a science as any that deals with matters of fact and existence, in so far as we know our own minds by introspection. Certainty goes along with abstraction; repetition of experience must imply abstraction. The principles of general psychology are certain in so far as they are abstract: the mechanism of association would presumably be the same even if human nature were to undergo a total change in every other respect.

In this context what is regarded as the weakness of Hume's psychology works in his favour: that it is so general and abstract as to be worthless as psychology: its 'experiments' are not genuine experiments because they are not exploratory, but merely elaborate illustrations of such platitudes as that we can only be proud of what is of some significance to us.[1] A conclusion so general can hardly be a menace to a 'historical conception of mind': it can accommodate any manifestation of pride in any culture. But if one says that Hume's psychology only achieves universality and certainty at the price of significance and psychological content, one can hardly criticize it for being the psychology of eighteenth-century European man universalized.

But as one traces matters lower, following the rivers downstream, one descends into ever growing uncertainty and unpredictability. The more concrete realms of human experience are more or less reducible to law and uniformity and general maxims.

---

[1] Cf. Passmore, *Hume's Intentions* (Cambridge, 1952), esp. 156–7. Passmore contrasts Hume with Hartley, in whom we constantly 'encounter hypotheses which we can test by the ordinary process of psychological enquiry'.

Thus uniformity must not be expected in those realms of experience where large numbers of men and the 'grosser', that is, more common, passions are not involved. So that the history of arts and sciences is largely, but not entirely, governed by 'chance...or secret and unknown causes', and civil or domestic history is more amenable to generalization than foreign affairs, subject as they are to such accidents as the health and personality of the few who conduct them (See the essay on *The Rise and Progress of the Arts and Sciences*, and *Of Eloquence*, § 1). If, in practice, Hume gives the impression of being a psychological uniformitarian, a historian with an 'unhistorical' conception of human nature, it may be because he was, for a number of reasons, especially attracted to the study of politics, in which, he thinks, the regularity of human nature is strikingly obvious.[1] In business and politics men's motives are sufficiently uniform to enable one to arrive at conclusions which, though they may not hold good 'to the latest posterity', nevertheless will be certain enough for practical purposes. The experienced observer knows what to expect, or rather what not to expect, from politics (*Enquiry concerning Human Understanding*, 85), and the fact that men in all ages are caught again and again by the same sort of baits, as Hume says towards the end of the essay on *Public Credit*, shows how necessary these general maxims are, though Hume knows very well that even the most experienced observer is liable to be confounded by utterly unaccountable phenomena, especially 'enthusiasm'; where religion is concerned, the experienced observer will be ready to expect anything. And in the famous paragraph in the *Enquiry*, it seems to be political 'experiments' which Hume has particularly in mind: history's 'chief use' is to provide 'materials'...these records of wars, intrigues, factions and revolutions, are so many collections of experiments etc.

It is because human nature in politics has this sameness that a science of politics concerned with universally applicable maxims is conceivable. This is not a tack on which Hume travels very far, nor does it seem to be going in the opposite direction to the historical and sociological one.

If the *History of England*, therefore, notoriously does not give its readers the *frisson historique*, this is not because Hume's philosophy is such that it prevents him from seeing that human nature in its

---

[1] 'In the end, he is prepared to abandon ethics and aesthetics to the realm of taste, if only he can preserve the status of politics, as a science at least as securely founded as physics', Passmore, *Hume's Intentions*, 11.

concrete historical manifestations is not everywhere the same, not because the science of man demands belief in a dogma or absolute presupposition about man's unchanging nature, but because of his dominating and anxious concern with politics and political experience. The *History* was not designed to give the reader a historical *frisson*; its purpose Hume regarded as much more serious and practical, viz: to enshrine for all time (at least as long as the English language lasted) a philosophy of political moderation. There is no single route leading directly from Hume's philosophy of human nature to his *History of England*. Even the technique of his historical portraits, so often criticized as mere mechanical assemblages of general psychological characteristics, could be explained, without reference to his psychology, as inspired by his classical models. Tacitus did not need a 'mechanical psychology'. Those who think that Hume's *History* is the sort of history one would expect from his science of man must be working with an abridged and oversimplified notion of the latter. There is enough social realism and sociological emphasis in Hume's philosophy of human nature to have provided (in theory, and forgetting the enormous technical difficulties in writing narrative history of a revolutionary nature) a quite different sort of *History* to the one actually written. Suppose a reader knowing Hume only from Book III of the *Treatise* and the *Enquiries* and certain of the essays, or parts of them, were to be told that Hume had also written a *History of England*, and then asked to hazard a guess as to what sort of a history he would expect it to be. Might he not be justified in replying: 'I note what Hume has to say about sympathy, social experience, national character, the evolution of morality, social rules and institutions, and "moral" causes; so on the whole I expect to see a social history, with the emphasis on the gradual evolution of English society and social institutions, on national character (and possibly its development), on the Common Law and manners and customs etc., neglecting "physical causes".' Would he not be surprised to learn that the narrative has often been criticized for being too narrowly political?

II *Philosophical Politics*

5
Scientific and vulgar Whiggism

In studying Hume's politics, it is helpful to begin by making a distinction between the political amateur observing the scene, or 'politician',[1] and the philosopher and philosophical politician whose 'chief business' is 'to regard the general course of things', especially in the domestic government of the state (*Of Commerce*, 260). Evidence of the former is to be found in Hume's private letters to his friends, which is what most of Hume's letters are; even here, whether, as especially in the 1740s and 50s he was simply observing, or whether as from 1763 to 1767 he was also employed by the 'public' and his 'situation and fortune' were closely involved, and he had 'from a Philosopher, degenerated into a petty Statesman...entirely occupied in Politics' (*Letters*, II, 128), he is remarkably detached. Indeed, as will be seen, there is a sense in which he is more detached as a 'politician' than as a philosopher. The desire to be, and the claim that he has been, independent of 'all connexions with the Great' (*Letters*, I, 295), and independent of the Establishment generally, as well as of all parties and sects, is a constant refrain in his letters.[2] Even so, there is a distinction between the 'philosopher' and the political 'man' – the famous recommendation to be a man in one's philosophy is a purely technical matter and not relevant here – which must be made, in order to ensure that the former does not disappear behind the latter, which is liable to happen if Hume's claim to be a philosopher above party is not accepted at its face value, as has usually been the case, both then and later, with the result that

---

[1] 'I am too great Politician to write any News', Hume from Paris in January 1764. *New Letters*, 79.
[2] 'The great Distance which I have always kept from all Party and Dependance' (*Letters*, I, 193); '...I attach myself to no great Man...' (*id*, 355); 'my Disdain of all Dependance' (*id*, 365); 'it would be easy to prevent my acceptance [of Hertford's invitation to go with him to Paris as Secretary to the Embassy] from having the least Appearance of Dependance' (*id*, 392); 'I, a philosopher, a man of letters, nowise a courtier, of the most independent spirit, who has given offence to every sect and every party...' (*id*., 504). Cf. *New Letters*, 26: in 1747, Hume is afraid of falling into 'necessity, perhaps, and Dependance, which I have sought all my Life to avoid'.

Hume's claim has not been thoroughly and properly investigated and explored.

The most sophisticated way of refusing to separate the philosopher and the politican is to point to the fact that the freedom from all political dependence and connexion on which Hume prided himself and made into a way of life for a man of letters, was itself an important political attitude in eighteenth-century England, and was often called 'Tory'; and further it could carry with it more or less of a 'country ideology', much of which can be seen in Hume, sometimes quite nakedly, as in his stubborn preference for militias over standing armies, or in some assumptions behind his economic theories – or so it could be argued; and that after 1760 what had been 'country' or 'opposition' slogans became a 'court' programme initiated by George III and Bute and carried on by the 'King's Friends', so-called, and were not two, at least, of Hume's oldest friends very famous 'King's Friends'? In this way Hume can be fitted neatly into eighteenth-century English political history; his thought can be related to contemporary events and shades of opinion and shown as something which changes and develops, and thereby a more historical interpretation of it can be offered than what is found in the more purely analytical commentaries,[1] which are unconvincing to the historically minded because the political background is so distant and hazy, or absent altogether perhaps, and Hume's thought seen and presented as unnaturally statuesque and all of a piece.

On the other hand, so cruel and capricious and paradoxical a mistress is Clio, that the more strenuously one hunts in the thickets of eighteenth-century English politics for the real, historical Hume, the more elusive he seems to become. The interpretation of the political background itself is a notoriously fluid and controversial matter among professional historians; the relating of the ideas and theories of a thinker of Hume's calibre to currents of political opinion is a hazardous business; and those who sail the seas of history under the flag of Duns Scotus will look for the distinguishing marks of individuality everywhere, eternally suspicious of the phantom similarities which are the sustenance of dogmatists – the fiercer the dogmatism, the more phantom-like the history. The spotting and listing of attitudes that *look* like 'Tory' attitudes, for example, Hume's approval of the established Church of England, his opinion of the National

[1] The most thorough attempt to do this is G. Giarrizzo's *David Hume politico e storico* (Torino, 1962).

Debt, his disapproval of the stock-holders and stock-jobbing (two years after his sharpest expression of this, added in 1764 to the essay on *Public Credit*, Hume wrote to his brother: 'I have sold out my four per cents in the Stocks, at 1545 pounds. I keep only the long Annuities, which I cou'd sell for between 4 and 500 pounds; so that I am a Gainer near 500 Pounds by the Stockjobbing' (*Letters*, II, 7)), his dislike of continental wars, etc. does not add up to a discovery of the historical Hume.

Nor is it easy to discover the views of Hume *qua* 'politician'. Taking the letters as evidence, one can mark out three fairly well-defined 'periods'. Up to August 1763, when Hume was invited by Lord Hertford to accompany him to Paris as Secretary to the embassy, and by which date Hume had virtually finished writing, as opposed to revising his published works for new editions, the topic of domestic politics (or for that matter, foreign politics) is in remarkably short supply. Out of 400 pages or so of letters, the references to politics would barely fill half a dozen: and what we have is largely exclamation, banter, anecdote or just plain fun.[1] The sort of detailed indication, brief as it is, that we have in the first letter to William Mure of Caldwell, of November 1742, of how Hume would vote on certain issues before Parliament, is unique in being specific and unusually serious in intention.[2] The reference in a letter of August 1747 about the dregs of Walpolian corruption being entirely purged away is ironical (*Letters*, I, 103); it was the comic side of the Wareham Election that appealed (briefly) to Hume (January 1748, to James Oswald, *id.*, 110); Dr Clephane is told in February, 1751: 'the present or expectant ministers I have no interest in' (*id.*, 148); two months later Hume told Gilbert Elliot of Minto that he would not sacrifice truth and reason, 'scarce even a Jest', to politics (*id.*, 156); on 15 May, 1759, the Pits and the Legs (sic) and the Grenvilles are 'all going by the Ears': with the first fair wind forty thousand French will 'probably settle the Ministry' (*id.*, 307). The Letter to Elliot of 2 July 1757 is especially revealing (*id.*, 252). At a crucial juncture in Elliot's own political fortunes, and as some would argue in the public interest as viewed by Hume – Pitt's 'coalition of parties' in

---

[1] As in the Letter of 6 July, 1759, to William Rouet, in which Hume mocks an invasion scare (*Letters*, I, 310).

[2] '...let all the Letters of my Epistle be regularly divided, they will be found equivalent to a dozen of *No's* and as Many *Ay's*. There will be found a *No* for the Triennial Bill, for the Pension Bill, for the Bill about regulating Elections, for the Bill of Pains and Penalties against L. Orford [Walpole] etc. There will also be found an *Ay* for the Standing Army, for Votes of Credit, for the Approbation of Treaties Etc...' (*Letters*, I, 44).

the Pitt–Newcastle ministry – a brief reference to these events in the first paragraph, in which incidentally Hume expresses apprehensions as to whether the ministry, being such a 'strange motley composition' can last (apprehensions on Elliot's behalf, although, as he says, according 'to the whimsical way of thinking in this Country, it is more difficult to rise than to fall with Reputation'), the rest of this 3½ page letter is taken up with literature and gossip. This is typical.

In the first three years of the reign of George III, the evidence of political interest in the letters concerns the extinction of party and the first round of Wilkes and Liberty. There are three references to the former. 'I was glad to observe what our King says', wrote Hume in November 1760, 'that Faction is at an end and Party Distinctions abolished' (*Letters*, I, 336). Two years later he tells David Mallet that 'happily, the Factions seem now to be almost entirely appeas'd' (*id.*, 368), and on 7 April 1763, Hume repeated to Mallet that 'Faction is in a manner extinguished, at least the Factions of Whig and Tory' (*id.*, 385). Whatever it was that occasioned these remarks, the accession of George III, the resignation of the remaining Newcastle old connection chieftains in October 1762, or the success of Bute in weathering the Peace and Cider tax storms (the last letter mentioned is dated one day before Bute's resignation), they all belong to the context of the effect of party politics on the writing of history and access to historical materials etc, and they refer to a general trend of opinion which Hume had noted in the essay on the *Coalition of Parties* of 1758; the dying-out of Jacobite or old style 'legitimist' sympathies which had hardened the division of parties in the nation at large. Hume was not, in these remarks about the ending of faction, thinking of Westminster politics, but of party division in a less narrowly party-political, a national, sense. They have nothing to do with any programme or political aspiration of governing without parties – if they did, they would be in contradiction with the findings of Hume's political science, as will be seen. It will be observed that what Hume wrote to Mallet was that faction was 'in a manner' extinguished. Otherwise an Opposition seems to be taken for granted, as Hume's political science would lead one to expect, as the letter to Adam Ferguson of March, 1767, for example, shows (*Letters*, II, 126), at least an Opposition that was not extra-parliamentary, as was that after 1768, even if 'storming the closet' is deplored (as seems to be implied in the letter to Smollett of July 1767, *id.*, 152. See below, p. 131).

As for Wilkes, Hume blamed him in March 1763 for indulging in 'national reflections, which are low, vulgar and ungenerous' (*Letters*, 1, 383); the passing remarks in letters to Wedderburn and Robertson in November and December respectively, condemning the 'factious barbarians under the appellation of Whigs' (in the letter to Wedderburn), and 'factious barbarians' (to Robertson), and presumably referring to the recently begun debates in Parliament anent Wilkes, and the championing of Wilkes by the Opposition, seem to be more literary and cultural, than political, in motivation, especially as they were written from Paris where Hume was now enjoying the renown and appreciation denied him in London. On 1 December he wrote to Andrew Millar that he was 'glad to see public Affairs likely to settle in favour of government' (*id.*, 418); as so often, the context is bookselling and literature, the remark very general, reflecting majority opinion in the House and in the country; it hardly allows one to decide how Hume felt about the constitutional issues raised by Wilkes and General Warrants. The evidence in the letters suggests that the important thing for Hume in this first political appearance of Wilkes was the rage against the Scots, which was barbarous and had the effect of hindering the sales of his *History* and further historical research (See, *id.*, 359, 378, 382). The use of the scornful expression 'under the appellation of Whigs' is worth noting. 'Under the appellation', because Whigs and Tories, strictly speaking, were no more: there was no longer a fort for the former to hold against the latter – this was what Hume meant by the extinction of parties – emergence from the garrison atmosphere caused by the dynastic question which had made it possible for some politicians to monopolize power and had caused Hume himself to be the prey of Whig prejudices in his view of the past, even when he had prided himself on his independence of the powers that be. It was in March 1763, that he told Elliot that he had corrected several mistakes and oversights in his *History* which had 'chiefly proceeded from the plaguy Prejudices of Whiggism' (*Letters*, 1, 379) – 'plaguy' is not necessarily a term of abuse: it can be taken in conjunction with Hume's very much stressed teaching about the power of 'contagion', and the difficulty of avoiding it. 'Plaguy prejudices of Whiggism' is not the snarl of a 'Tory historian': it represents a new degree of self-criticism and ability to get at the truth made possible by the removal of the pressing needs of self-preservation of the Hanoverian regime, which, for example, had made Hume twenty years before, say 'Aye' to the standing army, if one can assume that that was the reason; and can be regarded perhaps as an echo, more or less conscious, of Malebranche's teaching that the needs and faculties of self-preservation, 'contagion' or social sympathy being for Malebranche one of the most powerful of these, blind men to the truth. For a champion of Wilkes to call himself a 'Whig' was like abusing the word 'crusade', or having a *blitzkrieg* against the weeds in one's garden.

In September 1763 two letters of a new type, one to Mure and one to Adam Smith, appear in the collection: Hume is now in a position to retail political intelligence from inside – in this case it concerned the Bute–Pitt negotiations and the latter's two controversial interviews with George III in the late summer of 1763 – and obviously rather enjoys doing so, in spite of the 'reluctance' and repining at 'my loss of ease and leisure and retirement and independence' which he tells Smith are his underlying feelings. But from these, as from the few letters or sections of letters of the same sort which followed in the next four years or so (e.g. I, 393, 395; II, 18, 42, 126, 144–5, 152, 153), it is still not easy to tell where Hume himself stands in the political issues of the day. Indeed in the letter to Smith, Hume scrupulously plays the role of the impartial spectator, proceeding as he had done so often in his *History*. First he gives Pitt's version of what happened, then that of 'the other party', and finally his own conclusion, which is 'the best Account I can devise of the Matter, consistent with the Honour of both parties' (I, 396). (Bute emerges from Hume's account as having somewhat ineptly managed to arouse the displeasure of both Administration and Opposition, indeed more of the former than the latter – Hume may have got this from Elliot, who very much disliked Bute's meddling in an attempt to bring Pitt back – to the detriment of 'our countrymen' who are 'visibly hurt in this justle of parties, which I believe to be far from the intention of Lord Bute'). In the letter to Mure, Pitt is described as a 'formidable demagogue', and then occurs this phrase: 'I wish the high spirit of his M: may be supported'. If one takes this remark (it follows his report that he has reason to think that Halifax was 'proscribed along with the rest') as the tip of an iceberg of concealed support for, or sympathy with the 'King's Friends', what is one to make of the long and exclusively political letter to the Earl of Hertford of 27 February 1766, reporting the speeches and debates on America and reasons for the success of the repeal of the Stamp Act (II, 18–23)? For Hume himself this is presumably straight reporting of 'intelligence from good sources', except that he gives his own, rather mildly expressed opinion that the repeal is a good thing because otherwise the Americans would have been reduced to despair and obstinate resistance. But Hume also gives it as his opinion that everyone in the House was so convinced of the bad effect of the Act on trade etc., that 'no one voted against the repeal but from party', and in complete confidence of being outvoted. He then goes on to describe 'the intrigues of the Cabinet', and Bute's aim to use the opposition to the repeal to destroy the Rockingham ministry, whose members had made their hostility to him plain and who had assiduously courted Pitt. This looks very like what became the Rockingham party line: 'no one voted against the repeal but from party' implies that an inner cabinet was conspiring against the Ministry – Hertford's sympathies would be with the Ministry which included his brother, Conway. Hume writes as reporting the opinion of well-informed neutral observers. 'It is esteemed certain' that Bute planned to overthrow the Ministry, and still does, and the alienation of Bute, ascribed to the younger part of the ministry, is regarded as imprudent, because they could never support themselves by popularity alone, 'contrary to the Cabinet', and because Pitt would prove more domineering than Bute, who is called 'the King's favourite' here. The next letter to Hertford, presuming with the editor that it is to him, (8 May 1766), forecasts that owing to the dangerous state of affairs in America, Pitt will be sent for, and received on his own terms.

In February 1767 Hume was pressed by Conway and Hertford to be the former's Under-Secretary of State in the Chatham administration: he accepted out of friendship and a sense of obligation to Hertford (*Letters*, II, 123), and accordingly in the summer found himself involved in the crisis caused by Chatham's illness and withdrawal. Hume had only accepted with extreme reluctance and because, knowing the nature of British politics, he expected his continuance in place to be very short (*id.*), and was able to view the 'confusion' and negotiations for a new ministry with complete detachment. On July 18 he wrote to Smollett that 'Every thing is uncertain: there is a mighty combination to overpower the King. The force of the Crown is great; but is not employed with that steadiness which its friends would wish' (II, 152). This remark is *ad hoc*: it does not in itself provide evidence of subscription to a 'king-in-toils' political line: one did not have to be such a subscriber, or a 'King's Friend', to believe that 'mighty combinations to overpower the King' were unconstitutional and unacceptable: this was the generally accepted view. That presumably was why, as Hume reported in the following letter, to Mure, Conway being the 'most moderate Man of the whole' had great authority and credit with all parties and was likely 'to remain in power and even gain ground'.

Ennumerating Hume's friends and connections does not help much, either. Many of his closest friends were connected with Bute and very closely connected – as Hume wrote to Elliot, Bute was 'surrounded by all my most particular friends' (*Letters*, I, 428) – but Hume was extremely reluctant to use these friends to ask any favours of Bute, and his attitude to 'the Scotch Minister', 'the favourite', as he called him, was always somewhat detached and cool (*Letters*, I, 382, 440). Bute's power behind the scenes[1] which Hume believed was very real and active as late as 1771, he regarded as a very dubious blessing.[2] Being a 'King's Friend' did not necessarily mean being an admirer of Bute, of course, but what exactly constituted a 'King's Friend' is not an easy question. And one must remember that Hume had a very close friendship and connection after 1763 with Lord Hertford and his brother Conway, both men of unimpeachable Whig provenance. Hertford was Horace Walpole's cousin; Grafton was Hertford's nephew. Conway had been notoriously punished for voting against the Ministry over Wilkes and General Warrants in April 1764, when Hume was acting as his brother's Secretary in Paris, and was a member of the Rockingham confederation, and if some historians think of him as a rather luke-warm one, at this juncture, Hume at any rate seems to have had no doubts about his loyalty to that group and certainly did not regard him as any sort of traitor because he stayed on under Chatham.[3] In any case, Conway remained a

---

[1] 'Lord Bute is again all-powerful or rather...always was so...', April 1764. (*id.*, I, 439).

[2] Cf. October 1769: 'But is it certain that Lord Bute will abstain from tampering and trying some more of his pretty Experiments' (II, 210). June 1771: Lord North 'will not expose himself even in the best cause to the Odium of the populace, because he feels that he has no sure hold of the Cabinet, but depends for all his power on some invisible secret Being, call him Oberon the fairy or any other, whose Caprices can in a moment throw him off...' (II, 245).

[3] 28 July 1767, Hume reporting to his brother. 'About this time twelvemonth, when the last Revolution of Ministry took place, Mr Conway stay'd in, tho' Lord Rockingham and most of his Friends were turn'd out; but it was with Reluctance, and only on the earnest Entreaties of the King and Lord Chatham and on their giving him a Promise, that several of his Friends and Party should continue to hold their places.' Hume goes on to describe the breaking of this 'Engagement' and what followed, and how everybody thought that Conway had satisfied to the full

friend of Hume's till the latter's death, when there was no question of his loyalty to the Rockingham party.[1] When Hume accepted Hertford's invitation in 1763 he told Mure that he had thereby 'insulted Elliot, Sir Harry, Oswald and all our friends of that Administration' (Grenville's) – the invitation having come from the Opposition, Newcastle camp (*Letters*, I, 392). And what one is tempted to call, provocatively, Hume's connexion with the Rockingham Whigs, was far more profitable and useful to him personally than that of Bute ever was. It is worth noting also that Hume had a connection with Bedford, via Mme de Boufflers, which was more useful to him and which he was more prepared to use than that with Bute.[2]

Further, one can note that Hume's friends included Wilkes, whom he presumably first met in 1754 when Wilkes contested Berwick in the election of that year[3] – Berwick being within a few miles of Hume's family home at Ninewells – and whom he met in Paris in 1764 (I, 444); of Shelburne, both as a protégé of Bute, but later also, and of Barré (*New Letters*, 64–5, 85); of Wedderburn, 'always in opposition', as Hume wrote to Ferguson in March 1767; that in the same letter he regretted a poor speech by Burke – 'But Burke did very ill, which I am sorry for. It is pretended, that he rather sinks in Reputation' (II, 127); that he talked in a familiar way of 'Charles' (James Fox) – January 1774: 'And will Charles now draw the line and reform, and be frugal and virtuous?' (II, 285); and that with the whole weight of government, the greater part of public opinion and many of his friends against him he was 'American in my principles' and an advocate of total

the point of honour 'in which he is very scrupulous', and expected him to continue in office (II, 153–4). On 13 August, he wrote Elliot that 'Mr Conway's Delicacy of Honour was satisfy'd by bringing his old Friends, the Rockinghams, to have an Offer; and as it was impossible for them to concert a Ministry, he has agreed to act cordially with the Duke of Grafton' (II, 160).

[1] Conway visited Hume in Edinburgh in Autumn 1769. To Adam Smith: 'I expect General Conway here to-morrow, whom I shall attend to Roseneath, and I shall remain there a few days' (*Letters*, II, 207). To Straham in July 1771: 'But I am assur'd that Lady Aylesbury and Mr Conway are to be with the Duke of Argyle this Summer; which will oblige me to leave the Town for a fortnight and go to Inverara' (246). May 1776 to Blair: 'I promised to General Conway and Lady Aylesbury, that if I recovered my Health as to venture myself in Company, I should pass some weeks of the Autumn at Parkplace: this is the only Retardment I can forsee to my return to Scotland before winter' (320).

[2] 14 July 1765 to his brother: '...if the old Ministry return, I can look upon the Duke of Bedford alone as my Friend, by means of the Lady I mentiond to you. If the present Ministry stand, I have, by Lord Hertford's Means, many and great Friends...' (I, 512).

[3] See *Letters*, I, 194. To John Wilkes.

independence (Letters of Autumn 1775, II, 300-1, 303, 305).[1]

The last two examples have been taken from the other side of the boundary which marks the third and final 'period' as revealed by the letters. After '68 and in connection with the second round of Wilkes and liberty, the question as to where Hume stood becomes much simpler, because, for Hume at any rate, there was now a clearly defined battle line on fundamental issues, and from now on we get what we have not had before in the letters, a steady stream of passionate comment on political issues and unambiguous personal opinion, which is only too well known. The issues involved transcended the whole 'King's Friends' context: if Hume was a 'King's friend' here he was so in a sense which included everyone except the most extreme radicals and the contemporary lunatic fringe: like the young anti-Wilkite Charles James Fox, he was a friend of the parliamentary constitution now threatened from outside. The reason why Hume's stream of comment is so voluble and passionate is, paradoxically enough, as will be seen, because what was at stake transcended the mere politics he had been observing and taking part in (however obliquely) hitherto, and, in so far as the Wilkite eruption was not an 'absurdity' or outburst of 'madness' like the Popish plot, indeed even more absurd and unaccountable than that, because that at least was derived from religion, 'a Source which has, from uniform Prescription, acquired a Right to impose Nonsense on all Nations and all Ages' (*Letters*, II, 197),[2] it concerned the philosopher in the technical sense as Westminster politics had not, because even if the latter were not absurd or mad, they were nevertheless a 'whirl', not reducible to explanation on scientific principles. This very well known and much misunderstood phase of the allegedly reactionary Hume will be returned to again therefore, after an examination of his political science.

So much for the evidence provided by Hume's letters. When

[1] Caroline Robbins (*The Eighteenth Century Commonwealthman*, Harvard, 1961), leaning presumably on D. Fagerstrom, who has studied the matter in detail, says that 'the Scots were on the side of the colonists so far as the speculative philosophers were concerned. Not all supported the Americans, but an astonishing variety did' (197), and N. T. Phillipson talks of 'the remarkably widespread sympathy with which Scotsmen viewed the cause of the Americans'. (*Scotland in the age of Improvement*, p. 126). On the other hand, W. Ferguson in *Scotland, 1689 to the Present* (Edinburgh, 1968), says that 'to begin with, the war was generally popular...Little sympathy was shown for the colonists...' (p. 237).

[2] Hume was not alone in thinking the Wilkite phenomenon inexplicable. Franklin apparently thought so too. See Lucy Sutherland: 'The City of London in 18th Century Politics' in R. Pares and A. J. P. Taylor, *Essays presented to Sir Lewis Namier* (1956), 69. 'It struck contemporaries with astonishment.'

anyone who really starts asking questions about Hume's politics turns now to the published writings, he sees and is well-nigh confounded by a dazzling mosaic of the most baffling complexity and difficulty, in which it is impossible to distinguish well-marked phases in the development of Hume's political thinking because the evidence just does not allow one to do it in a convincing manner.[1] For no sooner has one gathered together an apparently satisfactory array of items to illustrate a particular 'phase', and which are said to be characteristic of a particular 'ideology', say 'Old Whig', 'Country' or 'King's Friend', than the eye discovers – if it is an innocent eye – other items belonging chronologically to the same phase which point in a quite different direction. Hume was perpetually revising his essays and *History* for new editions, and one must study all these revisions, but not only must one study the revisions, one must take account also, at any given moment, of what is left unchanged, because that may be equally significant. There may occasionally be some negligence in this, but not surely in any matter regarded as of urgent political importance? One must surely assume that if Hume leaves a clear and unambiguous statement or statements, for example, concerning the necessity in a constitution like that of Britain of court and country parties, unchanged in a later edition, then he meant it to be taken as his settled opinion then, and not what he had thought ten or twenty years before and no longer believed? And why, after all, should Hume have radically altered his teaching about the need for 'dependence', 'parties' etc after 1760? These things still were necessary, as George III quickly found out.

If one ranges over all the editions of the essays and the *History*, what one seems to see is not so much a river changing in appearance as it flows through different landscapes, that is, periods in Hume's development, as a glittering sea, composed of hundreds of points of light, now one colour, now another, giving the effect of a baffling *pointillisme* unless one stands well back. What matters and what is significant and uniquely Humian is what does not change: it may be true that Hume grew more 'conservative' as he grew older, but it may be equally true that this was only in the way in which 'everybody does' – and which is not significant for the historian of ideas. Even pessimism does not seem to have been peculiarly characteristic of a 'late period' in Hume, judging by the

[1] For examples of the sort of thing that one is forced to do with what to me is quite straightforward evidence, see my review of Giarrizzo's *David Hume politico e storico* (1962) in *The Historical Journal*, VI, 2 (1963), 280–95.

letter of October 1747 to James Oswald, in which Hume thinks 'the present times...so calamitous and our future prospect so dismal, that it is a misfortune to have any concern in public affairs...all accidents (beside the natural course of events) turn out against us. I shall not be much disappointed if this prove the last Parliament worthy the name we shall ever have in Britain.' The reference is to French military successes in the Low Countries (*Letters*, I, 106). There is far more consistency between the young and the old Hume than is generally realized, as will appear in due course.

As with the charming Jacobite relic in the Museum at Fort William, in order to make sense of the colourful confusion on the palette and get out of it a portrait of the rightful Prince, one has to put the polished cylinder in exactly the right place. And that, the uniquely and distinctively Humian thing in Hume's politics, is the attempt to rise above party and prejudice and friendship and attachments, personal or public, altogether, and bring the experimental method and the whole ethos of science or 'philosophy' to bear on English politics in order to promote moderation in the interest of an establishment not as secure as it might be, because at times racked by bouts of excessive party conflict, and, until the late 1750s at least, not accepted by a 'considerable' minority of malcontents.

It was in this sense that Hume was both a detached observer – the philosopher's 'trade' as Adam Smith said, was 'not to do anything, but to observe everything' (*Wealth of Nations*, ed Cannan, I, 14) – and politically committed at one and the same time: far from this being a contradiction,[1] it is the very essence of Hume *qua* 'philosopher' in politics. After all, some such attitude was that of the 'Tory' or 'country gentleman' or 'independent' in so far as he had a creed, and a passionate attachment to the constitution.[2] Elliot had that, and it was why he was an ardently anti-Wilkite supporter of the House of Commons; yet Elliot had written in

---

[1] G. Giarrizzo, 'Ancora su Hume storico' in *Rivista Storica Italiana* (1971), 440.
[2] See Betty Kemp, *Sir Francis Dashwood, an Eighteenth Century Independent* (1967). 'Independency was more than a group of independents. It was a constitutional creed' (1). As expounded by Betty Kemp, this creed is not that of Hume. For example, Hume deduced the necessity of *two parties* in the British Government, a court and country *party*. Whereas, says Betty Kemp, for the independent a division of the House into parties prevented the exercise of the critical function and so distorted the proper relation of the Commons to the government. But perhaps the distinction between this and Hume's country 'party' is too fine. The gap definitely widens if, with A. S. Foord (*His Majesty's Opposition* (1964), 234), one tacks on a Country party programme. Hume thought, for example, that in order to work at all, the British constitution needed parliamentary 'dependence'.

1754, at his entry on the political scene; 'I really flatter myself I shall be able to enter into the great game here with much the same indifference I sometimes play at whist...' (G. F. S. Elliot, *The Border Elliots*, Edinburgh, 1897, 335). 'Independency' is presumably something more basic than a 'country' programme; even when stripped to its essential minimum it can still be differentiated from the attitude of the 'philosopher', who observes everything, including independency and its role in the functioning of the British constitution, deduced from the principles of human nature in a mixed government.

It is another paradox of Hume's situation that he was more detached, in one sense, less seriously committed as a 'politician' or political amateur than as a 'philosopher', because what he observed and took part in in the former capacity was the unpredictable ministerial merry-go-round at Westminster (or the personal vagaries of Pitt playing his own game), and this was not an object for philosophy. 'Strange revolutions', 'whirl', 'confusion', 'extraordinary incident' are the sort of terms Hume uses to describe it.[1] This roulette wheel of 'chance', undependable and precarious from the point of view of a profession (*New Letters*, 26 June 1747), this curious British game of snakes and ladders in which it was almost more glorious and reputable for a minister to fall than to rise (*Letters*, I, 253, II, 146), amusing, boring or exasperating to watch, according to one's mood and expectations and the importance of the issues involved, 'frightening' when rising to a pitch of fury against Scotsmen (I, 492-3), profitable, potentially or actually, for one's friends, or even for oneself, when it was a question of righting injustice, as over the question of Hume's half-pay (numerous examples, see I, 103-4, 107, 263, 427-8, II, 130), was not reducible to 'general causes'. The detachment of ('experimental') philosophy was for the promotion of science and moderation in politics: the detachment of philosophy, in the classical sense, was for peace of mind; the sort of 'philosophy' Hume described in 1747 (I, 106), when he said that it was difficult to arrive at a proper degree of 'insensibility or philosophy when one is in the scene'.

In December 1754, Hume wrote to the Earl of Balcarres about the insubordination of Pitt and Fox in the Newcastle Ministry: 'This quarrel, I hope, they will fight out among themselves, and

[1] 'This rapid Revolution and Whirl of Fortune' (*Letters*, I, 510); 'strange revolutions' (I, 521); 'usual confusion' (II, 144); 'our annual confusions' (II, 151); 'our Ministers change so quick that we know not who is to be in Office next Post' (*New Letters*, 40, May 1757).

not expect to draw us in, as formerly, by pretending it is for our good. We will not be the dupes twice in our life' (I, 215). One is left to guess how or when he or 'we' had been duped before: 'twice in our lives' suggests something more resounding than recent, or even than the Granville/Broadbottom affair of 1744-6. If the reference is to the dashing of public expectations[1] after the fall of Walpole, when the politicians who had been so 'patriotic' and high-minded in opposition continued to play the game as before, then Hume was only duped *qua* 'politician', not *qua* 'philosopher', because in the latter capacity he would not or should not have expected any great change. Be that as it may, he had no illusions about 'the usual fluctuations of power in this country' (II, 123. March 1767, to the Comtesse de Boufflers). As he wrote to Montesquieu in April 1749: Bath (formerly Pulteney) is now in opposition: 'vous savez que ces distinctions ne sont pas souvent de longue durée parmi nous et sont très casuelles' (I, 138). And the same 'insensibility or philosophy' seen in this sort of remark later gave Hume consolation when he himself was personally involved; when, for instance, owing to the rage against Scotsmen, Hertford had to abandon his plan to take Hume with him to Ireland. Dazzling prospects, which Hume momentarily regarded as certain (II, 514) were thereby dashed to the ground. But Hume was well prepared: with the Rockinghams now in power, Hertford left Paris, where 'he was a man of no party', and got 'involved with his friends', thus endangering his, and therefore Hume's, position and prospects. As Hume wrote to his brother in July 1765: 'You know the fluctuation of English politics. Perhaps, before you receive this, the whole present System is overturn'd... All is turn'd topsy-turvy; and before next Winter, perhaps, I am at your Fireside without Office or Employment' (I, 511-12). When it was all over Hume wrote to Adam Smith: 'I have been whirled about lately in a strange Manner; but besides that none of the Revolutions have ever threatened me much, or been able to give me a Moment's Anxiety, all has ended very happily and to my wish...I have now Opulence and Liberty' (I, 520). Hume did not really want this sort of employment. In March 1767 he only accepted Conway's invitation to be Under-Secretary of State because among other reasons he knew it could not last long. (II, 128: 'I am too well acquainted with our usual Fluctuations and

---

[1] See W. Coxe, *Memoirs of the Administration of Henry Pelham* (1829), 33. After the downfall of Walpole, 'halcyon days were expected to smile upon the country and the golden age to be restored...'

Revolutions to believe that this Avocation will be durable') and indeed the boat was rocking violently four months later, in the summer crisis of 1767. Hume told his brother that the prospect of being out had left him cold. 'As the matter was nearly indifferent to me, I neither felt Anxiety for my past danger, nor do I experience any Joy from my present Establishment' (II, 153). 'All is come about again: and we seem to be more settled than ever' (II, 159). The Wilkes troubles, 1768–71, were qualitatively different: they involved philosophical considerations which went beyond the wheel of fortune and play of faction at Westminster.

To take Hume's claim to be a 'philosopher' in politics seriously and explore its meaning means playing down the element of change and the 'ideological' element in his thought. As for the first, even if one avoids the fallacies of the 'Whig interpretation' and realizes, for example, that to be anti-Wilkes in 1768–71 was not necessarily 'undemocratic' or 'reactionary', that what looks 'conservative' to us may be 'liberal' at the time and that in general these sorts of judgements are best avoided anyway, there are strikingly 'liberal' features in what is usually regarded as Hume's final 'conservative' or even 'reactionary' phase, and 'conservative' features in the early Hume, or what must pass for such if one is determined to play the game this way. But it is not 'conservatism' but the sceptical Whiggism involved in the philosophical approach to politics which gives Hume's thought its unity and continuity. Scientific Whiggism was sceptical because it questioned the value and holiness of the holy cows of the Whigs: the justification of the Revolution (this early example of sceptical Whiggism has been met already: a political philosophy designed to justify the present establishment in a manner which by-passed and played down the principles which kept the malcontents at arm's length could not justify the Revolution at the time it occurred, or could only do so tortuously and inconsistently); the contrast between English liberty and French 'slavery'; the 'ancient constitution' of the common lawyers and Commons' apologists in the seventeenth century and later modifications; the wickedness of the Stuart kings...It is hardly surprising that this sort of thing appeared in the eyes of a good Whig like Horace Walpole, as 'Toryism', or worse.

In this perspective, interpretation of Hume's politics is not primarily concerned with Whiggism, Toryism, court or country sympathies and affinities or 'conservatism'; an establishment political philosophy is not the same as a ministerialist one, or what we would call an 'establishment' one, it is beyond court and country as much as it is beyond Whig and Tory; and what matters, and the tool to be used in interpretation, is the contrast between philosophical or scientific (= sceptical) Whiggism and what is best called vulgar Whiggism: a contrast and tension which is seen in Hume himself; vulgar Whiggism being something which cuts right across the whole spectrum of politics from commonwealth-men to Tories and Jacobites,[1] in so far as they could subscribe to some or all of the old beliefs concerning the matchless constitution, French slavery etc.

This was not only a contrast between the scientific and the vulgar, but between the parochial and the cosmopolitan. And here it is especially necessary to remember that Hume was not, as he still appears in some English and foreign writings, an Englishman, but belonged to the most European of all the communities of Europe – its law based on Roman law to a considerable degree,[2] its people scattered all over Europe for centuries in the universities and the armies and in branches of Scottish families settled on the continent. These things cannot be weighed and measured, but Hume's love of France and French civilization is obvious to any reader of his letters, who will remember, for example, the long continued debate, which went on up to the last year of his life (II, 295), as to whether he would settle in France for good. As a 'citizen of the world' taking a metropolitan, European view of English politics and history, and a Francophil, therefore, as well as in his role of Newtonian philosopher appealing to experience, Hume was offended by a theory of political obligation based on an

[1] *Parliamentary History of England*, VIII (1811). Mr Shippen in 1732 on the British constitution: 'the best constituted, the best balanced government in Europe' (900). For 'vulgar Whiggism' in the poets, see B. Dobrée, *English Literature in the early 18th century* (1959), who shows, for instance, how the various national heroes in the long nature poems are 'mainly associated with liberty as a peculiarly British product'; and how this patriotic poetry cannot be dismissed as mere 'Whig panegyric', because the themes are equally 'fervently carolled by the most arrant Tories' (517).

[2] Stair, the Father of Scots law, 'under the guise of recording what the law of Scotland was in his day...gave the whole system a 'new look' – in a European style, which could be worn with urbanity in Paris or Leiden...Thus at the time of the Union with England in 1707 Scots law as administered in the Central Courts was cosmopolitan and comparative – in striking contrast to English law...The leaders of the Scottish Bench and Bar...could scarcely be other than cosmopolitan'. T. B. Smith, *British Justice: the Scottish Contribution* (1961), 12–14. Professor Smith points to the vastly different meaning of the words 'common law' in England and on the continent. In a scholarly context one objects to Hume being called English, as is done for example by G. R. Cragg on the first page of his *Reason and Authority in the 18th Century* (1964), because it blurs vital distinctions. It is equivalent to calling Walpole, or Bolingbroke, a Scotsman.

experience so limited as to exclude the civilized absolute monarchies of Europe. As has been seen, he seems, oddly, to have regarded the contract theory of government as a peculiarly English aberration, and was surprised to find an example of its use in France in 1715 – he does not seem to have realized what an ancient pedigree the theory had – but what destroyed its credibility was what Locke, the 'most noted of its partisans' had not scrupled to affirm: that 'absolute monarchy is inconsistent with civil society, and so can be no form of civil government at all'. So, according to this theory, France, the largest, most powerful and in many ways most civilized state in Europe, had no legitimate or proper government. 'What authority any moral reasoning can have, which leads into opinions, so wide of the general practice of mankind, in every place but this single kingdom, it is easy to determine' (*Original Contract*, 473). Twenty-five years later (the *Original Contract* essay was written in 1745) Hume burst out against 'those foolish English prejudices which all nations and all ages disavow' (*Letters*, II, 216) in the bitterness of his feelings about the 'popular leaders' in 1770, but he had always regarded these 'English prejudices' as unique (*qua* philosopher) and foolish (*qua* 'politician').[1] There is a whole science of comparative politics behind a remark which in itself looks like the petulance of an old 'reactionary', but which he might have made at any stage of his career. Contract theory for example was absurd not only because the reasoning was faulty, but because it was parochial, leading to paradoxes 'repugnant to the common sentiments of mankind, and to the practice and opinion of all nations and all ages'. The *reductio ad absurdum* of the 'fashionable system' was this: that put to the test of experience, it destroyed itself, in the *Original Contract* essay, at any rate. The Revolution of 1688 in no way involved the nation's choice or consent, but was the work of a tiny minority – the majority of

[1] Passing through Germany in March 1748, Hume, following in the footsteps of Marlborough, quoted some lines from Addison's poem, *The Campaign*, in which Addison describes the people of the country as *Nations of Slaves by Tyranny debased: Their Makers Image more than half defaced*, and went on: 'If any Foot Soldier cou'd have more ridiculous national Prejudices than the Poet, I shou'd be much surpriz'd. Be assur'd, there is not a finer Country in the World; nor are there any Signs of Poverty among the People. But John Bull's Prejudices are ridiculous; as his Insolence is intolerable.' (I, 121) Cf. 126: 'The common People are here, almost every where, much better treated and more at their ease, than in France: and are not very much inferior to the English, notwithstanding all the Airs the latter give themselves.' J. H. Burton says that one of Hume's characteristics was 'an inclination to doubt all authorities which tended to prove that the British people had any fundamental liberties not possessed by the French and other European nations', *Life and Correspondence of David Hume* (Edinburgh, 1846), Vol. I, 279.

seven hundred determined that change for near ten millions – as Hume pointed out in the *Original Contract* essay. On this reasoning, therefore, no examples of legitimate government were to be found anywhere.

According to Locke's *Second Treatise of Government*, absolute government could be no form of civil government and was inconsistent with civil society (§ 90), because the prince having the executive and legislative power in his own person, there is no common judge and no appeal possible from any action of the prince, who is therefore as much in a state of nature with his subjects as with the rest of mankind; civil government being designed to remedy the inconveniences of the state of nature where everyone is judge in his own case (§§ 13, 91). And so his subjects are slaves (§ 91). In § 57, liberty is defined as freedom under the rule of law – 'a Liberty to dispose, and order, as he lists, his person, actions, possessions and his whole property within the allowance of those laws under which he is' – and Laslett points out that Elrington, in 1798, used this statement about law and freedom to claim that men are free if governed by just laws, even if they were not consulted in their framing. But surely Locke takes it for granted that men have been so consulted – otherwise there is no liberty. 'The liberty of Man in society is to be under no other legislative power but that established, by consent, in the commonwealth... Freedom of men under government is to have a standing rule to live by, common to every one of that society, and made by the legislative power erected in it...' (§ 22).

Be that as it may, it was the essence of 'vulgar' Whiggism that the difference between free and absolute government was not one of degree, but of kind, an absolute qualitative difference, a chalk and cheese, sheep and goats type of distinction, which made any science of comparative politics or comparative study of constitutions impossible. On the one hand was liberty, the government of laws not men, which was a feature of free governments exclusively; on the other, slavery and absolutism (= tyranny, though there might, in the more refined versions, be degrees of this as between, say, France and Turkey; but again, there might not; for many France was no better than Turkey – at least it was the fashion to say so). The assumption behind this monolithic conception of liberty is that liberty of any sort in civil society is impossible unless all the people share in the making of laws and give their consent freely: that is why the French and the subjects of absolute government are 'slaves' and their governments 'tyrannical'. So there was the 'natural' liberty of the state of nature, and 'civil' or 'political' liberty – nor was there any need to distinguish 'civil' and 'political' liberty, because without the latter, there was no possibility of the former. When you wrote 'liberty', everyone knew what was meant, namely, for all practical purposes, England, and its matchless or 'singular' constitution, 'singular' because it had actually achieved the correct balance recognized as the ideal and mark of durable government by the classical theorists, the mixture declared by Tacitus to be impossible in practice.[1] This is the ground theme and cardinal tenet of vulgar Whiggism.

Thus Molesworth, in his Preface to his translation of *Franco-Gallia*, said that he was moved by a sincere desire of instructing 'the only possessors of true liberty in the world' what right they had to it (2nd edition, London, 1721, p. *v*. The first edition was published in 1711). Our constitution is a government of laws, not of persons (p. *x*). Defining true Whiggism, a true Whig, he said, 'will be for giving or restoring liberty even to France itself, were it in our power' (p. *xx*). Elsewhere he wrote that 'he must go out of these Kingdoms who would know experimentally the want of *Public Liberty*'; the only use English travellers can make of the French Tour is to learn from the misery and slavery of that people to set the higher value on our own happiness in so good a constitution which is 'already too perfect to want any improvement';[2] immature boys on the Grand Tour were deceived by appearances to prefer gilded slavery to coarse domestic liberty. The more polished and delicious countries of France, Spain and Italy dazzle the eye and disguise the 'slavery', but in the Northern kingdoms there is little or nothing to divert the mind from contemplating slavery in its true colours – hence his account of Denmark (Mr. Molesworth's *Preface, with historical and political remarks*, London (1714?) 2–7, 27). In Denmark slavery seems to be more absolutely established and more practised than in France, where there are *parlements*, an encouragement of trade, manufactures and learning, all tending to the good of the people, and where also the King has quarrels with the court of Rome, whereas in Denmark, there is not the least remnant of liberty remaining to the subject: all meetings of the estates in parliament entirely abolished; nay, the very name of estates and liberty quite forgotten (*An Account of Denmark*, 5th

---

[1] Cf. Blackstone's *Commentaries* (1765), I, 50–2: 'our own singular constitution' has achieved what Tacitus regarded as a 'visionary whim'.

[2] This for Oldmixon was the advantage an Englishman will derive from reading general history. *Critical History of England*, (3rd ed.), 12. The first edition was 1724.

edition, Glasgow, 1745, 33, 184). Thus Davenant wrote that in a government of the laws and not of men, princes are a part, but at the head of, the legislature, and either in person or by their ministers, execute what the constitution requires. But all this goes otherwise in an absolute monarchy, under which there is no legislative authority but the Prince's will (Essays upon Peace at Home and War abroad, Section XIII, of the Executive Power, in *Political and Commercial Works*, v, (1771), 2). Halifax, in *The Character of a Trimmer*, described the English government as a mean between the 'barbarous extremes' of a Commonwealth, which allows men no quiet, and a Monarchy, 'a thing that leaveth men no liberty' (*Complete Works*, ed. J. P. Kenyon for *Pelican Classics*, 54). For Sidney, 'whatever...proceeds not from the consent of the people, must be 'de facto' only, that is, void of all right' (*Discourses concerning Government* in *The Works of Algernon Sidney* [London, 1772], 446). The 'fabric of tyranny' will be much weakened if we prove that nations have a right to make their own laws and constitute their own magistrates – this is 'the public liberty' and he that oppugns that, 'overthrows his own'. As liberty solely consists in an independency upon the will of another, and by the name of slave we understand a man who can neither dispose of his person nor goods but enjoys all at the will of his master, there is no such thing in nature as a slave if 'these men or nations are not slaves who have no other title to what they enjoy than the grace of the prince, which he may revoke whenever he pleases'. On Filmer's principles, the ancient Greeks, Italians, Gauls, Germans were 'slaves', whereas the 'Asiatics' were free men, and liberty in its perfection now enjoyed in France and Turkey[1] (*op. cit.*, 6, 10, 11). Absolute monarchy, where the monarch will have no other law than his own will (196) cannot be introduced unless manners are corrupted (217). For Fletcher of Saltoun, arguing that 'slavery' is the natural consequence of standing armies, the 'French fashion of monarchy' is 'where the king has power to do what he pleases, and the people no security for anything they possess', and 'a government is not only a tyranny, when tyrannically exercised; but also when there is no sufficient caution in the constitution that it may not be exercised tyrannically'. 'I regard not names but things. We are told there is not a slave in France...but I say there is not a free man in France, because the king takes away any part of any man's property at his pleasure and that...there is no

[1] Cf. 128, 'If the people of Turky (sic) or France did rebel, I should think they were driven to it by misery, beggary or despair.'

remedy'. Fletcher then goes on to show how the Turks are all slaves to the Grand Seignior (*A Discourse of Government with relation to Militias*, 1698, 27, and *Two Discourses concerning the Affairs of Scotland*, 1698, 75, 91, in *Political Works of Andrew Fletcher of Saltoun*, Glasgow, 1749).

On 22 March 1707/8 Hoadly preached a sermon on 'the happiness of the present establishment and unhappiness of absolute monarchy', in which he said that the probable consequences of the establishment of the latter could be summed up in one comprehensive word: slavery. The great end of government is the happiness of the governed society and that consists in the enjoyment of liberty, property and the free exercise of religion. He was anxious to make a clear distinction between property and that 'nominal possession under absolute monarchy which consists in being tenants-at-will to one weak and passionate man'. This difference is ridiculed by those who say that subjects possess property under the most absolute monarchs as well as under other sorts of government. However, although they may have properties secure from the attacks of other subjects, except such as are protected by the monarch, these are only secure during his pleasure, which is as uncertain as his humour. In another sermon of 1708 Hoadly said that a lasting liberty is founded upon laws, and is the result of a good constitution of government as health is of a right constitution of body (*The Works of Benjamin Hoadly* (London, 1773), II, 110–13, 123). In the Sacheverell trial, Lechmere defined freedom as not being bound by laws to which the people did not consent (*An Impartial Account* [of the Trial of Sacheverell], London, 1710, 34–5). In *The Crisis* (1714), Steele defined liberty as the happiness of men's living under laws of their own making by their personal consent, or that of their representatives (*Tracts and Pamphlets* by Richard Steele edited by Rae Blanchard: Johns Hopkins Press, 1944, 137). And Addison chose the title of 'The Free-Holder' because 'it is what I most glory in...As a *British* Free Holder I should not scruple taking the place of a *French* Marquis. I consider myself as one who gives my consent to every law which passes... such is the nature of our happy constitution that the bulk of the population virtually give their approbation to every thing they are bound to obey...' (1715) (*The Free Holder or Political Essays*, London, 1761, 2). The *Spectator* of 29 January 1712 was on the British Constitution, and Addison wrote there that liberty, which is what exempts one man from subjection to another as far as the order and economy of government will permit, is best preserved where the Legislative power is lodged in several persons, especially if those persons are of different ranks and interests, for where they are of the same rank and consequently have an interest to manage peculiar to that rank, it differs little from a despotical government in a single person. The division of the three powers, regal, noble and popular, is most distinct and natural in the English form of government. In all despotic governments there is a natural degeneracy of mankind, even if the prince favours arts and letters, and about nine-tenths of the world are in the lowest state of slavery – European slavery being indeed a state of liberty, compared with what prevails in the rest of the world, so that it is no wonder that those who 'grovel under it' are not wholly barbarous, and have 'many tracks of light' not found elsewhere. 'Where absolute power is, there is no publick' wrote Shaftesbury. Morality and good government go together: there is no real love of virtue without the knowledge of public good. Those who live under a tyranny have scarce a notion of what is good or just other than as mere will and power have determined, but even so, even in the worst of magistracies, the mere despotic kind, there is still something of public principle, even when perverted and depressed – men imagine a 'public parent' even when they do not have one, and in place of a legal government, obey a tyrant. They are thrown back on the natural affection towards order and government among mankind. 'As for us Britons, thank Heaven, we have a better sense of government, delivered to us from our ancestors. We have the notion of a public and a constitution...We understand weight and measure in this kind and can reason justly on the balance of power and property...' (Essay on the Freedom of Wit and Humour in *Characteristicks*, I, 106–8.) In *Advice to an Author*, Shaftesbury explains why French tragedy is inferior: 'the high spirit of tragedy can ill subsist where the spirit of liberty is wanting', and where men 'in a long series of degrees, from the lowest peasant to the high slave of royal blood are taught to idolize the next in power above 'em, and think nothing so adorable as that unlimited greatness and tyrannic power, which is raised at their own expense, and exercised over themselves' – the genius of tragedy consists in the lively representation of the disorder and miseries of the great (*op. cit.*, 218–19). According to Shaftesbury, a free government is when a people is governed 'by such laws as they have themselves constituted, or to which they have freely given their consent' (*op. cit.*, III, 312). In *Cato's Letters* (1720), liberty is defined as government executed for the good of all and with the consent of all (6th edition, London, 1755, I, 179–80). In arbitrary countries, it is public spirit to be blind slaves to the blind will of the prince...but in Protestant free countries, public spirit is another thing (*op. cit.*, II, 12). Our constitution is the best republic in the world with a prince at the head of it, and much nearer to a commonwealth than any absolute monarchy (*id.*, 28). The whole globe cannot show five free kingdoms (107), but our lives and properties are secured by the best bulwark in the world, that of laws made by ourselves and executed by magistrates likewise made by us (112). Absolute princes are doomed to be tyrants in self-defence (256–7), and what absolute monarchy comes to in practice is rule by a multiplication of monarchs, the worst sort of oligarchy. In absolute monarchies the monarch seldom rules, but his creatures instead of him – that sort of government is a gradation of tyrants (III, 41, 44). This implies that there is no distinction between European and Asiatic monarchies or despotisms – all are equally tyrannical. 'In truth, government is a thing not so much as known in...by far the greatest part of the earth. Government supposes, on one side, a just execution of rational standing laws, made by the consent of society; and on the other side, a rational subjection to those laws' (50). The bulk of the earth being evidently almost a desert already, made so by tyrants, is a demonstration that the whole must soon be entirely so if the growth of tyranny be not restrained. Thus there will be an end of men, unless those states that are free preserve their freedom and people, and like the ancient Egyptians and Greeks fill the world again with colonies of free men (62).

In the *Craftsman*, the 'very essence' of free government 'consists in the regular execution of known laws made by the consent of the whole community' (*The Craftsman* (1731), III, 144); 'the first necessity of a free government' was that a representative of the people have a share in the legislature (VI, 72); whereas absolute monarchy consists in the arbitrary, unrestrained will of one man and can be supported only by armed force, whence it follows that absolute government is only another word for military government: without armed force there could never have been such a thing as absolute government in the world (III, 144–5). In the *Dissertation upon Parties*, Bolingbroke says that simple forms of government are governments of arbitrary will, and therefore of all imaginable absurdities the most absurd. These governments, which include absolute democracy as well as absolute monarchy, do not degenerate into tyranny: they are tyranny in their very institution (*A Dissertation upon Parties*, 206-7). In the *Idea of a Patriot King* he says that unlimited monarchy, in which arbitrary rule is the sole rule or un-rule, is a government fitter for savages than for civilized people (*The Works of Lord Bolingbroke*, II, 387). On this point Opposition and Ministerialist writers were in agreement. For instance, the *London Journal* of 25 September 1731 invited its readers to compare our government with that of a neighbouring nation, where all the laws of the Kingdom were swallowed up in two words, will and pleasure; and on 9 September 1732, it wrote: 'all governments in the world, where the people don't make their own laws, as in England, are unreasonable and unjust governments...not indeed governments but tyrannies, and are so far from being equally lawful with good governments...that they are absolutely against all Law'. The *Daily Gazetteer* of 11 September 1735 wrote that no man can doubt that the people of France are slaves by law, for what, wrote Osborne,[1] on 15 November, is liberty, but being governed by just and equal laws of the People's making? Is not this the highest liberty? Is not this the perfection of liberty? that the people should choose their own legislators and that the executive power of the kingdom should constantly govern by what these legislators institute? And on 29 October 1737, *Common Sense*, on English Liberty, said: that freedom consists in a peoples being governed by laws made with their own consent is a trite maxim. This did not stop *Common Sense* driving the point home yet again, that liberty involves giving one's consent, personally or by a representative, to the laws which one is obliged to obey. On 30 April 1737 it had said that the French have an air and a grace in their slavery...they sing to the jingle of their chains, and in some measure prevent tyranny by soliciting it. Hervey in *Ancient and Modern Liberty stated and compared* (1734), wrote that no government can be free but a mixed government (44).

There is a revealing story in Nichols' *Literary Anecdotes of the 18th Century* (II, 616) concerning Hooke, the historian of Rome, and a pamphlet by Warburton of 1746, in which the latter had written that 'when God in his justice weighs the fate of nations, he considers all arbitrary governments as paper and packthread in the scale'. What, said Mr Hooke, does Mr Warburton imagine that God Almighty considers the great monarchies of France and Spain only as paper and packthread? No one in the company

[1] 'Francis Osborne', who will be met again, was James Pitt. 'Walsingham' was William Arnall or Arnold. See R. L. Haig, *The Gazetteer 1735-97* (1960), and W. T. Laprade, *Public Opinion and Politics in 18th Century England* (1936), 318-20.

made any reply and the conversation dropped. But, says Nichols, we may suppose they took the fairness of the citation for granted. At the same time, according to Joseph Spence's *Anecdotes*, Hooke used to say that there were three reasons why a man would choose to live in England: liberty, liberty, liberty.[1]

Barrington in his *Observations upon the Statutes* quotes some fundamental maxims of French law as to the King's prerogative that will make an Englishman by comparison thankful for the noble constitution to which he is happily born. 'I can never be persuaded but that there is a necessary connection between slavery and misery and between freedom and happiness' (2nd ed, 1766, 163).

To end this brief selection of examples of some of the hardier varieties of vulgar Whiggism, which has not drawn on the poets or the parliamentary debates[2] or other sources, Blackstone quotes Locke on law and freedom and goes on to say that the idea and practice of 'this political or civil liberty' flourish in their highest vigour in these kingdoms, where it falls little short of perfection, the legislature and of course (i.e. in consequence) the laws of England being peculiarly adapted to the preservation of this inestimable blessing, even in the meanest subject, very different from the modern constitution of other states on the continent of Europe... (*Commentaries* (1765), I, 122–3). Blackstone in his Introduction quoted Montesquieu to the effect that England is a land, perhaps the only one in the universe, in which 'political or civil liberty' is the very end and scope of the constitution, without any of Montesquieu's misgivings (6), and in his lectures showed precisely how and why this was so, viz: because the three great primary rights, to personal security, liberty (that is, against arbitrary imprisonment, as 'practised daily' in France by the Crown) and property were secured by the constitution in various ways which he listed, (122–41).[3] 'This review of our situation' justified

---

[1] I owe these references to Hooke to Addison Ward, 'the Tory view of Roman History' in *Studies in English Literature*, IV (1964), 443–5.

[2] See, e.g. *Parliamentary History*, VIII. In the debate on Walpole's Excise scheme of 1733, Sir Paul Methuen said: the neighbouring nations in Europe once free, are most of them at present reduced to a state of slavery. They have no liberty, no property or law, etc. See Vol XI: Wyndham in a debate on a Place Bill (1740) defines 'free government': it must consist of two distinct powers: the legislative and the executive, the latter always subordinate and subject to review by the former. 'The very essence of a free government' consists among other things in the accountability of the executive, otherwise what benefit in the people making their own laws? (370). Vol. XIII (1036), Pelham in 1744: under a despotic government there is no property and no liberty etc.

[3] Including the constitution, powers and privileges of Parliament, the strict and known limitation of the king's prerogative, etc.

Montesquieu's remark (141). Blackstone did not distinguish between 'absolute' and 'despotic' governments: the 'main principle' of the constitution of absolute monarchies was 'that of governing by fear' (395);[1] 'in absolute and despotic governments...no real liberty exists' (404) – the context is the danger 'in a land of liberty' of making a distinct order of the profession of arms. If France ever recovers 'its former liberty', it will owe it to the efforts of the *parlements*; it is owing to the independence of the judicial power vested in the latter that the absolutism of the French monarchy is more tolerable than that of the 'eastern empires' (260).

All these judgements and comparisons rested on somewhat superficial views as to the nature of French government and law, let alone Turkish or 'Asiatic' or 'eastern' 'despotism'. There were few who knew any better about the latter;[2] as to France, how much of the sort of thing quoted was merely rhetoric or propaganda makes no difference. It was the sort of loose thinking and talking, symptomatic of and adding fuel to the anti-French chauvinism which Hume detested (which does not mean that he was unaware of the danger of French hegemony in Europe) which it was his aim, *qua* philosopher, to correct; and this can be regarded as part of his programme of promoting political moderation.[3]

But there was vulgar Whiggism in Hume too: many instances

[1] Cf. *Letters of Junius*, Letter XXXVIII of 3 April 1770. The spirit of the modern French consitutution requires that the King should be feared, and the principle, I believe, is tolerably supported by the fact. When the *parlements* venture to remonstrate, the tyrant comes forward and answers absolutely for himself.

[2] For an exception see Vol. II of the *Lives of the Norths* (London, 1890): Sir Dudley North had lived in Turkey and made a close study of the legal system, which he contrasted very favourably with that in England; thereby refuting the 'common opinion that Turkey hath no law nor property' as well as the prevailing notion that the English legal system is a much better guarantee of liberty. Apparently he was in the habit of pointing out how hard it was to 'come at' a true knowledge of the Turkish government even for those who lived there: that Sir Paul Rycaut's book was very superficial and full of errors (59–60, 63–5, 156–7). Hume says that Turkish 'justice' is slavery 'in the full and proper sense of the term', being the decisions of 'bashaws' and 'cadis' unrestrained 'by any methods, forms, or laws', that is to say the 'altogether ruinous and intolerable' exercise of 'despotic' (changed to 'arbitrary' in 1770) power 'contracted into a small compass', by men whose tenure of authority is limited and uncertain (*Rise of Arts and Sciences*, Essays, 117). In *Populousness of Ancient Nations* (*id.*, 443), the government of the Turks is not 'very favourable to industry and propagation; yet it preserves at least peace and order among the inhabitants'. That is the minimum any government can do in order to exist at all.

[3] To Abbé Le Blanc, September 1754: 'You wou'd have remark'd in my Writings, that my Principles are, all along, tolerably monarchical, and that I abhor that low Practice, so prevalent in England, of speaking with Malignity of France.' (*Letters*, I, 194). On the danger to Europe of 'enormous monarchies', see the final § of the essay on the *Balance of Power*. In the editions 1752–64, after 'enormous monarchies',

can be found in his political and historical thinking, and they can cause glaring inconsistency. There may have been an element of calculated 'prudence' in it sometimes, and there was policy in glorying in the name of North Briton. But many of these expressions of good Whig-British sentiment, examples of which have been met already, seem genuinely from the heart and perfectly sincere. For instance, in *Whether the British Government inclines more to Absolute Monarchy or to a Republic*: 'these considerations are apt to make one entertain a magnificent idea of the British spirit and love of liberty; since we could maintain our free government, during so many centuries, against our sovereigns etc'. And in the essay on the *Protestant Succession*, there is a great paean of praise in favour of the revolution settlement: 'the glory of the nation has spread itself all over Europe... So long and so glorious a period no nation almost can boast of: nor is there another instance in the whole history of mankind, that so many millions of people have, during such a space of time, been held together, in a manner so free, so rational and so suitable to the dignity of human nature'

Hume had 'such as Europe is at present threatened with'. Hume was anxious that England, from interfering too much and unnecessarily in European affairs (and thereby adding enormously to the national debt) would be led to the opposite extreme of taking no part at all. 'These excesses to which we have been carried... may, perhaps, in time, become still more prejudicial another way, by begetting, as is usual, the opposite extreme, and rendering us totally careless and supine with regard to the fate of Europe.' 'Enormous monarchies' soon destroy themselves, but are also 'destructive to human nature'. See also the conclusion of the essay on *Public Credit*. From 1752-68, after 'foreign enemies', Hume had written 'or rather enemy (for we have but one to dread)', which is of course France. Our children, he says, may sit down and see our neighbours oppressed and conquered till at last they themselves lie at the mercy of the conqueror.

In the editions 1752-68 of the essay on the *Protestant Succession* (*Essays*, 493), Hume had after 'the glory of the nation has spread itself all over Europe': 'while we stand the bulwark against oppression and the great antagonist of that power which threatens every people with conquest and subjection'.

Cf. the note in *Essays*, 345 (*Balance of Power*) which was in the text of all editions from 1752 to 1768. 'The greatest force that ever perhaps was formed by the civil or political combination of mankind'. Hume says that there remains some hope of maintaining the resistance 'so long, that the natural revolutions of human affairs, together with unforeseen events and accidents, may guard us against universal monarchy, and preserve the world from so great an evil'. All these remarks on the danger of French hegemony were withdrawn after 1768. The dislike of anti-French chauvinism and the fear of French military hegemony are perfectly compatible. 'Our jealousy and our hatred of France are without bounds; and the former sentiment, at least, must be acknowledged reasonable and well-grounded' (*Balance of Trade*, *Essays*, 322). 'But everything connected with France is supposed, in England, to be polluted beyond all possibility of expiation' (*History*, x, 147n). Cf. *History*, III, 98: the English though commonly the aggressors, 'have always retained a stronger tincture of national antipathy; nor is their hatred retaliated on them to an equal degree by the French'.

(*Essays*, 493-4). In both these instances, Hume is not in fact speaking directly in the first person; he is presenting a one-sided argument, (the first quotation would seem to be an echo of Bolingbroke's *Dissertation upon Parties*), so there may be an element of exaggeration, but even so, there is no reason to suppose that Hume himself did not endorse the gist of these remarks. In Appendix III of the *History of England*, in the section on Government in Elizabeth's reign, he says that 'on the whole, the English have no reason, from the example of their ancestors, to be in love with the picture of absolute monarchy; or to prefer the unlimited authority of the prince and his unbounded prerogatives to that noble liberty, that sweet equality and that happy security, by which they are at present distinguished above all nations in the universe' (VI, 429-30). (Hume left this passage untouched. In the light of what he had to say about the 'civilized monarchies' of modern Europe, the operative phrase here would seem to be 'from the example of their ancestors': one must lean heavily on that if one wants to lessen the effect of the vulgar Whiggism produced by the sugary adjectives – in fact one cannot help feeling that Hume has his tongue in his cheek just a little.) No other government has a law of Habeas Corpus, a consideration which 'alone may induce us to prefer our constitution to all others' (*History*, IX, 232: this is genuine enough). In 1772 he wrote to Strahan, his publisher, asking him to restore the words 'and happy' to the phrase 'that singular and happy Government which we enjoy at present', which he had struck out of the proofs of his *History* in a fit of disgust with the 'licentiousness of our odious patriots'. After all, he wrote, 'the English government is certainly happy, though probably not calculated for duration by reason of its excessive liberty'. But if the sheet in question was already printed, it wasn't worth bothering about (*Letters*, II, 260-1). Other examples of vulgar Whiggism in conflict with scientific Whiggism will be seen later.

So all-pervasive and powerful was the stereotype: English liberty versus French 'slavery', that Hume was himself its victim, and could speak of 'slavery' in connection with absolute government,[1] and the Jansenists as keeping alive 'the small sparks of the love of liberty, which are to be found in the French nation' (*Of Superstition and Enthusiasm*, conclusion). But there is very little, in Hume's published writings, about the French nation, its history

---

[1] See the penultimate § of the essay *Whether the British Government inclines etc.* Although liberty was 'infinitely' (withdrawn after 1758) preferable to slavery in almost every case, yet he would rather see an absolute monarch than a republic in Britain.

and institutions. Perhaps because he knew enough to feel that he was not on very firm ground in the controversial matters involved (he knew Boulainvilliers)[1] what he has to say about the 'civilized monarchies' of Europe is brief and general and in broad historical perspective (the progress of civilization).

But *qua* philosopher, Hume set himself to correct the excesses of vulgar Whiggism with respect to the contrast between the 'free' government of Britain and the absolute monarchies of the continent. Unlike the 'fashionable system' of politics, his theory of political obligation, as set out in *Treatise* III is such that it can accommodate the latter: for the object of government is simply to maintain what Hume calls 'justice', the 'peace and liberty' which in the *Enquiry concerning the Principles of Morals* becomes 'peace and order' (Section IV, § 1): the liberty and security of the individual under the rule of law – not political or public liberty in any further sense, not a liberty which has anything to do with specific forms of government or types of constitution, and observation and 'experiment' show that the absolute monarchies at the present time in Europe do in fact maintain 'justice' and therefore, for all practical purposes, they answer the purpose of government as such.

Where 'public liberty' is mentioned in *Treatise* III, it is in the special context of mixed monarchy; Hume is making the point that in this particular type of government it is allowable to resist the chief magistrate 'even when he would encroach on the other parts of the constitution', and goes on: 'For besides that nothing is more essential to public interest than the preservation of public liberty ...' (564). That is, in this form of government, public liberty is the guarantee of the personal liberty and security of the individual.[2] The latter is guaranteed, perhaps not quite so well but anyway differently, in the absolute monarchies. So all the civilized monarchies pass the test, even if they are not 'free governments'.

For an actual definition of 'free government' one has to go to Hume's last essay (written in 1774) on the *Origin of Government*. All governments Hume says there are more or less free: no government is absolutely free because 'a great sacrifice of liberty must necessarily be made in every government'; and no government is

---

[1] Boulainvilliers' *Etat de la France* is cited in Hume's *Early Memoranda*.
[2] If the sentence quoted is meant to be taken as a general statement, not referring only to mixed governments, and if 'public liberty' here equals political liberty or 'free government', representative institutions etc, then we have an example of vulgar Whiggism which is contradicted by Hume's political philosophy in general and his account of the civilized monarchies.

wholly absolute, because there will always be limitations of some sort on the power of the ruler. The sultan, even though he is master of the life and fortune of his subjects cannot impose taxes at pleasure; the king of France can do that, but 'would find it dangerous to attempt the lives and fortunes of individuals'. And other principles or prejudices act as barriers – to say nothing of religion. What therefore is meant by a so-called 'free government'? It is a government in which power is divided 'among several members, whose united authority is no less, or is commonly greater, than that of any monarch; but who in the usual course of administration, must act by general and equal laws, that are previously known to all the members, and to all their subjects. In this sense, it must be owned that liberty is the perfection of civil society.'

The absolute monarchies fall short of the perfection of civil society; they do not enjoy what Hume calls on different occasions, 'regular liberty', or 'regular established liberty', or 'public liberty', or 'political or civil liberty', or 'political liberty', or 'civil liberty', or sometimes just 'liberty'. These terms are interchangeable and apply to different aspects of 'regular' liberty: for example, sometimes to the jury system, sometimes to parliamentary institutions or privileges, sometimes to laws guaranteeing personal freedom; they are used nearly always in connexion with England and English history, and never with any great precision.[1]

But if the absolute monarchies do not actually enjoy 'civil' or 'political' liberty, they enjoy 'some of the most considerable advantages of it' (*History*, IV, 52).

In the essay which after 1754 was called *Of Civil Liberty*, Hume

[1] Since Hume's notion of liberty is what is being discussed, all that needs to be said here is that his various usages may or may not include the sort of 'liberty' enjoyed also in absolute monarchies (Cf. *History*, II, 303: the formalities of justice are found requisite to the support of 'liberty' in all monarchical governments). E.g.: 'public liberty' could do so, as used in IV, 89, where Henry VIII's royal prerogative was allowed to 'break all bounds of law and to violate public liberty', especially as in the first 1759 edition (p. 17) this reads to 'break all bounds of law and order', but not as used in VI, 485, where it is used in connection with a parliamentary privilege essential to 'public liberty'. Since in the English constitution this 'public liberty' is necessary to maintain 'liberty' in a broader sense, Hume does not need to be more specific. Thus in VI, 554, 'liberty' means popular assemblies entering into every branch of public business: it is equivalent to the 'regular established liberty' of VI, 614, meaning the parliamentary institutions of the present constitution. 'Civil liberty' of VII, 133 includes parliamentary consent to taxation as well as absolute security for property. In VIII, 248, the deists are said to have had no other object than 'political liberty'. This would have been better as 'liberty', or the 'general liberty' of VI, 514n, or the 'civil and religious liberty' of V, 108. 'Political' is presumably here being used in contrast with 'natural'.

undertook a comparison of Liberty and Despotism (that was the original title of the essay), in which he produced 'experiments' from modern history to counter the teaching that the arts and sciences could only flourish in a free government: the teaching of Longinus, which was based on the 'two experiments, of which each was double in its kind', of Greece and Rome, followed by 'several eminent writers in our country', like Shaftesbury and Addison, who had either confined their view 'merely to ancient facts', or been led astray by 'too great a partiality in favour of that form of government established among us' (*Essays*, I, 91).[1] The chief of Hume's experiments consisted simply in looking across the Channel, where France 'which scarcely ever enjoyed any established liberty...yet has carried the arts and sciences as near perfection as any other nation. The English are, perhaps, better [later changed to 'greater'] philosophers...but the French are the only people, except the Greeks, who have been at once philosophers, poets, orators, historians, painters, architects, sculptors and musicians. With regard to the stage they have far [later withdrawn] excelled even the Greeks...' And they have in a greater measure perfected the most useful and agreeable art of any: *l'art de vivre*. In comparison, the English are rather backward and rustic (*id.*, 92).

The 'established opinion' that commerce can only flourish in a free government seems to be better founded, 'on a longer and larger experience'. But even in this, our great jealousy of France seems to prove that this maxim is no more certain and infallible than that of Longinus, just refuted, and that the subjects of an absolute prince are as capable of becoming our rivals as much in commerce as in learning and the arts (93).

In the essay on the *Rise and Progress of the Arts and Sciences*, Hume maintains that the arts and sciences originate in republics (after 1770 changed to 'free states'), because, however barbarous, a republic infallibly gives rise to law, 'even before mankind have made any considerable advances in the other sciences'. 'From law arises security: from security curiosity: and from curiosity knowledge' (*Essays*, 119). In a monarchical government, on the other hand, law does not arise necessarily from the form of government. 'Monarchy, when absolute, contains even something repugnant to law. Great wisdom and reflexion can alone reconcile them. But

---

[1] For the conventional liberty and letters theme at this time in England see, for example, R. Wellek, *The Rise of English Literary History*, (1941), 34, *et seq*. Chesterfield rejected it (1749).

such a degree of wisdom can never be expected, before the greater refinements and improvements of human reason' (119). Law, however, once it has taken root, is a 'hardy plant' (125) and, unlike the arts of 'luxury' and the more liberal arts, which depend on a refined taste and sentiment, can scarcely fall into oblivion, except by the total subversion of society and such barbarian invasions as obliterate all memory of former arts and civility. These coarser and more useful arts, too, are transported by imitation from one climate to another, and 'from these causes proceed civilized monarchies; where the arts of government, first invented in free states, are preserved to the mutual advantage and security of sovereign and subject' (126). The reconciliation of absolute monarchy and law is thus brought about by the progress of reason and civilization; monarchy borrows its laws, methods and institutions, and consequently its stability and order, from free governments, and a new type of government, the 'civilized monarchy' emerges.

These 'civilized monarchies' were 'despotic' – as has been seen, the essay on *Civil Liberty* was originally called *Of Liberty and Despotism*. Hume changed the title, and in this essay, and elsewhere, he later changed 'despotic' into 'absolute',[1] but not consistently, and in the *History of England* he talks of 'despotic government exercised in the legal manner of European nations' (VIII, 273).[2] 'Despotism' could have a bad meaning as well as a purely neutral one;[3] it was presumably to avoid the bad connotations that Hume made his changes. But he made a clear distinction between absolute government in the Eastern style, 'the maxims of Eastern

---

[1] E.g., 'Having...intended in this essay to make a full comparison of liberty and despotism', was changed in 1758 to 'civil liberty and absolute government' (*Essays*, 90).
[2] For the European manner, see *That Politics may be reduced to a Science* (*Essays*, 20).
[3] See, for instance Hutcheson, *Short Introduction*, Book III, Chap. 4 (conclusion): 'the very notion of civil life, or polity, is opposite to despotism, or the power of masters over slaves'. Rutherforth (*Institutes*) says despotic power is a bad name because commonly used to convey what is arbitrary and tyrannical (II, 121), and the constitution is called despotic where the compact has established both the legislative and the executive powers in the same person or body. If both are vested in one man, it is an absolute or despotic monarchy; there is also despotic aristocracy and democracy (II, 92). In order to take off the bad meaning of 'despotism', Rutherforth calls the civil power originally inherent in the community or collective body but entrusted by their tacit or express consent with the governing part of each community, 'civil despotism' (II, 121). Blackstone talks of 'that absolute despotic power which must in all governments reside somewhere' residing in Parliament (*Commentaries*, I, 156). In the essay on *Liberty of the Press*, Hume describes the English government as a mixture of despotism and liberty, where the liberty predominates.

tyranny' (*History*, VIII, 273) or the barbarous Turkish monarchy, 'where the judges are not restrained by any methods, forms or laws', which Hume had originally called 'despotic power' but after 1770 called 'arbitrary' (*Essays*, 117), and the 'civilized' absolute monarchies of Europe. In the former, full powers are delegated to every subordinate official: only in an advanced state of political knowledge is it realized that the inconveniences which attend the application of general laws to particular cases are fewer than those resulting from full discretionary powers in every magistrate. A people arbitrarily governed in this way are 'slaves in the full and proper sense of the word' (117). They are at the mercy of the wills of particular individuals. In a 'civilized monarchy', on the other hand, only the prince is unrestrained in the exercise of his authority, and possesses a power not limited by anything but custom, example and the sense of his own interest.[1] Every minister or magistrate, however eminent, must submit to the general laws which govern the whole society. No one apart from the prince has any discretionary power. The people depend on none but their sovereign for the security of their property. But he is so far removed from them, and is so much exempt from private jealousies or interests, that this dependence is scarcely felt. 'And thus a species of government arises, to which, in a high political rant, we may give the name of *Tyranny*; but which by a just and prudent administration, may afford tolerable security to the people, and may answer most of the ends of political society.' The people have as much security for the enjoyment of their property in a civilized monarchy as in a republic (*Essays*, 126–7).[2] There is 'a long train of

[1] It is perhaps worth noting here that Dugald Stewart thought that Montesquieu, led by an excusable partiality for the form of government under which he had been educated, and probably in some degree by prudential considerations, had insisted too much on the distinction between monarchy and despotism; if by monarchy he had meant that of England, the contrast would have been complete, but what he meant by it acknowledged no legal or constitutional checks, and wherever it could safely exert its authority exhibited all the spirit of despotism (*Collected Works*, IX, 409). Cf. also 353. In his enumeration of the forms of government Stewart rejects Montesquieu's classification, excludes limited monarchy from the list of simple forms, because the limitations of the sovereign power can only arise from a mixture in the government, and employs the word Monarchy as synonymous with Despotism.

[2] Cf. *Of Civil Liberty*: 'Private property seems to me fully as secure [changed in 1753 to 'almost'] in a civilized European monarchy, as in a republic', nor is any danger apprehended in such a government from the violence of the sovereign more than we commonly dread harm from thunder, or earthquakes, or any accident the most unusual or extraordinary (94). Robert Wallace found this 'surprising', and argued that men's safety does not depend on what they may apprehend, but on the real nature of their condition: a man may be in great danger when he does not

dependence from the prince to the peasant, which is not great enough to render property precarious or depress the minds of the people' (128).

Indeed, although 'all kinds of government, free and absolute, seem to have undergone, in modern times, a great change for the better, with regard both to foreign and domestic management', it is monarchical government 'that seems to have made the greatest advances towards perfection. It may now be affirmed of civilized

apprehend it. Whether one is in safety must be determined not from what does, but from what may happen. A subject in France has not an equal security with one in Britain, of not being thrown into prison never more to be heard of. See *Characteristics of the present political state of Great Britain*, (1758), 215–16n. A writer in *Common Sense* (1737) agreed with Hume. See below, p. 197n. Thomas Blackwell, Principal of Marischal College, Aberdeen, and an ardent Whig and propagandist for the blessings of 'our matchless constitution' (I, 150), and the administration of Pelham (I, 196–7), whose 'chief aim' in his *Memoirs of the Court of Augustus* (Vol. I, 1753) was to show that liberty, virtue and true grandeur are indissolubly linked by nature, in order to account for the greatness of the French armies under absolute monarchy, while the free Venetian republic hires foreign troops, said that it would be necessary to show from their history how a tyrannical, enslaving rule has 'prevailed in the one, though called a commonwealth; and that the other has been, in many respects free under an arbitrary government'. France's wars with England and her civil wars formed her soldiery, and the general civility and forms of justice originally introduced by their abolished or despised laws, stand them instead of a constitution. Civil war is a sort of liberty; and a prevalent custom is a law without a sanction. It is neither law nor justice (which their princes trample upon at pleasure) but precedent and a kind of political humanity that protects them from the ravages of absolute power, yet in effect they are frequently protected, and under a tolerable administration, enjoy several of the blessings of a better state. This may look somewhat similar to Hume's remarks, but is really different and more grudging. Blackwell says that France has many natural advantages which require great abuse and vast misrule to nullify. Also, what prevents a king of France from cutting off his subjects' heads and seizing their estates with as much impunity as the Grand Signior is that it would be 'unpolite', if not illegal; some pretence like religion is needed; it is not 'so usual in the one country as in the other' (*Memoirs*, I, 39–40). By a 'civilized monarchy' Hume means something much more than this. Blackwell was not thinking in terms of the progress of society; Hume was, and so was Sir James Steuart in his *Inquiry into the Principles of Political Economy* (1767). Liberty for Sir James Steuart is a European phenomenon because it is the transition from military to modern commercial society, which is 'a better scheme for limiting the arbitrary power of princes than all the rebellions that ever were contrived' (I, 504), and under most forms of which every industrious man who lives with economy is free and independent (I, 10). So he talks of 'our free modern governments' (I, xiii), 'the spirit of European liberty' as a living presence, not something that almost everywhere except in England has been 'lost', (I, 169), the 'civil and domestic liberty introduced into Europe' (I, 150) by 'the revolution', which is not 1688, but the dissolution of the feudal form of government. No term is less understood that that of liberty, he says, but by a people's being free, 'I understand no more than their being governed by general laws...' In so far as any ruler has the power of dispensing with, restraining or extending these laws, liberty is, not necessarily hurt, but rendered precarious. According to this definition of liberty, a people may be found to enjoy freedom under the most despotic forms of government (I, 237–8).

monarchies what was formerly said in praise of republics alone, *that they are a government of Laws, not of Men*. They are found susceptible of order, method, and constancy, to a surprising degree. Property is there secure; industry encouraged; the arts flourish; and the prince lives secure among his subjects, like a father among his children' (95). In 1753 was added a calculation to the effect that out of 2,000 monarchs great and small in 200 years of modern European history, there had not been one so bad as Tiberius, Caligula, Nero or Domitian, who were four in twelve amongst the Roman Emperors.[1]

However, although monarchical governments have approached nearer to popular ones in gentleness and stability, they are still 'much inferior' – 'much' was withdrawn in 1770. Our modern education and customs instil more humanity and moderation than the ancient, but have not as yet been able to overcome entirely the disadvantages of that form of government (95–6). Commerce, for instance, is 'apt to decay' in absolute governments, not because it is less secure, but because it is less honourable – a subordination of ranks based on birth and title being absolutely essential to that form of government, notwithstanding the efforts, and considerable success, of the French.[2] Another disadvantage is that monarchies, receiving their chief stability from a superstitious reverence to priests and princes, have commonly abridged the liberty of reasoning with regard to religion and politics and consequently metaphysics and morals – that is, the most considerable branches of science, because what remains, mathematics and natural science, are 'not half so valuable' (127).[3] On the other hand, free governments are ruinous and oppressive to their provinces and conquered territories (compare the *pays conquis* of France with Ireland), whereas to an absolute monarch all his subjects are to him

[1] No 75 in Section III of Hume's early memoranda says that within the last 2000 [200?] years [almost] all the despotic governments of the world have been improving and the free ones degenerating; so that they are now pretty near a par. See *Hume's Early Memoranda*. Mossner judges Section III to date from, say, 1737–40.

[2] For French commercial success see also *Balance of Trade* (322–3), *Taxes*, 2nd §: 'Trade came late into France and seems to have been the effect of reflection and observation in an ingenious and enterprizing people.' Towards the end of the essay *Of Commerce*, Hume says that the poverty of the common people is a natural, if not infallible effect of absolute monarchy; but their wealth is not an infallible result of liberty. 'Liberty must be attended with particular accidents, and a certain turn of thinking in order to produce that effect' (272).

[3] It is odd that Hume does not mention standing armies as an inherent defect of absolute monarchy. It is not easy to see how Hume's virtually lifelong subscription to the belief that standing armies are incompatible with liberty can be reconciled with his view of the civilized monarchies as a government of laws not men etc.

the same, except for a few friends and favourites, and he does not therefore make any distinction between any of them in his general laws (*Politics a Science*, 17, 19).

The central fact however is that the civilized monarchies adequately fulfil, for all practical purposes, the functions of government: they are 'regular monarchies', governments of laws not men. In the *History of England* (IV, 91) Hume remarks that Scotland in the fifteenth century 'had not yet attained that state which distinguishes a civilized monarchy, and which enables the government by the force of its laws and institutions alone, without any extraordinary capacity in the sovereign, to maintain itself in order and tranquillity'. These civilized monarchies are recent phenomena, and that helps to explain the weaknesses of Machiavelli's political science, and why his reasonings 'especially upon monarchical government' have been found so defective, and why most of the maxims in the *Prince* have been refuted by subsequent experience (*Civil Liberty*, 1st §). The example Hume gives concerns prime ministers, an essential feature of all 'regular monarchies' (*History*, III, 23).[1] A 'regular' monarchy normally runs itself without the interposition of the monarch; Henry III would have been a 'proper pageant' in such a government, instead of being a failure (*History*, II, 350).[2]

If the civilized absolute monarchies of Europe were to be accounted governments of laws and not of men, there must be personal liberty, if not 'political or civil' liberty, in these types of government; and there must therefore be a distinction, implicit at least in Hume's thought, between personal liberty and 'political or civil' liberty; you can have the former without the latter, that is, in a government which is not a 'free government', although in the English constitution, the latter is necessary to maintain and guarantee the former. This may be why Hume altered his remark in the essay on *Civil Liberty* about France, 'which never enjoyed any shadow of liberty', to 'France, which scarce ever enjoyed any established liberty' (1758). The revised form of words shows a certain cautious timidity. Montesquieu would have insisted that

[1] At the beginning of the fourteenth century the European kingdoms were unacquainted with the office of a prime minister 'so well understood at present in all regular monarchies'.
[2] Cf. *History*, VI, 430. On the English Government in the reign of Elizabeth: the most that can be said in favour of it is that the power of the prince, though unlimited, was 'exercised after the European manner, and entered not into every part of the administration; that the instances of a high exerted prerogative were not so frequent as to render property insensibly insecure, or to reduce the people to a total servitude...'

Hume went much further. But at any rate, to talk of French 'slavery' was political rant: for one thing, it obscured the vast superiority of a modern civilized monarchy to even the republics of antiquity.[1] The distinction in Hume is liable to be obscured by the fact that there is no corresponding verbal distinction between 'civil' and 'political' liberty, a distinction which vulgar Whiggism did not make because it did not need to: the one implied the other, though Bolingbroke in the *Dissertation upon Parties*, made a verbal distinction between 'private liberty' and 'public liberty' which would have been useful to Hume if he had adopted it.[2]

Such a distinction is implicit in Hutcheson, for although he says that 'under an absolute hereditary monarchy nothing is secure' (*Short Introduction*, Book III, Chap. 6, Section IV), and that none of the simple forms of government are well adapted to preserve any state happy, yet he takes it for granted that absolute monarchy is a legitimate form of government (Book III, Chap. 6, Section

---

[1] Some passionate admirers of the ancients and zealous partisans of civil liberty 'brand all submission to the government of a single person with the harsh denomination of slavery'. But to anyone who considers coolly on the subject it will appear that human nature, in general, really enjoys more liberty at present, in the most arbitrary government of Europe, than it ever did during the most flourishing period of ancient times. Hume is here thinking of domestic slavery. *Populousness of Ancient Nations* (385).

[2] '...as private liberty cannot be deemed secure under a government, wherein law, the proper and sole security of it, is dependent on will; so public liberty must be in danger, whenever a free constitution, the proper and sole security of it, is dependent on will; and a free constitution like ours is dependent on will, whenever the will of one estate can direct the conduct of all three' (279). Thomas Blackwell, in *Memoirs of the Court of Augustus* (Vol I, 1753), comparing the British and Roman constitutions, said that while the security of every man's private liberty, property and life seems to have been nearly equal, the security of public liberty, the liberty of the state on which private liberty, property, life and everything depends, is incontestably greater in the British constitution (143-4). John Dalrymple, *Considerations upon the policy of Entails* (1764) wrote that conversion of leases into feus was the best way in Scotland to diffuse 'civil liberty', by making tenants independent of their landlords; and it was also one of the best ways to diffuse 'political liberty' by paving the way to the extension of the number of voters in elections (94). *The Edinburgh Magazine and Review* (Vol. IV, 1775) pointed out that De Lolme distinguishes between 'general liberty', that is of the rights of the nation as a nation, and of its share in the government, and 'private liberty', the liberty of individuals, 'without which the general liberty, being absolutely frustrated in its object, would be only a matter of ostentation, and even could not long subsist' (598). De Lolme's *Constitution de l'Angleterre* was published in 1771. For his distinction between *la liberté politique* and *la liberté civile*, see G. Bonno, *La Constitution Brittanique devant l'opinion française*, (1932), 124-5.

For Bentham it was 'unfortunate that individual and political liberty have received the same name'. He was anxious to distinguish 'personal liberty' meaning 'security against a certain species of injury which affects the person', and 'political liberty' which is 'another branch of security – security against the injustice of the members of the government'. Quoted by M. P. Mack in *Jeremy Bentham* (1962), 95.

II), and his general definition of a 'state or civil society' is 'a society of free men united under one government for their common interest', and, he goes on, the very notion of civil life or polity is opposite to despotism or the power of a master over slaves (Book III, Chap. 4): it follows that absolute monarchy, even if it is 'least of all' adapted to promote the prosperity of the community (Book III, Chap. 7, Section VII), is a 'society of free men' and not a 'despotism' as just defined. This is reinforced by what he has to say about the right of resistance in every government, including absolute governments, 'for even slaves, adjudged to the most miserable subjection for their crimes, may have a right to defend themselves against certain injuries...' The whole paragraph makes it clear that the subjects of absolute governments are not to be regarded as 'slaves' (Book III, Chap. 7, Section II). Absolute monarchies are the 'monarchies only limited by laws, without any council sharing in the supreme power', described in Hutcheson's *System of Moral Philosophy*, II, 254.

The 'Whimsical philosopher' in his first dissertation in the *London Magazine* (April 1749), wrote that the subjects of an absolute monarch may enjoy 'public liberty' and be 'free', while those of a commonwealth or limited monarchy, both of which are usually called a 'free' government, may not, although the latter have a more certain tenure in that blessing, so long as he neither enacts any laws or appoints any magistrates but such as are, from public motives, approved by a majority of the people. 'Public or social liberty', according to this writer, consists in no free man being obliged to submit to any law or magistrate but such as are, from motives of a public nature, approved of by a majority of the people; it does not consist in the constitution or form, so much as in the execution and administration of government.[1]

The best and fullest contemporary treatment of this topic seems to be that of Rutherforth in his *Institutes of Natural Law* (1754), which were the 'substance' of a course of lectures on Grotius' *De Jure Belli ac Pacis* given at Cambridge. Rutherforth distinguished two kinds of civil liberty established by the social contract: (1) of the parts and (2) of the whole collectively. (1) implies a freedom from all except civil subjection, and (2) a freedom from all subjection whatever. Whether both were present or not in civil society depended on the type of government. In 'free states' both are present, because 'the collective body of the whole society is free or is not under any subjection'. 'Free states' does not mean

---

[1] I have taken this from a report in the *Scots Magazine*, XI, 211 *et seq*.

only perfect democracies, but also mixed governments, which have the essence of a free state, whether common usage gives them the title or not, notwithstanding the king may be a constituent part of the legislative body and vested with executive power, provided the collective body is not bound by any act of legislation in which it does not concur either immediately or by its representatives. In absolute governments, the collective body is in a state of subjection to its constitutional governors, because as far as their power extends, their act is binding on the collective body, as well as upon the several members. In absolute governments only civil liberty in the first sense is present, because the collective body is bound to act for the purposes of social union by a judgement and will which is not of its own keeping, and is therefore in a state of civil subjection which is consistent with freedom in the first, but not with freedom in the second sense. But in all forms of government, freedom in the first sense remains as of right. Why then, asks Rutherforth, should one prefer any one type of government to any other, a 'free' to an 'absolute' government? The reason is because where freedom in the second sense is lacking, freedom in the first sense is not so secure. There is a wide difference between the right of individuals to civil liberty and their enjoyment of it in fact: the absolute monarch is in a situation which gives him the opportunity and arms him with strength enough to treat his subjects as if they were his slaves, that is to advance a separate interest of his own. Since in the nature of the thing there is a possibility, and from the general temper of mankind some likelihood that the trust will be abused when all is left to the will of one man, it is necessary in order to secure the civil liberty of the several members in fact, to preserve and maintain the civil liberty of the collective body, by giving it so much weight and influence in the legislature, that nothing can be done without its consent or that of its representatives. When we say that a nation has lost or given up its civil liberty, what we mean is civil liberty in the second sense; but this is the support of civil liberty in the first sense. Loss of (2) in right will commonly be attended with loss of (1) in fact.

In a mixed form of government, where the agents or representatives of the people make a distinct and constitutional part of the legislative body, it is commonly said that the civil liberty of the people consists in their right of thus acting in the legislature by their representatives. But this means their right so to act as a collective body, not as separate individuals: otherwise many people even in a perfect democracy, who for one reason or another are excluded from acting in the legislative body, would have no 'civil liberty'. The essence of civil liberty therefore does not consist in this right, although this right is, as seen already, the support of civil liberty (Vol. II, Chap. VIII, 'Of Civil Subjection and Civil Liberty').

Grotius therefore was right, and Locke was wrong: absolute government, even if it is attended with more inconveniences than any other form of government (II, 124) and a mixed form of government is 'vastly preferable' (II, 107), is a perfectly legitimate form of government, and civil subjection to such is not 'slavery', though technically the constitution is called 'despotic' where the compact has established the legislative and executive powers in the same person or body, and if both are vested in one man it is 'an absolute or despotic monarchy' (II, 92). Rutherforth shows how Locke's reasoning in the exclusion of absolute monarchy (want of a common judge between subjects and monarch) will go to prove that any form of government is inconsistent with civil society, so that there cannot be such a thing as civil government at all (II, 100 *et seq.*). Every legislative body, being supposed to have all the legislative power in itself alone, is on Locke's reasoning in a state of nature with all under its authority – there is no appeal against it, no common judge. In whatever sense a legislative body is incapable of doing an injury, an absolute monarch may be said likewise to be incapable of doing any; he is equally commissioned to act for the people as their representative; his authority is derived from the same source ultimately. The people do not feel the want of a common judge, either where the legislative body is simple or mixed, till the trust committed to it is abused, but there is no more common judge in the one form of government as in the other. Therefore if absolute monarchy is an impossible form of government, so is every other. The fact that a mixed government is less likely to abuse its trust, does not alter the fact that absolute monarchy is possible and consistent with the nature of society. Rutherforth's moral in all this is that you cannot prove a constitution to be popular by abstract arguments 'from general reasonings upon the nature of civil government, without recourse to records and history, custom and usage' (II, 107). Want of a common judge between the body of the society and its monarch can be no reason for concluding that these two parties are necessarily in a state of nature, because there is the same want of a common judge between the government and the body of the society in all constitutions whatever, except such, if there be any, that are perfectly democratical. The reason why a monarch and the collective body of the society are not in a state of nature is because this body has entrusted him with such an authority over it as the state of nature knows nothing of: it is a limited authority in its own nature, as intended for the security and advancement of the common benefit. The state of nature properly speaking only appears when the monarchical constitution is dissolved (II, 109–10).

As for Montesquieu, vulgar Whigs saw him as one of themselves and interpreted him accordingly. But Montesquieu's ideas of liberty and the English Constitution were not what vulgar Whigs, then and later, took them to be. Liberty was the direct aim of the English Constitution, but for that very reason, liberty was as precarious as it was extreme: 'le plus haut point de liberté, où la constitution d'un État peu être portée', and Montesquieu did not favour extremes of any sort (see *L'Esprit des Lois*, XI, 6 – the last two paragraphs). The English 'pour favoriser la liberté', had destroyed its surest foundation: the intermediary powers of the nobility. Whereas in France a more moderate freedom, suited to a nation in which there was more *esprit* and sociability and civilization and less politics and barbarism (of climate and of manners), was the indirect result of a constitution which aimed at something else (*la gloire*), and was guaranteed in a different fashion. There is, roughly speaking, the same distinction that is more or less implicit in Hutcheson, Hume and Rutherforth, between 'civil' and 'political' liberty. The phrase Montesquieu used most frequently in *L'Esprit des Lois* is 'political liberty'; in so far as there is a difference between 'political' and 'civil' liberty, the latter is used as the opposite of legal slavery: thus in 'despotism', as defined by Montesquieu, there is 'civil liberty' because the people are not literally and legally slaves, but there is no 'political liberty', because despotism is by definition the rule of one, unrestrained by law.[1] There is, however, 'political liberty' in monarchy, because

---

[1] See XV, 6. Montesquieu says that in despotic governments, political slavery has destroyed civil liberty ('*l'esclavage politique y anéantit en quelque façon la liberté civile*'). This does not mean the destruction of free institutions. This is made clear by XV, 13. The point Montesquieu is making is that for practical purposes there is little difference in a despotic government between a legally 'free man' (so-called) and a 'slave'. Political slavery, meaning that the so-called 'free man' is at the mercy of the despot's whim, makes one's 'civil liberty' valueless, whereas in *gouvernements modérés*, 'political liberty' makes 'civil liberty' precious; so that he who is deprived of the latter is deprived of the former. This shows that by 'civil liberty' Montesquieu means the freedom of men who are free in the sense of not being slaves – literally, not metaphorically. By 'political liberty' he means the rule of law, which is absent in the despotic form of government. In a despotism, a free man has 'civil liberty',

monarchy is a *gouvernement modéré*, that is, according to law, and 'political liberty' consists in security, or at least in the opinion that one has security (XII, 2), and depends essentially on the goodness or badness of the criminal laws. This is why it is possible for the individual to enjoy *la liberté politique* in a state which is not 'free', and to be unfree in *un État libre*, as, for example, in the ancient republics, where the laws against debtors were peculiarly harsh, or where the father of the family had the power to sell his children into slavery. (Montesquieu might have used as another example the political oddity which Hume noticed: the existence in England of the press gang.) This is why Montesquieu makes a distinction between the free constitution, and the freedom of the citizen, between the laws which 'forment la liberté politique dans son rapport avec la constitution', and those 'qui la forment dans son rapport avec le citoyen', devoting Book XI to the former and Book XII to the latter. At the beginning of Book VII, he says that it can happen that the constitution is free and the citizen not; and that the citizen can be free and the constitution not free.

Therefore although France is not a 'free state', which postulates a legislature representing the nation as a whole and a separation of powers between legislature and executive, its citizens enjoy what Montesquieu calls *la liberté politique* (as well, of course, as civil liberty), guaranteed especially by the fundamental and crucial separation of the executive and judicial powers. 'Political liberty' is only found in *états modérés*, that is not despotically governed, and France is an *état modéré*, if not an *état libre*.

If any of this rubbed off on to Hume, it was there already, in essentials, before the publication of *L'Esprit des Lois*. And the same line of thinking is seen later in Dugald Stewart, who seems to have been more heavily indebted to Hume's political science, or more willing to acknowledge specific obligations, than the other political thinkers of the Scottish Enlightenment, and who was on more than one occasion at pains to insist that mistaken notions of political liberty, widely disseminated by Locke and his followers, had helped greatly to divert the studies of political thinkers from the proper object of their attention, namely, the science of political economy. Not that the share of political power vested in the people is of trifling moment, but that its importance to their happiness depends on the protection and support it provides for

but no 'political liberty'; he is at the mercy of the whim of the despot and has no protection by law; that is, his lack of 'political' liberty renders him little better off than a real slave.

their civil rights. Happiness is the only object of legislation which is of intrinsic value, and what is called political liberty is only one of the means of obtaining that end. With the advantage of good laws, a people not possessed of political power, may yet enjoy a great deal of happiness. Stewart goes on to say that the only effective and permanent bulwark against the encroachments of tyranny is to be found in the political privileges secured by the constitution to the governed. However, the want of political privileges does not, like that of civil liberty, necessarily affect the happiness nor impair the natural rights of individuals, for their value is founded entirely on considerations of political expediency, and therefore the measure of them which a wise man would desire for himself and his fellow citizens is determined not by the degree in which every individual consents, directly or indirectly, to the laws by which he is governed, but by the share of power which it is necessary for the people to possess, in order to place their civil rights beyond the danger of violation; in so far as this is attained under any establishment, the civil liberty rests on a solid foundation, and their political power accomplishes completely the only purpose from which its value is derived. Nor must it be forgotten, how often a people, losing sight of the end, in blind pursuit of the means, have forfeited both (*Collected Works*, VIII, 23-4). And according to John Craig, however highly Millar valued civil liberty, he considered personal freedom as infinitely more important; had Pitt vigorously prosecuted the abolition of the slave trade, Millar might have been brought to overlook the manner in which his power was acquired – and Millar certainly felt most strongly about that – in consideration of its beneficial exertion (Craig's *Life of Millar* in the 4th edition of the *Origin of Ranks*, p. cxi).

In all the civilized governments of Europe, then, whether free or absolute, Hume saw the end and purpose of government realized, the life and property of the individual secure. But in England 'the perfection of civil society' was realized: the life and property of the subject were dependent not on a monarch, however civilized, remote and disinterested and unlikely to interfere with the impartial administration of justice, but exclusively on the laws. No one is above the law, unrestrained by it in the exercise of his authority; the rule of law is absolute: in a mixed monarchy the king can be allowed no discretionary powers which threaten the lives and liberties of his subjects; 'an eternal jealousy must be preserved against the sovereign, and no discretionary powers must ever be entrusted to him by which the property or personal liberty of any subject can be affected' (*History*, VII, 5).[1] In England no prerogative of the king, no power of any magistrate, nothing but the authority alone of laws could restrain the 'unlimited freedom' of the subject. 'The full prosecution of this noble principle into all its natural consequences... at last, through many contests, produced that singular and happy government which we enjoy at present' (VI, 649). In this, the English constitution is unique, 'singular' (cf. IX, 231), 'the most perfect and most accurate system of liberty that was ever found compatible with government', 'the complicated fabric of the most perfect government' (IV, 54–5), 'the best civil constitution where every man is restrained by the most rigid laws' (*Politics a Science*, last §). In all editions before 1758 this read: 'the best constitution of the world, where every man etc.', and in the preceding paragraph occurs the phrase 'a good constitution'. This change and the insertion of 'civil', the difference between 'a good constitution' and 'the best civil constitution', suggests that Hume is aware that some sort of distinction should be made and pointed up between the political constitution and form of government, and the legal constitution or rule of law, 'where every man is restrained by the most rigid laws'. The former is 'good', the latter is 'the best'. Whether this is so or not in this particular instance, such a distinction is implicit in Hume's comparative study of constitutions; and it might explain the remark in the final chapter of the *History of England*, that since the revolution of 1688, England has enjoyed, 'if not the best system of government, at least the most entire system of liberty that was ever known amongst mankind' (IX, 520). This is not to be taken as showing a change in Hume's political beliefs (it dates from the first edition, of 1757), a symptom of his earlier conventional praise of the matchless constitution gone, or in process of going, sour. It summarizes the findings of comparative politics. The best system of government in pure theory is the republican, judging by the essay on the *Idea of a Perfect Commonwealth*; the best

[1] Hume says that branches of power like the dispensing power, the power of imprisonment, of exacting loans and benevolences etc., 'if not directly opposite to the principles of all free governments, must at least be acknowledged dangerous to freedom in a monarchical constitution, where an eternal jealousy etc'. The true philosopher, however, takes note of exceptions and irregularities; in this case the pressing of seamen. The exercise of an irregular power is here tacitly permitted in the crown, because the very irregularity seems to be the best safeguard against abuse of it. So we get the extraordinary spectacle of authority armed against the law in times of full peace and concord: a renewal of 'the wild state of nature... in one of the most civilized societies of mankind'. This is Hume's third and last political oddity in the essay *Of Some Remarkable Customs*.

model of a limited monarchy would be the British government, with certain alterations which are given in that essay, but even this would be exposed to certain unavoidable inconveniences (*Essays*, 513); 'the best of all governments', it is suggested in a note, appended (1748) to the essay on the *Rise of Arts and Sciences*, on the Chinese government, is 'perhaps, a pure monarchy of this kind', (that is, where 'the sword... may properly be said to be always in the hands of the people'), because it has 'both the tranquillity attending kingly power, and the moderation and liberty of popular assemblies' (123). In any case, to search for the best of all governments in practice as opposed to pure speculation is not very 'philosophical'; on the other hand the phrase 'the most entire system of liberty' is, in Hume, no mere 'hurrah word', but has a very precise and determinate meaning.

Why England has 'as much liberty and even perhaps licentiousness' as imperial Rome had of slavery and tyranny, including a unique freedom of the press not indulged in any other government whatsoever, is explained in the essay on the *Liberty of the Press*. (The gist of what is essential in the present context dates from 1741.)[1] It is due to our mixed form of government, prevailingly republican, but with 'a great mixture of monarchy', so that the republican part 'is obliged, for its own preservation, to maintain a watchful *jealousy* over the magistrates, to remove all discretionary powers, and to secure every one's life and fortune by general and inflexible laws'.[2] On the other hand, the two extremes of absolute monarchy and republic 'approach very near to each other in the most material circumstances' (After 1758 'very' was withdrawn and 'some' substituted for 'the most'). In a government such as that of France, which is 'entirely absolute' ('entirely' withdrawn in the last edition), the monarch cannot entertain 'the least' (after 1770, 'any') jealousy against his subjects, and 'therefore is apt to indulge them in great *liberties* both of speech and action'.[3] In a government altogether republican, such as that of

---

[1] The orientation is worth noting. 'Nothing is more apt to surprize a foreigner...' Hume begins.

[2] 'No action must be deemed a crime but what the law has plainly determined to be such: no crime must be imputed to a man but from a legal proof before his judges; and even these judges must be his fellow-subjects, who are obliged by their own interest, to have a watchful eye over the encroachments and violence of the ministers' (*Essays*, 10).

[3] In *Parties of Great Gritain*, § 3, liberty of thought and expression 'can never be enjoyed, at least has never yet been enjoyed, but in a free government'. The context is ecclesiastical parties: priests have always been enemies to liberty, and have a propensity to 'despotic power and the government of a single person' ('despotic power and' withdrawn after 1758).

Holland, 'where there is no magistrate so eminent as to give *jealousy* to the state, there is no danger in intrusting the magistrates with large discretionary powers, and though many advantages result from such powers, in preserving peace and order, yet they lay a considerable restraint in men's actions and make every private citizen pay a great respect to the government'. In pure monarchies, the magistrate has no jealousy of the people: in pure republics, the people have none of the magistrate, 'which want of jealousy begets a mutual confidence and trust in both cases and produces a species of liberty in monarchies and of arbitrary power in republics'.

But the perfection of civil society, the most entire system of liberty, demands a form of government which is for a number of reasons not 'the best'. No other government has been known which has 'subsisted without the mixture of some arbitrary authority, committed to some magistrate'; in the event it has been found that the advantages of the 'noble principle' (the absolute rule of law) overbalance the 'inconveniences': for the last edition of the *History* (VII, 360) Hume wrote 'sensible inconveniences', and 'that noble though dangerous principle'. As so often with his numerous alterations in the later editions of the *History* and the essays, he is underlining a point made previously, or implicit in earlier editions, not changing his point of view. There is a similar underlining in the final version of his remarks on the Habeas Corpus Act. The first edition says: 'This law is essentially requisite for the protection of liberty in a mixed monarchy.' In the last edition this becomes: 'This law seems necessary'. But both editions go on to point out the dangerous consequences: it is difficult to reconcile with 'such extreme liberty' the 'full security and the regular police of a state, especially the police of great cities' – Hume added 'full security' later, but otherwise the remark dates from 1757[1] (*History*, IX, 232).

The noble principle of the absolute rule of law, therefore, the perfection of civil society, is in practice inconvenient and even dangerous, because it may hamstring a government in the necessary exercise of its functions in times of crisis.

Another disadvantage inherent in the English government was that there was necessarily, in a mixed monarchy of this type, a kind of constitutional no man's land between king and parliament:

---

[1] To the essay on *Public Credit* he added, in 1770, this passage: 'The immense greatness, indeed, of London, under a government which admits not of discretionary power, renders the people factious, mutinous, seditious, and even perhaps rebellious' (359).

a 'circumstance in the English constitution, which it is most difficult, or rather altogether impossible, to regulate by laws, and which must be governed by certain delicate ideas of propriety and decency, rather than by any exact rule or prescription'. Obviously parliament must have the right to complain about the king's government; equally obviously, if this right is not to be totally meaningless, it must have the power of withholding supplies in order to force the king, if necessary, to redress grievances. To deny parliament this right would be to virtually change the constitution into an absolute monarchy, but in its very nature it cannot be defined and limited by law. And given human nature, this right will be exerted to its full extent. When human ambition so often breaks through all the restraints of law and justice, it is not likely to be deterred by the 'weak limitations of respect and decorum'. But fortunately 'the wisdom of the English constitution, or rather, the concurrence of accidents', has, at different times, provided certain 'irregular checks' to this privilege of parliament, and maintained the dignity and authority of the crown 'in some tolerable measure'. In our present constitution, government having become more expensive everywhere, has 'thrown into the hands of the crown the disposal of a very large revenue' which has enabled the king 'by the private interest and ambition of the members, to restrain the public interest and ambition of the body' (*History of England: Pelican Classics*, 388–9, X, 175–7. The text of the 1754 edition later became a note).[1]

On the other hand, the king no longer possesses the discretionary powers which he formerly enjoyed, and the result of a comparison between the constitution as it now is and as it was at the accession of James I is to reveal a curious paradox. The monarchy then was possessed of a very extensive authority, but this was founded solely on the opinion of the people, and not supported by money or force of arms. 'By the changes which have since been introduced, the liberty and independence of individuals have been rendered much more full, entire and secure; those of the public more uncertain and precarious' (*History*, VII, 9). Two years later (1759) he took up the theme again. After describing the almost despotic authority and power of the monarchy in the reign of Queen Elizabeth, he pointed out that as 'the prince commanded no mercenary army, there was a tacit check on him' and 'this

[1] No. 40 of Section III of Hume's early memoranda notes that the government of England is perhaps the only one, except Holland, where the legislature has not force enough to execute its laws without the good will of the people. 'This is an irregular kind of check upon the Legislature.'

situation of England, though seemingly it approached nearer, was in reality more remote from a despotic and eastern monarchy than the present government of that kingdom, where the people, though guarded by multiplied laws, are totally naked, defenceless and disarmed' (VI, 430). That is to say, personal liberty is seemingly more secure now, but the political or public liberty which in England guarantees it, is more precarious, because in place of the discretionary powers enjoyed by the Tudors, the king now has a standing army, and a large revenue. And in the last edition of the *History* Hume tacked a sentence on to the first of the passages quoted: 'And it seems a necessary, though perhaps a melancholy truth, that in every government the magistrate must either possess a large revenue and a military force, or enjoy some discretionary powers, in order to execute the laws and support his own authority.' This seems to represent a rather half-hearted death bed conversion to the opinion of his friend Adam Smith, concerning the necessity of standing armies in modern states; the 'melancholy' in the truth is an echo of Hume's older belief that standing armies and liberty are incompatible. From 1752–68 there had been a passage in the *Perfect Commonwealth* essay describing the standing army as 'a mortal distemper in the British Government of which it must at last inevitably perish'.

This paradox of English history, that the struggle for public liberty in the seventeenth century, has in fact resulted in a situation in which public liberty is rendered precarious, because the prize for which the patriots fought has been won and the discretionary powers of the crown abolished, can be regarded as the addition of an historical dimension to Hume's comparison of the English free government and the absolute monarchies of the continent, reducing still further the gap between them.

The political scientist looking back sees that English and French political experience began to diverge in the seventeenth century, but on closer inspection the divergence is not so great as appears at first sight. Any suggestions as to future developments can only be extremely tentative, a point which Hume is at pains to make on more than one occasion and which is related to his acute awareness – among other things – of the complexity of political phenomena that is an aspect of his 'scepticism'. It is worth noting that his well-known 'suspicion' that 'the world is still too young to fix many general truths in politics which will remain true to the latest posterity', because we have not yet had experience of three thousand years and do not know what degree of refinement human nature is susceptible of or what may be expected from any great revolution in education, customs or principles, is the preface to his comparative study of free and absolute governments (*Of Civil Liberty*). Having intended to make this comparison, he says, and to show the great advantages of the former above the latter,[1] he began to entertain a suspicion that no one in this age was sufficiently qualified for such an undertaking, and 'that whatever one should advance on that head would, in all probability, be refuted by further experience and rejected by posterity'. The implication seems to be that any one trying to demonstate the truth of the Englishman's belief in the superiority of his free government will 'in all probability' be refuted by the continued progress of civilization in general and the 'civilized monarchies' in particular. Absolute government will become as advantageous as civil liberty, perhaps more so, though at the moment this form of government is 'still inferior'. And looking tentatively into the future he can descry in monarchical governments a source of improvement and in popular governments a source of degeneracy 'which in time will bring these species of civil polity still nearer an equality'. In France, 'the most perfect model of pure monarchy', the greatest abuses arise not from the number or weight of the taxes 'beyond what are to be met with in free countries', but from the expensive, unequal, arbitrary and intricate manner of levying them, which benefits no one apart from the *Financiers*, a race of men odious to the whole kingdom. If a prince or minister should arise, with sufficient intelligence to know his own and the public interest and force of mind to break through ancient customs, 'we might expect to see these abuses remedied; in which case, the difference between that absolute government and our free one, would not appear so considerable as at present' ('be more nominal than real', in the editions 1741-53). This is the more likely since the principal losers under the present system are the nobility, and it is natural in such a constitution that their interests should be more consulted than those of the people. The source of degeneracy in popular or free governments is the practice of contracting debt and mortgaging the public revenues, by which 'taxes may in time, become altogether intolerable and all the property of the state be brought into the hands of the public' whereas the subjects of an absolute prince can never be oppressed by his debts, because he can make a bankruptcy when he pleases: a remedy which in a popular government is difficult, and however necessary sometimes, always cruel

---

[1] In the editions 1741-8 this read 'the advantages and disadvantages of each'.

and barbarous. The national debt is an 'inconvenience which nearly [= closely] threatens all free governments; especially our own, at the present juncture of affairs...a strong motive...to increase our frugality of public money; lest, for want of it, we be reduced by the multiplicity of our taxes...to curse our very liberty, and wish ourselves in the same state of servitude with the nations which surround us'. This was written in 1741; the warning was repeated at the beginning of the essay on Public Credit in 1752, in which the practice of mortgaging the public revenues is described as 'ruinous beyond all controversy', leading inevitably to 'poverty, impotence, and subjection to foreign powers', and in the additions to that essay in 1764. What Hume foresaw in the latter was an 'unnatural state of society', in which 'the only persons who possess any revenue beyond the immediate effects of their industry are the stockholders...men who have no connexions with the state', the consequent destruction of 'the several ranks of men which form a kind of independent magistracy in a state, instituted by the hand of nature', every man in authority deriving his influence from the sovereign's commission exclusively, 'and the middle power between king and people being totally removed, a grievous despotism must prevail', which the landholders would be unable to oppose. 'Adieu to all ideas of nobility, gentry and family' (362–3).

This addition of 1764 to the essay on *Public Credit* has been seen as typical of Hume 'in his late pessimistic Tory period': the essay 'epitomizes the despair that he shared with such earlier Augustan writers like Bolingbroke. It describes an England oppressed with a huge debt etc.'[1] If instead of singling out this eminently quotable paragraph for special and exclusive attention as an echo of Bolingbroke's 'politics of nostalgia', one looks at the essay as a whole, one can see that it is in fact in the key not of domestic, but of foreign politics: the 'situation of foreign affairs' is where the thrust of the argument lies; it is the effect of the national debt on the ability of the nation to defend itself in war and negotiation that is what chiefly matters. To say that Hume's main emphasis lay on the political consequences of the debt is true: to say that he was mainly concerned with the difficulties which must arise from the political power which the stockholders would acquire is only half of this truth.[2] In his enumeration of the disadvantages of the debt, Hume

[1] Isaac Kramnick, *Bolingbroke and his Circle. The Politics of Nostalgia in the Age of Walpole* (Harvard University Press, 1968), 82. Kramnick's note refers the reader to Giarrizzo for Hume's 'decisive turn to Toryism'.
[2] See E. L. Hargreaves, *The National Debt*, (1930), 75.

says that the not inconsiderable injury to commerce and industry is 'trivial' in comparison with the prejudice 'to the state considered as a body politic, which must support itself in the society of nations, and have various transactions with other states in wars and negotiations' (*Essays*, 360). The ill there is pure and unmixed without any favourable circumstance to atone for it; and it is an ill 'of a nature the highest and most important'. In fact the two added paragraphs (for there are two that are relevant in this context) concerned with the social and political aspects of the debt are woven into this line of argument: for Hume goes on to say that even when every fund is mortgaged, great commerce and opulence will remain, and how are they to be defended? (*Essays*, 363-4): what is at stake, Hume is saying, is not just liberty supported by a 'natural' magistracy, but the country's very existence. 'We have always found, where a government has mortgaged all its revenues, that it necessarily sinks into a state of languor, inactivity and impotence'.[1] This seems to be the point which Hume is particularly anxious to drive home, in order to shake the complacency of 'all ranks of men'. (The danger that France might manage to rid herself of her burden of debt quicker than England and be in a position to give the law to all Europe was one of the most powerful arguments used by contemporary writers – such fears survived the Seven Years War.)[2]

This aspect of the debt is present at the end of the essay on *Civil Liberty* of 1741. But the other, the probable socio-political consequences, is surely present also implicitly, in that Hume foresaw the possibility of all the property of the state being brought into the hands of the public, which is equivalent to a 'Turkish despotism' or worse – nor has that actually happened in 1764. Hume is not 'describing' the condition of England in the addition to the *Public Credit* essay. He says 'suppose' certain things – land taxed at eighteen or nineteen shillings in the pound, etc. – then, 'adieu to all ideas of nobility, gentry and family'. The threat may be nearer, the warning more urgent, which is hardly surprising when the debt itself increased in a fashion which filled nearly all his contemporaries with the utmost alarm and despondency. But there is nothing peculiar to a 'late pessimistic', 'Tory' Hume which was not in essence present as early as 1741, nor indeed was there anything especially 'Tory' in Hume's arguments.

[1] Cf. the end of the essay: 'our children, weary of the struggle, may sit down...and see their neighbours oppressed and conquered, till at last, they themselves and their creditors lie both at the mercy of the conqueror'.
[2] Cf. P. G. M. Dickson, *The Financial Revolution in England*, (1967), 21-3.

It may be objected that something fundamental in Hume's beliefs had changed: that the 'middling rank of men', which in a passage later withdrawn from the essay on the *Parties of Great Britain*, are described as peculiarly prone to Tory principles, have become in the essay on *Luxury* of 1752 (later *Of Refinement in the Arts*), 'the best and firmest basis of public liberty' (*Essays*, 284). But this does not alter the fact (1) that as early as 1741 Hume saw the national debt threatening the national existence, and therefore all ranks of men, whatever he may have thought of some of them, and (2) that the 'middling rank' in the essay on the *Parties of Great Britain* of 1741 is seemingly narrower in scope than that of 1752, and is certainly not the same as the 'middle power' of 1764. 'Middle' and 'middling' was used with no more precision in a social sense in the eighteenth century than at any other time: it can mean very different types of people. For instance, Dorothy Marshall thinks that the eighteenth-century 'middling sort' excluded gentry, as well as those dependent on manual skill for their livelihood (*English People in the 18th century*, (1956), 58). Lucy Sutherland equates 'middling men', as contemporaries called them, with the class of small merchants, tradesmen and master craftsmen. But she later quotes Alderman Beckford saying in 1761 that by the 'middling people of England' he means 'the manufacturer, the yeoman, the merchant, the country gentleman'. He does not mean either the mob or the nobility, 'about 1200 men of quality' ('City of London in 18th century Politics' in R. Pares and A. J. P. Taylor: *Essays presented to Sir Lewis Namier* (1956), 54, 66).[1]

In Hume, 'middling rank' in 1741 excludes 'gentlemen who have some fortune and education' as well as the 'meanest, slaving poor', and abounds in England, both in cities and in the country more than in any other part of the world. The essay on *The Middle Station of Life* of 1742 is not much help here. It is a slight performance, withdrawn in the next edition, and is not 'sociological'. Happiness, virtue and wisdom are to be found between the 'great' who are too much immersed in pleasure, and the 'poor', too occupied with the necessities of life: Hume talks of lawyers and physicians, and the 'common professions': he seems to have professional people in mind. In the *History of England* (v, 383, 1759 and all later editions) 'gentry' and 'the middling rank of men' are

[1] In Guthrie's *History of England* (Vol. 1, 1744), the 'middling rank...live at a distance from the vices and hurry of great cities'. The hospitality of the ancient Germans is still to be found among them (1, 123). Later on 'that middle rank of people... compose the bulk of the nation' (1, 428).

distinct.[1] In 1752, in the essay on *Luxury* (later *Refinement in the Arts*) the middling rank, who are the best and firmest basis of public liberty, are neither 'peasants' nor 'barons' – the perspective is a long, historical one. Peasants become 'rich and independent', while 'tradesmen and merchants acquire a share of the property and draw authority and consideration to that middling rank of men...' They 'covet equal laws' to preserve them from monarchical as well as aristocratical tyranny (*Essays*, 284). Hume then goes on to refer to the 'lower house' and the 'Commons', and the increase of commerce throwing the balance of property into their hands. 'Middling rank' in this perspective seems, therefore, to include 'gentry', especially as the House of Commons is composed chiefly of proprietors of land (*Public Credit*, penultimate §).[2]

What then is the social composition of 'the middle power between king and people' threatened by the debt in the addition of 1764 to *Public Credit*? In Bolingbroke, this 'middle power' is the House of Lords, which mediates between the King and the Commons.[3] Hume's 'middle power' is more than this and includes 'gentry', in fact Hume talks of 'several ranks of men' constituting 'a kind of independent magistracy', but this could mean simply the nobility and gentry – no one else in fact is mentioned in this connexion. But perhaps Hume would include the 'merchants', who together with the 'gentry', are said, in the essay *Of National Characters*, to compose 'the people in authority' in England (212), and whose interests are not distinct from those of the 'landed part' of the nation – and never will be until the debt becomes 'altogether oppressive and intolerable' (*Of Parties in General* (58): incidentally Hume left this passage untouched in the later editions). This is presumably compatible with the fact that the House of Commons is composed 'chiefly of proprietors of land' (*Public*

---

[1] '...the preachers, finding that they could not rival the gentry, or even the middling rank of men, in opulence...' In a letter to Turgot, of 1766, Hume refers to a class which besides Merchants, includes 'all shop-keepers and master-tradesmen of every species'; they are distinct from proprietors of land, and the labouring poor, but Hume does not give them a name (*Letters*, II, 94).

[2] In *History*, IX, 98 (anno 1674), Hume says that a great part of the landed property belonged 'either to the yeomanry or middling gentry'.

[3] Hardwicke in 1736, on the Mortmain Act, reviewing the course of English history, said that the power of the barons was broken, the constitution brought to a truer balance, trade and arts increased and liberty was diffused through the whole body of the people, while the nobility became 'a middle class', at once a security to the throne against encroachments and a protection to the people (P. C. Yorke, *Life and Correspondence of Philip Yorke, Earl of Hardwicke*, (Cambridge, 1913), Vol. I, 148).

Here one sees both the emergence of the 'middling rank', and at the same time that of the nobility as a 'middle class' or 'middle power'.

Credit, penultimate §),[1] and even with the outburst in the letter to Strahan of October 1769, in which Hume hopes to see a public bankruptcy, the total revolt of America, the diminution of London to less than half, and 'the Restoration of the Government to the King, Nobility and Gentry of this Realm' (*Letters*, II, 210).

But one cannot simply equate the 'middling rank of men' of 1752 with the 'middle power' of 1764, calling them both a 'middle class' in roughly the sense we use it.[2] For one thing such a large body could hardly mediate between king and 'people', given the eighteenth-century use of 'people': such a body, if it was not just gentry and the larger merchants, would be virtually the 'people'.[3] The 'middling rank' of 1752 are the basis of liberty because they 'covet equal laws': the 'middle power' is a matter of constitutional balance and political liberty in a narrower sense, and indeed it is quite likely that Hume did not mean to include the merchants in this context, but only the 'landholders'.[4]

At least ten years later (because it is not in the edition of 1773 and there was no further edition in Hume's lifetime), Hume added a sentence to the passage in Appendix III of the *History of England* (VI, 430), part of which has already been quoted, comparing the English government now and in the reign of Queen Elizabeth, in which he says that the people, though guarded by multiplied laws, are totally defenceless and disarmed. In the final version it concludes: 'and besides, are not secured by any middle power, or

---

[1] Cf. in editions 1752–68 of the essay *Of Taxes*: 'the landed gentlemen, in whose hands our legislature is chiefly lodged'. This variant is not in *Essays*. See *Hume: Writings on Economics* (ed. E. Rotwein), 86n.

[2] As Rotwein does in a note to 'middle power between king and people' in the 1764 passage of the *Public Credit* essay, in which he says that elsewhere (i.e. in 1752) Hume 'calls attention to the central importance for liberty and parliamentary government of a prosperous middle class, in particular the merchant class' (*op. cit.*, 99).

[3] Cf. The *Vicar of Wakefield*, Ch. XIX. 'In this middle order of mankind are generally to be found all the arts, wisdom and virtues of society. This order alone is known to be the true preserver of freedom, and may be called *the people*.' They 'subsist between the very rich and the very rabble'.

[4] Guthrie distinguishes between 'the middling state' of his Dissertation V who were encouraged by Henry VII against the barons (III, 1393), and a 'middle order' consisting of the 'great nobility' (II, 390–1), afterwards saying that Henry VII knew that trade and manufactures were chiefly cultivated by 'the middling order of commons' (II, 788–9). Echard calls them 'the middle sort' *History of England*, (1707), 593. Blackstone uses 'middling rank' in this context: 'the other two estates' that formerly balanced the prerogative were weakened (*Commentaries*, IV, 427). The nobility necessary in monarchies between prince and people is 'a nobility or intermediate state' (*id.*, 407). Blackwell's 'middle order' between the 'two great bodies of men, Nobles and Commons, into which nations naturally divide', and without which nations are 'seldom of considerable standing', are 'the gentry' in Great Britain, corresponding to the Equestrian Order in the Roman state (*Memoirs of the Court of Augustus* (I, 73).

independent powerful nobility, interposed between them and the monarch'. (It will be noticed that the 'middle power' here is a nobility.) Anyone who did not know how late this sentence was added would presumably regard it as a straight reference to Montesquieu's remark in *L'Esprit des Lois*, II 4, about the English having abolished the intermediary powers, and his warning that as a result, if they lose their liberty they will be the most enslaved people on earth, especially as the context is a historical retrospect, and also because Montesquieu's remark had originally made such an impression on Hume. It was the first thing which he singled out for comment in his letter to Montesquieu in April 1749, with particular reference to the abolition of the hereditary jurisdictions in Scotland two years before. The parliament of England had abolished them because it thought that the 'penchant violent au gouvernement monarchique' of the Scottish nation, 'venoit de ce que la noblesse avoit conservé les juridictions gothiques féodales. Cela fait voir combien les Anglais ont été uniformes et conséquents dans leur manière de raisonner sur ce sujet. Les conséquences que vous prédisez arriveroient certainement dans le cas d'une révolution dans notre gouvernement' (*Letters*, I, 134).[1] If, in addition the sentence added to Appendix III has a connexion with his thoughts on the national debt (though the reader has to make the connexion himself) then he is saying that something has already happened which elsewhere, at least not until the last year of his life, he never goes beyond saying is only highly likely. (But he had done it before, at the start of his career as a political writer, when he had taken a chance on what looked like another inevitable trend or march of history and had stated dogmatically in 1741 that Jacobitism was no more in Scotland.) Or it may be that Hume simply wanted to strengthen his paradoxical contrast between Elizabethan

[1] John Dalrymple said in 1757 that it had been urged against Hardwicke's law, abolishing the heritable jurisdictions, that they are barriers against the power of the crown, with Montesquieu cited in support. This was so in absolute monarchies, but in limited monarchies the abolition of them tends to establish and diffuse law and liberty (*Essays towards a general history of Feudal Property*, 4th ed., 306). Whig historians conveniently forget what 'law and liberty' came to mean for Highlanders, but that is another story. They nearly always look down the wrong end of the telescope at Hardwicke's law. There were good arguments in favour of the heritable jurisdictions at that time, or certain aspects of the system, some of them put forward by no less a person than Duncan Forbes of Culloden (See G. Menary, *Life and Letters of Duncan Forbes* (1936), 317-18). Arguments and speeches for and against can be read in the *Scots Magazine*, Vols. IX and X. The main trend of Hume's thinking of course was in the direction indicated by John Dalrymple, although the fact that 'many inconveniences must necessarily result from the abolishing of all discretionary power in every magistrate' (*History* VI, 530) is a constant theme in Hume's political thinking.

and modern England, and remembered Montesquieu, however late in the day – which is certainly how the passage reads.[1] It is a question of just how much of an obsession the national debt was, or became; and how much reading between the lines is allowable.[2]

The inevitability of the progress of the national debt and its consequences is deduced from the principles of human nature. This is what is 'philosophical' in Hume's treatment of this topic: 'there seems to be a natural progress of things, which may guide our reasoning'. As the present state of affairs could have been foretold 'from the nature of men and of ministers', so now the consequences may without difficulty be guessed at: either the nation must destroy public credit, or public credit must destroy the nation (*Public Credit*, 366).

The national debt apart, the tendency of the British government was towards absolutism in any case. Hazarding the risks of political conjecture in the essay, *Whether the British government inclines more to Absolute Monarchy, or to a Republic?*, after giving the arguments on both sides, Hume concluded that the tide having long run to the side of popular government is just beginning to turn

---

[1] Not necessarily Montesquieu. There is a passage rather similar to Hume's in Appendix III in Lyttleton's *Letters from a Persian in England*. Lyttleton says that the difference between the 'ancient plan' of the constitution, and that which has taken place since the expulsion of the Stuarts is that the first was less perfect, but better secured, because the nobility had the sword in their hands, whereas the last is 'more regular' and 'more free', in the frame of it, but ill secured, the sword being only in the hands of the king, to which is added a vast increase in the wealth of the crown etc. (*Lyttleton's Works*, 1774, 239. His *Persian Letters* were published originally in 1735.) It will be noticed that Hume's addition follows the words 'defenceless and disarmed', so that his 'middle power' could be an echo of Lyttleton and mean the swords of the nobility. Its provenance could be Harringtonian. Hurd expressly refers to *Oceana* in this context, when Arbuthnot in one of the dialogues on the Golden Age of Queen Elizabeth 'occasioned by a view of Kenilworth Castle in 1716', replying to Addison's remark that the interest of the great was but another name for the slavery of the people, says that their destruction was at the same time the destruction of the people's shield. When this 'counterpoise to the power of the sovereign' was destroyed, it was discovered too late that 'public freedom throve best when it wound itself about the stock of the ancient nobility'. It was the defect, not the excess of patrician influence that made way for the miseries of the seventeenth century. Richard Hurd, *Moral and Political Dialogues*, 133-4.

[2] A few pages further on Hume added a note to the effect that in the present year, 1776, all the revenues of the island north of Trent and west of Reading are mortgaged or anticipated for ever. Could the small remainder be in a worse state if those provinces were seized by Austria and Prussia? Hume says we have now 'completely reached' the goal of 'national ruin' as a result of the increase of the national debt (vi, 436). Cf. *Letters*, ii, 301. Hume, writing in October 1775, talks of the 'over-loaded or rather overwhelm'd and totally ruin'd State of our Finances'. Hume added a note in Vol. iii (526) anno 1461, sometime after 1762, because it is not in the first edition, noting the commencement of the 'pernicious practice'. The ruinous effects 'threaten the very existence of the nation'.

towards monarchy; although its progress is very slow and almost insensible, the power of the crown 'by means of its large revenue, is rather upon the increase'; and the easiest death for our present mixed government would be absolutism rather than a republic, because that would certainly be chaotic and lead after many convulsions and civil wars to absolute government anyway. Perhaps it was the spectacle of the 'civilized monarchies' which allowed Hume to contemplate the 'euthanasia' of the British government with such cool detachment; though the point of the essay was to be a 'lesson of moderation in all our political controversies': if we have reason to be more 'jealous' of monarchy because the danger is more imminent from that quarter, we also have reason to be more jealous of popular government because that danger is more terrible.

There were other reasons why 'the most entire system of liberty' was not also 'the best form of government'. There were certain inherent disadvantages in that mixed form of government which postulated the absolute rule of law and absence of discretionary powers in the executive. Firstly, without what the opposition called 'corruption' or 'dependence', the balance between the republican and the monarchical part of our mixed government could not be maintained; given the natural love of power, the commons, having the control of the purse, the king's veto in practice meaning little, and the lords having no force or authority to maintain themselves alone without the support of the Crown, would be all-powerful. But the ambition and interest of the commons as a corporate body in usurping all the powers of government is restrained by the interest that the majority of its members have, as individuals, in the offices and pensions etc. at the disposal of the crown. We may call this corruption and dependence, but 'some degree and some kind of it are inseparable from the very nature of the constitution, and necessary to the preservation of our mixed government' (*Independency of Parliament*). This is 'an unavoidable disadvantage...attending that species of government',[1] because the power of the crown is lodged in a single person, either king or minister, and as this person may have a greater or less degree of ambition, capacity, courage, popularity or fortune, the power which is too great in one hand may be too little in another. It is a variable and unstable factor, altogether too dependent on personal character; whereas in a pure republic, where the power is distributed among several assemblies, the

[1] Cf. also *Perfect Commonwealth* (513).

checks and controls are more regular in their operation. But added Hume in 1748 (and apart from this addition, the essay continued to be published as in 1741, with only a few minor alterations) a 'limited monarchy admits not of any such stability; nor is it possible to assign to the crown such a determinate degree of power, as will, in every hand, form a proper counterbalance to the other parts of the constitution' (*Independency of Parliament*, penultimate sentence).

The evidence in fact suggests that Hume regarded the republican as the best form of government, though it was not practical politics in Britain (See the conclusion of *First Principles of Government*).[1] In a letter of December 1775 to his nephew, then living with and studying under John Millar at Glasgow, Hume wrote; 'I cannot but agree with Mr Millar that the Republican Form of [Government] is by far the best.' The ancient republics were 'somewhat ferocious' and torn by factions, but were still much preferable to the monarchies or aristocracies which seem to have been quite intolerable. 'Modern Manners have corrected this Abuse; and all the Republics in Europe, without Exception, are so well governed, that one is at a Loss to which we should give the Preference. But what is this general Subject of Speculation to our Purpose?' The result in Britain of attempting to establish a republic would be anarchy, the immediate forerunner of despotism (*Letters* II, 306). One great advantage of the republican form of government was that, as seen already, liberty was tempered by the discretionary powers possessed by the magistrates. As Hume wrote in the letter just quoted: '[One] great Advantage of a Commonwealth over our mixt Monarchy is that it[woud considerably abridge our Liberty, which is growing to such an Extreme, as to be incom[patible wi]th all Government. Such Fools are they who perpetually cry out Liberty: [and think to] augment it, by shaking off the Monarchy.' In the last edition of the essay on the *Populousness of Ancient Nations* he notices the superiority of the modern republics to those of antiquity: 'At present there is not one republic in Europe from one extremity of it to the other, that is not remarkable for justice, lenity and stability, equal to, or even beyond...the most celebrated in antiquity.' They are almost all 'well-tempered aristocracies' (413: the remark appeared first in the edition of 1777). In the second paragraph of the essay on the

---

[1] See John Allen in the *Edinburgh Review* (April 1825) Vol XLII, p. 4: 'Paradoxical as the assertion may seem, it has always appeared to us that Mr Hume was in reality an admirer of popular government in preference to monarchy. But though in his speculative tenets a republican . . .'

Protestant Succession (1752), he says of 'monarchical government' (which here includes limited or mixed monarchy) that it is and always has been the most common, 'though, perhaps not the best'. And the Perfect Commonwealth is, of course, a republic, resembling, though improving on 'the wise and renowned government' of the United Provinces (512),[1] and inspired by *Oceana*. And it is interesting to notice that in this essay Hume rejected the almost universally accepted belief of his time that a republic is suited only to a city or small territory, and 'that no large state, such as France or Great Britain could ever be modelled into a commonwealth' (513-14), though in the letter to his nephew of 1775 one of his reasons why republicanism is a purely academic subject of speculation in Britain is that it 'is only fitted for a small State'.

The liberty of the press was also necessary to the proper functioning of our mixed monarchy, and in England the press was free to a degree found nowhere else. Hume did not at first regard this as a disadvantage; at least the earlier editions of the essay conclude with a long section claiming that liberty of the press 'is attended with so few inconveniences that it may be claimed as the common right of mankind', which 'ought to be indulged them almost in every government except the ecclesiastical', and arguing that however much abused, it can never be dangerous, or cause popular tumults or rebellion,[2] even though it is true that men will always be prone to believe anything to the disadvantage of their rulers; and that increasing experience shows that the people are no such dangerous monster as they have been represented; that like Holland for religious liberty, England has set an example of civil liberty, which it is to be hoped will result in the education and improved judgement of the people.

This long section was withdrawn in 1770, and in the final edition of *Liberty of the Press* Hume concludes that 'the unbounded liberty of the press, though it be difficult, perhaps impossible, to

---

[1] From 1752-68 this was 'formerly one of the wisest and most renowned governments in the world'. In the essay on *Jealousy of Trade* (1748) the Dutch 'having mortgaged all their revenues, make not such a figure in political transactions as formerly'; but their commerce is surely equal to what it was in the middle of the last century, 'when they were reckoned among the great powers of Europe' (337-8).

[2] 'A man reads a book or pamphlet alone and coolly.' Hume does not discuss the issues raised by the Stage Licensing Act of 1737, which had caused a pamphlet war in which some argued that to limit the freedom of the stage endangered liberty of the press. Colley Cibber defended the Act by pointing out the far greater and immediate impact of a dramatic over a printed libel. John Loftis, *Politics of Drama in Augustan England* (1963), 128 et seq. The section Hume later withdrew is in *Essays*, 11-12n.

propose a suitable remedy for it, is one of the evils attending those mixt forms of government'. This is perhaps the most striking example of a retreat in the later Hume from a liberal to a less liberal position. And yet certain things should be noted. What has been surrendered is not the thing itself – and an 'unbounded liberty', if Hume really meant that, is going much further than most of the most liberal-minded would be prepared to go – for after all, liberty of the press is not an absolute, not an end in itself,[1] but almost unqualified remarks about its harmlessness which Hume must have come to regard, for example in the light of the mean-minded chauvinistic press campaign against Scotsmen, and the manifestations of 'mobbish' nationalism which he certainly did not regard as harmless (e.g. *Letters*, I, 491, 492), as somewhat uncritical.[2] And the enthusiasm of these earlier statements in the section that was withdrawn are somewhat blunted by a remark in his *Character of Sir Robert Walpole*, of 1742, that he wished for the honour of our country that he had found any one character of the fallen statesman drawn with such judgement and impartiality as to have credit with posterity, 'and to show that our liberty, has, for once at least, been employed to good purpose'. Also in the essay on *Liberty of the Press*, Hume talks of it as an example of the 'liberty and even perhaps licentiousness', to be found in Britain.[3]

There was, finally, the disadvantage of political parties, an evil which was to be found in all governments, more especially in free ones,[4] and in a mixed monarchy like that of Britain, they were

[1] The reason why it is impossible to remedy the unbounded liberty of the press is explained in the section Hume withdrew, where he says that the general laws against sedition and libelling are at present as strong as they can possibly be made (12n.).
[2] In November 1766 he wrote to Suard, who had envied England's liberty: 'be assured that the Indifference, and I may say Barbarism, of England is more discouraging than all the Persecutions of France which sometimes tend only to give a Lustre to an Author, and to render him more interesting' (*Letters*, II, 104). The letter of June 1768, to Turgot, blames liberty of the press as chiefly responsible for the Wilkite disturbances (*Letters*, II, 180).
[3] The remark in the first volume (1754) of the *History* (Pelican Classics, 347-8) to the effect that liberty of the press, 'so necessary in every monarchy confined by legal limitations' was in the seventeenth century something unheard of and generally esteemed incompatible with good government, so that we should not judge that age by the maxims prevailing in our own, was left untouched in all later editions (VII, 204), and the short paragraph on the very late introduction of this liberty in England (IX, 535-6) was added to the last edition and is entirely dispassionate. If Hume had felt as strongly about the evils of this liberty as some writers of his age, one might have expected some sign of it to show in one or the other of these references to it in the *History*.
[4] Cf. *Populousness of Ancient Nations*: 'To exclude faction from a free government, is very difficult, if not altogether impracticable' (405).

inevitable.[1] This was deduced from the principles of human nature. Where the balance between the monarchical and the republican parts of the constitution is so extremely delicate and uncertain, different opinions are bound to arise in the working of it. In general, all reasonable men will agree to support our mixed government, but when it comes to particulars, some will consistently incline one way, some another. There will be two parties catering for two types of men: the bold, passionate lovers of liberty as opposed to those of mild temper who love peace and order; the latter will incline to the monarchical side and constitute a court party; the former will form a country party. Hume distinguishes three main types of 'real', as opposed to 'personal' parties: those divided on interest, principle and affection;[2] it appears that there are 'parties of principle involved in the very nature of our constitution which may properly enough be denominated Court and Country'. Hume explained that he was using the terms in a purely neutral, scientific sense (*Essays*, 64n, passage withdrawn in 1768) without meaning to imply that measures proposed by the court were necessarily against the true interests of the country or those pressed by the country party necessarily in the country's best interests. The strength and violence of these parties will depend on the particular administration, 'but however the nation may fluctuate between them the parties themselves will always subsist, so long as we are governed by a limited monarchy' (*Parties of Great Britain*, 64).

The two parties, Court and Country, are not exclusively parties of principle; interest is also involved, by which Hume means ambition for office and the spoils of government, and it is this

---

[1] Cf. Hume to Montesquieu: 'Nos compatriotes sont fort vains de l'approbation que vous donnez à leur forme de gouvernement, dont ils sont, et avec quelque raison, si amoureux. Mais ne peut-on pas remarquer que, si les formes simples de gouvernement sont par leur nature sujettes à l'abus, parce qu'il n'y a aucun contrepoids, d'un autre côté les formes compliquées où une partie réprime l'autre, sont, comme les machines compliquées, sujettes à se déranger par le contraste et l'opposition des parties' (*Letters*, I, 138).

[2] Hume clearly has the Jacobites in mind in his description of parties from affection. See the conclusion of the essay on *Parties in General* (61–2). He thought that the Tories were more a party of affection than one of principle. 'I will venture to affirm that it was not so much principle...that attached the Tories to the ancient family as affection, or a certain love and esteem for their persons.' The same cause divided England formerly between York and Lancaster, and Scotland between the followers of Bruce and Baliol, *Parties of Great Britain*, 72n. This was in the texts of all editions up to and including that of 1768. A 'personal' as opposed to a 'real' faction is where the party division is the result exclusively of friendship and enmity, as especially in Renaissance Italy. The Jacobites are a 'real' party 'from affection', not a 'personal' party.

which exacerbates political controversy and pushes men into extreme positions. The leaders of the parties are generally motivated mainly by interest; the rank and file by principle.

This opposition of court and country parties is an 'inconvenience' inseparable from a mixed government.[1] Hume does not regard it as an unmitigated evil; it cannot be, if it is necessary to the proper functioning of the British constitution. Thus in the *History of England*, referring to the opposition or 'patriot' attitude of mind, a 'general cast of thought which has, more or less, prevailed in England, during near a century and a half', he says that it has 'been the cause of much good' as well as 'much ill in public affairs' (VII, 259). In the *Idea of a Perfect Commonwealth*, 'the chief support of the British government is the opposition of interests... that, though in the main serviceable, breeds endless factions' (510). The context makes it clear that he means the opposition which is the result of the mixed form of government. (As seen already, there is no opposition between the landed and trading interests until the national debt becomes altogether intolerable.) Hume's sketch in this essay of the British government so corrected as to make it 'the most perfect model of limited monarchy', does not remove entirely, 'though it may soften', the parties of court and country (513). In the *History* he goes so far as to say that the parties of court and country, 'while they oft threaten the total disolution of the government, are the real causes of its permanent life and vigour' (x, 151; in the 1754 text, *Pelican Classics*, 169).

Qua philosopher (and cosmopolitan Scotsman) Hume viewed the British Constitution with scientific detachment: it was 'singular', as all observers agreed, and in some respects 'happy', but (1) its very singularity as the most entire and perfect system of liberty ever seen – entailing a rule of law more absolute than in any other type of government, whether absolute monarchy or republic,

[1] Cf. *History of England* (VI, 618), anno 1621: The 'wise and moderate in the nation' regarded the very rise of opposite parties as a happy prognostic of the establishment of liberty; 'nor could they ever expect to enjoy, in a mixed government, so invaluable a blessing, without suffering that inconvenience, which, in such governments, has ever attended it'. Cf. IX, 248, anno 1679, 'State of Parties'; 'In every mixed government, such as that of England, the bulk of the nation will always incline to preserve the entire frame of our constitution; but according to the various prejudices, interests and dispositions of men, some will attach themselves with more passion to the regal, others to the popular, part of the government.' Cf. *The History of Great Britain*, Vol. 1 (1754): 'While the opposition (for we must still have an opposition open or disguised)...' (*Pelican Classics*, 389. This was part of a section which later became a note, Vol. x, 177.)

ancient or modern – brought disadvantages and dangers, and (2) it was not so much happier and superior to the absolute monarchies of Europe, especially that of France, as to be qualitatively different: the superiority was real enough, but absolute government was not only a perfectly possible and legitimate form of government, answering the ends of government as defined by Hume, but the gap between it and 'free governments' could be seen to have narrowed as the result of the progress of civilization,[1] which had improved absolute governments faster than free ones and produced the 'civilized monarchies' of modern Europe, and in the light of certain visible developments the process could reasonably be expected to continue,[2] always provided that the national debt did not put an end to British freedom, or even national independence, altogether.

One is now in a better position to understand and see what lies behind the notorious outbursts in connection with Wilkes and Liberty in Hume's letters of 1768–71, which by themselves appear to be simply the unthinking reaction of outraged conservatism. When Hume says that the English have too much liberty, he means something definite and precise, which he has studied with objectivity and explained in some of his earliest political essays. It is the judgement of an impartial spectator with a European and metropolitan point of view. This characteristic note is struck in the first reference in the letters to the Wilkite disturbances in the Spring of 1768. Writing in May to the Marquise de Barbentane, Hume says: 'There have been this spring in London a good many French gentlemen, who have seen the nation in a strange situation, and have admired at our oddity', that is, 'mutinies...founded on nothing', which have caused 'but little mischief and seem now entirely dispersed. I believe most of your countrymen return very happy, that they are born under a government not liable to these inconveniences; which is a fortunate way of thinking' (*Letters*, II, 178). Writing to Turgot in June, Hume used the riots to demonstrate,

[1] The scandal of the execution of the Chevalier de la Barre in 1766 shocked Hume deeply. 'Such of my friends as are not over favourable to France, insult me on this occasion', he wrote to the Marquise de Barbentane. 'It is strange, that such cruelty should be found among a people so celebrated for humanity, and so much bigotry amid so much knowledge and philosophy' (*Letters*, II, 85). He was pleased that indignation was as general in Paris as in all foreign countries.

[2] Reporting on France to Blair and his Edinburgh friends from Paris in 1765, Hume wrote: 'Shall I begin with the Points in which it most differs from England, viz. the general Regard pay'd to Genius and Learning...Or shall I mention the Points in which the French begin to concur with the English, their Love of Liberty for Instance?' (*Letters*, I, 497).

against Turgot's belief in the perpetual progress of society towards perfection, the defects of 'the... perfection of our Government, carried to an Extreme': firstly, 'a People thrown into Disorders (not dangerous ones, I hope) merely from the Abuse of Liberty, chiefly the Liberty of the Press; without any grievance...'[1] and secondly, a point which Hume did not make publicly: in a government so perfect, where there is so little difference between the governors and the governed, and where every abuse is checked, where a minister cannot make any money or even revenge himself on his enemies because everyone is 'entrenched in laws and privileges', men of great rank and fortune are very indifferent about being ministers, having little to gain, not even reputation. They either decline high offices or serve with obvious reluctance and negligence, sentiments which 'loosen the attachment of their inferiors' (*Letters*, II, 180-1).[2]

In March 1769, Hume described the Wilkes affair as a peculiarly English extravagance, unlike the Popish plot. '... the present Extravagance is peculiar to Ourselves and quite risible' (*Letters*, II, 197). As the affair developed it became less 'risible', however, and Hume's tone becomes so urgent and despondent that in retrospect it appears exaggerated and pessimistic to the point of absurdity. This is notorious. Certain things have to be borne in mind in this connexion, however, and given their proper weight; even when one has made allowances for a certain amount of coat-trailing and playing to the gallery, Hume's state of health, and so on. For example (and these two things are linked), there is Hume's concern for literature and his dislike of the English: both these themes come through loud and clear in the letters; the latter, rising to a pitch of *Schadenfreude* at times, is, among other things and especially, an inflammation of a life-long complaint against the 'great men' of England and his fierce desire to be independent of them, his dislike of English snobbery and the hauteur of the

[1] Hume ignores the economic grievances which caused unrest in the Spring and Summer of 1768, but according to Rudé, these were not really connected with the political movement and only merged with it in exceptional circumstances. (*Wilkes and Liberty*, (1962), 90 *et seq*). 'They roar Liberty', Hume wrote, 'tho' they have apparently more Liberty than any People in the World; a great deal more than they deserve; and perhaps more than any men ought to have'.

[2] The letter of September 1767 to Gilbert Elliot makes the same point. Nobody wants to have any share in the Administration except adventurers. The pecuniary emoluments are of no consideration to men of rank and fortune: there is often more personal regard from being in opposition; the protection of the law is at all times sufficient for one's security; and by acquiring authority one is exposed to insults, instead of gaining the power to revenge them. 'Such is the Defect that arises from the Perfection of the most perfect Government' (II, 161).

English ruling class[1] – the same sort of thing that Hume may originally have found attractive in Rousseau.[2] When Hume talked about the English 'barbarians', it was often the great men, not the mob, that he had in mind.[3] The London 'mob' was by no means his sole or main target.[4] It was the 'great men' who indulged in the faction that destroyed literature,[5] and exploited Wilkes.

Hume does not explicitly and as a 'philosopher' connect, or see any causal relation between English 'barbarism' and English liberty, as Montesquieu does. But the theme of excessive English liberty is strictly philosophical. In December 1768 Hume could claim, at a time when 'licentiousness, or rather the frenzy of liberty, has taken possession of us', that 'in all my writings I have always kept at a proper distance from that tempting extreme, and have maintained a due regard to magistracy and established government, suitably to the character of an historian and a philosopher!' (*Letters*, II, 191–2, to the Comtesse de Boufflers).[6] For Hume, as for Montesquieu, modern English liberty was a somewhat precarious achievement, and he had always thought so. It implied a form of government which lacked power to deal adequately with abuses of liberty without endangering that liberty. Hence the remark quoted earlier from the *History of England* about the modern state needing either discretionary powers or a large revenue and standing army.

The philosophical view of British liberty and the British con-

---

[1] Oswald's wife, Hume reported to Kames, in 1747, 'seems to be a sensible Woman, but...also dry and reserv'd, like the foolish English women' (*New Letters*, 28).

[2] In his description of the Peasants Revolt of 1381, Hume quoted 'When Adam delv'd and Eve span, Where was then the gentleman?', verses 'which, in spite of prejudice, one cannot but regard with some degree of approbation'. This footnote (III, 245) is not in the first edition of the *History* (November 1761, but dated 1762).

[3] Cf. the letter to Oswald of April 1763: '...those barbarians (your great men, I mean)...' (*Letters*, I, 385).

[4] June 1770: 'The Madness and Wickedness of the English (for do not say, the Scum of London) appear astonishing...' (*Letters*, II, 226). The 'mob' and 'scum' included the city radicals.

[5] January 1773. '...as to any Englishman, that Nation is so sunk in Stupidity and Barbarism and Faction that you may as well think of Lapland for an Author. The best Book that has been writ by any Englishman these thirty Years (for Dr Franklyn is an American) is Tristram Shandy...' (*Letters*, II, 269). March 1776: Hume tells Gibbon that for 'almost a whole Generation' the English 'have given themselves up to barbarous and absurd Faction, and have totally neglected all polite Letters'. He no longer expected any valuable production ever to come from them (II, 310). To Adam Smith he said that he hoped Gibbon had not taken amiss 'the national reflection'; 'it is lamentable to consider how much that Nation has declined in Literature during our time' (II, 312).

[6] Cf. October 1754 to the Abbé le Blanc: 'that I am a Lover of Liberty will be expected from my Country, tho' I hope, that I carry not that Passion to any ridiculous Extreme'. (*Letters*, I, 198).

stitution involved also a doctrine not mentioned so far, that belongs to the weak, 'mechanical' side of Hume's philosophy[1] and may bear a large measure of responsibility for his attitude of despondency; that 'the growth of everything, both in arts and nature, at last checks itself' (*Letters*, I, 143, November, 1750). 'Great empires, great cities, great commerce all of them receive a check, not from accidental events but necessary principles' (*Letters*, I, 272). It is an aspect of Hume's economic theory, for instance, seen in the letter just quoted (271) and the essay on the *Balance of Trade* (*Essays*, 329). It is a swinging pendulum variety of determinism, according to which a movement or historical process, like the dark ages after the German invasions and fall of the Roman empire, reaching an extreme in one direction must start moving in the opposite way.

But one does not need this theory of natural 'checks' to understand why the cry of the London radicals and their allies for 'liberty' was so exasperating and fatuous to Hume. Not only did they constitute a tiny minority of the whole country (the Edinburgh apprentices burnt Wilkes in effigy); they were jeopardising the very liberty for which they roared so mindlessly. For, as Hume had always insisted, and did so again at the conclusion of his last essay, *Of the Origin of Government*, if 'liberty is the perfection of civil society...authority must be acknowledged essential to its very existence.'[2] And that authority, in the English form of government, was uniquely and dangerously narrow anyway, and in the reign of George III had been eroded still further. As Hume wrote to Strahan in June 1771: 'Only consider how many Powers of Government are lost in this short Reign. The right of displacing the Judges was given up; General Warrants are lost; the right of Expulsion the same; all the co-ercive Powers of the House of Commons abandon'd; all Laws against Libels annihilated...the revenue of the civil List diminish'd' (*Letters*, II, 244–5).[3] Modern

[1] Commentators tend to call this sort of thing 'mechanical'. 'Classical platitude' would serve equally well.
[2] The reason why Hume wrote this last, isolated essay so late in his life (it was not published till the year after his death) was presumably to fill a gap in his published writings: he had not in fact treated this important topic in essay form (that is, turned the treatment of it in the discarded *Treatise* into an essay) except indirectly, and in what by 1774 had, in Scotland at any rate, become a somewhat old-fashioned and artificial manner.
[3] Cf. November 1775: 'Government...has already but too little Authority.' This was one of the reasons why Hume advocated the grant of total independence to the American colonies, which is the context of the remark just quoted: the loss of America, which would be inevitable, would be detrimental to the credit and reputation of Government: the result will probably be anarchy, the best consequence of

historians would endorse this view that powers like that of the use of General Warrants were powers that had been traditionally exercised by government: that the innovation was on the part of those who aimed at abolishing them.[1] The trouble was that this excessive liberty could 'scarcely be retrench'd without Danger of being entirely lost', as Hume wrote to Elliot in February, 1770, but on the other hand the road to republicanism was also, in Britain at least, the road, via anarchy, to despotism (*Letters*, II, 306).

This was why Hume advocated 'vigorous measures' and a show-down 'between the Mob and the Constitution' (March 1770, *Letters*, II, 218), and blamed the government for remissness and pusillanimity. The rule of law as it had been achieved in England, was a unique and dangerous experiment: leniency to those who openly defied it was 'a new Experiment to reconcile such extreme Licence with Government' (April 1770, to Gilbert Elliot. II, 221). Still, he was glad of the 'victories' of Lord North and the 'King's Friends', though he did not expect much from them in a government 'which has become a Chimera...too perfect in point of Liberty, for so vile a Beast as an Englishman...corrupted by above a century of Licentiousness' (II, 216).

What was involved was more fundamental than anything which the 'King's Friends', as such, stood for, and to say that Hume was on their side does not get to the heart of the matter at all. One could, for instance, be against the radicals, precisely because one was so hot for *parliamentary* opposition, 'the ordinary parliamentary Arts of Opposition' as Hume called them in January 1770.[2] The issues raised were outside the context in which 'King's Friends' had been relevant: the radicals made that clear enough themselves. The question was whether King, country, or factions could survive, because without authority, you could not have liberty, and that included factions, detestable as they could be.

To write off Hume's attitude to the political crisis of his last years as the aberration of an old and world-weary man, not to be taken too seriously, by his admirers, or to see it as the expression of a final phase of reactionary conservatism, does not do Hume

which would be 'a settled Plan of arbitrary Power; the worst, total Ruin and Destruction' (*Letters*, II, 305, Cf. also 300-1, 303).

[1] For example, see Rudé: *Wilkes and Liberty* (28-9) on the case for General Warrants, and I. R. Christie: *Myth and Reality in late 18th century British Politics* (1970), 199-203. Junius, in Letter LIX, said that if the *manners* of the people were not republican enough, the *form* of the constitution was, if anything, too much so.
[2] *Letters*, I, 212-13. Given the King's resolution to support his Ministers, men 'will either acquiesce, or return to the ordinary, parliamentary Arts of Opposition'.

justice. Beneath the violence, at times, of his language – and after all, one is listening in to what is virtually private conversation – there is his philosophically grounded view of the crisis as one of extreme seriousness, for reasons which should now be clear. He expressed himself strongly precisely because the continuity of his thought was unbroken: what he had foreseen as likely in his earliest writings had come to pass. And yet, towards the end of the day, after the political 'man' had let himself go in his letters and pulled no punches about the 'vile' English 'barbarians' and 'mob' and their excessive love of liberty, leading either to absolute government or ruin, after all he had been through in the 60s and early 70s, what *qua* 'philosopher' is his valedictory conclusion, at the very end of his last essay? Authority, he says, must be acknowledged essential to the very existence of civil society, and 'in those contests, which so often take place between the one and the other, the latter *may* [my italics], on that account, challenge the preference. Unless perhaps one may say (and it may be said with some reason) that a circumstance, which is essential to the existence of civil society, must always support itself, and needs be guarded with less jealousy, than one that contributes only to its perfection, which the indolence of men is so apt to neglect, or their ignorance to overlook' (39). If this final sentence is not an example of philosophical self-control and a triumph of scientific detachment and objectivity, one would like to know what is. The 'philosopher' is still at the wheel, the 'man' in the smoking-room.

6
Applied philosophy, genuine and false: Hume and the Court and Country parties in 1741–2

The occasion of Hume's first batch of political essays, published in the autumn of 1741,[1] was the controversy generated by Walpole's administration and Bolingbroke's opposition, the violence and extremism of which gave Hume the opportunity to show how philosophy could be applied to politics, and what that really meant. The essays were therefore written when the long sustained opposition was on the eve of success: that however was not known to Hume, who admitted as much in the Advertisement to his *Character of Sir Robert Walpole,* which was first published in the second volume of essays, which appeared in January 1742. (These were mostly non-political.) Walpole resigned in February. And sometime in the summer of 1742, a second, corrected edition of the essays appeared.

Hume must have learnt much of his domestic English politics from this debate. The political topics he took up in his essays were discussed at much greater length in the journals and pamphlets of the 30s and 40s. And there were some very live contemporary issues which he ignored, notably those connected with foreign policy which traditionally divided 'Whigs' and 'Tories': the question of continental 'entanglement' in general, the still bitterly controversial Peace of Utrecht – and the events of the last years of the reign of Queen Anne in general[2] – the 'Old System' of alliance with Austria versus 'Tory' leanings towards France, the much discussed Treaty of Hanover of 1725 etc.[3] This was pre-

---

[1] It appears now that these essays were published not in Spring 1742, as T. E. Jessop thought (A *Bibliography of David Hume and of Scottish Philosophy* [1938], 15) nor late in 1741, as Mossner supposed (*The Life of David Hume* [1954], 138), but in June or July 1741. See M. M. Goldsmith, *History*, Vol. 64, No. 210 (1979) p. 16. Certainly it must have been before October 10, because the *Craftsman* of that date printed Hume's essay on *Whether the British government inclines* (see below).

[2] As T. W. Perry says, the extent to which the events of the latter half of Anne's reign influenced the political attitudes of 40 years later is remarkable, and has not been sufficiently noted. *Public Opinion, Propaganda and Politics in 18th century England. A Study of the Jew Bill of 1753* (Harvard, 1962), 29.

[3] Hume touched on 'foreign politics' in passing in his attempt to distinguish the Whig and Tory parties. 'Holland has always been most favoured by one and France

sumably because he thought that foreign politics was less amenable to philosophical treatment than domestic (*Essays*, 113, 260). Nor did he immerse himself in those debates which involved detailed knowledge of constitutional theory, as for example the meaning of prerogative, or sovereignty, or the question of the division of powers. (The Ministerialist writers had attacked the Opposition on this issue: how, they asked, could the government function at all if the three powers had to be as independent as the opposition demanded? See *The Craftsman*, Vol. VII, 86 *et seq.*) This may have been due to ignorance of English constitutional law and theory, or to the belief that such matters consorted ill with polite literature and the appeal to a wide public, or both.

His aim of using philosophy to promote moderation in politics was all the more necessary because the foremost political writer of the day claimed that he was writing as a philosopher and not a party man. (Hume said later, in 1754, that Bolingbroke's posthumous productions showed that he owed his inflated reputation to 'his being a man of Quality, and to the Prevalence of Faction' (*Letters*, I, 208).) But the Opposition idea of what constituted political moderation was not Hume's. In the *Craftsman* 'true' moderation was defined as not opposing the measures of government, except when great national interests were at stake; any other kind was 'false' and a symptom of the lack of 'public spirit' without which liberty was doomed (*Craftsman*, VII, 346). That no doubt was why Hume insisted that 'public spirit or' a 'regard to the community', without which a man is 'deficient in the most material part of virtue', and moderation, as he understood it, are the same thing: that the surest way to promote moderation 'in every party' is to increase our zeal for the public (*Politics a Science*, 23–4).

For Bolingbroke, too, 'public spirit' and philosophy were practically the same thing; in the *Letter on the Spirit of Patriotism* he compared the 'intellectual joys' of 'real patriotism' with the meditations of Descartes, or even Newton (*The Works of Lord Bolingbroke*, II, 360) and claimed that he was using 'reason and truth' to silence 'the drummers and trumpeters of faction', overthrow Walpole and promote, above all, zeal for the constitution (*A Dissertation upon Parties*, 16, 198).

'Reason and truth', in Bolingbroke's political writings, spoke with many voices; notably those of Locke, for the notion of

by the other.' *Parties of Great Britain*. The section was in the editions from 1741 to 1768 (*Essays*, 71).

government as a trust and rulers as trustees, Machiavelli and Harrington; on the whole, Bolingbroke relied on history, philosophically considered, and the theory of the British constitution, because it was this sort of ignorance which allowed men to accept Walpole's flouting of the constitution as normal (*On the Spirit of Patriotism*). In the *Dissertation upon Parties* he wrote that 'they who talk of liberty in Britain on any other principles than those of the British constitution, talk impertinently at best, and much charity is requisite to believe no worse of them' (192), which is implicitly a rejection of natural law, and in this work Bolingbroke does not in fact make any use of natural law. The Ministerialist writers fell back on natural law, because they could not regard the ancient constitution and ancient liberty, which the Opposition kept appealing to, as historical fact (See, for example, *Daily Gazetter*, 5 July 1735). The Opposition believed that the ancient constitution was a firmer basis of English liberty, and a writer in *Fog's Journal* (13 May 1732) regarded natural law as so broad a basis for political obligation that it could render any form of government, Christian or non-Christian, despotic or free, legitimate. 'Nothing is so absurd as a recourse to the Law of Nature which Mr Osborne will have to be the basis of government and the rock on which the revolution stands. The Law of Nature is an uncertain and dangerous direction in matters of government, civil and ecclesiastical, and makes no difference between martyrs for an onion or the Christian religion...By the Law of Nature a Papist is as fit to govern a Protestant people as any other...' Bolingbroke subscribed to a theory of natural law (see Kramnick, *Bolingbroke and his Circle*, Ch. IV), and the Patriot King, we are told, will reverence the constitution 'as the law of God and man' (*The Idea of a Patriot King* in *Works* II, 392), but if he did not make use of it in the campaign against Walpole, or only very indirectly, one cannot help feeling that it must have been a somewhat pale and academic affair. He saw the British Constitution itself as an original contract, because it was a balance of three 'orders', which presupposed a contract or bargain between king and people, and between the representative and collective body of the nation. In most other countries the original contract or 'consultation and composition between men' from which 'all public regiment hath arisen' (Hooker is the authority Bolingbroke appeals to in this instance) has been forgotten or grown so obsolete that it has been denied by those whose interest it is to deny it (*Dissertation upon Parties*, 199–202). Kings may have preceded lawgivers and government by will been established before government by constitution: this does not disprove Hooker, for men soon discovered their error, instituted commonwealths and limited monarchies. The depravity of the many, together with men's mutual wants, made government necessary, the depravity of the few obliged men to subject government to constitution (*Craftsman*, XII, 102–3). Bolingbroke insisted on the distinction between government and constitution.

He took it for granted that 'liberty' meant and implied 'free government', or government by laws made with our own consent, in fact a parliament, consisting of three estates equally balanced. Without this, men were 'slaves'. History and the comparative study of constitutions showed that the British constitution is 'brought nearer than any other constitution ever was to the most perfect idea of a free system of government' (*Dissertation*, 187). Hereditary monarchy, he says in the *Patriot King*, is the best monarchy, and limited monarchy the best of governments (*Works*, II, 381). What Tacitus had thought possible only in theory and as an ideal, had been realized in practice in Britain, because since the sixteenth century, with the shift of the balance of property in favour of the commons, the constitution had been firmly settled on the correct necessary balance of property and power, or rather, re-settled more securely on its original Saxon basis. As a result the British Constitution was uniquely free and excellent (two things which coincide, for Bolingbroke), and uniquely long-lasting,[1] in spite of incessant attempts to destroy it.

The peculiar excellence of the British Constitution was made clear by a comparison with other governments, especially that of France (*Dissertation*, 247). For instance, the Roman commonwealth and the French monarchy both suffered from the great original defect of having only two orders or estates to share the supreme power: of the three simple forms of government, monarchy, aristocracy and democracy, Rome lacked the first and France the last. The Roman Commonwealth, insecurely based on a faulty balance of property and power, because the people did not possess sufficient of the former to match their share of the latter, never arrived at a method of preventing disputes between the two orders; the people had recourse to sedition; the senate to a dictator, which was legal, but as inconsistent with a free constitution of government as the former. Want of a third estate (meaning a king) and of a representative body to act for the collective body, kept up a

---

[1] The Romans maintained their liberty little more than seven centuries; Britain was a free nation 1700 years ago and is so still (*Craftsman*, VII, 50).

perpetual ferment. Had it not been for the 'public spirit' of the Romans, the Commonwealth would have succumbed much sooner: when that was lost, the constitution destroyed itself via the dictatorial power. In France the people have had no share in the supreme power, either collectively or by representation, since the foundation of the Frankish monarchy by Clovis (*Dissertation*, 209–14 (Rome), 233–46 (France)).[1]

But in Britain, government had always been 'free' (*Dissertation*, 187); the legislative or supreme power is vested in three estates, of which the king is one, the peers constituting a 'middle order', mediating between king and people (202, 205). It was by this balance that our free constitution had been preserved for so long inviolate, or brought back to its original principles and renewed and improved by frequent and salutary revolutions (205). The correct 'poise of our constitution' (202) depended on the independence of parliament, a principle which had always been maintained through all the variations which the Saxon constitution had undergone; 'parliaments were never interrupted, nor the right of any estate taken away, however the exercise of it might be disturbed' (250–2). It was the 'essence of our constitution' (277); on this depended the correct balance of the constitution, because that balance was such that the commons could never preponderate: the king and nobility would unite to prevent any such attempt; whereas there was always the real danger that the king could win

---

[1] In *Common Sense or the Englishman's Journal* (18 June 1737) there is a variation on the theme of the warning to Britons provided by the absolute monarchies of Europe. The writer begins by amending Harrington, pointing out that since he wrote, a new sort of wealth has been invented, upon which all the absolute monarchies in Europe depend, viz: that of taxes, posts and employments. In these countries, private property, either in land or money or goods, is as secure and as generally dispersed among the people, as it is in England: in every country of Europe, except Turkey, a man's property is secured to him by the laws of his country: those laws are as public and well known, though perhaps not so good, as the laws of this kingdom, and no private man can be divested of his property without a legal trial and formal condemnation. But the taxes, posts and employments at the king's disposal give him so large a share of wealth as to overbalance that of the nobles and people; and though in most of those countries, no tax or very few can be imposed without the consent of the assembly of the states, or Parliament, yet by means of the posts etc. at the disposal of the king, the majority of members so 'hang by their teeth' upon the king that the assembly never refuses any tax or free gift he may demand. In this country we are not yet in danger of such an absolute government as Turkey, where the Grand Seignior is proprietor of all the land, but when we consider the number of taxes and employments at the disposal of the king and his ministers we are in danger of becoming an absolute monarchy like that of France... *Common Sense or the Englishman's Journal* (London, 1738), 141–2. The subjects of the absolute monarchies are not regarded by this writer as 'slaves' in the usual manner of vulgar Whiggism.

over members of the other two orders and tip the balance in his favour (261, *Craftsman*, 115–16, 119–20). Therefore 'Parliaments are the true guardians of liberty' (*Dissertation*, 151), and always have been (256–7). In Bolingbroke 'parliamentary slavery' corresponds to the state of nature: by the 'absolute influence of a king or his minister on the two houses, we return into that state to deliver us and secure us from which parliaments were instituted, and are really governed by the arbitrary will of one man' (151). 'Parliamentary slavery' means the destruction of government by constitution and the return to government by will. By the corruption of Parliament our whole constitution is at once dissolved...independency of parliament is the keystone...if this be taken away our constitution falls into ruin. The integrity of Parliament is a kind of palladium, a tutelary Goddess, who protects our state (*Craftsman*, XII, 108). Anyone who doubts this has only to consult the history of England and observe how kings with designs against liberty have always tried to gain parliament or govern without it (*Dissertation*, 158). The frequency, integrity and independency of parliaments are the essentials of British liberty; any defect here will soon destroy the constitution, even if every other part of it is preserved (163).

But parliamentary freedom and the constitution can only be destroyed if the people allow it to happen; nothing can destroy the constitution of Britain but the people of Britain (270–6): they will never submit to slavery unless they fall into a state of universal corruption, and if this happens no constitution will avail (181–2).

The danger however is very great. 'This necessary independency of parliament in which the essence of our constitution and by consequence of our liberty consist seems to be in great, not to say imminent, danger of being lost' (277). It is true that up till now the spirit of liberty handed down from our Saxon ancestors has always prevailed in the end: Charles II had tried to corrupt parliament but had failed. But since then, and especially since the revolution, the means at the disposal of the crown had vastly increased. Had Bolingbroke heard of the law of the transformation of quantity into quality, no doubt he would have used it in connection with what had occurred as a result of the establishment of the new system of finance at the revolution. With the new taxes, the increase in the king's revenue, and the new system of borrowing, something hitherto unheard of had suddenly appeared in English history. The men who made the Revolution had their eye on the royal prerogative: they did not see and so did not provide against the new and much greater danger; though very soon after men began to realize it, and to demand those measures, place bills, more frequent parliaments etc, which had been neglected in 1689, and which were needed in order to complete the return of the constitution to first principles.

But the constitution was threatened also on the other side, because liberty did not depend simply on the constitution; the constitution in turn depended on the 'spirit of liberty' which had never been totally extinguished, but was now in danger of being undermined by the growth of 'luxury', producing 'corruption' in the Machiavellian sense of the loss of 'public spirit' or 'patriotism'. 'Spirit of liberty' versus 'spirit of faction' was a cardinal principle of historical interpretation as well as a maxim of political practice; and this theme of 'patriotism', which is so conspicuous in the *Patriot King*, where 'patriotism' is said to be the cardinal virtue of society, is related to the theme of the balanced constitution, because that has a foundation in the Harringtonian maxim that power follows property: the correct balance depends on a certain diffusion of wealth which in turn demands 'an ancient economy and simplicity of manners' (*Craftsman*, XII, 64) which is threatened by the growth of 'luxury'.

The *Craftsman* of 28 February 1730 had pointed to the superficial way in which the 'vulgar' look no further for the cause of national evils like heavy taxation than the persons whose conduct has been the immediate instrument of them; even if these men do deserve the reproaches of the vulgar, there is always 'some more remote cause as either the want of some good laws or some error or defect, in the constitution itself, which serves as an inlet to these misfortunes; for governments may be so formed, or laws so framed, as will necessarily produce virtue, and make good ministers even of bad men' (VI, 72). In September what was being stressed was the fact that no laws can secure liberty if public spirit is lacking; that was why the Romans lost their liberty: the spirit of liberty had gone down before the spirit of faction: the principal men considered themselves now as *individuals*, not as *citizens* (VII, 18–20). The object was not to take the blame off Walpole's shoulders, but to make it heavier.

How far the process of corruption had gone Bolingbroke was not prepared to say (*Dissertation*, 304), but Walpole was accused of undermining the constitution both by corrupting parliament and by encouraging 'luxury' and selfishness,[1] and doing it under cover

[1] In the *Patriot King*, Walpole is accused of having corrupted the minds of men:

of the smokescreen of a division of parties which he was using for his own sinister purposes. (Otherwise there would have been no need to sound the alarm: Walpole's 'faction' would be seen by all to be what in truth it was.) In order to unmask Walpole's 'wicked conduct' and reveal the true state of the nation, Bolingbroke undertook an historical analysis or 'deduction of the state of parties' (194). An 'enquiry into the rise and progress of our late parties' will help us to make a true judgement of our present state, and point out remedies (16–17). This was philosophical history in action on the most immediate and crucial political front; this 'history of Torism [sic] and Whiggism from their cradle to their grave' was one of those complete examples which only history can provide, in which 'the whole example is before us and consequently the whole lesson' (See Letter II in *Letters on the Study and Use of History*. Bolingbroke uses the Revolution of 1688 to illustrate his meaning. To make it a 'complete example', and so to be able to develop all the salutary lessons involved, it is necessary to go back, perhaps even to the beginning of the reign of James I.) The lesson in the *Dissertation upon Parties* is precisely that the parties are purely and exclusively *historical* phenomena: if they were not simply that and were still truly alive their history could provide no lessons, because only in so far as any chapter of history is closed can it do so.

What this 'example' showed was that the Tory and Whig parties, as such, had never reflected a real division in the nation except in so far as they coincided with the real division between the court and the country:[1] these were national 'parties', a misfortune enough, but at least they were the expression of a genuine disagreement as to what was in the national interest. When the 'parties' succumbed, as parties tend to do, to self-interest (*Patriot King, Works*, II, 402), they ceased to be 'parties', and became mere 'factions'; only when that happened, was the constitution seriously endangered, to the point of actual subversion in one instance, but in the other great crisis, which culminated in 1688, the Tories saw the danger in time, and coaliting with the Whigs, helped to save and restore the constitution. Thus their conduct spoke louder than

---

narrowed them to personal regards alone, and confined their views to the present moment. This was his 'greatest iniquity'.

[1] Cf. *The Craftsman* (I, 100–1). Since 1660 the two parties have chopped about and reciprocally changed sides, just as their leaders have happened to be in or out of power. Great numbers who now (1726) flourish as Whigs would for the same actions have been esteemed arrant Tories forty years ago; others are branded as Tories for actions which once made the Whigs popular.

their professed principles of passive obedience and divine hereditary right, but unfortunately they did not abandon their principles and thus perpetuated a distinction which was more nominal than real, because 'the bulk of both parties are really united...on principles of liberty' (*Dissertation*, 6), and gave Walpole the lever he needed. If one ignored outmoded labels and party slogans, and observed men's actual behaviour since the revolution, the true situation was that the only real and meaningful divisions of parties were those between Churchmen and Dissenters and Court and Country, and the Dissenters really belonged to the latter (10–11). In fact it was not really a question of parties but of a division between constitutionalists and anti-constitutionalists, friends of liberty and friends of Walpole, the whole nation representing the 'spirit of liberty', versus a faction.

As soon as this was sufficiently realized, a 'coalition of parties' would be able to complete the restoration of the constitution to first principles which had been left unfinished at the Revolution, and by fully securing the independence of Parliament would perfect 'the most perfect idea of a free system of government' (264).

The historical deduction showed that parties and factions, if, given human nature they were unavoidable, especially in free government (*Patriot King: Works* II, 412), were always pathological, the result of some extraneous disturbing factor – in English history, the result of rulers endeavouring to govern against the will and sense of the whole nation, or more specifically, James I's new-fangled notion of divine right. The Whig and Tory parties were not the natural result of the British constitution: they were the creation of the Stuart kings who chose to govern by faction (*Craftsman*, VII, 192).

For any one trying to discover whether the British government was functioning properly, or what was disturbing its proper functioning, the problem of the parties was crucial. It was also extremely difficult. To determine the nature of the Whig and Tory parties was, Hume said, 'one of the most difficult problems that can be met with, and is a proof that history may contain questions as uncertain as any to be found in the most abstract sciences'. We have seen the conduct of the two parties for seventy years in a vast variety of circumstances, in and out of power, in peace and war; we meet people who profess to belong to one side or the other every day, in business and pleasure; 'we ourselves are constrained, in a manner, to take party'; and we live in a country where everyone can express himself fully and freely. And yet we are 'at a loss to tell the nature, pretensions and principles of the different factions'. (Hume later changed 'factions' into 'parties': he did this and also the reverse so frequently that it is clear that he did not, like Bolingbroke, make a distinction between them. He also withdrew, after 1768, a passage to the effect that the question had been made even more difficult by party prejudice and violence. *Parties of Great Britain*, 69n.)

Bolingbroke's 'deduction' of the state of parties had been purely historical, confined to English history since 1603, at the earliest. In good 'philosophical' style, Hume begins with a study of 'Parties in General', casting his net as widely as possible, and classifying parties into 'personal' and 'real', and subdividing the latter into parties from interest, principle and affection. He then, using psychology, constructs a model, or ideal type, of the party system of Britain. As seen already, factions or parties are an evil, and the founders of sects and factions are detestable (55), and Hume speaks as though legislators ought to try and 'prevent' parties from interest, however difficult that may be – many philosophers regarding it as impossible in practice (58), nevertheless the British government is such that it necessarily gives rise to Court and Country parties catering for two different types of men. Similarly the psychology of 'superstition' and 'enthusiasm', which Hume expounds in the essay with that title, will ensure that churchmen will naturally gravitate to the court and dissenters to the country party. 'Enthusiasm being the infirmity of bold and ambitious tempers' is naturally accompanied with a spirit of liberty; 'superstition' the product of ignorance and fear of the unseen generates priestly authority and power. Normally, therefore, 'while things are in their natural situation' (added in 1748) one can expect to find Court + established clergy versus Country + dissenters. They are parties of principle, but interest is also involved, especially where the leaders of the parties are concerned, and it is this which makes them dangerous and violent (*Parties of Great Britain*, 64–5).[1]

The first rise of parties in England conformed to this 'general theory': 'the species of government gave birth to them, by a regular and infallible operation'. Cavaliers and Roundheads were a court and country party inflamed into a civil war by an 'unhappy concurrence of circumstances': neither disowned either monarchy or liberty, but the former inclined to the monarchical, the latter to the republican part of our government. Since the hopes of

[1] See above p. 186.

success were equal on both sides, 'interest' was not involved; they were exclusively parties of principle. The established clergy, as one would expect, joined the king; the Presbyterian non-conformists the parliament (66–7). They were the ancestors of the Whigs and Tories, the main difference being that the latter professed principles, not much heard of among the Cavaliers, of passive obedience and indefeasible right, which were absurd and illogical, as was proved by the conduct of the Tories at the Revolution, which showed them to be, in spite of their professed principles, a genuine court party in a mixed government such as ours. However they never really accepted the settlement made at the Revolution or that which has since taken place. This contradicts their behaviour in 1688, but no more so than that contradicted their professed principles. 'But the heart of man is made to reconcile contradictions.' Their principles are strongly monarchical, but for the last fifty years, except for four years at the end of Queen Anne's reign, and this is easily enough explained, they have consistently opposed the court, which shows that their quarrel has not been with the throne, but with the persons who sat on it. Tory and Whig began as court and country parties: the natural product of the type of government, but the Tory principle of attachment to monarchy had in a natural manner degenerated into an attachment to the person of the monarch and the royal family ('natural', that is, according to Hume's psychology and theory of the working of the 'imagination'), the connexion between monarchy and the monarch being so close and the latter being so much the more natural and familiar object. 'How easily does worship of the divinity degenerate into worship of the idol!' It became a matter of affection rather than principle, at least with men of sense, who could hardly be expected to subscribe to the absurdities proclaimed from pulpits, though no doubt the party leaders acted from purely interested motives – though, says Hume, it is difficult enough to penetrate into the thoughts and sentiments of a particular man, let alone those of a whole party. The connection between the divinity of the Whigs, which was liberty, and any monarch or royal family not being so close, worship of the one is not so easily 'transferred from the one to the other', though even that would be no great miracle. (This section of psychological explanation was added to the essay on the *Parties of Great Britain* in 1748, and withdrawn when the essay was considerably pruned to its present concise shape in 1768.) Love of liberty is professedly the predominant inclination of the Whigs, whereas with the Tories it was not their monarchical principles, but their affection for the house of Stuart that was the predominant inclination of the party. That explains why they have at times acted like republicans. Thus the succession of the crown is the chief point with the Tories; the security of our liberties with the Whigs, and if the latter have taken steps dangerous to liberty under pretext of securing the succession, it must be that, since the body of that party have no passion for the succession other than as the means of securing liberty, they have been betrayed into these steps by ignorance or frailty, or the interest of their leaders. So, since the Revolution, a Tory may be defined as a lover of monarchy, though without abandoning liberty, and a partisan of the family of Stuart; and a Whig as a lover of liberty, though without renouncing monarchy, and a friend to the settlement in the Protestant line. These views were accidental, but natural additions to the principles of the court and country parties, which are the genuine divisions in the British government. A passionate lover of monarchy is apt to be displeased at any change in the succession; a passionate lover of liberty thinks that liberty must have priority.

In Scotland there were properly speaking no Tories, and never had been; and the division there was into Whigs and Jacobites; a Jacobite being a Tory who has no regard to the constitution, and is either a zealous partisan of absolute monarchy, or at least willing to sacrifice our liberties to obtain the succession in that family to which he is attached.

It must be confessed that the Tory party has of late decayed much in their numbers, zeal and still more in their credit and authority; there is no man of knowledge or learning who would not be ashamed to be thought of that party, and the name of Old Whig is in all companies mentioned as an 'incontestable appellation of honour and dignity'. That is why the enemies of the ministry call the courtiers Tories, and those in opposition the true Whigs. However, there are 'very considerable remains of that party in England with all their old prejudices' (this sentence was never withdrawn) while the 'monstrous' spectacle of an established episcopal clergy in declared opposition to the court is proof that they have espoused monarchical principles too high for the present settlement, and causing the equally unnatural behaviour of the non-conformists, who, from fear of the prevalence of these principles, adhere to the court. Court and country are thus not our only parties; different views with regard to the settlement of the crown have kept alive the old division between Whigs and Tories, and this is the 'extrinsic weight' or 'bias' which 'still hangs upon our constitution' and 'turns it from its natural course, and causes a confusion in our parties'.

Bolingbroke's deduction of parties and diagnosis of the present political situation was therefore faulty. To assert, as this 'celebrated writer' does, that the real distinction between Whigs and Tories was lost at the Revolution, and that since then they have been mere personal parties, like Guelfs and Ghibellines after the Emperor had lost all authority in Italy, 'would turn our whole history into an enigma'. Even those who do not go as far as this and who 'seem inclined to think' that things are returned to their natural state of court versus country parties are refuted by 'what every one may have observed or heard concerning the conduct and conversation of all his friends and acquaintance on both sides. Have not the Tories always bore an avowed affection to the family of Stuart, and have not their adversaries always opposed with vigour the succession of that family?' The succession of the crown is a point of too great consequence to be absolutely indifferent to persons who concern themselves in any degree about the fortunes of the public, and the Tories, who never valued themselves upon moderation, can hardly be expected to maintain a stoical indifference on a point of such importance, or were they zealous for Hanover? Or was it not more likely that they kept an opposite zeal from appearing from prudence and a sense of decency?

So what for Bolingbroke is a pathological symptom is for Hume a sign of the normal functioning of the constitution, and what according to Bolingbroke exists no more is just what is disturbing the proper functioning of the system: the distinction between Whig and Tory caused by the dynastic issue.

This presumably was the 'dangerous' distinction of parties, symptoms of whose disappearance Hume saw and welcomed in the essay on the *Coalition of Parties* of 1758. 'To abolish all distinctions of party may not be practicable, perhaps not desirable, in a free government. The only dangerous parties are such as entertain opposite views with regard to the essentials of government, the succession of the crown, or the more considerable privileges belonging to the several members of the constitution; where there is no room for any compromise or accommodation, and where the controversy may appear so momentous as to justify even an opposition by arms to the pretensions of antagonists...'

There is nothing in the essay to indicate a conversion to a 'King-in-toils' political programme or philosophy of coalition inspired by Bolingbroke and advocating abolition of political parties as such. Hume is observing and welcoming signs, including no doubt Pitt's experiment in coalition government, of a 'universal desire to abolish these party distinctions', that is, the 'dangerous' ones, as analysed in his essay on the *Parties of Great Britain*. To feel that this is too simple, and that the succession question was irrelevant as late as 1758 only goes to show that the historian of ideas must do his own history, and that the quest for 'how it actually was' can mean different things: the historian of ideas is concerned with 'how it actually was' in the eyes of contemporaries; and one has only to be slightly familiar with the diaries, debates, journals, letters etc of these days to see that 'Jacobitism' was an unconscionable time a' dying. Even if what that meant is by no means always clear, as when for example Horace Walpole endorsed the remark in the House of Commons in 1755 by the son of Campbell of Cawdor that there were more Jacobites in Middlesex than in the Highlands of Scotland (*Memoirs of the Reign of King George II* (1846), Vol. II, 15); and granted that the term was often used simply as a smear or scare or political ploy, nevertheless there were people who did not accept that the Hanoverian regime had any moral right to be, and that undeniable fact was a source of real or potential political division, and could be and was manipulated to the hurt of many worthy people, especially Scotsmen. This is the 'background' of Hume's essay on *Coalition of Parties*.[1]

[1] Smollett in his *Complete History of England*, published 1757–8, wrote that since the revolution, 'these kingdoms have been divided and harassed by violent and implacable factions...exposed to plots, conspiracies, civil wars and successive rebellions', and are 'still subjected to all those alarms and dangers which are engendered by a disputed title to the throne' (Smollett's *History* (London, 1834), x, 6–7n). The review of Smollett's History in the *Critical Review* (Vol. 5, 1758) begins by remarking on the difficulty of writing modern English history in 'a nation, divided as we are, into two inveterate factions...' (1). This sort of thing gives one a better understanding of Hume's coalition essay than any amount of modern history of the Namier school. In Vol. 6 (1758) a review of *The Case of the Royal Martyr considered* expresses apprehension that such controversies, instead of healing divisions, will, by irritating both parties mutually, rather help to widen the unhappy breaches which faction has made (293). In November 1758 Dr Shebbeare was pilloried and imprisoned for his *Letters to the People of England* (Horace Walpole, *Memoirs of the Reign of George II*, 152). Walpole in a letter of May 1759 says that it is certain that the Jacobites' spirit and projects revive, and France is preparing an invasion (Vol. 16 (1951) of the Yale edition of Walpole's *Correspondence*, 30). Tom Tempest and Jack Sneaker of the *Idler* (17 June 1758), the former a steady friend to the House of Stuart and the latter wishing that some better security could be found for the succession of Hanover than the present oaths, which are not sufficiently birfding, consider themselves neglected by their parties and are presented as somewhat high and dry, but they are there. Johnson would not have caricatured unreal phantoms in order to illustrate the credulity of party men. In January 1757 Hardwicke wrote

Another important subject of controversy between the Ministerialists and the Opposition in the 30s and 40s was the question of the balance of the constitution: was it inclining more towards the King or the People, or to quote from *A Letter from a By-Stander to a Member of Parliament*, dated 26 February 1741/2, (the date on the title page is 1741), 'whether the weight of power in the regal or popular scale now preponderates'. The Harringtonian maxim that power follows property was crucial here: and was used to support the argument on both sides. As has been seen, Bolingbroke used it to show how the constitution had been settled in the sixteenth century in such a way that the Commons could never preponderate (*Dissertation*, 266–7), and also to reveal the threat which resulted from the great increase of royal revenue since the Revolution. There was also the 'unanswerable argument' against governing by a party, that such a party by continuing in employments of profit might succeed in buying up all the lands in the kingdom and turning the government into a real oligarchy (*Craftsman*, IX, 99–100). The Ministerialist writers argued that by the events in the sixteenth century which shifted the balance of property and power in favour of the commons, the latter, from being slaves of the king, nobility and church had become their masters: that ever since the reign of Henry VII, the natural strength of the English monarchy had been decreasing, and if the king did not possess the 'influence' which the Opposition attacked as 'corruption', he

to Newcastle: 'I find the measure of raising 2000 Highlanders alarms many of the best affected...' (*Life and Correspondence of Philip Yorke, Earl of Hardwicke*, 383). Shelburne in his autobiography tells how 'all Scotland was enthusiastically devoted to the exiled family', and how in 1756 he had heard many of them avow it in the most unreserved manner (Fitzmaurice, *Life of Shelburne* (1912), I, 38). Blackstone in Vol. IV of his *Commentaries* (1769), writes that perhaps the time is not very distant when all fears of a pretender shall have vanished (57). As late as November 1775, Boswell, talking of the family of Stuart, observed 'that there is now an end of the party for them. In this reign omnes eodem cogimur' (Boswell: *The Ominous Years* (1963), 174). In 1777 Boswell made notes of an argument in which Dr Johnson maintained that a majority of the people of England would vote for a restoration of the Stuarts, and said that we will never have a stable government in England till all the branches of the royal family nearer to the House of Stuart than the family in possession be extinguished (*Private Papers of James Boswell* (1928), Vol. 13, 26–7). These very few random examples are merely to remind any reader who needs reminding that Jacobitism was taken far more seriously and for much longer than most general histories of the period seem to suggest. In 1770 Hume added a short section to the essay on *Public Credit* in which he gives 'Jacobitish violence' along with 'democratical frenzy' as an example of the sort of menace that would make the stockholders rally to the support of the government (360), nor for that matter did he ever withdraw the remark in the *Protestant Succession* essay (1752) to the effect that 'the claims of the banished family, I fear, are not yet antiquated; and who can foretel, that their future attempts will produce no greater disorder' (494).

would be a mere cipher; the constitution would cease to be a mixed monarchy and become wholly republican. The balance was strongly on the side of the commons, because the wealth of the kingdom was in their hands.[1]

In his essay *Whether the British Monarchy inclines more to Absolute Monarchy or to a Republic*, Hume does not just summarize the Opposition and Ministerialist arguments: what he does, as in the essay on *Coalition of Parties*, and at times in the *History of England*, is to make out a case for both sides as economically as possible, he presents each side impartially with what he thinks are the best arguments. Thus he improved Bolingbroke's case by resting it on a modification or 'limitation' of the Harringtonian thesis (because, he says, the general maxim that the balance of power depends on

[1] Cf. *London Journal*, 16 March, 28 September 1734. The debates continued after Hume's contribution in 1741. The bystander, mentioned above, argued against the *Dissertation upon Parties* that Harrington's maxim may prove true in the long run, but that prerogative, in full power, will command money, and as late as the reign of Charles I gave the crown an almost unlimited power over the lives and properties of the subjects; before the Revolution the Crown had an 'absolute uncontrollable power' of the whole standing public revenue, and that since the Revolution the Crown cannot command this revenue by means of corrupt officers, because the nature of the original contract and the reciprocal obligations are too well understood at present by the people of Britain, to make these things pass for jests, as formerly (35). It does not follow that because the income of the Crown is greater now than at any time since the Revolution, its pecuniary influence is greater, unless it can be shown that the income of the people has not been equivalently increased in the same time. The author's argument is that if the income of the Crown and of the people be respectively doubled, trebled or equally augmented to any amount, though the wealth of the Crown will be still in the same proportion to that of the people, as before, yet its power and influence will be much diminished. His proof is to compare a lord of the manor worth £500 a year with a thousand cottagers with £10 a year, with one worth £5,000 with farmers worth £100; the cottagers gain upon the lord in *ability*, which is the chief constituent article of power (56). His investigation of the respective incomes of Crown and People since 1660 shows a very extraordinary increase in the latter's 'ability', and that our present tendency lies much stronger to democracy than to absolute monarchy. The balance of our government is in danger of being upset unless the increasing *ability* of the people is tempered with a new moderation and just sense of the felicity of their present situation (58). This account of the situation of regal and popular power was answered (*A Proper Answer to the Bystander*, London, 1742, 53 *et seq*), by an elaborate distinction between different types of power. In modern times only the king has 'political military power', but he also has 'political civil power of a mercenary nature', which according to the constitution he should not have, though it is impossible to abolish the effect of it entirely. The pecuniary influence of the Crown will prevail over that of rich private men though the latter be twenty times as large as the former (62). As for the manor argument, every one does not grow equally rich, and even if simple men 'unite to form a purse' what can they do with it? The people have no power against the crown except in a sudden mob or insurrection (67). The debate continued in 1743. A lengthy section of the famous *Faction detected by the evidence of Facts* was devoted to the topic, (7th edition, 1744, 134–61), and was answered in *The Detector detected*.

the balance of the other 'must be received with several limitations'), which by-passes Bolingbroke's failure to meet the argument that the commons did possess the greater part of the wealth of the country and were therefore the preponderant power in the constitution. Bolingbroke simply asserted the contrary: his display of facts and figures showing how the revenue and power of the crown had increased since the Revolution was not accompanied by similar and equally cogent evidence with respect to the wealth and power of the commons.[1] Presumably the Machiavellian 'corruption' argument comes in here: if the commons are getting wealthier, they are also becoming more prone to corruption and easier for the Crown to win over to its side. At any rate without this argument and without facts and figures about the wealth of the commons since 1688, Bolingbroke's case is not very powerful. But Hume rejected the corruption argument: he did not regard the Machiavellian moralism so common in eighteenth-century English political thinking as 'philosophical'. He cuts out the need for either by pointing out that much less property in a single hand can counterbalance a greater property in several, because property when united causes much greater dependence than property when dispersed: a man with £100,000 a year can acquire more influence and power than 100 persons with £1000 a year each. The wealth of the Medici made them masters of Florence, though it was probably not considerable when compared with the united property of that opulent republic.

This modification of the Harringtonian maxim makes the British spirit and love of liberty appear an even more remarkable achievement, since 'we could maintain our free government during so many centuries against our sovereigns, who besides the power and dignity and majesty of the Crown, have always been possessed of so much more property than any subject has ever enjoyed in any commonwealth'. (It must be remembered that Hume is making out a case for those who assert that the balance of the British government inclines towards absolute monarchy.) Another modification of Harrington's maxim which might have helped the

[1] Such as Percival presents in *Faction detected*. He argued that since 1688 the revenue of the people had increased from 42 to 70 million (134). The answer to this in *The Detector detected* was that 'property of itself gives no *social* power, nor indeed any great *natural* power when it is divided among *such a number* as can never enter into *a general concert*'. So the power of the people cannot be said to have increased, even if they now have a greater share of property than at any time from the Conquest to the Restoration (8). But such a total dismissal of the power follows property maxim as this makes nonsense of Bolingbroke's thesis as to how the present Constitution came to be settled on its present foundation in the sixteenth century.

Opposition to meet certain objections is found in the essay on the *First Principles of Government*, where it is pointed out that the House of Commons is not always supported by the people: there are instances where this has happened even when the House has been in opposition to the crown, e.g. the Tory House in the reign of King William. Its weight in the scale is not always proportioned to the property and power of those it represents (32). If Members of Parliament were simply delegates with instructions, it might be so, but then the constitution would be republican.

Having made a stronger case for Bolingbroke than that set out in the *Dissertation upon Parties*, Hume now tacks this on: can the British love of liberty continue to prevail against the immense and increasing revenue of the crown, together with the increasing luxury of the nation, our 'proneness to corruption' etc? He does not mention the national debt here, but this may, as it does in Bolingbroke, come under 'pronenness to corruption'. He then proceeds to give his own reply to this line of reasoning, not the Ministerial one. (Hume does not, for example, consider the history of the royal revenue or the ministerialist use of the Harringtonian thesis.) The very fact that this immense property is joined to the dignity of the first magistrate, and to many other legal powers and prerogatives, which should naturally give it greater influence, in fact renders it less dangerous to liberty, than a much smaller property would be in the hands of any private man in a republic, because in this case the prospects of a successful coup are very inviting; successful usurpation has no limits, partisans expect more, violent opposition makes the usurper go further through fear, whereas a legal authority, though great, always has bounds; the magistrate has less to hope, more to fear from any excesses he may be tempted to commit, less temptation and opportunity to extend his legal authority further, when it is quietly submitted to. Hume adds one of his favourite psychological 'laws' or maxims: the power of novelty. Like novelties in philosophy and religion, ambitious new aims and projects spread faster and further than what is old and established, and are opposed and defended with more vehemence. Such is the nature of novelty that anything new doubly excites either pleasure or aversion, and the violence of enmity is favourable to ambitious projects as well as partisan zeal. Finally, Hume points to the changed climate of opinion in the last fifty years, which favours the republican trend. 'The mere name of *king* commands little respect.' This does not matter in times of tranquillity: the crown continues to support its authority, by means of its large revenue, upon private interest and influence, but not being supported by the settled opinions and principles of men, the least shock which breaks this chain of interest must be fatal to the royal power.

Hume's essay was reprinted in full in the *Craftsman* (10 October 1741), but in fact Hume's own conclusion does not really support the opposition case. In line with the extreme caution with which the essay begins, with Harrington held up as one whose forecast was almost immediately falsified by the turn of events, and an awful warning to all 'politicians', Hume's conclusion can hardly be said to come down on one side or the other, which is presumably why he does not bother to expand his own conclusion, or really argue it. The point of the essay, in fact, is 'to teach us a lesson of moderation in all our political controversies'. Daring to venture his own sentiments, Hume says that 'the power of the crown, by means of its large revenue, is rather upon the increase; though, at the same time, I own, that its progress seems very slow and almost insensible. The tide has run long, and with some rapidity, to the side of popular government, and is just beginning to turn towards monarchy.' For the opposition writers, the tide turned in 1688, or rather a new royal tide began to flow, and had been flowing with alarming and increasing rapidity ever since. 'Just beginning' does not mean 'has turned': and Hume could leave his conclusion unrevised in all later editions. And this essay must be taken in conjunction with that in *The Independency of Parliament*, in which Hume argues that the Commons are only prevented from being all-powerful by the system of parliamentary dependence: for 'the share allotted by our constitution to the house of commons, is so great, that it absolutely commands all the other parts of the government'.

Related to the question whether the power of the crown was on the increase was the question of the standing army. This was a hotly debated topic, on which strong opinions were held, and a large number of considerations was involved. The government case was a strong one: some sort of disciplined force which the Militia could not provide was necessary to keep order and defend the country, especially in view of the possibility of insurrection and the power of France. The Militia is now useless and regarded as a burden by the people themselves. Ours is not properly a standing army, which is raised and maintained at the will of the prince: it is the nation's and cannot be used against the nation (*London Journal*, 12 February 1732, 13 January 1733, *Free Briton*,

9 March 1732. Cf. also *A Letter from a Gentleman in Worcestershire* (1727), 12, *A Letter from a By-Stander* (1741)). One might have expected Hume to have argued for moderation in this very important debate: instead of condemning the standing army outright, as the opposition notoriously did, they should have discussed its size, composition etc. Considering the importance of the question he might have written an essay on it, debating the pros and cons in his usual manner. But in 1741/2 he avoided the subject altogether, except for a brief mention in the essay *Whether the British Government inclines*: but this is part of Hume's case for those who fear the growing power of the crown: in his own conclusion he does not mention the standing army, only the crown's large revenue. In November 1742 he votes 'aye' for the standing army (*Letters*, I, 44) but no reason is given. In 1748, in a note on the Chinese government added in that year to the *Rise of Arts and Sciences*, Hume says that it is not properly speaking an absolute monarchy because the standing forces are mere militia of the worst kind, so that the sword may be said to be always in the hands of the people, which is a sufficient restraint on the monarch. Hume says that perhaps a pure monarchy of this kind, given proper defence against foreign enemies, would be the best of all governments (123). From now on, and especially in essays published in 1752, Hume often expresses opinions in favour of militias and against standing armies.[1]

As for the other controversial political topics of the day, Hume

[1] In the *Protestant Succession* essay (1752) Hume says that one of the disadvantages of the Hanoverian regime is that with a disputed succession the prince dares not arm his subjects: 'the only method of securing a people fully, both against domestic oppression and foreign conquest' (494). This is Hume himself speaking, showing 'the temper', at least, 'of a philosopher' (493). In *Public Credit* (1752), standing armies are the beaten road to arbitrary government: it is one of the 'baits' which always catches 'mankind' (369). The Perfect Commonwealth (1752) has a militia on the Swiss model (506), and Hume says that 'without a militia, it is in vain to think that any free government will ever have security or stability (511). In the plan of limited monarchy suggested as an improved version of the English government, one of the weaknesses still remaining is that the 'sword is in the hands of a single person, who will always neglect to discipline the militia, in order to have a pretence for keeping up a standing army' (513) and in all editions from 1752 to 1769, Hume goes on to say that this is a mortal distemper in the British government, of which it must at last inevitably perish. He confesses however that Sweden seems to have remedied this inconvenience, and has a militia along with its limited monarchy as well as a standing army which is less dangerous than the British. Hume does not say precisely why the British standing army is so dangerous. Only in an addition to the last version of the *History* (that is, after 1773) does Hume reluctantly accept the 'melancholy truth' that the magistrate must either enjoy some discretionary powers in order to execute the laws and support his own authority, or possess a 'large revenue and a military force' (VII, 9).

was in some closer to the Country position, in others to that of the Court. He was, for example, in 1741, in favour of complete liberty of the press; nor, for that matter, did he ever argue that it had gone far enough and should be checked.[1] On the question of instructions to Members of Parliament, a characteristic 'country' nostrum, he agreed with the Court writers that this would 'introduce a total alteration in our government, and would soon reduce it to a pure republic', and if, in theory, this might be a change for the better, 'perhaps...a republic of no inconvenient form', in practice it was better to 'cherish and improve our ancient government' than to encourage a passion for 'such dangerous novelties' which were not practical politics in Britain (*First Principles of Government*, 33). The earlier editions, 1741-60, concluded with an argument designed to show that the whole debate on instructions was futile: the country party did not really want Members of Parliament to be 'absolutely bound to follow instructions as an ambassador or general is confined by his orders', (but this is precisely what some of them did want); nor did the Court argue that they should act in complete independence of their constituents, and therefore the question became one of degree ('the degrees of weight which ought to be placed on instructions'), and as such admitted of no solution (33-4n). In dismissing this debate as futile, Hume seems to have missed the force of the ministerialist argument, later used by Burke, that Members of Parliament are legislators, not 'attorneys of the people'.[2] Hume did not discuss the question of more frequent parliaments; that this was unnecessary follows from what he has to say about the need for parliamentary 'dependence'; and in the letter of November 1742 he tells Mure to vote against the Triennial Bill (*Letters*, 1, 44). He agreed with the Court that Bolingbroke was wrong to say that the distinction between Whigs and Tories no longer had any meaning, that the

[1] See, for instance, *Common Sense* of 7 January 1738. The article defending 'this palladium of our rights' was in answer to one in the *Gazetteer* calling for an immediate check to it. 'I know how much the furnishing the People with the means of forming any judgement in public transactions has of late been ridiculed amongst us, but this is the effect of narrow and interested politics...' (333 *et seq*).

[2] *London Journal* (5 May 1733): To regard them as such is to change our government into a democracy. (1 September 1733): They cannot be chosen to represent the sense of the people, because it is impossible for the sense of the people about future transactions to be known. See *Faction detected*, 101. It is the constant principle of our constitution that no man after he is chosen is to consider himself as a member for any particular place but as a representative for the whole nation, without which there could be neither freedom of judgment or speech, and all debate entirely unnecessary, and as a consequence the Legislature torn with faction and contrariety of interests.

latter no longer believed in their old principles of passive obedience and divine hereditary right.[1] But he was careful to distinguish Jacobites and Tories, as the Court was not; nor did he agree with their argument that there was no need for a country party in a legal administration, besides what was always to be found whenever you had men and governments.[2] He did not join in the debate about the king's prerogative, but presumably he would have agreed with 'Osborne' that if by the king's prerogative one means what that meant before the Revolution, that is, powers more than or besides the law, then the king since 1688 has had none.[3]

As for the question of Church and State, Hume's approach was that of the psychologist: the psychology of 'superstition' gave rise to priestly power which naturally gravitated to the side of established government, while 'enthusiasm' had the reverse tendency. This was giving a political dimension to an essay in the *Old Whig* of 9 March 1738, on the parallel between Superstition and Enthusiasm, which is in many ways remarkably similar to Hume's more famous one.[4] The versions of Hume's essay from 1741-60

---

[1] Cf. *London Journal*, 24 November 1733. The fact that the Tories acted against their principles in 1688 is no argument that they did not believe them to be true. As soon as the danger of Popery was over Tories and Jacobites resumed their old principles and invented the distinction of kings *de jure* and *de facto*.

[2] See *London Journal*, 21 July 1733. Why must we have a country party? against what? A country party against the Court will be against the country. See (W. Arnall) *Opposition no proof of Patriotism* (London, 1735), 11, 18. All opposition is not to be discouraged and abolished, but where the Laws rule and Liberty flourishes and where a legal administration prevails, *General Opposition* ought to be out of countenance and cease. As to the Opposition's distinction between court and country, that is as old as men and governments, and will last as long.

[3] 'Osborne' argued that prerogative as defined by Locke and Bolingbroke meant nothing that no ordinary citizen did not possess: a power to act for the good of the people, but never contrary to law and always subject to the limitations of the law. Bolingbroke replied that the Crown was still possessed of several prerogatives sufficient to counterbalance the other parts of the legislature without those additional powers created by our debts and taxes since the Revolution. The dispute is about the king's power – and he has rather an overbalance than otherwise. See *Daily Gazette*, 19 June 1736, *Craftsman*, 3 July 1736. Cf. also *Craftsman*, 2 September 1733.

[4] The writer of the article in the *Old Whig* says that superstition presupposes a meanness of spirit, whereas enthusiasm proceeds chiefly from pride of heart and excess of imagination. The one debases the soul below, the other exalts it above reason. The one submits to anything imposed with a solemn aspect, the enthusiast disdains everything which springs not from himself. (1) produces ignorance through a dread of knowledge, (2) through a disdain of all information. The operations of (2) are sudden and violent, but of short duration; the workings of (1) are insinuating and slow but generally lasting – it spreads through the multitude, while (2) intoxicates only a few. Hence (2) frequently sets up a new religion while (1) always corrupts an old one. (2) is full of vigour at its birth, but when the storm has spent its force, it settles into a calm, uniform (1). Hence most superstitions are the

have a note making a distinction between 'priests' and '*Clergymen*, who are set apart by *the laws* to the care of sacred matters and to the conducting our public devotions with greater decency and order. There is no rank of men more to be respected than the latter.' And in the text of the essay there is a brief passage (inserted 1748, withdrawn 1768) in which the Church of England is said to 'retain a strong mixture of Popish superstition', and therefore 'partakes also in its original constitution, of a propensity to priestly power and dominion; particularly in the respect it exacts to the priest'. Considering what Hume says elsewhere in the essay about the tendency of superstition to steal in gradually and insensibly, 'till at last the priest, having firmly established his authority, becomes the tyrant and disturber of human society...', whereas enthusiasm like a violent storm soon exhausts itself, leaving the air 'more calm and serene than before', there is a hint of menace in the remark quoted which Hume presumably came to feel was not justified, though one should point out that Hume says that as superstition is a considerable ingredient in almost all religions, even the most fanatical, priests are to be found in almost every religious sect. The more powerful the ingredient of superstition, the higher will be the authority of the priesthood (77). He ended with considerable respect for the Church of England. He does not discuss the question of whether the Church of England was acquiring too much land and therefore power, as 'Osborne', for instance, had argued in the *London Journal* (26 February 1732). 'Osborne' says he has the utmost regard for the Church of England, but a higher value for the state: the clergy ought to be restrained from increasing in lands: they are buying great livings and perpetual advowsons all over the kingdom and so in time may get such an overbalance of lands as to become independent of the Crown. T*he Daily Gazetteer*, on 8 November 1735, extended the campaign of the government writers in favour of the superiority of the modern over the ancient constitution to the 'ecclesiastical part' of the constitution: the modern ecclesiastical constitution,

---

dregs of some preceding enthusiasm. (1) is therefore to be considered the more stubborn and permanent evil as (2) is more speedily destructive to society. (1) is the evil most to be guarded against because (2) is more local and temporary, and more easily cured: it being more practicable to bring the mind down from too exalted a condition than to raise it from a depressed stupidity. (1) must consider that he is at least a man and (2) that he is at most a man. I have taken this from the précis in the *Gentleman's Magazine* (Vol. 8, 148): I have not seen the original version in *The Old Whig*. Unless there is something missing from the version in the *Gentleman's Magazine*, what Hume had to add was the political dimension, and the historical examples.

though not perfect, was excellent, and its excellence lay in its absolute dependence on the civil power – speaking politically, and 'not as a divine'. The 'dreadful independency of the Church' was at an end. Hume did not express any such opinion in the essays of 1741–2, except indirectly and fleetingly, but judging from his later views, he would have agreed.[1]

But if the core of the opposition case was, as Bolingbroke argued in the *Dissertation upon Parties*, the independence of Parliament, then Hume should have appeared to the Opposition as little better than a government mercenary, repeating an argument which Bolingbroke regarded as fatal to liberty: that anyone could actually argue in favour of corruption or dependence was a dreadful sign of the decay of public spirit (*Dissertation*, 305). Hume agreed in principle with the ministerialists that some degree and some kind of court influence or parliamentary dependence was inseparable from the very nature of the constitution and necessary to the preservation of our mixed government. At the same time he hinted that the Court might be exaggerating the amount of dependence necessary, because after a calm investigation of the question, the advantage 'might possibly remain to the *country party*'. Instead of undertaking such an investigation, the opposition had destroyed its case by the extremism typical of party zeal. (The root and branch attack on dependence as such necessarily occasioned a whole chain

[1] In *Parties in General* 'the separation of the civil and ecclesiastical powers' is one of the causes which has contributed to render Christendom the scene of religious wars and divisions (61). Hume's views, and clash of opinion with Adam Smith on the question of the virtues of an established church, are well known. In the *Perfect Commonwealth* 'the Presbyterian government is established'; this follows from the republican form of government (506). 'Without the dependence of the clergy on the civil magistrate...it is in vain to think that any free government will ever have security or stability' (511). Cf. *History*, I, 267: 'those dangerous principles, by which the church is totally severed from the state...' Cf. *id*, II, 27. Hume (the occasion being Henry II's quarrel with Becket) says that the union of the civil and ecclesiastical power 'serves extremely' to maintain peace and order in every civilized government. It does not matter whether the supreme magistrate who unites these powers is called prince or prelate, because the 'superior weight which temporal interests commonly bear in the apprehensions of men above spiritual, renders the civil part of his character most prevalent'. Hume's longest discussion of this topic is in the *History*, anno 1521, (IV, 282–4). This is where Hume says that 'every wise legislator' will study to prevent 'the interested diligence of the clergy'. The clerical profession is one of those which it is not in the best interests of the state to leave to itself: the civil magistrate will find that 'he has paid dearly for his pretended frugality in saving a fixed establishment for the priests'. It is in his best interests 'to bribe their indolence'. Cf. VI, 1–2: 'Of all the European churches which shook off the yoke of the papal authority, no one proceeded with so much reason and moderation as the Church of England; an advantage...derived partly from the interposition of the civil magistrate in this innovation, partly from the gradual and slow steps by which the reformation was conducted in that kingdom' (cf. V, 84).

of mistakes about the nature and history of the constitution.) In other words the *Dissertation on Parties* (which Hume here refers to in a footnote), was not the work of a philosopher, as it claimed to be, but the pseudo-philosophical voice of party. (*Independency of Parliament*, 45. *Essays* does not have the footnote: 'See *Dissertation on Parties*, throughout'.)

Presumably also Hume sympathized with the ministerialist writers in so far as they made it their aim to modernize the thinking of the establishment and to stop its supporters perpetually looking over their shoulders. For they can be regarded in this light. For one thing, they complained that the 'patriots' or opposition were constantly preaching the general doctrine of resistance to governments, as though they were still living in the seventeenth century.[1] Although the 'true Whigs' made a great show of claiming that resistance to established government was only a last resort, and that the people never did resort to it unless they absolutely had to etc.,[2] they were always talking about it; Hervey deplored this: in a post-revolutionary establishment, it only helped the Pretender.[3]

Moreover, the ministerialist case against the opposition presupposed a notion of social progress, though this was not fully fledged. The court writers rejected both the Machiavellian moralism which diagnosed a society corrupted by the progress of

---

[1] *London Journal*, 16 November 1734: our patriots seem to infer that because the revolution was founded in resistance, therefore resistance is our constant duty, and the situation in which we ought always to keep ourselves whether oppressed or not, in order to preserve our liberties. This is a doctrine contrary to common sense, because if it were put into practice no government could subsist anywhere. If this general doctrine of resistance is at all times to be preached, and to operate equally under the best and worst kings, it must tend to make the prince and people act as natural enemies.

[2] *Craftsman*, 111, 13: Indeed the greatest advocates for resistance do not contend for it but in cases of the utmost extremity, when fundamentals are concerned.

[3] *Ancient and Modern Liberty stated and compared* (1734). 'When the people are injured and oppressed, let them resist...What I consider is the general doctrine of resistance now so industriously preached and inculcated . . .it must tend to mutual enmity between prince and people and *at this time* it is opening a gate to the ruin of both by making way for the Pretender' (47). Cf. *The Conduct of the Opposition and the Tendency of Modern Patriotism* (1734). This family and government, I am very ready to agree, can only be supported by men acting on Whig principles, but not such as prevailed in the middle of the last century... but the only honest and good Whig principles, those of preserving a limited monarchy in the shape and fashion we now enjoy it' (37). 'When [the *Craftsman*] says that the Act of Settlement is a Contract between King and People and that the latter are the sole judges whether it be broken or not, and that the whole nation now complains of the want of observance of it, what is and must be the inference but that the people now actually are absolved from any allegiance, and are at liberty to take what king they please' (55).

'luxury', and the constitutional primitivism; the conception of a pristine freedom to which the constitution, and society, had to be 'brought back'. We are not more corrupt now than of old, asserted the *London Journal* (1 April 1732); there is more sense, civility, humanity and integrity at this time than in any age before us. Men who practise virtue on a principle of reason must be more virtuous than when they blindly submitted to authority. And liberty, these writers argued, had never existed in the modern sense, or in any sense so far as the people were concerned, before the seventeenth century, and was only properly established in 1688. As the idea of ancient liberty was unhistorical and the 'ancient constitution' historiography of the Opposition an outmoded solecism, there could be no question of a return to the first principles of our Government: it would be a return to civil and ecclesiastical tyranny, and the 'slavery by law established' that had been the fate of most Englishmen for the greater part of their history. The ministerialist writers claimed to be vindicating modern Britain and the Revolution, since when we had been as free as laws can make us, 'or as human nature will perhaps admit of.'[1]

The historical debate went on all through the 1730s in the Opposition and Ministerialist journals and pamphlets, and was summarized blow by blow in the *Gentleman's Magazine*.[2] One can only guess what sort of impression it made on Hume. There are

[1] *Daily Gazetteer*, 5 July 1735. 'Osborne' in his introductory discourse on the *Craftsman's* view of the ancient constitution says his design is to show that New England (as Lord Shaftesbury calls it) is infinitely preferable to Old England, and the modern constitution vastly excels the ancient, and so vindicate the wisdom and justice of the revolution. The line taken by the *Craftsman* makes people indifferent to it. Cf. *Daily Gazetteer*, no. 174 (1736): the Craftsman had been doing the work of Jacobites and Papists. 'This was the reason of my entering into the debate...to vindicate the Revolution.' Cf. *The Parliamentary History*, IX, 401–32. In a debate in 1734 on a motion to repeal the Septennial Act, more than one speaker attacked the Opposition's notion of the ancient constitution and said that if they really understood it, they would not be so anxious to return to it. Sir Thomas Robinson said that he did not understand what was meant by this indefinite term; that he knew of no settled constitution till the Revolution: 'it is from that happy period that I date our having any at all': that there was no such thing as a House of Commons for 200 years after the Conquest or if there was, it seldom met; that Queen Elizabeth's use of Parliaments was hardly exemplary etc. Lord Somerset in favour of the motion was then driven to say that when we now talk of our ancient constitution, we mean as it was settled and reformed at the Revolution: that meant repeal of the Septennial Act.

[2] The more specifically historical aspects of this debate will be dealt with in Part III, Philosophical History, below. I do not give page references to the *Gentleman's Magazine* since my quotations often are taken direct from the Journals themselves and might not be found in the *Magazine*. Anything of interest in the magazine was checked and enlarged by reading the journal in question, as far as possible.

some possible clues. For example, in the essay *That Politics may be reduced to a Science*, in all editions from 1741 to 1770, there occurs, after the phrase 'All absolute governments', this remark: 'and such in great measure was that of England, till the middle of the last century', and in 1748 he added: 'notwithstanding the numerous panegyrics on ancient English liberty'. There is also this phrase in the essay *Of Eloquence*, which dates from 1742: 'during the civil wars, when liberty began to be fully established...' (106). This is not necessarily incompatible with Queen Elizabeth's 'happy' government, in *Liberty of the Press* (9) although 'happy' was omitted in 1748: because Elizabeth's government was happy for the ministerialist writers – though they did not make so much of it as Bolingbroke.

What distinguishes Hume's political essays of 1741/2 from the other political writings of this time is that their point of view is that of the impartial spectator, observing both sides in complete detachment, and even improving their arguments, and the fact that this itself is a political commitment and a lesson in moderation. In the Advertisement to the *Essays Moral and Political* Hume hopes that the reader will approve of his 'moderation and impartiality in my handling political subjects' – public spirit means loving the public and not hating half our countrymen under colour of loving the whole. It is the programme of the *Spectator*, given new power and subtlety, reinforced by experimental philosophy used as political hygiene.

The impartial spectator is seen very strikingly in the opening paragraphs of the essay on *The Independency of Parliament* (withdrawn after 1760, presumably as part of a general process of pruning, to give the essay better balance), in which Hume observes and explains the contrasting political manners and behaviour of members of the two parties: an essay in the psychology of politics. The court party is less dogmatic in conversation, more apt to make concessions, and 'if not perhaps more susceptible of conviction, yet more able to bear contradiction' than their opponents, who regard any attempt at cool impartiality or concessions to their adversaries as mercenary and designing. The country party explain this behaviour as due to public spirit and zeal, which cannot easily endure doctrines pernicious to liberty; the court party quote Shaftesbury's clown, who could only tell who was wrong in a dispute which he did not understand by observing who was the first to get angry. Hume's neutral explanation is that the country party, being at present, and perhaps in most administrations, the more popular, is accustomed to prevail in argument and therefore cannot easily brook opposition: the courtiers are so used to being 'run down by your popular talkers' that they feel obliged by any show of moderation and reciprocate it. In general, the defenders of established and popular opinions are always 'most dogmatical and imperious in their style'; their adversaries affect gentleness and moderation in order to soften prejudice. Freethinkers of all denominations are more moderate than their opponents, as the Deist controversy shows, as were those who defended the 'Moderns' in the controversy between the Ancients and the Moderns in France. (The rather fascinating and perhaps perennially valuable implication is that the popular, country party is a kind of 'establishment', equated not with the free thinkers but their opponents, the established clergy, and not with the Moderns, but the Ancients, a paradox no doubt intended by Hume to pull them up sharp.) Hume hastens to add that his generalization only applies to the 'gentlemen' of the court party: the hired scribblers indulge in scurrility on both sides, the *Gazetteer* as well as *Common Sense*. His essay, he concludes, will illustrate his thesis by showing how the reasoning of the country party concerning the independence of parliament suffers from rigidity and the refusal to make any concessions to their opponents (40–2n).

Hume's conscious straining to be impartial is seen in his sketch of the character of Walpole added to the volume of essays published in January 1742. In the Advertisement he admits that the 'antipathy which every true born Briton naturally bears to Ministers of State' inspired him with some prejudice against Walpole: the impartial reader, if any such there be in posterity, will best be able to correct his mistakes. In the essay itself he hopes that his sketch of a man whose actions have been more earnestly and openly canvassed than those of any other, is impartial enough to be adopted by future historians, and Mossner thinks that posterity has generally accepted it as such, as 'a fine example of the dispassionate moderation sought after by Hume' (*Life of Hume*, 143). But Hume eventually decided that posterity ought not to see it at all, because after 1768, he withdrew it altogether: his dispassionate moderation, one suspects, got the better of his fondness for a 'literary gem' in the style of Tacitus. For this style leaves an impression of harshness and severity, rather than dispassionate impartiality. 'The private character of the man is better than the public...his fortune greater than his fame...He would have been more worthy of his high station had he never possessed it [capax imperii, nisi imperasset], and is better qualified for the second than the first place in any government. His ministry has been more advantageous to his family than to the public...' Hume says that during his time trade has flourished and 'liberty declined'; but that can only mean as much as Hume allows it to mean in the other essays – which is not very much.[1] The only way to see this *Sketch* as a contribution to political moderation and the allaying of party rage is to remember the sheer fury of those who wanted to impeach and destroy Walpole: in such an atmosphere what looks coldly harsh may be regarded as an attempt at a moderating influence as well as an impartial judgement fit for posterity. At any rate, by 1748, Hume was regretting it; he added a footnote to the effect that the only great error of 'this great man' was in not paying off more of the national debt. The *Sketch* itself had become a footnote at the end of the essay on *Politics reduced to a Science*.

This in itself is significant: suggesting that this essay must not be judged in a vacuum, but against the background of the 'party rage' of 1741. The challenging title is notoriously not matched by the weight of the contents, so that the essay has appeared to most commentators and critics as a rather slight performance. Seen in the light of the immediate needs of the political situation in which it was written, however, it seems that what matters is not so much the scientific content, as the application of the scientific or 'philosophical' attitude of mind as a moderating influence in political controversy. What is stressed in this essay is the point of view that is not content to impute blame to individual politicians and rulers, but seeks to understand their actions in the light of the circumstances which condition or determine them: this, for Hume, means largely the prevailing form of government. Applied to the seventeenth century, it is seen in the *Parties of Great Britain*, in so far as Hume implies that the species of government was such that it allowed an 'ambitious, or rather ignorant' king to act in defiance of liberty, thereby giving rise to the two parties by 'a regular and infallible operation'.

The lesson of moderation which Hume wished to drive home in the essay *That Politics may be reduced to a Science* is that where government does not depend very much on the administration, as in free and republican governments as opposed to all absolute

[1] In the answers to the queries of the *Newcastle Journal* of 13 February 1742, printed in the *Scots Magazine* in March, which may or may not be by Hume, the instances of 'the declension of liberty' are said to be 'many, tho' I hope, none fatal; such as, the increase of the civil list, votes of credit, and too large a standing army etc' (Mossner's *Life*, 143-4).

governments (and this is one of the great inconveniences attending that form of government), statesmen and rulers will be good or bad, in their public capacity, according to whether the frame of government, the system of checks and controls, is good or bad, skilfully constructed or not. Politics can be treated as a science to the degree that it is independent of the humours and temperament of particular men; in so far as there is a more or less regular form of government. Since the revolution, the English constitution has been regular, the powers of its various parts accurately defined. Therefore there must be a contradiction in the accusation and panegyric of those who accuse or defend the minister in the extreme manner which our freedom allows, and without which they would not be able to push the argument to extremes. Because if the constitution is as good as Bolingbroke says it is, 'the pride of Britain, the envy of our neighbours etc', it would never have been possible for a weak and wicked minister to govern for twenty years when opposed by the greatest geniuses in the nation, who have enjoyed a complete liberty with which to present their case to the people. And if it is so faulty in its original principles as to allow such a thing to happen, then he cannot be charged with undermining the best constitution in the world; a constitution is only so far good as it provides a remedy against maladministration, and if ours does not do so, then we are 'beholden to any minister who undermines it and affords us an opportunity of erecting a better in its place'. On the other hand, if, as Walpole's defenders hotly assert, the constitution is as good or even better now than when he assumed office, then the prospect of his departure cannot be so disastrous; and if the constitution is very bad, 'then so extraordinary a jealousy on account of changes is ill-placed...public affairs, in such a government, must necessarily go to confusion, by whatever hands they are conducted...'

There is more than one lesson of moderation or type of lesson in these essays. There is the doctrine of circumstances, just mentioned; there is the warning at the end of the essay on *Whether the British Monarchy inclines*, that republicanism in Britain would be such as to lead to absolute monarchy via anarchy; there is the political style, the Addisonian insistence on good manners and the civilized conduct of literary and political controversy, the calm balancing of pros and cons.

There was finally the argument that it was not Walpole's administration that was endangering the constitution, but the heat and violence of party strife; the fact that the controversies were being treated as though they were a matter of life and death for the constitution: men were contending as if *pro aris et focis* (a favourite expression of Bolingbroke's, and, for example the heading of an article on liberty of the press in the *Craftsman* in 1728 (III, 228) (*Politics a Science*, penultimate §). The mixed monarchy of Britain was a form of government which called especially for the virtue of moderation, all the more so at a time when there were still 'very considerable remains' of a party which did not accept the present regime. And all the more so as the English, so Hume seems to have believed, were peculiarly prone to excess and extremism.[1]

[1] Cf. the dialectic of England's religious history, added to the essay *Of National Characters* in 1753/4: 'our ancestors, a few centuries ago were sunk into the most abject superstition; last century they were inflamed with the most furious enthusiasm, and are now settled into the most cool indifference with regard to religious matters, that is to be found in any nation in the world' (211). In the *History* Hume says that it is obvious from many incidents that in 1625, 'of all European nations, the British were at that time, and till long after, sunk into the lowest and most odious bigotry' (*Pelican Classics*, 264). This was later changed to: 'the most under the influence of that religious spirit which tends rather to inflame bigotry than increase peace and mutual charity' (VII, 73). In upholding the balance of power, too, the English have been too passionate, 'more possessed with the ancient Greek spirit of jealous emulation, than actuated by the prudent views of modern politics', pushing war with France too far, from 'obstinacy and passion' and 'imprudent vehemence' (*Balance of Power*, 345-6).

7
The primacy of political institutions

What has just been seen in action in the essay *That Politics may be reduced to a Science* is a cardinal principle of Hume's science of politics: the importance of the constitution or form of government in determining human behaviour in politics and national character. 'How could *politics* be a science, if laws and forms of government had not a uniform influence upon society?' (*Enquiry concerning Human Understanding*, Section VIII, Part I, 90).

For this, he was taken to task by John Brown in his *Estimate of the Manners and Principles of the Times* (Vol. I, 1757, Vol. II, 1758). Brown's political science derives from Machiavelli, 'the greatest political reasoner upon facts that hath appeared in any age or country', and Montesquieu, the only other writer who ever fully comprehended and penetrated the secret springs of government and who owed much to the *Discourses on Livy*. Political science meant ceasing to regard public misfortunes as due to the 'particular and accidental conduct of individuals' and searching out the 'general causes' (I, 12–13): for Brown that meant studying the manners of the ruling class, or rather those 'predominant' ones that affect the 'permanency or duration' of the state, which is his main concern in the *Estimate* (I, 24–5, II, 105). Political writers had generally attributed the decline and fall of states to some defect in the original constitution of their laws, but this, to the extent that it is generally affirmed and understood, seems an entire mistake. Thus, in contrast to Hume, he says that it is only manners and the principle of honour that give the French many of the blessings of liberty in a despotic political constitution. Bolingbroke and Hume, the first of them esteemed a capital writer in politics, have written whole systems of policy, without so much as mentioning, or seeming to regard, this ruling circumstance. He classes both among 'the many superficial pretenders to the political science' who totally overlook the state of the manners and principles of a commonwealth (II, 20–2).

This seems a bit unfair to Bolingbroke, but Hume at any rate was wholly untouched by that Machiavellian moralism, or the political pathology concerned with the degree of corruption and lack of public spirit in a state, which was so all-pervasive in eighteenth-century Britain, and which took many forms, more or less sophisticated. When tempted to talk of Hume's 'social pessimism', it is worth remembering that he never fell for this form of it, fashionable as it was: his awareness of the precarious nature of civilization is something quite different: a much more salutary mental and moral hygiene. He said that under Walpole, learning had 'gone to ruin': not manners and morals. He shows some concern for 'excess of refinement' in literature, but not in society, 'degeneration of taste' but not of manners (*Of Simplicity and Refinement in Writing*). 'Where riches are the chief idol, corruption, venality, rapine prevail', but also 'arts, manufactures, commerce, agriculture flourish' (*Enquiry concerning Morals*, Section VI, Part II, conclusion). It is a passing remark, a piece of social observation, and has nothing to do with the problem of decadence. In the perfect commonwealth 'the first year in every century is set apart for correcting all inequalities which time may have produced in the representative' (508): this is as near as Hume ever comes to the notion of a return to the first principles of the constitution – nothing is said about a restoration of manners, because the question of manners is irrelevant: the ideal republic will function in any state of manners, and will last, if not literally for ever, because all states have their term like everything mortal, at least 'for many ages'; it is even said to be feasible in a large state like France or England, and presumably therefore in an advanced stage of commercial civilization: a very unorthodox speculation in the eighteenth century. Hume has virtually no affinities with the Machiavellian moralists and corruption mongers of his age.

Thus, for example, the fate of the ancient Britons was not, as in the 'monkish historians', due to 'luxury', but to 'cowardice or improvident counsels' (*History*, I, 20).[1] Nor was the Norman conquest due to the general corruption and lack of public spirit of the people and the luxury and private factions of the nobility and gentry, as in Carte (*General History of England*, I, 382), and Guthrie (*op. cit.*, I, 325). What some see as the corruption of a 'simplicity of manners, so highly and often so injudiciously extolled', ought says Hume, to be regarded as an advantageous contact with foreigners

---

[1] This is a criticism not only of the 'monkish historians', but, e.g. of Guthrie, who is concerned with the 'degree of degeneracy' of the Britons. The 'last crisis' of their virtue, due to 'the loss of public virtue in private luxury and personal indolence', was 'the third and last era of British degeneracy'. W. Guthrie, *General History of England*, I, 37, 40.

(*History*, I, 167). They were totally conquered by the Normans because the Normans were more civilized, and because there were 'several vices in the Anglo-Saxon constitution, which rendered it difficult for the English to defend their liberties in so critical an emergency'. Hume says the people had lost all national pride and spirit by their recent and long subjection to the Danes: he does not say they were corrupted by luxury (I, 308).

In Hume's science of politics, political institutions and forms of government were the crucial 'moral causes' and determining agents. In *National Characters*, 'the nature of the government' comes first in Hume's list of examples of 'moral' (as opposed to 'physical') causes (202–3). Thus, as has been seen, whereas Bolingbroke traced the rise of parties to James I's importing of new-fangled notions of divine right into England, for Hume 'the species of government gave birth to them, by a regular and infallible operation'. And it was 'the unstable form of the constitution' which gave rise to 'the turbulent dispositions of the people derived from it' which made the situation of the medieval kings so 'perilous', a situation for which a man like Edward II was wholly unqualified (*History*, III, 2).

The form of government is the crucial factor in Hume's account of the origin of the arts and sciences; they do not emerge naturally and spontaneously, but can only take their rise in free governments which infallibly produce laws and the necessary security. And the difference between England, where the chief source of distinction is present opulence, and most continental countries, where it depends on inherited wealth and titles and birth, is due, in the final analysis, to the different types of government which 'vary the utility' of the different customs (*Enquiry concerning Morals*, Section VI, Part II, conclusion). The prejudice in favour of birth, being favourable to military virtue, is more suited to monarchies, the other being the chief spur to industry, agrees better with a republican government. But, as he says in the essay *Of National Characters*, it is difficult to generalize about the English national character, because 'the English, of any people in the universe, have the least of a national character, unless this very singularity may pass for such'. This again is due to the form of government – a mixture of monarchy, aristocracy and democracy – to the mixed nature of the people in authority, 'composed of gentry and merchants', and to 'the great liberty and independency which every man enjoys' which 'allows him to display the manners peculiar to him' (212). At the beginning of the seventeenth century, on the other hand, when the government was more like a simple monarchy, the English character was more uniform. 'The manners of the nation were agreeable to the monarchical government which prevailed; and contained not that strange mixture which at present distinguishes England from all other countries' (*History*, VII, 15). The vital factor in this example of a changing national character is the form of government. And in a large country like China, one finds 'the greatest uniformity of character imaginable', due to the establishment there for many centuries of a 'very extensive government...the same national character commonly follows the authority of government to a precise boundary; and upon crossing a river or...mountain, one finds a new set of manners, with a new government' (*National Characters*, 209). In the essay on the *Standard of Taste* he thinks it worth remarking that differences of taste will be found 'even where the persons have been educated under the same government and have early imbibed the same prejudices' (231).

But if the constitution has a great effect in determining manners, manners have not the same influence on the proper functioning or otherwise of a constitution. Correctly modelled constitutions function independently of the manners of men, and the goodness or badness of rulers, making it the interest even of bad men to act for the public good (*Politics a Science*, 14). The science of politics was concerned with political machinery, checks and controls. And the political scientist, in contriving such a system of checks and controls, assumes that everyone is governed by self-interest. It is a just *political* maxim that every man must be supposed a knave, a maxim which is true in politics though false in fact, because of the distinction between human nature in public and private life. Men acting in groups or political parties consider only the interests of the party; every senate or court is determined by the majority and the majority of men are self interested; so that the psychology of political man is relatively simple and uniform (*Independency of Parliament*, 39–43). This 'natural depravity of mankind', that is, of political man, being taken for granted, means that the political scientist is not concerned with manners and morals, but with the balancing of separate interests and the skilful division of power in order to best secure the public interest. There is a distinction between public virtue and private virtue: the former does not depend on the latter, on the manners and morals of a nation, but on well-conceived and well constructed political machinery.

That institutions not manners are the primary, if not exclusive, concern of the political scientist, is proved by the fact that 'one part of the same republic may be wisely conducted, and another weakly, by the very same men, merely on account of the difference of the forms and institutions by which these parts are regulated'. In Genoa, for example, the bank of St George, 'which had become a considerable part of the people' was honestly and wisely administered, while the rest of the state was full of sedition, tumult and disorder. The stability and wisdom of the Venetian government through so many ages can only be ascribed to the form of government; while the ruin of the Athenian and Roman republics was due to 'defects in the original constitution'. The most illustrious period of Roman history, 'considered in a political view', when the balance of the constitution was working most effectively, was an age of rampant immorality; 'so depraved in private life were that people, whom in their histories we so much admire'. They were probably more virtuous during the time of the Triumvirates, 'when they were tearing their common country to pieces... merely for the choice of tyrants'. Thus 'the ages of greatest public spirit are not always most eminent for private virtue. Good laws may beget order and moderation in the government, where the manners and customs have instilled little humanity or justice into the tempers of men' (*Politics a Science*, 22). The downfall of the Roman republic is the knockout argument of those who denounce luxury and refinement in the arts: 'all the Latin classics whom we peruse in our infancy, are full of these sentiments, and universally ascribe the ruin of their state to the arts and riches imported from the East... But it would be easy to prove that these writers mistook the cause of the disorders in the Roman state, and ascribed to luxury and the arts what really proceeded from an ill-modelled government...' (*Refinement in the Arts*, 282). Although 'the maxims of ancient politics contain, in general, so little humanity and moderation that it seems superfluous to give any particular reason for the acts of violence committed at any particular period', he cannot forbear observing that the bloody violence of the Roman factions in the last years of the republic was the necessary and inevitable result of laws 'so absurdly contrived that they obliged the heads of parties to have recourse to these extremities'. Because the laws did not provide for capital punishment and the most criminal and dangerous citizens could only be banished, 'it became necessary, in the revolutions of party, to draw the sword of private vengeance'. Excessive lenity in the laws 'naturally produces cruelty and barbarity' (*Populousness of Ancient Nations*, 412). And the cruelty of the Roman emperors was due to the fact that the government was a mixture of despotism and liberty, with the despotism prevailing; it was chiefly excited by their jealousy of the great men of Rome who bore with impatience the dominion of a family which shortly before was in no way superior to their own (*Liberty of the Press*, 10).

This idea that the fate of nations depends on the 'modelling' of its government was related to the classical notion, rejected by Ferguson and other leading social theorists of eighteenth-century Scotland, that political institutions are made by 'Legislators and Founders of States'. As Hume says in *Politics may be reduced to a Science*, legislators ought to make constitutional laws that will last for ever: 'provide a system of laws to regulate the administration of public affairs to the latest posterity. Effects will always correspond to causes; and wise regulations, in any commonwealth, are the most valuable legacy that can be left to future ages' (22). Hence the need for a science providing maxims of universal validity, such as that a hereditary monarch is better than an elective one, a nobility without vassals is the best form of aristocracy, a people voting by their representatives the best form of democracy; hence the value of the model of a perfect commonwealth which can be used as an idea or standard, 'that we may be able to bring any real constitution or form of government as near it as possible, by such gentle alterations and innovations as may not give too great disturbance to society' (500).

This notion of a science of politics, emphasizing the importance of the fabric and modelling of political institutions, and dissociating that from the question of manners and morals throws a question mark over three great commonplaces of British eighteenth-century political thought: (1) that without virtue there can be no liberty, and without liberty no virtue – meaning political liberty, free or republican institutions; (2) closely allied to this, that political science is primarily concerned with the manners and morals of a nation, because what is to be done will depend on the state of its moral health, the degree of public spirit or 'corruption'; (3) that power follows property, a maxim ascribed to Harrington, as (2) was ascribed to Machiavelli.

It has been seen that Hume's political scientist is not concerned with the moral health of a people at all because the fate of nations depends on their institutions, not on manners and morals. As to the balance of property, this too was subordinate to the modelling of the constitution; and so the maxim that power follows property is not universally true. If it were, the British government would now be republican: there could have been no restoration of the monarchy in 1660 – Hume uses this event as a classical instance of the danger of formulating general principles in politics; Harrington was proved wrong almost immediately after he had published his theory (*Whether the British government inclines*, 48). In fact, 'a government may endure for several ages, though the balance of power and the balance of property do not coincide'. Power follows property, only if the original framework of the constitution allows it to happen: if the original constitution allows any share of power, however small, to an order of men who possess a large share of the property it is easy for them to gradually extend their authority and bring the balance of power to coincide with that of property. This was the case with the House of Commons in England. But an order of men who had no original share of power would never be able to usurp any; the public being commonly much attached to their ancient form of government, would not stand for it. Opinion therefore and the form of the constitution are more fundamental than the balance of property (*Principles of Government*, 31–2).

III Philosophical History

8
The History of England: philosophical history as establishment history

(i) *Ancient constitutionalism: Rapin, Bolingbroke, the government journalists, Lyttleton, Blackstone, Guthrie, Hurd*

There was a widespread belief in the republic of letters in the first half of the eighteenth century that the division of parties made it impossible for Englishmen to write their own history impartially. In *L'Esprit des Lois* this is given as a general principle of social science.[1] It seems to have been fairly widely agreed also that the best and most impartial general history of England was that of Rapin, a foreigner writing for foreigners baffled by the party conflict which had impinged so dramatically on the history of Europe in the last years of the reign of Queen Anne.[2] Rapin's *History* was not only regarded as authoritative by Bolingbroke, it was also acclaimed by the *London Journal*.[3]

---

[1] 'Dans les monarchies extrêmement absolues, les historiens trahissent la vérité, parce qu'ils n'ont pas la liberté de la dire: dans les États extrêmement libres, ils trahissent la vérité à cause de leur liberté même, qui, produisant toujours des divisions, chacun devient aussi esclave des préjugés de sa faction, qu'il le seroit d'un despote.' This is the penultimate paragraph of Chapter 27 of Book XIX. Hume thought that if there was more candour and sincerity in ancient historians, but less exactness and care than the moderns, this was owing to the 'speculative factions' that were a unique feature of modern history (*Populousness of Ancient Nations*, 419n). In the essay on *Parties in General*, parties from *principle*, especially abstract speculative principle, are 'known only to modern times', and are described as perhaps the most extraordinary and unaccountable phenomenon that has yet appeared in human affairs (58). Christianity is to blame, as Hume says here and in the *Natural History of Religion*.

[2] There is a monograph on Rapin by Nelly Girard d'Albissin: *Un précurseur de Montesquieu: Rapin-Thoyras* (Paris, 1969). As the title indicates, this is mainly concerned with Rapin's political thought. References to Rapin's *History* are to the translation by Tindal, in 15 vols, 1726-31.

[3] This 'Essay (28 October 1732) on the usefulness of History, particularly Rapin's History', contains a passage on historical evidence which is so Hume-like as to be worth quoting. We cannot arrive at certainty in history, says the writer, but one can arrive at probability. The one rule is never follow any historian beyond the pillars of probability, for the credibility of the things related must be considered; we must never give up the credibility of things to the credibility of any person on earth, because 'we are more sure that all men and human affairs were ever much the same as they are now, than we can be that any man speaks truth'. Bolingbroke's use

It was Rapin's recognition of the existence of the Whig and Tory parties as the dominant fact of modern British politics, and his acute awareness of its implications for the study of English history, that was largely responsible for the exceptionally sophisticated critical tone and professional approach of his *History*. Since the parties which arose in the seventeenth century are still with us, there is 'scarce any hopes of seeing an impartial history of England, from the beginning of King James the First's reign, to our time. Let a historian turn which way so ever he pleases, he will be looked upon as partial, by one or other of the two factions' (IX, 377). This applied not only to the seventeenth-century conflict itself, but to all those historical topics which had become controversial as a result. Rapin's plan, therefore, ideally, was to present the reader with the facts and the arguments on both sides, so that he could draw his own conclusions (e.g.: IX, 607–8, X, 95, 211, XI, 401). Hence the large amount of documentary material embodied wholesale in the text and breaking the flow of the narrative for pages on end; hence his awareness of the history of the historiography of a topic like the reign of James I (IX, 377); hence the critical bibliographical essay at the beginning of Volume XI ('Considerations on the Authors who have writ the History of the Reign of Charles I'); hence his candid confessions of what are merely his own conjectures, concerning, for example, the rise of the Independents (XII, 290–2). The reader is constantly reminded that there are difficulties of interpretation, of the need for care in handling the evidence, and of apparatus, including (in 1621) the sort of mock debate giving a summary of the royalist and the popular case (IX, 498–502), which Hume took over and made peculiarly his own, and Rapin's 'scheme' for the interpretation of the reign of Charles I, which is not that of the parliamentary nor that of the royalist historians (XI, 15).

All this apparatus of critical impartiality, however, rests on the presupposition which Oldmixon made absolutely explicit when he

of Rapin did not do the latter much good in the eyes of government writers later. In the *Daily Gazetteer* of 9 August 1735, 'Walsingham' accused the Craftsman of knowing little history except what he has gleaned from the dullest of all dull writers, Rapin, who had an honest intention and love of liberty to recommend him, but wrote without genius or perfect knowledge of the subject. In his *Essays on British Antiquities* (1747), Kames described Rapin as 'a most judicious historian', but frequently at a loss through want of a sufficient knowledge of the constitution of England (126). Robert Wallace said that Rapin 'appears the most impartial of our historians' (Papers of Robert Wallace in Edinburgh University Library, Laing II, 97, No. 5, p. 11, a paper entitled an address to the Jacobites of Scotland, written soon after the '45 but never published).

said, in a *Critical History of England* whose object was to counter the dangerous effects of Echard's *History*, which according to Oldmixon, vindicated or extenuated all King Charles the First's invasions of the rights and liberties of the subject, that to write on the side of the constitution is to be impartial. For party is what separates and divides itself from the public interest, that is, the religion, laws and liberties of our country.[1]

For, according to Rapin, the only way to make sense of the course of events leading to the Civil War, and in particular the fact – not properly explained by Clarendon or any English historian hitherto – that a minority of Presbyterians (for Rapin, Puritans and Presbyterians are the same thing, x, 258–9) was eventually able to get control of the House of Commons, thus precipitating the war, was to realize that the first two Stuarts held and propagated principles of monarchical government and hereditary right which were entirely new to the constitution, and when applied, wholly destructive of it (IX, 236–7, 252 – 'James I's notion of the English Constitution was very different from what had passed for current hitherto'). In this, there was no difference between James I and Charles I: 'there was nothing new but the King's person'; 'Charles I trod exactly in the steps of the King his father' (x, 1, 7, cf. 117–18). Both kings set out from the very beginning of their reigns to subvert the constitution and set up a despotic power; 'had formed a design to establish in England an arbitrary government': if this is not taken for granted, it would be impossible 'to understand fully' the reign of Charles I, and particularly the second part (XI, 140).

The English constitution was such that the powers of the king and the privileges of the commons could never be accurately determined. They do not owe their origin to the laws and can neither be limited nor enlarged but as warranted by precedents, but as these precedents are so contrary to one another, there is no way of forming any sure and certain rules. The question is made still more difficult by the ambiguity of the terms 'parliament' and 'prerogative'. Since, therefore, the bounds of prerogative and privilege cannot be defined, the only way to make the constitution work is for both sides to avoid the issue altogether, to 'avoid as a rock the engaging in such disputes', and this had always been the

---

[1] Oldmixon: *The critical History of England ecclesiastical and civil* (London 1728), 148. This is the third edition. The first is 1724. The remark about Echard comes from the Preface, but in the advertisement at the end of the book, Oldmixon says that the publication of Echard's and Clarendon's Histories was designed to bring disgrace on the glorious Revolution.

policy of the wisest and best kings of England, to the great advantage and prosperity of themselves and their people. 'A wise and prudent King of England, who is acquainted with his own interest, will never quarrel with his parliament' (IX, 494–8, X, 6) – for no absolute monarch can be as powerful and wealthy as a king of England who makes himself beloved by his subjects, and to do that is easy: he need only respect the constitution and observe the laws. 'For supposing a king of England should render himself absolute, he would never be able by oppression and violence to get from his people what he may draw from them with their consent, by submitting to the laws and constitution of the government' (X, 246–7). The catastrophic reign of Richard II shows that 'in a government such as that of England, all the endeavours used by the king to make himself absolute, are but so many steps towards his downfall' (IV, 453).

This is the lesson of Rapin's *History*, and it is brought home by the contrast between the reigns of Elizabeth and her successors. Elizabeth 'caused the English to enjoy' a state of almost unprecedented felicity (IX, 225);[1] in the reign of James I, ''tis certain England never flourished less' (IX, 612). The maxims of government adopted by Elizabeth to gain the love of her subjects, as catalogued by Rapin (economy, impartial administration of justice and so on – VIII, 261–3), are not in fact incompatible with an enlightened despotism or absolute monarchy as such, but what he stresses is that Elizabeth made no attempt on the liberties of Englishmen as traditionally received; not thwarting the national will meant this especially – that was why she was so popular and successful. '...the English in her reign were the happiest people under the sun. They saw no designs upon their liberties...' (IX, 215–16). In such a ruler, even considerable stretching of the royal prerogative will be overlooked.

What was new about the Stuart kings was that their stretching of the royal prerogative was systematic and a matter of principle: the application of a theory that monarchy admitted of no degrees, and according to which all kings were equally absolute (X, 5). They therefore assumed powers never before claimed or exercised by any English king – only Richard II had declared that a king of

---

[1] 'Let a man turn over the whole History of England, and he will find no reign wherein Justice was administered so impartially, or the subjects enjoyed their privileges more peaceably, or were freer from wars abroad and at home, or from extraordinary taxes and impositions, in a word, wherein the kingdom was more flourishing' (IX, 23). The Eleven Years Tyranny of Charles I was marked by 'the decay of trade' (XI, 18).

'THE HISTORY OF ENGLAND'

England could act contrary to the laws. It followed that parliament was a royal concession, entirely at the king's disposal to summon or not as he pleased; this was going further even than Henry VIII, 'the most absolute of all the kings of England since William the Conqueror' (XI, 112), who was able to manage a parliament rendered entirely submissive by religion, but never claimed to base his authority on such principles (IX, 323). 'Religion was the sole cause' of Henry's power, because the king steered a middle course between adherents of the old religion and supporters of the new, and both parties 'striving to make him their friend, there followed for him an authority which none of his predecessors had ever enjoyed and which he would not have been able to usurp in any other circumstances without endangering his crown'. But Henry did nothing contrary to law; he made use of his power to get such laws passed as he wanted (VII, 498-9).

It was the new plan of monarchy, proceeding from the dubious claim to hereditary right of James I, that gave rise to the two parties later known as Whig and Tory.[1] And the royal policy of treating everyone who opposed these innovations as a 'Puritan' or 'Presbyterian', whether they were actually so or not (IX, 396, X, 283, XI, 61-2, 518-19) drove the 'political Puritans' who were concerned with political grievances and whose aim was to restore the government 'according to its true and ancient constitution' (XI, 19), into the arms of the 'religious Puritans', who wanted to subvert the (monarchical) constitution in order to achieve their religious objectives. And after the political grievances had been redressed in 1641, the Presbyterians were able to work on the majority's fear and distrust of Charles I (XI, 193-8), and 'this distrust was the stumbling block and immediate cause of the war between the king and parliament' (XI, 48).

This was Rapin's 'scheme' to explain the events leading to the civil war and commonwealth. No system he claimed, without this, could do so 'so as to satisfy the impartial and unbiassed' (XI, 518).

[1] 'This supposed hereditary right, and the consequences drawn from thence, were the spring and fountain of the divisions which began in this reign and which continued during the three following reigns. This very thing likewise gave birth to the Tory and Whig factions, who worry one another to this day' (IX, 237). '... James I, resolving to assert this supposed hereditary right, was the first cause of the troubles which afflicted England, and which are not yet ceased' (IX, 239). 'It was properly in this third parliament [1621] that two parties were formed, one for the court, the other for the people... these were the same parties which are still in being... James I gave birth to these two parties... by the haughty manner wherein he would have established prerogatives, which perhaps would never have been called in question, had he not built them upon principles that opened a door to arbitrary power' (IX, 452-3).

James and Charles were the innovators and aggressors[1] and their attempt to 'alter the government' (XI, 112), was wholly responsible for the subversion of the constitution which the Independents, who remained concealed in the Presbyterian party till the time was ripe, were eventually able to bring about.

This 'scheme' presupposes the ancient and continuous existence of some sort of parliamentary constitution as old as the monarchy, even if parliament as we know it cannot be proved to be of great antiquity. Rapin was not competent to defend the more exposed salients of ancient constitutionalism, so heavily attacked by Brady,[2] nor did he regard these controversial topics as very important or relevant to the rights and wrongs of the conflict in the seventeenth century. He makes a show of giving both sides of the question (often at considerable length), and confessing the difficulties involved, but he did not have the knowledge or expertise to be able to do this very convincingly. What most seriously weakens his whole account is the almost unbroken silence with respect to feudalism, feudal law and tenure. He refuses to discuss the 'original of fees', because it would lead him too far, and because there is nothing peculiar to England about it (II, 197); and the next (and last) mention of the subject is when we are told that William the Conqueror 'seized upon all the baronies and all the fiefs of the Crown in general' of the English, and distributed them among the Normans (II, 252). That is all. Tindall comes to the rescue here, and refers the reader to the recently published essay of St Amand, where it could be seen how the feudalism which Brady had employed in the royalist cause could be used to bridge the chasm of the Norman Conquest, or rather, to argue it away altogether, and thus restore the continuity of the ancient constitution (II, 141–3n, 174–7n).[3] Rapin says that 'the Normans introduced a

[1] If we consider what passed in the first two parliaments of James' reign, 'the commons did not begin to attack the king, but the king himself gave the parliament cause to complain' (IX, 447).

[2] The classic study of these controversies is J. G. A. Pocock's *The Ancient Constitution and the Feudal Law* (Cambridge, 1957). It, alas, does not carry the story beyond the Revolution, which, admittedly, is anti-climax. See also S. Kliger, *The Goths in England* (1952).

[3] St Amand's *Historical Essay on the Legislative Power of England* (the version used here is that printed in Vol. II of *A Complete Collection of the Lords' Protests*, London, 1767) argues that the feudal law and tenure, which was 'as solemn an original contract as it is possible to devise' (xxv) prevailed in Saxon England, and the Saxon government, which equalled or even excelled all others in preserving the people in a real and unbounded liberty, the only end of civil government (xxxiii) – freedom consisting in the being bound to no laws but such as one has given one's consent to (xcv), was derived from it, as in the rest of Europe: or at least, if not in its per-

new system of law into the kingdom', but he does not explain what this was (III, 150); what William actually did to the laws of England is far from clear in Rapin's brief account – 'he made several innovations in the English laws' (II, 295); as to his title by conquest, Rapin follows Echard very closely (Rapin II, 303, Echard *History of England* (1707), 152): it is an uncertain matter, like that of the Emperor Augustus, but William certainly acted like a conqueror (II, 256) and deprived the English of their estates, and whatever he and his sons did to the English laws, it was not long before the Norman lords, having 'put on the English genius, wholly addicted to liberty', and become completely anglicised, feeling their possessions insecure under arbitrary kings, were demanding their revival. What gave them a plausible right to do so, which otherwise was dubious, were the solemn promises of Henry I, Henry II and Stephen to restore the Saxon laws (III, 221–2). Not feudalism, but the confirmation of the laws of Edward the Confessor, is the context of Magna Carta in Rapin. He gives the full text, but does not discuss it, except to say that the barons compelled John to give up all the prerogatives which his predecessors had enjoyed since the Conqueror (III, 157), and that it was the foundation of English liberty henceforth (III, 227). As for the question of the commons in Parliament: the Saxon government was a mixture of monarchy and aristocracy: the question as to whether it was partly democratical as well is a knotty problem, says Rapin, who gives the arguments for and against at some length in order to show that they are unsatisfactory on either side, and also because the question is important to some, though he cannot agree, unless it is important to be able to show that the royalist argument that the existence and privileges of the commons were due to concessions on the king's part cannot be conclusively proved (II, 142–3, 163–74). Rapin favours the late origin of the commons in the parliament of de Montfort – the famous 49 Henry III. The whole question is full of uncertainties, but what is indisputable is that the commons enjoyed the privilege of sending representatives to parliament in the reign of Edward I, and have continued to do so ever since (IV, 2–3, cf. III, 438–4, 461, 466, 492

> fection, yet sufficiently so to prove that the Norman Conquest – which gave William no right *a priori*, nor did he act as if it had (Ch. III) – made no real difference to the Legislature which continued to include representatives of the boroughs as before. As all proprietors of land were represented, 'the commons as now understood was ever part of the legislature' (lx); that is the gist of St Amand's thesis, without pursuing him any further into such thickets as the meaning of the word 'baron' etc.

and XIV, 404. The last reference is from Rapin's *A Dissertation on the Origin of the Government of England*, which is a translation of the *Dissertation sur les Whigs et les Tories*, first published in 1717. Tindall put the reader firmly back on the rails of sound ancient constitutionalism by referring him to Petit, Tyrell and Hody (III, 466n)).

This still left Rapin with some two hundred years before the accession of James I of firmly settled constitution and 'uninterrupted possession of the privileges of Magna Carta', to which the people of England were so accustomed 'that it seemed impossible to make any alteration without throwing the kingdom into confusion' (XIV [*Dissertation, op. cit.*], 405); that is to say, a parliamentary constitution for all practical purposes the same as in Rapin's day. That he thought so is made clear enough by his critique of the defects and dangers of the parliamentary constitution as such: in pointing them out he makes no distinction between the fifteenth, sixteenth and eighteenth centuries. If the constitution was not settled and regular, there would have been no point in using it to illustrate a present weakness, or comparing Richard II's technique in subverting it with that of the Stuarts (IV, 434).[1]

But in essentials English freedom was at least as old as the Saxon constitution. 'The maxim that no laws are binding but what the whole nation has consented to, has all along been looked upon in England, as the foundation of liberty and the basis of government' (II, 180). As Tindal said in his dedication of his translation of this volume, all who are not blinded by prejudice may here be convinced, that our liberties are interwoven in the original frame of our government.

Bolingbroke made much use of Rapin's *History* in giving the opposition case against Walpole a historical dimension. Rapin had

[1] In IV, 433-4, Rapin points out that while the institution of parliament is the only support of the liberty of the people, it is liable to become very dangerous when influenced by popular factions or the cabals of an ambitious prince; and the evil is all the harder to cure, because what is done by parliament is supposed to be done with the unanimous consent of the whole nation. It can only be cured by equally violent means; this is one of the principal causes of the domestic troubles which have all along afflicted England more than any other European state. Cf. V, 71-2. Henry IV's packing a parliament leads to an anticipation of Montesquieu. 'This is a thing of so fatal a consequence that one may venture to affirm, the liberty of the English will no longer have a being than whilst the privilege of freely electing their representatives in Parliament stands inviolated.' Cf. VIII, 30-1. Since MPs are not given instructions by their constituents, a Parliament does not necessarily reflect the general will – a favourite criticism of Rapin's. The context here is the reign of Edward VI: the Court did its utmost to get members elected who would be of the same mind: this is practised 'even at this day and will always be so, until some way be found out to remedy this inconvenience' (cf. 143).

stressed the ever present danger in the British constitution of the corruption of parliament by court influence; he had also made the point that since the king has no real interest in trying to make himself absolute, for this in the English government is merely self-defeating, the only thing that may make him lose the advantages he may naturally draw from the constitution are the pride and avarice of favourites and ministers (x, 246-7), and in the *Dissertation*, it is the Duke of Buckingham, not James I, who bears the blame as 'the first author of the troubles which have so long infested England, and continue to infest it to this day' (xiv, 406). Much of Bolingbroke's English history is diluted Rapin (whom he frequently quotes), converted or abridged into the spirit of liberty versus spirit of faction thesis, with the Harringtonian infusion which is entirely lacking in Rapin.[1]

Bolingbroke's use of English history set off a renewed controversy over the ancient constitution, this time inside the Whig camp, between 'new' and 'old' Whigs, but as in the Convocation controversy at the turn of the century, Atterbury versus Wake and Kennett, it was the opposition who appealed to the ancient constitution.[2]

Bolingbroke was no antiquarian; he may have been influenced by Rapin's hesitations. The ancient constitutionalism in the more technical sense of his *Remarks on the History of England* is a thin and rather vague Norman Yoke thesis. We are told that 'the principles of the Saxon commonwealth were... very democratical', that the Witan, 'composed of the king, the lords, and the Saxon freemen... that original sketch of a British Parliament' examined and controlled the conduct of the kings. William, though it may be disputed whether he was strictly a conqueror, 'imposed many new laws and customs' and 'made very great alterations in the whole

[1] I call it and have throughout called it 'Harringtonian', because I am adopting the standpoint of Bolingbroke and his contemporaries. Professor Pocock would call it 'neo-Harringtonian'. See 'Machiavelli, Harrington and English Political Ideologies in the 18th century' in J. G. A. Pocock, *Politics, Language and Time* (1972). Anyone who knows *Oceana* moderately well will recognize echoes in much of what follows. I am not concerned with Harrington's influence on these writers.

[2] Atterbury found it convenient to deny that there had been any change in the constitution in Henry III's reign, whereas Kennett argued that that was when commoners first had the right to be constantly summoned to parliament, which had hitherto been a council of King and great barons. The crucial factor in the development was a diffusion of property: liberty and property kept equal paces, they are the twins that have lived and will die together. The commons were summoned as proprietors, 'not barely as the people of England'. White Kennett: *Ecclesiastical Synods and Parliamentary Convocations* (1701), 225-7. See G. V. Bennett: *White Kennett 1660-1728* (1957), 33-42, 166-7.

model of government', and, as did his two sons after him, ruled on many occasions like an absolute monarch. 'Yet neither he, nor they could destroy the old constitution; because neither he nor they could extinguish the old spirit of liberty' (52-4), of which Magna Carta was a triumph.[1] For two and a half centuries after the Conquest, the 'present constitution of our government' was forming itself; 'a rough building raised out of the demolitions which the Normans had made, and upon the solid foundations laid by the Saxons'. The 'commonalty had little or no share in the legislature and made no figure in the government', but numbers were on their side, the spirit of liberty was diffused through the whole mass, and in all the disputes between king, lords and clergy it was necessary to apply to them, so that although king, lords and clergy were enemies to liberty, and so many factions in the nation, yet all helped in their turns to establish liberty (56-7). Bolingbroke says further on that 'in the early days of our government, after the Norman invasion, the commons of England were rather formidable in their collective, than considerable in their representative body, by their numbers in extraordinary emergencies, rather than by their weight in the ordinary course of government'. They acquired weight by degrees, but before that time 'they had too much of the dependency of tenants, and the king, the nobility and the clergy too much of the superiority of landlords' (134). This suggests that the commons were represented all along, even if, owing to the balance of property, they were not influential in the government.[2]

Bolingbroke's amateurish excursion into medieval history exposed a weakness which the government writers were quick to exploit, thereby forcing the opposition to be more specific and fly closer to the guns of genuine scholarship. For Brady, they insisted,

[1] 1215 was, almost comically in Bolingbroke's *Remarks*, a rehearsal of 1688. John's 'electors...found themselves deceived in their expectations; for he governed in the most extravagant manner. But they soon made him feel whose creature he was. The contests between the laity and an ambitious usurping clergy ran very high at this time. John had made his advantage of these divisions. But the spirit of liberty prevailed and that of faction vanished before it. Men grew ashamed of being the tools of private ambition, when public safety was at stake. Those of the high church and those of the low church united in one common cause. The king blustered and drew out his army; but it was a British army. No wonder therefore, if the king submitted and Magna Charta was signed' (54-5).

[2] This tallies with Hume's remark in the essay on *Principles of government* that the property/power maxim applies 'where the original constitution allows any share of power, though small, to an order of men who possess a large share of the property'; they can stretch their authority and bring the balance of power to coincide with that of property. 'This has been the case with the house of commons in England.'

however mistaken he may have been in his royalist principles, was right in his facts:[1] the alleged primitive purity of our government was that the people had no share in the government whatsoever. There was no question of liberty for the people; when the great mass of them were vassals or bondsmen of the lords, parliaments were composed only of ecclesiastical and civil tyrants; the king may not have been absolute over the barons, but king and barons were absolute over the people. This is the logic of what Bolingbroke admits about the overbalance of land being in the hands of king, church and nobility: the people were absolute slaves, and the *Craftsman* is ignorant about the ancient constitution, and what it really was;[2] because he does not know the meaning of the words he quotes from old records and histories. The 'people' means different things at different times, and in the feudal government the 'people', even in the exclusive sense of landholders, were 'slaves by law', bound in one continued chain of vassalage from the King down to the meanest 'slave' (*Daily Gazetteer*, 12 July 1735). Consequently, Magna Carta was no contract with, or grant to, the people; only some concessions to the churchmen and barons, which their swords wrested from the king. Nor does it provide any evidence that the commons were represented in parliament[3] – on the contrary. In those days, parliament men were standing men and parliaments standing parliaments indeed – a 'standing parliament' was a favourite opposition and country slogan. During the eight or nine hundred years which 'Osborne' calls the ancient constitution, that is from the Saxon government to the end of the reign of Henry III, there is no trace that the people chose their own legislators; the contrary is almost certain. The form at least of the present constitution dates from 49 Henry III (*London Journal*, 1734, March 17, 23, April 13. In this number, Rapin is quoted in support of the late origin of the House of Commons). Its substantial privileges were established much later than Rapin and Bolingbroke assume: for long it was the prerogative of the prince to explain and determine them, as Elizabeth's conduct makes quite plain. The House of Commons was hardly a free assembly if the king had the right to create parliamentary boroughs – an advantage well understood by James I. ('Walsingham' in *Daily Gazetteer*, 11 September, 1735.)

---

[1] *Daily Gazetteer*, 5 July 1735. *Hyp Doctor*, 17 June 1735: the controversy turns on facts; not Dr Brady, but the fact, is the enquiry.
[2] *London Journal*, 1 September 1733, 16 March 1734. ('A Defence of the Present Constitution of Great Britain against the Ancient Constitution').
[3] As the *Craftsman* argued (e.g. XII, 185).

If the government writers accused the *Craftsman* of failing to understand the ancient constitution, the opposition, or those among them who insisted that the question was not purely speculative,[1] retaliated by accusing their opponents of expounding 'a novel and pernicious doctrine, first advanced by the Tories and since adopted by our modern Whigs, that liberty is not an ancient inheritance, but only an acquisition since the Revolution, or the Restoration at furthest' (From the Dedication of Volume VIII of the *Craftsman*, London, 1737), and of licking up the spittle of Brady and other slavish writers (*Craftsman*, XIV, 21). Entrenched behind the authority of Selden, Sidney, Petit, Hody, Tyrrel, West, St Amand 'and others', the *Craftsman* stubbornly repeated the old arguments; appealing to Hunt's *Argumentum anti-Normanicum* to show that William I made no absolute conquest etc.; that his parliament was in substance the same as before, with the commons a constituent part: a truth confirmed by Hales in his *History of the Common Law*, where he says that William made the laws of Edward the Confessor the rules of his government and added very few new ones. If 'baron' is explained properly, it coincides with our use of commons, that is, people of property. So that, substantially at least, the Revolution was a 'renewal of our ancient constitution' (*id.*, 2-21, 99-103).

There were varieties of ancient constitutionalism depending on how far and how dogmatically (and from the point of view of modern scholarship how dangerously) a writer was prepared to extend his lines. As Oldmixon said, no one ever pretended that the form of parliaments was in old times exactly the same as it is now. 'But the main of the matter...is as old as the Gothic government' (*Critical History*, 45). But although the 'main of the matter' could be more or less precise and detailed to a very great degree, and carry a larger or smaller load of historical, or pseudo-historical, scholarship, the essence of ancient constitutionalism is the idea of a unity and continuity behind the vicissitudes of history and the differences of constitutional forms. A statement to that effect is how Bolingbroke opened his review of English history in the *Craftsman* in 1730. Few nations have gone through more revolutions; if we are free men it is because the spirit of liberty has never been quite extinguished among us. We have been surprised, betrayed, forced into situations little better than downright slavery,

---

[1] *Craftsman*, 7 June 1735. This was in answer to Lyttleton's *Letters from a Persian in England*. Public rights, insisted the *Craftsman*, acquire strength by long prescription and people are by nature more tenacious of their ancient birthright than of recent acquisitions (*Craftsman*, Vol. XIV, 2).

but these usurpations have never become settlements. They have disordered the frame, but not destroyed the principles of a free government...that uniformity of spirit which created and has constantly preserved, or retrieved, the original freedom of the British and Saxon constitutions (*Craftsman*, VII, 49).

Of all the vicissitudes of English liberty and breaks in the essential continuity of the English constitution, the most significant and instructive was that which was brought about by the innovations of James I; roughly half the *Remarks on English History* is concerned with this episode. Henry VIII's absolute rule was a 'tyranny by law', and was due, as Rapin explained, to the religious divisions in the nation (*Remarks*, 125). It is a useful warning that tyranny need not abolish parliaments (*Craftsman*, XII, 108). But Bolingbroke was particularly concerned to bring out the lessons of Queen Elizabeth's reign and its disastrous successors. No part of our annals, nor perhaps of the annals of any other country, deserves more to be studied or to be oftener called to remembrance than that of Elizabeth (*Remarks*, 144–5). And the contrast between her reign and those which followed, which Bolingbroke was so anxious to make as dramatically as possible,[1] will appear stronger and be the more instructive when it is made to 'centre in one single point', which is that Elizabeth, with far greater disadvantages than James, was successful and her reign prosperous because her conduct was 'wisely suited to the nature of our government', whereas the conduct of James, who 'had many and great advantages which his predecessor wanted' made his reign miserable, and led to the civil war (234), 'because it was ill-suited to the nature of our government, and founded on principles destructive of liberty' (145).

There was no break in the continuity of the government between the reigns of Elizabeth and James, except that which James himself was responsible for. The shift in the balance of property in favour of the commons, which settled the foundations of the present constitution, had occurred earlier; Elizabeth had realized what had happened ('her penetration discovered the consequences of that great change in the balance of property', 209), wisely accommodated her notions and conduct and whole character to it,

---

[1] 'The scene we are going to pen will appear vastly different from that, which we have just closed. Instead of an uninterrupted, pleasing harmony of government, we shall meet with a perpetual jarring dissonance; instead of success and glory abroad, disappointment and contempt; instead of satisfaction, prosperity and union at home, discontent, distress and at last civil war will present themselves to us in all their horrors' (*Remarks*, 204).

and thereby notwithstanding that the prerogative, which she had inherited from her father and grandfather, 'ran high in those days' (137), provided a shining example of the lesson that is valid for all time in a constitution of this sort, whose smooth working depends on 'the union of interest and affection between the king and his subjects' (203–4, 230–1).

James, on the other hand, introduced new principles of government wholly foreign to the constitution, derived from the absurd and mistaken doctrine of hereditary right (243, 248), found many people ready to adopt them, because there are always many people who are ready to be deceived and corrupted (232), made his government a faction, because there can be conspiracies against liberty as well as against prerogative (205), and thus gave rise to a division in the nation which alone could render the religious ones fatal (233), and made impossible any union of crown and people (260–1). And Charles I naturally 'came a party man to the throne' (233). Thus James I, by attempting to govern England by foreign maxims, was entirely to blame for the disorders, 'which in a few more years destroyed the whole constitution' (261), and in which the people had reason to be jealous of the designs of the court, but the king had none to be jealous of the parliament and people (259). 'The constitution was the same in his time as in the time of Queen Elizabeth: and the people claimed under him, no other privileges nor powers, than they had enjoyed under her' (262). 'The sum of all is this. We were destroyed by faction; but faction prevailed at court near forty years before it prevailed amongst the people. It was the original principle on one side. It was an accident on the other. Churchmen and royalists attacked the constitution. Puritans and commonwealthsmen, and above all, a motley race of precise knaves and enthusiastic madmen ruined it. But the last could never have happened, if the first had not; and whoever will dispassionately trace the causes of that detestable civil war, will find them laid in the conduct of James the first, as early as his accession to the throne of England' (234).

Against the continuity of English history which is the core of the Opposition case, as of ancient constitutionalism generally, the government writers argued an essential discontinuity, seen for example in the title of an essay in the *London Journal* 'on the different constitution of England from the Conquest to this time...' (20 November 1731), in which it is pointed out that because the English government has always been monarchical does not mean that it has always been the same. From 1066–1485, we were under 'a sort of Polish nobility'. This continual emphasis in the government writers on the 'slavery' of the Gothic constitution[1] is not the discontinuity of the Norman Yoke thesis: it is not a question of anything being interrupted but of a government bad in the beginning, made better by degrees and brought to perfection at the last (*London Journal*, 1 September 1733). The core of the Ministerialist case in the 1730s is that the substance of liberty is modern, dating from the Restoration at the earliest, and in any settled or regular form only from the Revolution, as Bolingbroke complained. This thesis was most forcibly presented in Hervey's *Ancient and Modern Liberty stated and compared* (1734), which was presumably an answer to Bolingbroke's remarks on English history: it is a survey of English history reign by reign in order to prove the opposite of what Bolingbroke's similar survey was designed to prove: viz: that before the 'banishment, abdication, deposition of whatever people please to call it' of James II, there cannot be said to have been any real liberty in England (40). To talk of the liberty of Old England in comparison with that now subsisting is to show one's ignorance: till the Restoration there was no such thing, and after the Restoration it was nothing compared with the strength it gained at the Revolution. 'I never hear any body harangue with enthusiastic encomiums on the Liberty of Old England, that I am not either ashamed of my ancestors for deserving these economiums so little, or of my cotemporaries for bestowing them so ignorantly' (7). Any change in the government that took place between the Conquest and the Restoration was 'nothing more than from one tyrant, or kind of tyranny, to another...sometimes it was the *regal* tyranny of the Prince; sometimes the *aristocratic* tyranny of the Barons; sometimes...the ecclesiastical tyranny of the *Clergy* and sometimes all together...' (6-7). The famous struggle for liberty in John's reign was not for the liberty of the people; the struggle lay between a king who had a mind to be sole tyrant and the barons who had long tyrannized in their particular districts over their inferiors and now wanted to tyrannize over their superior too (10). The arrival of the commons in parliament made no difference: in Edward I's reign the gates of liberty were

---

[1] They made a point also of stressing the spiritual slavery which was the result of the ecclesiastical constitution and 'dreadful independency of the Church'. 'The ecclesiastical part of our old constitution was a monstrous tyranny erected over the souls, bodies and estates of the laity', *Daily Gazetteer* (8 November 1735). This made the slavery of the ancient constitution even worse. In the previous number, 'Osborne' had argued that the tyranny of the secular ancient constitution explains the ignorance and therefore the religion of medieval England. Destroy the Bastille and you destroy Popery.

as closely shut and strongly barred as ever (12). Queen Elizabeth's reign is justly extolled as great and glorious, but not when it is called a reign in which the people enjoyed the least shadow of liberty. Never was the yoke of slavery faster bound upon the people's necks: Elizabeth's subjects possessed every good but that of being able to make the good they possessed the effects of their own election (23–5). The only difference between her government and that of James I and Charles I was that she ruled despotically for the good of the people, whereas that 'equally unhappy and undeserving race of Stuarts' thought that they had a right 'to keep up the prerogative at the mark they found it', even if they ruled to the nation's infamy and ruin, instead of for their glory and prosperity (29).

Nor was it until the Bill of Rights that the boundaries of prerogative and liberty were properly defined. Notwithstanding Magna Carta, until this 'explanatory renewal of it, or rather till this supplemental ingraftment on the great Charter', the bounds of liberty and prerogative were so 'indistinctly marked out and so indeterminately known, that the names of *Liberty* and *Prerogative* were made use of by both *Prince* and *People*, just as opportunity favoured the arbitrary views of the one or the licentious disposition of the other' (41). (In the *Daily Gazetteer* [6 July 1735], 'Osborne' showed that we never had fixed boundaries, nor a full and complete establishment of our liberties, so that we could say to our kings thus far and no further, till the Revolution.) Nobody knew the just degrees of either, and the result was the kind of contention which Machiavelli says is ruinous to most states: king and people, jealous of each other and fearing encroachments if they remained quiet, were always guilty of injustice themselves to avoid suffering it from the other (42). 'As therefore no government can be free but a mixed government, and no mixed government peaceable, but where the particular jurisdictions are allotted and the bounds of each part fully known and settled, so...one may affirm, this government was never on so free and so desirable a foot, as after the Bill of Rights was passed...' (44).

There is one important difference in Hervey's presentation of the case for modern liberty and the modern constitution – what 'Osborne' called 'vindicating' the Revolution: he was prepared to draw conclusions from his thesis for the conflict in the seventeenth century, if only tentatively, which the other writers were careful to avoid. They were not prepared to apologize for the Stuart kings in any way, perhaps because that would have been sailing too close to the wind of Jacobitism, and it was an important part of their case that Jacobitism was still very much a danger which the opposition were trying to pretend no longer existed. They combined their notion of liberty and the constitution as essentially modern and their destruction of the ancient constitutionalism of the opposition with subscription to a view of James I and Charles I similar to Rapin's. The *London Journal* accused the *Craftsman* of 'slavishly passing over' the reign of Charles I for fear of offending the High Church party and damaging the sales of the paper: Charles I had the most arbitrary and tyrannical views of any English king (20 November 1731); the reigns of James I and Charles I were one continued violation against the laws of the land and a continued conspiracy against the English constitution. To say that Charles I only imagined himself defending his own rights while notoriously invading those of the people, is to make him a weaker man than his father (17 April 1731 – 'Osborne'). But Hervey, although he described the reigns of the first two Stuarts as one continued series of folly and injustice, also said that Queen Elizabeth was the cause of most of the misfortunes that befell either them or their people, because they inherited her notions of the prerogative (*op. cit.*, 29). When Hume elaborated this view some twenty-five years later there was an outcry from the Whigs as though the ark of the covenant had been defiled.

For in spite of Hervey, 'Osborne' and 'Walsingham', ancient constitutionalism was Whig orthodoxy in the eighteenth century, meaning by this a compelling need to assert and defend the essential continuity of the English form of government – hence the search for feudalism, or at least something like it, in England before the conquest, hence the notion of William I as not a usurper, but a tyrant, a man who was forced to act like a conqueror later, but who never claimed a right of conquest, hence the view of Magna Carta as not merely or mainly a feudal document of post-conquest provenance and so on.

Thus Lyttleton enshrined the ancient constitutionalism of the opposition against Walpole, which he had supported at the time,[1]

---

[1] In his *Persian Letters* of 1735, where there is a section on English history. The great article on which English historians differ is the ancient power of the crown and that of parliament: the point is debated with great warmth, but is not so important as some think. (As seen above, the *Craftsman* objected to this remark, although Lyttleton adds that a long possession of freedom serves to establish and strengthen original right, or at least makes it more shameful to give it up.) Worth noticing is Lyttleton's use of the idea of the spontaneous origin of the Gothic government in the Whig cause. Governments are often the result of chance and force of circumstances, not of the refinements of human wisdom and 'deep-laid systems and

in his monumental and long awaited *History of Henry II* (on which he had apparently begun work at least as early as 1741),[1] whose 'Whiggery' and 'piety' Hume invited Smith to admire (*Letters*, II, 150). The 'best principles and some of the great outlines of our present constitution', including a legislative power in the king and general assembly of the nation, and a right in the latter to call the king and his ministers to account, derive from our Saxon ancestors, and were confirmed by the Charter of Henry I, which was a model for Magna Carta (*Henry II*, I, 160, 99). William I altered the laws of Edward the Confessor by the introduction of 'those tenures which were derived to us from Normandy' (II, 212), by the 'more complete introduction of a strict feudal law', and as a result the constitution became more aristocratical than before, 'more unequally balanced' (I, 42), and this was only rectified 'many centuries' later, when 'great alterations having happened in the balance of property, from many causes combined, a more extensive, more equal, and more regular system was happily established' (I, 160). But William, who was far from grounding his title on a supposed right of conquest and who may be said to have acquired his title from the consent of the nation cheerfully given (I, 29) did not destroy the liberty of the subject. However it is from the reign of Henry I that 'we must date the first regular settlement of the

plans of policy'. Such was the origin of the celebrated Gothic government all over Europe. 'It was produced not in a cabinet but a camp.' (Did Hume echo this in *Treatise* III?) It owes less to the prudence of a legislator than to the necessity of the times which gave it birth. Lyttleton goes on to say that it was all the better for this reason: there was 'more of nature in it', and less of 'political mystery', which is the bane of public good. A government so established could admit of no pretence of a power in a king transcendent to law, or an unalterable right in the succession; or of a reason of state distinct from the common reason of mankind. However he says that the Saxon government, perhaps the most free of all the limited monarchies ever known in the world – like Rapin (II, 157) he compares its excellence, with special reference to the tything-system, to the government of China – 'received its final perfection' by 'the wisdom and virtue of two or three great kings'. The ancient constitutionalism of Lyttleton's Persian Letters is in the style of Bolingbroke: the Saxon constitution was never wholly subdued; the Norman newcomers relished slavery no more than the old inhabitants, 1688 saw the extinction of the phantoms of hereditary right and power superior to law, which James I had conjured up in his attempt to 'break the balance' of government so wisely fixed by Elizabeth. However Lyttleton also says that till the revolution, the prerogatives of the crown were so ill-defined that the full extent of it was rather stopped by the degree of prudence in the government, or impatience in the people, than by the letter of the law, and indeed in some instances the law allowed a power to the king entirely destructive of itself. To this extent, the constitution is modern. (*The Works of Lord Lyttleton* (1774), 219–35.)

[1] The first extant reference to the *Henry II* dates from a letter of June 1741 (R. M. Davies, *The Good Lord Lyttleton* [1939], 326). It was published in 1767, in three volumes (one of notes).

Anglo-Norman constitution', because the rough draft sketched out by William I was defaced by his tyranny and that of his successor, and 'the principle of it was founded in liberty', because feudal tenure meant a reciprocal obligation incompatible with arbitrary power (I, 158–9). This constitution, a mixture of Norman institutions mitigated and tempered by Saxon customs, and the best feudal government in the world at that time (II, 16), 'modelled' by Henry I (I, 160) was restored by the patriot king Henry II, after the anarchy of Stephen's reign.[1] The Anglo-Norman constitution was the seed-plot of our present constitution and liberty, even if the commons were much overbalanced by the clergy and nobles in property and power, because another great benefit of the feudal law was the uniting of power to property, which is the surest basis upon which all liberty stands, so that as property gradually diffused itself wider, the power united to it extended itself further, and produced that comprehensive system of freedom which the whole nation enjoys under our present constitution (II, 205). As to the origin of the house of commons, Lyttleton agreed with Rapin that this was a matter of curiosity rather than real importance, because the right of the commons to a share in the national councils, 'even according to the hypothesis of those most unfavourable to them, has antiquity enough to give it all the establishment which can be derived from long custom...' (II, 273). However he mobilizes arguments against the late origin of the commons (49 Henry III): it was not in de Montforts' interest to make distasteful innovations, no institution begun in such a way would have been confirmed and perpetuated by Edward I, there was no reason for such an important change in the constitution: for example, trade was no more esteemed then than in Saxon times – on the contrary, and the age was turbulent and unfriendly to the increase of trade and industry, the feudal powers of the nobility were not relaxed etc (See the discussion in Vol. III, 72 *et seq.*). His conclusion is that we must presume that the right of the commons must have been incontestably established by custom and 'interwoven into the original frame of our government' (II, 277).

In Blackstone's *Commentaries* (1765–9) what one gets is not an Anglo-Norman constitution which is the germ of a full liberty

---

[1] Henry II obtained the highest glory a king can obtain, that of having reformed a depraved and corrupted state. He might have taken advantage of the lull after Stephen's reign to make himself despotic; however he had read Rapin and Bolingbroke, and he knew that even if he succeeded, 'the master of a race of slaves must himself sink' (II, 15–17).

which matured with the diffusion of property, but a classic Norman Yoke – the nation groaned under slavery (IV, 411–12) – which had to be lifted off the Saxon free constitution, 'the policy of our ancient constitution as regulated and established by the great Alfred' (III, 30), in stages, beginning with Magna Carta, or rather the exact observation, not just the making of Magna Carta, in the reign of Edward I (IV, 420) – the earlier charters were not a thorough restoration of King Edward's or the Saxon laws – and ending in 1679, which is the point at which Blackstone fixes the theoretical perfection of our public law and the full vigour of the English constitution – although practical oppression followed – by which time the 'slavish' tenures had been finally removed, and the 'people had as large a portion of real liberty as is consistent with a state of society', and sufficient power in their own hands to assert and preserve it, if invaded by royal prerogative – as 1688 showed (IV, 432–3).

Nevertheless Blackstone was most anxious to show that this feudal yoke, which as a rigorous system and as part of the constitution dates from the reign of William I, was not imposed by the arbitrary will and power of a conqueror: Blackstone lent his authority to the old Whig myth that William conquered Harold, not the nation, that 'conquest' in its feudal acceptation means 'acquisition', and the conqueror's seizure of all the land of the English was an error of monkish historians (I, 192, II, 48). The introduction of the feudal tenures was a military necessity, the result of an invasion scare from Denmark, freely accepted as such by the whole nation, and freely consented to (II, 48–50). But what was 'originally a plan of simplicity and liberty' (II, 58), was transformed by 'metaphysical' Norman jurists into a complete and well-concerted scheme of servility (II, 51–2, 408 *et seq.*). Magna Carta was a restoration of that ancient constitution of which our ancestors had been defrauded by the art and finesse of the Norman lawyers rather than deprived by the force of the Norman arms (II, 52). In general, although Blackstone refused to enter into controversies about the composition of parliaments and origin of the commons, merely saying that our present parliamentary constitution has subsisted in fact from 49 Henry III at least (I, 145), he is clear that the absolute rights of Englishmen are coeval with our form of government, and although that has been subject to fluctuations and changes, 'the vigour of our free constitution has always delivered the nation from these embarassments', a constitution, that is, which includes the powers and privileges of parlia-

'THE HISTORY OF ENGLAND'

ment without which these rights would have no protection (I, 123, 136).

Of the general histories of England published around mid-century[1] that of William Guthrie (in three volumes, 1744, '47, '51) is probably the least known. It seems to have suffered an early eclipse.[2] In some ways it is closer in intention to Hume's than the others, in that the customary claim to impartiality (impartiality was probably the strongest obsession of eighteenth-century English historians) can be seen as an application of an establishment political philosophy which combined what was true in the political systems of both parties to the controversial issues of English history. There are other similarities. Hume presumably knew Guthrie's *History of England*, though his reference to Guthrie in a letter of 1754 to the Abbé Le Blanc is not flattering.[3] Hume in 1751 associated him with his wild Jacobite friend James Fraser,[4] and Boswell describes him as 'an adherent of the unfortunate house of Stuart'.[5] This did not prevent him from getting a pension from Pelham, and in 1755 he was made a J.P. When the pension

[1] Carte's was published in four volumes (1747, '50, '52, '55). From around 1755 Smollett was working on his. It was published 1757-8. L. M. Knapp says that it is not clear why he undertook the project (*Tobias Smollett: Doctor of Men and Manners* [Princeton, 1949], 186). It sold well and was translated into French (1759-64).

[2] Thomas Gray, writing to Horace Walpole in 1768, said of Guthrie, who had reviewed Walpole's *Historic Doubts* in the *Critical Review*, 'His *History* I never saw, nor is it here, nor do I know anyone who ever saw it. He is a rascal!' *Horace Walpole's Correspondence* (Yale edition), Vol. 14, 180. Ramsay of Ochtertyre, writing some time during the last quarter of the eighteenth century, said of Guthrie's *History* that it was 'much neglected ever since the new fashion of writing history was introduced by Voltaire, Hume and their imitators', *Scotland and Scotsmen in the 18th Century*, (ed. A. Allardyce (1888)), II, 548.

[3] 'I have not seen Guthrie's Book against you: But I have seen his other Works, which makes me conclude, as you do, that it will make more against himself' (*Letters*, I, 209). Guthrie was not personally known to any of the Edinburgh literati. There is a letter of 20 March 1752 to a friend in Edinburgh, now in Edinburgh University Library, in which Guthrie says that he is 'next to an utter stranger' there and acquainted with nobody but his correspondent (a Dr Harie).

[4] See Hume, *Letters*, II, 340, Appendix A. 'That the said James Fraser associating himself with...William Guthrey Esq, and other evil intentioned persons...' For the practical joke designed to cure Fraser of his Jacobitism in which this pseudo-petition played the main part, see Mossner's *Life*, 237. Fraser would not have appreciated what Guthrie said about the Highlanders in Vol. I of his *History* (1744). The cruelties practised by the army of David I, composed mainly of Highlanders, were due to 'that spirit which intervening ages have in vain attempted to humanise and to that polity which succeeding governments have ineffectually tried to reform', (I, 469-70).

[5] *Life of Johnson*, ed. Birkbeck Hill, (1934), I, 116. Guthrie was the first parliamentary 'reporter', working in collaboration with Johnson for the *Gentleman's Magazine*. Boswell thought that 'his writings in history, criticism and politics had considerable merit', and Johnson described him as 'a man of parts'.

was confirmed by Newcastle on Pelham's death, Guthrie wrote that this was 'owing I suppose to the memory of his brother not regard for me, who never did the government a shilling's worth of service nor was ever required to do it'.[1] There are aspects of Guthrie's *History*, however, which could be interpreted as a continuation of the ministerial anti-*Craftsman* historiography of the 1730s. He is best regarded as what he prided himself on being: an 'author by profession', one of the first, if not the first, of the great clan of London-based Scottish full-time professional writers and journalists, and his *History of England* was the first example of what was soon to become a typical Scottish product. He genuinely aimed at impartiality, and a clue to what that meant is provided by his Preface, where he describes Brady's history as a shameful attempt to support the schemes of his patron, James II, and Tyrrel's an ill-judged one to weaken the principles of hereditary right.[2] It has been 'the unhappy fate of the nation, in its political tenets, to be distracted by diametrically opposite writers, who have sought truth everywhere but where she is to be found, in a candid mean'. The context is the succession of the Saxon kings: the preference was generally given to primogeniture, yet in many cases succession was conferred on the most worthy, but never without regard to family. The facts are so stubborn that systematic writers, whether advocates for primogeniture or popular rights, may dash their foam about the basis of this rock, but can never shake a truth so deeply founded in the English history and constitution that it has grown with their growth and strengthened with their strength (I, 295). Guthrie did not think that Rapin had struck the 'candid mean': he is accused of inaccuracy and want of genius, and the success of his *History* is explained by its appearance 'at a time when the principles on which he wrote were useful to a party', who therefore powerfully recommended it from the press of which they were then masters, and by the ridiculous prepossession that a foreigner was best fitted to write the English history (I, Preface, iii). This suggests that Guthrie set out to write an impartial

---

[1] See the Letters to Dr Harie in Edinburgh University Library. As D. J. Greene says, a Jacobitism so easily quieted could not have been particularly vigorous. *The Politics of Samuel Johnson*, (1960), 82.

[2] Among the letters in Edinburgh University Library there is a page entitled *Mr Tytler's opinion, April 1752* which concerns Guthrie's proposal for a History of Scotland. Tytler says that its merit is strict observance of truth without attachment to party, but this will disgust numbers on both sides. Exposing the falsities of Buchanan will offend the presbyterian and anti-monarchical folks...on the other hand the attacking the prerogative will render it as little agreeable to the bigoted of the other sort.

'THE HISTORY OF ENGLAND'

establishment history to supersede Rapin. Like Rapin, he gives the reader a critical survey of the literature of the seventeenth-century conflict – a miniature history of the historiography (Vol. I, Preface, III, 1225–6) – pointing out in particular the danger of relying on memoirs and the value of the journals of the House of Commons, which Guthrie was the first historian to use extensively: 'they are in themselves, if I may be allowed the expression, facts' (III, 1226). He brings out clearly what Rapin ignores and Bolingbroke skates over: the arbitrary, despotic nature of Elizabeth's happy government and the existence of men like Peter Wentworth who realized this. If Elizabeth had been succeeded by rulers of equal ability and fewer virtues, the liberties of England 'must have been irretrievably ruined'. Elizabeth had continued or taken up again the policy of her wise grandfather (Henry VII); in the meantime the property of the soil of England had reverted too much to its former channels, so Elizabeth, fearing that the balance would again preponderate in favour of the nobility, had taken every opportunity to add to the property of the commons by introducing manufactures and encouraging the extravagance of the nobility, but not 'national luxury'. As a result, the people, secure in their property and not burdened with taxes, almost lost sight of their constitutional rights: 'the generality of the people, pleased with their easy situation, did not reflect upon the consequences' (III, 378–81).

Guthrie refuses to accept the contrast between Elizabeth and James I which Bolingbroke found so instructive. 'In contradiction to all former authorities', he regards James' foreign policy as having shown no common degree of genius: whether it was due to indolence or policy he will not say, but it laid the foundation of England's commercial greatness; her enemies, at any rate, thought that James was pursuing her real interests (III, 647).[1] He criticizes 'the ridiculous assertion of modern writers' that commerce suffered under James (III, 821); on the contrary, his care for trade deserves the eternal gratitude of the English nation (III, 683), and he adds that the great increase of the commerce and manufactures of England under Elizabeth and James could not have been effected but by the force of prerogative, which was sometimes usefully and beneficially applied (III, 821). But James I did not sufficiently reflect on the vast difference between his situation and that of the Tudor monarchs: the ignorance and consequently the tameness of

[1] When occasion calls, he justifies the foreign policy of Charles I, e.g. in 1638; thus spotlighting truths which have been smothered by the ingratitude of historians (III, 953).

the English had gone; they were resolved to defend with courage what they had acquired with industry (III, 819). And England never saw an abler House of Commons than the reign of James I produced. The transactions of the parliamentary session of 1614, never before mentioned by historians, explain the foundation of the constitutional opposition now formed against James and his family. The 'patriots of those times', who were aware of the reverence which the people were apt to entertain for government, saw that what James claimed, threatened all property amongst subjects (III, 703), and Guthrie can find no ground to support the notion that they had gone too far in their distrust of James (III, 775). The general impression left by Guthrie's account is that English liberty was saved by the foresight of an exceptionally able group of patriots, ('the opposition' to Charles I 'was composed of the greatest mean that England has, to this day, ever seen' (III, 896)) who had to contend not only with the royal claims, but the people's indifference, due to the flourishing condition of the country, 'far beyond what had ever been known...they who chiefly tasted the sweets of commerce were willing to enjoy it in peace'. Besides, the nation had seen so high an exercise of the prerogative for so long that it was unable to appreciate the 'blessings to which it was restored' by the Petition of Right, and the people had a high opinion of the king's probity, and were not very apprehensive that he would make an ill use of his prerogative (III, 896), in which opinion Guthrie thought they were perfectly justified (III, 903, 1222). The merchants, who generally take the lead in these matters, were 'too sensible of the sweets of commerce to risk them' in opposing the intention to make ship-money general, which did not alarm the nation as much as was expected (III, 925), and the people, continuing still at ease, in peace and plenty, shewed too great insensibility at the discontinuance of parliaments and the unconstitutional measures of the government (III, 970). The patriots were eventually rewarded by the opposition of the Scots, which in Guthrie's opinion was totally unjustified: and the Solemn League and Covenant an act of defiance and barefaced rebellion (III, 942-3), which forced Charles to call a parliament. All this forms an important part of the story as told by Hume also.

Guthrie adds an element of 'class-conflict' which is lacking in Hume's interpretation. Like Clarendon and Hume he points to the propertied men of commerce who could not brook the insults of the landed interest – the 'idolatry' paid to the nobility was wearing off in those parts of the country that were supported by trade and men became sensible that in a regulated government power ought to follow property. But Guthrie goes on to emphasize the importance of the huge gulf in manners and way of life and language and sentiments between the merchants and the court: at that time arts and learning did not, as now, raise traders and merchants above the sentiments of mechanics (III, 1071). The result was that the king and the court looked down on them as the drudges of the state, who were to acquire what noblemen and gentlemen were to spend, although James I and Charles I owed more to commerce than any king of England had ever done. Charles thought all power acquired by property and not communicated to the court to be unlawful (III, 1065).

Guthrie's impartiality is still that of a basic ancient constitutionalism. The historian, he says, is 'obliged to point out the gradual progression in the civil system of our government from these principles first introduced by our Saxon ancestors' (I, 80),[1] a constitution which has perished in the hands of the Germans and the French. In his account of the Saxon government, Guthrie is looking out for 'consistency' between the ancient and the modern constitutions (e.g. I, 140). He finds the present English character in Tacitus' account of the German manners (I, 119). The Germans may have been 'rude'; 'barbarous' they cannot be called, because although destitute of other arts, they possessed the vivifying principle of all arts; the art of government, which they had long been used to (I, 103). Their hospitality 'still survives in the middling rank of the English, who live at a distance from the vices and hurry of great cities' (I, 123). Guthrie's *Third Dissertation*, printed at the end of Volume III, is on the 'Norman Engraftments upon the English Laws and Government'. The 'stock of the feudal law' was imported by the Saxons, the Norman engraftments constituted a 'dreadful feudal yoke' from which the people gradually obtained relief, and a return to the original principles of the Saxon constitution (III, 1384-7). But William's title did not rest on conquest: he had conquered Harold, not the people of England. The solution of the famous dispute is that though William's right was evidently not founded on conquest, he later exercised it as though it were. Though no usurper, he became a tyrant. His acquisition of regal power may be vindicated on the best of all principles: the invitation and consent of the people; his exercise of it condemned

---

[1] Marie Schütt deals with this aspect of Guthrie's historical thinking in *Das Germanenproblem in der Englischen Geschichtsschreibung des 18 Jahrhunderts*, (Hamburg 1960), 27-38.

upon the most obvious of all reasons: his breach of solemn engagements (1, 356).

When Guthrie comes to Magna Carta, he pulls out all the stops, and the result at first hearing is a loud noise somewhat lacking in precision.[1] But when he does get more precise about its value and meaning, what he emphasizes – rather unusually in the history of the interpretation of Magna Carta – is the institutionalization of the right of resistance, so that he is able to see and present Magna Carta as the truth and essence of the constitution as finally restored in 1688; enshrining the twin doctrines of hereditary right and resistance which the parties have unnaturally rent asunder. What was lacking in William I's contract with his people, and what the behaviour of the Norman kings taught them to demand, the barons who 'opposed John upon principles of regulated liberty', now fixed: not only the principle of resistance, to compel the king if necessary to fulfil his engagements with his people, but its very manner. But they were careful also to preserve the mode of succession. 'The whole act rests upon two principles, that of resistance, and hereditary right; principles which long lurked in our constitution', even if only the spirit survived, and 'on which our present happy constitution now rests'. The barons of Magna Carta, 'our forefathers...looked upon them as not only united, but inseparable. They looked upon the object of their obedience to be an object of resistance upon every deviation into wrong; and even when their resistance was exerted in facts, their obedience rested upon principle. This insensibly insinuated itself into the vitals of our constitution, and at the time the late revolution took place, its force directed every step of the newly-modelled establishment... The same scheme of resistance and right continued and the government of England is now founded upon both' (1, 678).

Hurd, writing shortly after and partly in answer to Hume's Stuart volumes – his Dialogues on the constitution, first published in 1759, afford, he says, a 'seasonable antidote to the poison of this new history' (315n) – agreed that the Tudor monarchy was despotic, and that if Elizabeth's government was 'in many instances

[1] 'Such was the glorious instrument by which the rights of Englishmen were declared, explained and confirmed. From this period of our history, as from a pinnacle, we may descry the promised land of liberty; we view, at once, the more than Egyptian bondage from whence this nation was delivered, and the more than Roman privileges to which she was entitled. This charter is a nobler, a more express, and more extensive, instrument of constitutional freedom than any people ever could boast of: it removes all altercations, all doubts, concerning the compact between king and people...and is perhaps the only instance on record, when a king talked and treated with the whole body of his free subjects' (1, 677).

oppressive and highly prejudicial to the ancient rights and privileges of her people', this was because 'the English constitution as it then stood, as well as her own nature had a good deal of that bias' (211, 218). Since the majority of Englishmen consider the enquiry into the constitution of their own government as a question of fact, to be tried by precedents and authorities only, and decided by the evidence of historical testimony, not by the conclusions of philosophy or political speculation,[1] the two hundred year long interlude of despotić rule from Henry VIII onwards has to be shown as an essentially unconstitutional lapse and its existence explained. This task, 'the most difficult part', of explaining why the government of England was for so long not in accordance with the system of the constitution as one of 'civil liberty' expounded in Dialogue V, and 'reconciling the fact to the right', is given to Burnet, presumably because Hurd is anxious to stress what he regards as the most important and yet most neglected factor: the royal headship of the church 'was the circumstance of all others which most favoured the sudden growth of the imperial power in this nation' (349). But as Maynard says in Dialogue V, the question is not under what form the government has appeared at some particular conjunctures, but what we may conclude it to have been 'from the general current and tenor of our histories': whether 'the genius of the government' has not always been free, however despotic the administration at times. And Maynard goes on to show how the key to the continuing freedom of the constitution is feudalism. This was 'improved and corrected', not introduced, by William I in such a way that 'our Saxon liberties were not so properly restrained as extended by it' (260), and the system was not imposed on, but accepted by, the nation – William's claim to the crown was not conquest etc. However, what happened before the Conquest and even the Conqueror himself are relatively unimportant: what matters is the government he established. The vital fact to be demonstrated is that the constitution of England is laid in the feudal tenures, and that the very changes it has undergone were the natural and almost unavoidable effects of those tenures (271). The genius of the feudal system was 'oligarchical in a high degree', yet founded on

[1] Dialogues V and VI on the Constitution are set in 1689, between Sir John Maynard, Somers and Burnet, but are not to be read simply as a piece of historical reconstruction, though they could pass quite creditably for such. The two previous dialogues on the Golden Age of Queen Elizabeth are, among other things, expressly directed against factious use of the glories of her reign by Bolingbroke (128n). *Moral and Political Dialogues* (2nd ed., 1760).

principles of 'public liberty' – villenage concludes no more against the feudal, than slavery against the Greek and Roman constitutions (262, 273). In a military age, when the strength of the nation lay in the soldiery, and no one else was of much account, the king's council of tenants-in-capite was representative. Its defects became obvious with the growth of arts and commerce and security, and gradually made way for the introduction of a better system, which was not so properly a new form, as the old one amended and set right, conducted on the same principles and pursuing the same end by different methods (251, 266–70). The gradual change in the legislature was more properly an extension than a violation of the ancient system (267–8): the late rise of the Commons serves to illustrate the fact that the feudal constitution was uniquely capable of growth, that it readily gave way and fitted itself to the varying situations of society, like the skin on a growing body;[1] so it was not the House of Commons that violated the constitution, but the constitution demanded, or rather generated the House of Commons (276–7). It is as unnecessary as it is unhistorical to search for the origin of the House of Commons in the British or even the Saxon annals (277–8).

If therefore what is best is what is usual, as Hume asserts in his apology for the Stuarts, Tudor and Stuart sovereigns are equally to blame, or rather the latter are more blameworthy for trying to turn irregularities into precedent and extravagancies into system, and fix the chains forged by their predecessors permanently on the necks of their subjects (313–15). Otherwise, if use is to be estimated only from immediately preceding times, how could any country support a free constitution? No attempt to free itself from usurpation would ever be justified.

(ii) *The philosophical revision of ancient constitutionalism*

When in a letter of 1755 (*Letters*, I, 221–2) Hume said that the impartiality he had achieved in his History of James I and Charles I[2] represented a victory over 'some of the prejudices of my education', presumably he had in mind not only the view of the Stuart

---

[1] Cf. *id.*, 272. The change from the aristocratical to the more free and popular constitution of our day is compared to what naturalists observe of the human body, which in its maturity does not perhaps contain a single particle of its original matter, and yet the system is accounted the same under all changes. Just so we seem to have shaken off the constituent parts of the feudal constitution, yet as liberty was always the informing principle, time and experience have rather completed the old system, than created a new one.

[2] Hume's *History of Great Britain, Volume One*, containing *the reigns of James I and Charles I* was published in 1754. The second volume, going up to the Revolution,

kings as the aggressors in the conflict of Crown and Parliament, but also the ancient constitutionalism behind that view of them, and in particular, ancient constitutionalism in its most sophisticated form, that of Rapin. He had begun by admiring Rapin. He asked for 'the last Volume of Rapin' as early as 1730 (*Letters*, II, 337). In the essay on the *Original Contract*, he called him 'our historian' (469) in such a way as to confer a kind of official status, especially as the 'our' does not refer to nationality. (This was part of a section added to the essay for the edition of 1753.) In the essay on the *Protestant Succession* (1752), he is 'the most judicious of historians' (491n), and it is not difficult to see why Rapin should have appealed to Hume, in spite of literary defects, the perpetual references to Providence and God's vengeance, and Rapin's subscription to the fashionable consent theory of government. Hume would have appreciated the anti-clericalism which is so prominent a feature of Rapin's *History*, the critical approach to the sources, the prevailing air of scepticism about, for example, the (mostly interested) motives of rulers and politicians and leaders of parties, and the careful analysis of the parties. Rapin seems to be behind Hume's short and very general account of the events leading to the Civil War in the essay on the *Parties of Great Britain* of 1741. He does not name or distinguish James I and Charles I: 'an ambitious or rather ignorant' (later 'misguided') 'prince arose, who deemed all these privileges to be the concessions of his predecessors...'; distrust of Charles' motives plays a large part in causing the fatal division after 1640 in which it is still so difficult for the impartial to decide 'concerning the justice of the quarrel', the extremists on both sides 'lay concealed in both parties and formed but an inconsiderable part of them' (66–7). There is however an important difference: Rapin had made it abundantly clear that the Stuart kings with their new-fangled notion of government were to blame for the rise of the parties and all the evil consequences. Hume says that 'the species of government gave birth to them'. The English constitution had 'lain in a kind of confusion', with the subjects, however, possessing 'many noble privileges' which, if not exactly defined by law, were deemed to be their 'birth-right'. 'An ambitious or rather ignorant prince arose...' What he means by the 'species of government' giving

is dated 1757, but was published in December 1756. A second edition, revised and corrected, of the History of the Stuarts was published in 1759, the year of the publication of *The History of England under the House of Tudor*. Two volumes from the invasion of Julius Caesar to 1485 were published in November 1761, dated 1762, and in 1763 the history was published as a whole, in 8 vols, for the first time.

birth to the parties is made clearer by the conclusion of the *Passive Obedience* essay (1748): in a limited monarchy the king is tempted by 'imprudent ambition', as an absolute sovereign is not, to abuse his power in such a way as to provoke rebellion. And this is what Charles 'evidently' did. (In the edition of 1770, the passage is altered to 'this is frequently supposed to have been the case with Charles the First'.) Both Charles I and James I, 'mistaking the nature of our constitution and engrossing the whole legislative power, it became necessary to oppose them with some vehemence'. When Charles was eventually brought to book (to return to the account in *Parties of Great Britain*), in 1640, there were those prepared to trust him and those who were not; hence, as in Rapin, a polarization which helped the extremists. In 1741 (*Parties of Great Britain*) Charles is ambitious or rather ignorant, in 1748 (*Passive Obedience*) he is both. In 1752 (*Protestant Succession*), if we can take the arguments for the advantages of the Hanover succession as expressing Hume's own opinion at that time, it was not extraordinary that the first Stuart kings 'mistook the nature of our constitution and the genius of the people' ('and' was changed in 1770 to 'at least'), because they were encouraged in their mistake by the example of the princes on the continent. They regarded the constitution as a simple monarchy (489–90).[1] But they are not to be blamed – and to this extent, and in so far as the 'species of government' was responsible, Hume's earliest published account of the seventeenth-century conflict is more 'philosophical' than Rapin's. The description of Rapin in *Protestant Succession* as 'the most judicious of historians' is qualified to this effect: he is criticized for treating James I and Charles I 'with too much severity' on that account (491n). A few months later, in January 1753, 'even Rapin during this latter period [from 1603] is extremely deficient' (*Letters*, I, 170), and by June, 'Rapin, whom I had an esteem for, is totally despicable' (*id.*, 179).[2] And a note appended to the *Parties*

---

[1] In the essay *Of Some Remarkable Customs* (1752) what Hume says about the much greater danger to liberty of the magistrate acquiring an authority, however inconsiderable, from violence and usurpation than from the law – a thin end of the wedge argument – and the 'heroism of Hampden's conduct', implies that the Stuarts were encroaching illegally: 'hence the care of all English patriots to guard against the first encroachments of the Crown; and hence alone the existence, at this day, of English liberty' (378–9). Hume never revised this passage.

[2] In July 1757 Hume asks the Abbé Le Blanc to note a correction. Where he had called Rapin 'the most judicious of our historians...please to say. "*And Rapin, suitable to his usual Partiality and Malignity, seems etc*". To tell the truth, I was carry'd away with the usual Esteem pay'd to that Historian, till I came to examine him more particularly, when I found him altogether despicable; and I was not asham'd to acknowledge my Mistake' (*Letters*, I, 258).

of Great Britain after 1758 confesses to opinions 'with regard to the public transactions in the last century' which were (in 1741) 'almost universal in this kingdom', which Hume says he 'found reason to retract in his *History*'.

What Hume came to believe 'on more accurate examination' (*id.*), was that the first two Stuarts were not so obviously mistaken about the constitution, and therefore not so 'ambitious' as he, following Rapin, had originally thought. But this change is implicit in remarks in the essays of 1741 noted earlier. Especially, for example, where, in the essay *That Politics may be reduced to a Science*, he says that England was 'in great measure' an 'absolute government' till the middle of the seventeenth century, unless he is using Bolingbroke's distinction between 'government' and 'constitution'. This would seem, from the context, to be too generous a concession to those who might not like to think that Hume could hold two contradictory opinions at the same time, and even so, there are other signs that Hume's later interpretation was present in germ from the beginning, at least from his first published essays; what he did, in the *History*, was to draw the logical consequences which the government writers in the 1730s had refused to draw, and Hervey only hinted at: that if liberty and the constitution are modern, the Stuarts, or the first two at least, could hardly be blamed for trying to destroy something which did not then exist.

When Hume discovered the unsatisfactory nature of orthodox ancient constitutionalism – which was presumably a gradual process[1] – he must have come to realize that the need for a decent general history of England was no longer merely a literary one: a proper history was required as part of the political foundations of the establishment. This, in general, is the political significance of Hume's *History of England*: it represents the third and final phase of his philosophical politics. The *History* is the non-party History which Hume came to realize Rapin had failed to provide. At the same time, the question of the rights and wrongs of the struggle in the seventeenth century became more complex. Most of Hume's contemporaries failed to understand this, and could only conclude that a History which was not obviously and fashionably Whig, must be Tory, or worse.

[1] The 'Memoranda for my History of England' in the National Library of Scotland throw little light on this process. We are told that William I 'introduced the feudal law into England', but there is no discussion of his title by conquest. On the whole the Memoranda do not provide sufficient evidence to enable one to draw any conclusions as to Hume's opinions in the standard controversial topics of English historiography.

It is true that the *History of England* was 'written to teach lessons directly relevant to contemporary politics', and to 'exorcise irrational hostility between the Whigs and the Tories'. But to call it 'primarily a tract for the times', and 'in an important sense anti-historical' is going too far.[1] It is an exaggeration, however, of an important truth about the *History*. It was an establishment history: the application of a theory of political obligation designed for a post-revolutionary establishment to the events of the seventeenth century, with the necessary allowances made (a) for the great difference between the constitution then and now; the failure to realize this was one of the greatest weaknesses of orthodox Whig history – at the same time, the philosophical historian is on the watch for signs of the emergence of our present form of government,[2] and (b) for the vital part played by religion, and 'enthusiasm', which is unaccountable and altogether beyond the ken of the philosopher.[3] In so far as the English owe their freedom to the Puritans,[4] they owe it to something wholly contingent and inexplicable.

[1] J. B. Stewart: *The Moral and Political Philosophy of David Hume* (1963), 298–9. Stewart remarks that 'it is notable that when he had finished his essentially negative task, he did not undertake another historical work'. He did not, it is true, but it is probably also true that no historian has ever spent so much time revising and correcting a single work. Hume was doing this vigorously right up to his death. I agree that there is an important sense in which the *History* is anti-historical – that is true of most histories, probably, and cannot be discussed here. Much of the usual criticism of Hume's as 'anti-historical' is mistaken.

[2] In addition to the examples below, cf. Hume's *History*, VI, 613–14. In 1621 a powerful opponent of the court in the House of Commons was made comptroller of the household, a privy counsellor, and soon after a baron. 'This event is memorable; as being the first instance, perhaps, in the whole history of England, of any king's advancing a man on account of parliamentary interest, and of opposition to his measures. However irregular this practice, it will be regarded by political reasoners, as one of the most early and most infallible symptoms of a regular established liberty.' Cf. VII, 172: Charles I does the same thing in 1630: 'a sure proof that a secret revolution had happened in the constitution, and had necessitated the prince to adopt new maxims of government'.

[3] *History*, VI, 569. 'But it is an observation suggested by all history, and by none more than by that of James and his successor, that the religious spirit, when it mingles with faction, contains in it something supernatural and unaccountable; and that, in its operations upon society, effects correspond less to their known causes than is found in any other circumstance of government.' This is a warning to rulers not to innovate lightly in 'so dangerous an article' and an apology for those who fail in their projected undertakings. Cf. VII, 171: in 1630, 'the spirit of enthusiasm being universally diffused, disappointed all the views of human prudence, and disturbed the operation of every motive which usually influences society'.

[4] As Hume says in VI, 46–7. In Elizabeth's reign, the precious spark of liberty had been kindled by the puritans alone, 'and it was to this sect, whose principles appear so frivolous and habits so ridiculous, that the English owe the whole freedom of their constitution'. Cf. also the *Pelican Classics* edition of the 1754 volume, 172–3:

An establishment history in a mixed monarchy must try to do justice to both sides in the dispute: each stood for a vital principle of the present constitution,[1] but as the implementation of one of these involved what was at the time a most violent innovation, it could only be justified retrospectively; an impartial history, therefore, doing justice to both sides, must have more than one point of view, viz: the constitution as it is now and the constitution as it was then. If one applied a proper theory of political obligation to the seventeenth-century conflict, a strong case could be made out for the Stuart kings at the time. It was not in the true interest of the Whigs to deny this, and, in history as in political philosophy, to cling to outmoded and unscientific views. The fashionable system of history was as unphilosophical as the fashionable system of politics, and equally self-defeating. This Hume endeavoured to point out in the essay on *Coalition of Parties*, which in effect is an apologia for the first volume of the *History* published four years previously. The essay brings out clearly another facet of the *History* considered as an establishment history: that it was designed, as Hume claims, to hasten the 'coalition of parties', meaning by that the abolition of the 'dangerous' distinction of Whig and Tory, of which Hume in 1758 saw 'the strongest symptoms of an universal desire'.

Just as the object of the essays on contract and passive obedience had been to show that neither party had a monopoly of truth and reason with regard to the 'philosophical and practical controversies between the parties', so, Hume says, a similar exercise of moderation with regard to the historical disputes between the parties will

the spirit of civil liberty reaped so much advantage and so little honour from its religious associate and VII, 314-15, 393, X, 182-3: theological zeal and religious controversy are the immediate cause of the civil war. Far from owing anything to the Puritans for our modern constitution, Carte sees them as ultimately responsible for its gross over-representation of the boroughs at the expense of the landed interest, and therefore for the venality and corruption of the modern House of Commons. They would have been an inconsiderable minority if they had not been patronized by powerful courtiers in Elizabeth's reign, who maintained that a practice used by Edward I of summoning demesne towns, many of them mere villages, was a right of representation and used it in favour of their protégés. The Puritans were introduced into the Commons by the increase of these pocket boroughs, and according to Carte their factious aim to reduce the king to the position of a doge was the cause of the war. See Carte IV, 5-6.

[1] The Whigs who have for nearly seventy years enjoyed the whole authority of government, have extolled only those who 'pursued as their object the perfection of civil society', at the expense of their antagonists, 'who maintained those maxims that are essential to its very existence' (IX, 524). This sentence was added in the last edition of the *History*, replacing one which accused the Whigs of assuming a right to impose their history as well as their political philosophy on the public and representing the other party as 'governed entirely by the lowest and most vulgar prejudices'.

show that there were powerful arguments on both sides – or at least that each side now can make out a strong case 'to justify the conduct of their predecessors, during that great crisis'. We owe our liberty and greatness to the views of those who resisted the Stuarts, but as the consequences could not have been foreseen, the royalists had a very powerful, perhaps the stronger, case, and Hume's presentation of it forms the bulk of the essay. It was the royalists, not their opponents, who were defending the ancient constitution, that is the constitution that had been 'incontestably established' and accepted since Henry VII at the very least – as long a period as that from Augustus to the Emperor Hadrian, and would it not have appeared ridiculous to have talked of the republican constitution in the reign of the latter? It was nonsense for the popular party to talk of recovering the ancient constitution, if by that they meant the 'ancient barbarous and gothic [after 1770, changed to 'feudal'] constitution', because under that the people had 'no authority, and even little or no liberty', and control of the kings was placed in the barons, not the commons. And before Magna Carta there was a constitution in which the barons themselves possessed few 'regular, stated privileges' and 'the house of commons probably had not an existence'.[1] This talk of recovering ancient liberty shows that the popular party themselves admit that innovation is dangerous, that the only rule of government is use and practice, and the 'true rule of government is the present established practice of the age'. The arguments of the popular party have been justified by the event, 'if that can be admitted as a reason', but 'beforehand', the views of the royalists 'ought...to have appeared more solid, more safe and more legal'.

The essay ends with an appeal to the 'malcontents' to 'acquiesce entirely in the present settlement of the constitution', especially since 'they must be sensible that the very principle which made the strength of their party and from which it derived its chief authority, has now deserted them and gone over to their antagonists'. Now that the plan of liberty is settled, the argument of the royalists against those who first proposed it has become an argument for it. And for the Whigs to reject this interpretation of the seventeenth-century conflict is not only 'contrary to the clearest evidence of facts', but inept, because 'there is not a more effectual method of betraying a cause than to lay the stress of the argument in a wrong place; and by disputing an untenable post, ensure the adversaries

[1] In the *History* published three years later, in the medieval section, there is no 'probably' about it.

to success and victory'. This sort of over-active zeal keeps the conflict going on a front where the Whigs cannot win anyway, and helps to turn the moderate opposition to the establishment of their enemies into an implacable hostility.

As can be seen from the essay on *Coalition of Parties*, an apology for the governments of James I and Charles I from the point of view of the present establishment – and this was the real novelty of Hume's *History* and the rock of offence to Whig orthodoxy, and the first volume to be published was the crucial one and the hinge of the whole *History* – involved a radical revision of the accepted theory or theories of ancient constitutionalism. It was James I and Charles I who adhered to the ancient constitution, 'that which prevailed before the settlement of our present plan of liberty'. There was a more ancient constitution where, though the people had perhaps less liberty than under the Tudors, the king had less authority: the barons both checked him and oppressed the people. But there was a still more ancient constitution before the signing of the charters, when neither the people nor the barons had any regular privileges. 'The English constitution, like all others, has been in a state of continual fluctuation' (*History*, VI, 404–5n). This note on the ancient constitution was added to the *History* in 1763: it echoes, in Appendix III of the Tudor section, the essay on *Coalition of Parties* and the last three paragraphs of the *History* (because the writing, as opposed to revising, of the *History* ended with 1485), in which Hume gives a brief summary of the fluctuations of the constitution, up to 1485, and points the moral: that the more ancient the constitution, the more primitive and barbarous and unworthy of imitation it is (IV, 52–5). The Remarks on English History in the *Craftsman* begin, and Hume's *History* ends with a picture of a constitution continually changing, but Bolingbroke does not describe change at all, but the attempts to subvert and destroy something which (so far) has managed triumphantly to survive: the fluctuations conceal an essential continuity. In Hume, there is no single ancient constitution, but several, constituting a progressive series.

According to Hume, the Saxon government, originally 'free' and 'democratical', became progressively aristocratic (IV, 53 and below) a trend which was checked by the Norman Conquest, which introduced the feudal law and feudal government, a system unfavourable to the liberty of the people,[1] and with a strong bias

---

[1] 'If the feudal government was so little favourable to the true liberty even of the military vassal, it was still more destructive of the independence and security of the

towards aristocracy and depression of the monarchy, which however in England was checked by the peculiar circumstances of the Conquest (II, 240, 287), until the 'epoch' of Magna Carta, after which the king was theoretically at any rate limited by law, but in fact the feudal government was a mixture of regal tyranny and aristocratical 'licentiousness' (II, 376). It was this tug of war between the king and the great barons which increased the power of parliament; in Edward III's reign, even the House of Commons 'began to appear of some weight in the constitution' (III, 217).[1] If Edward III's reign deserves to be studied in order to show the true genius of the kind of mixed government then established in England, it was not for the reason put forward by Bolingbroke, for whom Edward III is one of the great heroes of the constitution, but because it was a confusion of opposite and incompatible 'systems', that of the king, that of the nobles, that of the clergy, and that of the commons, the latter being by far the weakest and least important, even if their weight and authority was on the increase, especially under the Lancastrians (III, 234–5, 401).

The reign of Henry VII constitutes another 'epoch in the English constitution' (IV, 177): the power of the greater nobles – 'the mighty barons who rendered the people incapable of any regular system of civil government' (III, 481) – was curbed, so that the government of Henry VII, more absolute than that of any previous king, at least since the establishment of the great charter (IV, 176–7), was so much the less burdensome in that he was the sole oppressor in his kingdom (IV, 136). In the interval between the decline of the barons and the rise of the commons, the Tudors were able to establish a 'more regular system of government':[2] with the reformation the four competing 'systems' seen earlier were reduced to one, that of the king: Henry VIII was able by the courtship paid him by both Catholics and Protestants to assume an unbounded authority (IV, 417: Hume follows Rapin here), and 'the king, by being able to retain the nation in such a delicate medium, displayed the utmost power of an imperious despotism of which any history furnishes an example' (IV, 470). Parliament was reduced to being an instrument of the king's will, to convert

other members of the state, or what, in a proper sense, we call the people' (II, 284, cf. 285–7, 5, 128–9, I, 478, IV, 45).

[1] For Hume's account of the late origin of the Commons, see below.
[2] X, 153. In 1754 this was part of the text. See *Pelican Classics*, 170. In the editions of the *Coalition of Parties* from 1758–70, Hume says he believes he is the first writer to have advanced the thesis that the Tudors possessed in general more authority than their immediate predecessors (482n).

tyranny into law (IV, 503). The very fact that Henry could not impose taxes without consent of parliament – a rule fixed under the princes of the house of Lancaster (III, 400) – made the government more 'Turkish', because the king adopted the most oppressive expedients, 'which destroyed all security in private property', to get round the difficulty (IV, 166–7).

Henry could have extinguished English liberty for ever and changed the constitution into an absolute monarchy; so servile was the parliament that he had no need to. Given the support of the houses of parliament his authority was 'more absolute than any prince in a simple monarchy, even by means of military force, is ever able to obtain' (IV, 470). The people were so little jealous of their liberties, so anxious to make the crown quite independent and remove from themselves as much as possible the burdens of government, that they would have regarded a large standing army and fixed revenue on these conditions as great blessings, and the English 'owe all their present liberty' to Henry's prodigality and confidence that the power of the crown could never fail (X, 67).

In the reign of Elizabeth can be seen the 'faint dawn of the spirit of liberty among the English' (VI, 33–4), the 'dawn of liberty' (VI, 105), but so absolute was the authority of the crown that it was only the Puritans, 'actuated by that zeal which belongs to innovators and by the courage which enthusiasm inspires' (VI, 47), who dared to kindle and preserve 'the precious spark of liberty'. Otherwise her great popularity proves that her wholly arbitrary maxims of government were 'conformable to the principles of the times, and to the principle generally entertained with regard to the constitution' (VI, 46), and that 'she did not infringe any *established* liberties of the people' (VI, 405. The italics date from the last edition).

In a letter of September 1757 Hume wishes he had begun his *History* with the Tudors, so that he could have shown how absolute was the authority which the English kings possessed, and that 'the Stuarts did little or nothing more than continue matters in the former tract', thereby escaping the reproach of Jacobitism (*Letters*, I, 264), and dishing the Whigs in advance (Letter of January 1759 to Robertson, I, 294), who 'have long indulged their prejudices against the succeeding race of princes, by bestowing unbounded panegyrics on the virtue and wisdom of Elizabeth. They have even been so extremely ignorant of the transactions of this reign, as to extol her for a quality which, of all others, she was least possessed of; a tender regard for the constitution, and a concern for the liberties and privileges of her people.' (Beginning of Appendix III, VI, 403.)[1] He agrees with Bolingbroke that 'in order to understand the ancient constitution of England, there is not a period which deserves more to be studied than the reign of Elizabeth' (VI, 405), but for diametrically opposite reasons; to show that her prerogative was so extensive as to be 'incompatible with an exact or regular enjoyment of liberty' (VI, 420), and that 'in the two succeeding reigns it was the people who encroached upon the sovereign; not the sovereign who attempted, as is pretended, to usurp upon the people' (X, 111). For the plain fact is that those branches of prerogative which rendered the authority of the Tudor sovereigns virtually absolute were done away with. Whatever the rights and wrongs of the matter, no one can deny that this was what actually happened. The Stuart kings were deprived of powers which they had inherited from their immediate predecessors. And these powers are totally incompatible with 'all the ideas which we at present entertain of a legal constitution', so much so that 'there is a danger lest the public should run into the opposite extreme and should entertain an aversion to the memory of a princess who exercised the royal authority' in this way (VI, 403). In fact it becomes necessary to make out a case for the government of Elizabeth, especially as the exercise of many of these powers was not technically legal: there was more than one act on the statute book, besides Magna Carta, which prohibited them, as Charles I later discovered, to his surprise (VII, 100).[2]

There were branches of power, such as the dispensing power, the power of imprisonment, of exacting loans and benevolences, of erecting monopolies, which, if 'not directly opposite to the principles of all free governments, must, at least, be acknowledged dangerous to freedom in a monarchical constitution', but the kings of England had constantly exercised them, and if on any occasion they had had to submit to laws enacted against them, they

[1] Cf. *Pelican classics*, 204–5n. Certain writers 'from a shameful ignorance' represent Elizabeth's government as 'the model of liberty'. Cf. VI, 390. Hume wrote in a letter of 1765 that to describe Queen Elizabeth's maxims of government as arbitrary, and as arbitrary as those of the Stuarts, 'tho now an undoubted and acknowledged truth, is contrary to the Principles of sound Whiggery' (*Letters*, I, 502). Nevertheless it was the view of, among others, Hurd and Blackstone. Perhaps he means among politicians: he goes on to say that Grenville took exception to him for that reason.
[2] '...the king was astonished to observe that a power exercised by his predecessors, almost without interruption, was found, upon trial, to be directly opposite to the clearest laws...'

had always eluded these laws and returned to the same arbitrary administration. For almost three centuries before the accession of James I the regal authority, in all these particulars, had never once been called in question (VII, 5).[1] These technical irregularities had for so long been regarded as necessary that they had acquired a sort of regularity, though Hume says that 'though established for several centuries', they 'were scarcely ever allowed by the English to be parts of their constitution' (II, 534).[2] In this way Elizabeth's government is justified by the application of Hume's general theory of political obligation. 'In the particular exertions of power the question ought never to be forgotten, *What is best?* But in the general distribution of power among the several members of a constitution, there can seldom be admitted any other question than *What is usual?*' (changed in the final edition to '*What is established*') (VI, 404). Or, as Hume said in his concluding survey of the history of the constitution, or constitutions, at the end of the reign of Richard III: 'in each of these successive alterations, the only rule of government which is intelligible, or carries any authority with it, is the established practice of the age, and the maxims of administration which are at that time prevalent and universally assented to' (IV, 54).

It should be noticed that Hume says: 'in the general distribution of power among the several members of a constitution', the rule is not what is best, but what is usual, or established. He does not here, as he does elsewhere, breach his general theory of political obligation and make an exception for the case of a limited monarchy. And on this ground, it is not easy to see how there could be a case for the House of Commons in the reigns of James I and Charles I at all: their resistance could only be justified retrospectively. Even if the king exercised power much beyond what was 'usual', even if he aimed to make his government absolute, and Hume gives the impression that he would not have had very far to go in order to turn the quasi-absolute monarchy of Elizabeth

---

[1] Cf. VII, 98–100. The kings of England had not been able to prevent the enacting of various statutes (which Hume lists) in favour of personal liberty, but had sufficient authority, when the 'tide of liberty was spent', to obstruct their regular execution, and deemed it superfluous to attempt the formal repeal of statutes which they found so many expedients and pretences to elude. The safety of the people absolutely required the exercise of special powers in turbulent times. Cf. VI, 154: the fines levied by the Court of High Commission were discretionary and often contrary to the established laws of the kingdom.

[2] The affection of the nation for liberty prevailed over all precedent and even all political reasoning and the exercise of these powers was, in fullness of time, 'solemnly abolished as illegal, at least as oppressive, by the whole legislative authority' (*id.*).

into a simple monarchy,[1] there would still have been no right of resistance – neither James nor Charles was a Nero.

But the situation is complicated by the fact (a) that what was 'usual' and 'established' under Elizabeth was by 1600 beginning to be seriously questioned: it was no longer generally accepted, and (b) Hume does not apply his general theory when he comes to the conflict of King and Commons in the seventeenth century. According to that, as has been seen, the Commons had no case. He applies the special theory of what is justified in a mixed monarchy, and that is why it becomes difficult to decide the justice of the quarrel.[2] Although the Stuart kings were defending the ancient constitution from what they regarded as encroachment on their authority, their power, however great, was not unlimited. However 'inaccurate the English constitution was, before the parliament was enabled by continued acquisitions or encroachments, to establish it on fixed principles of liberty' (VI, 528), however 'confused and uncertain' men's ideas of the constitution may have been (VII, 202), however much 'the ambiguous nature of the English constitution' may excuse Charles I's high notions of prerogative (VII, 68), and even if many people regarded it as absolute, it was not in fact an absolute monarchy, but had always been limited, however inaccurately. It was therefore possible to see the king as claiming and exercising powers incompatible with limited monarchy, however ill-defined and inaccurate. And this the first two Stuarts undoubtedly did. It was possible, therefore, for Hume to say that James I, 'while he imagined that he was only maintaining his authority...in a few of his actions, and still more

[1] 'I have not met with any English writer in that age who speaks of England as a limited monarchy, but as an absolute one, where the people have many privileges. That is no contradiction. In all European monarchies the people have privileges; but whether dependent or independent on the will of the monarch, is a question, that, in most governments it is better to forbear' (X, 103). In the edition of 1754 this is also part of a note, but the note itself is slightly shorter, (*Pelican Classics*, 224). 'By a great many, therefore, monarchy, simple and unmixed was conceived to be the government of England' (VII, 6). In the *Protestant Succession* essay (1752–68), these notions were 'very common, though not, perhaps the universal notions of the times' (491). 'Upon the whole, we must conceive that monarchy, on the accession, of the house of Stuart, was possessed of a very extensive authority: an authority, in the judgement of all, not exactly limited; in the judgement of some, not limitable (VII, 8).
[2] As Hume says when discussing the character of Cromwell. His enemies violently reproach him, but that he should prefer the parliamentary to the royal cause 'will not appear extraordinary; since even at present, some men of sense and knowledge are disposed to think that the question, with regard to the justice of the quarrel, may be regarded as very doubtful and uncertain', (VIII, 335, The 'very' was later withdrawn).

of his pretensions...somewhat encroached on the liberties of his people' (VI, 662), even if his 'despotism was more speculative than practical' (VI, 533), and Charles I 'never respected sufficiently the privileges of the parliament' (*Pelican classics*, 387, VII, 268). It is possible for Hume to say that Charles 'never sufficiently respected the constitution' (*Pelican classics*, 393) without subscribing to ancient constitutionalism, or to the 'system' of Rapin, according to which he, like his father, designed to subvert the constitution: their actions plainly show that they had formed no such plan.[1] However, Hume says quite clearly that they were not acting always on the defensive,[2] that they 'encroached' and went too far (especially Charles I): too far, that is, when judged from the point of view of what is legitimate in the special case of a mixed monarchy. Hume makes this as plain as any orthodox Whig could desire, and the fact that he later toned down and qualified many of the more forthright remarks of the 1754 edition to agree better with what he had discovered concerning the exercise of royal power in earlier reigns, does not alter the fundamental condemnation. For example, Hume says that had Charles I possessed a standing army, ''tis likely that he had, at once, taken off the mask [in 1626] and governed without any regard to the ancient laws and constitution' (*Pelican classics*, 275–6; in later editions this becomes 'without any regard to parliamentary privileges', VII, 93). In 1627, 'moderate men' could not 'esteem the provocation which the king had received, though great, sufficient to warrant all these violent measures. The commons, as yet, had no-wise invaded his authority: they had only exercised, as best pleased them, their own privileges' (VII,103). In 1628, 'there is nothing which tends more to excuse, if not justify, the extreme rigour of the Commons towards Charles, than his open encouragement and avowal of such general principles as were altogether incompatible with a limited government' (VII, 133). During the time that he ruled without parliaments, Charles levied money 'either by the revival of obsolete laws, or by violations, some more open, some more disguised, of the privileges of the nation' (VII, 184), and 'too lightly moved by the appearance of necessity, the King had assumed powers altogether incompatible with the principles of limited government, and had rendered it impossible for his most zealous partisans to justify his conduct, except by topics so odious that they were more fitted to inflame

---

[1] 'James...had certainly laid no plan for extending his power' (VII, 18).
[2] James' violent letter to the Commons of 1621, in which the king, 'may be thought not to have acted altogether on the defensive'. In later editions Hume added 'though he here imitated former precedents' (VI, 609).

than appease the general discontent' (*Pelican classics*, 396. In later editions, after 'the King' Hume inserted 'perhaps', VII, 280). Charles had stretched the rights of his prerogative beyond former precedent (*Pelican classics*, 420; later versions have 'perhaps', VII, 320). The King 'had stretched his prerogative beyond its just bounds: [in the last edition 'in some instances' is added (VIII, 239)] and aided by the church, had well nigh put an end to all the liberties and privileges of the nation' (*History of Great Britain containing the Commonwealth etc.*, London, 1759, 45). 'Their violations of law [i.e. of James I and Charles I] particularly those of Charles, are palpable, and obvious, and were, generally speaking transgressions of a plain limit, which was marked out to royal authority' (*Pelican classics*, 390. The latest edition has, after 'Charles', 'are in some few instances, transgressions of a plain limit' [X, 178]. The note was originally part of the text.)

The corollary of this is that the Commons were on the defensive: defending established liberties from the encroachments of royal authority, so that, for example, one finds Hume saying (in connexion with Goodwin's case in 1604) that 'a power like this' – to judge their own election returns – 'so essential to the exercise of all their other powers, themselves so essential to public liberty, cannot fairly be deemed an encroachment in the commons; but must be regarded as an inherent privilege, happily rescued from that ambiguity which the negligence of former parliaments had thrown upon it' (VI, 485). Discussing ship-money, Hume says that although there were some precedents for it, it would be rash to affirm that Charles' maxim, that national privileges must give way to supreme power in the public good generally and not only in cases of extreme necessity, was derived from the uniform tenor of English laws, and 'public liberty must be so precarious under this exorbitant prerogative as to render an opposition not only excusable, but laudable, in the people' (VII, 198). This clashes with the justification of Elizabeth's quasi-despotic government in Appendix III: the Commons' case is now grounded on Hume's special, not general, justification of resistance.

As has been seen, an opposition in the people cannot be justified on Hume's general theory of political obligation. In the reign of James I, the growth of trade and industry for which Elizabeth is so dubiously praised[1] really got under way, the country was pros-

[1] '...as her monopolies tended to extinguish all domestic industry, which is much more valuable than foreign trade, and is the foundation of it, the general train of her conduct was ill calculated to serve the purpose at which she aimed, much less to promote the riches of her people' (VI, 438, cf. 490).

'THE HISTORY OF ENGLAND'

perous, the burden of government so light as to be virtually non-existent, the condition of the gentry (the class which constituted the House of Commons) as happy as human affairs allow.[1] And of the Eleven Years Tyranny, Hume wrote: 'The grievances, under which the English laboured, when considered in themselves, scarce deserve the name:[2] nor were they either burthensome on the people's revenues, or any way shocking to the natural humanity of mankind. Even the taxation of ship money, independent of the consequences, was rather an advantage to the public; by the judicious use which the King made of the money levied by that expedient. And tho' it was justly apprehended, that such precedents, if patiently submitted to, would end in a total disuse of parliaments, and in the establishment of arbitrary authority; Charles dreaded no opposition from the people, who are not commonly much affected with consequences, and require some striking motive, to engage them into resistance of established government... Peace too, industry, commerce, opulence, along with justice and lenity of administration: All these were fully enjoyed by the people; and every other blessing of government, except liberty, or rather the present exercise of liberty, and its proper security.'[3]

But in so far as in Hume's political philosophy, 'liberty' and 'justice' are virtually the same thing: the liberty and security of individuals under the rule of law, then the object of government as envisaged by Hume was realized in England on the eve of the civil war. 'Present exercise of liberty and its proper security' applies only to mixed monarchies.

But the crucial point of the story as told by Hume is that the commons were not simply on the defensive. They, or their leaders (i.e. the political as opposed to the religious Puritans, or Puritans in so far as they were politically motivated)[4] were able to

[1] 'Could human nature ever reach happiness, the condition of the English gentry under so mild and benign a prince, might merit that appellation' (VII, 20). The prince is James I. Cf. VI, 661: 'the prosperous and pacific reign of James'. For the lightness of the burden of government, see VI, 493, VII, 536. 'It may...be affirmed, that during no preceding period of English history, was there a more sensible increase than during the reign of this monarch, of all the advantages which distinguish a flourishing people' (VII, 33).
[2] Cf. VI, 300. It was only after the assembly of the Long Parliament that 'the nation caught new fire from the popular leaders, and seemed now to have made the first discovery of the many supposed disorders in the government'.
[3] *Pelican classics*, 357. In the latest edition after 'administration' was inserted 'notwithstanding some very few exceptions', and 'fully' was removed; 'rather an advantage' becomes 'a great and evident advantage' (VII, 220–1).
[4] Hume is at pains to point out that religious enthusiasm and civil ability are not

275

see that a new situation had arisen which called for a new, more regular type of free government. They aimed at a 'new plan of liberty'. By this Hume does not mean something that sprang fully-fashioned from the heads of the commons' leaders, in the sort of 'unhistorical' mode that was once regarded as typical of eighteenth-century historians.

The 'new plan of liberty' involved a change in the climate of opinion due to the progress of society and civilization and the emergence of the 'middling rank', which refused any longer, because it was no longer in their interest, to tolerate anomalies and irregularities and evasions of laws in favour of liberty and parliamentary privilege, which were useful once and generally accepted in the interests of good order and good government, or because they were essential to any sort of government at all, but which had outgrown their usefulness and necessity, i.e., existing laws could and should be made into real laws which were systematically and universally enforced without discretionary powers on the part of the magistrate, as was essential in a regular mixed monarchy. Hume says several times in the course of his *History* that the illegalities which had been so consistently practised by kings were never, after the 'epoch' of Magna Carta, regarded as constitutional and legal. He was anxious, for example to show that the government of Edward III (one of Bolingbroke's constitutional heroes) was extremely arbitrary: he openly and avowedly imposed taxes without consent of parliament. But, says Hume, one must distinguish between the *right* and the *practice* of the times; the *right* seems to be on the side of the commons, whose repeated remonstrances 'served to prevent the arbitrary practices of the court from becoming an established part of the constitution' (III, 221–4). In the feudal constitution the prince 'naturally proceeded, from the acquiescence of the people, to assume, in many particulars of moment, an authority from which he had excluded himself by express statutes, charters or concessions, and which was, in the main, repugnant to the general genius of the constitution' (II, 320–1). 'Accordingly we find that, though arbitrary practices often

necessarily incompatible; 'though the religious schemes of many of ['many of' is lacking in the first edition] the puritans, when explained, appear [first edition inserts 'many of them'] pretty frivolous, we are not thence to imagine that they were pursued by none but persons of weak understandings [first editions has 'fools']. Some men ['many men'] of the greatest parts and most extensive knowledge that the nation at this time produced, could not enjoy peace of mind; because obliged to hear prayers offered up to the Divinity by a priest covered with a white linen vestment', (VII, 64–5, *Pelican classics*, 259).

prevailed, and were even able to establish themselves into settled customs, the validity of the Great Charter was never afterwards formally disputed; and that grant was still regarded as the basis of English government, and the sure rule by which the authority of every custom was to be tried and canvassed' (II, 534). In the Tudor despotism, 'there remained at that time (1547) in England an idea of laws and a constitution...' (V, 86). The impression one gets is that there were two constitutions, or two levels of constitutional thinking: unconstitutional practices accepted as necessary and hallowed by custom and customary acceptance are 'constitutional' in that sense, and at the same time illegal and recognized to be so. But this is part of the irregularity which after 1600 the commons, increasingly, would stand no longer, when it came to be more generally understood what the nature of law and constitution was and implied. It is not inconsistency in Hume; it is part of the story: viz: that before 1600 the people had 'a very feeble sense of law and a constitution' (III, 490n), as is shown by the repeated confirmations of Magna Carta, 'a precaution which...discovers some ignorance of the true nature of law and government' (II, 534) because it was not understood that a law 'instead of acquiring, was imagined to lose force by time' (III, 219).

The 'new plan of liberty' was thus not new in the sense of a new discovery or invention, nor, on the other hand was it simply a restoration or renewal. It was the result of a new attitude to law and government in general, as 'rigid', systematic and uniform, not a matter of picking and choosing the favourable, and ignoring the unfavourable precedents; the government of laws, not men. This was the significance of the Five Knights case of 1626: they were the first who claimed the protection of the constitution against the will of the sovereign. 'It was not till this age, when the spirit of liberty was universally diffused, when the principles of government were nearly reduced to a system, when the tempers of men, more civilized, seemed less to require those violent exertions of prerogative, that these five gentlemen...ventured in this national cause, to bring the question to a final determination. And the king was astonished to observe, that a power exercised by his predecessors, almost without interruption, was found, upon trial, to be directly opposite to the clearest laws...' (VII, 99–100). And with regard to martial law, 'men, now become more jealous of liberty, and more refined reasoners in questions of government, regarded as illegal and arbitrary, every exercise of authority which was not supported by express statute or uninterrupted precedent'

(VII, 102). Thus tonnage and poundage as previously levied, without consent of parliament – and Hume came to see that this had been the rule rather than the exception (V, 62, VI, 524) – was now regarded as an intolerable incongruity in a free constitution (VII, 321), as was neglect of the statute of Edward III calling for annual parliaments; a defect supplied by the Triennial Bill (1640), than which 'nothing could be more necessary...for completing a regular plan of law and liberty', but which was at the same time a great innovation (VII, 322–3).

The ancient constitution was now seen to be an 'inconsistent fabric' in which liberty somehow managed to exist alongside the most arbitrary authority in the king. The former royal prerogatives, especially the dispensing power – and nothing shows more clearly 'the irregular nature of the old English government than the existence of such a prerogative, always exercised and never questioned till the acquisition of real liberty discovered at last the danger of it' (IX, 423n) – were seen to be absolutely incompatible with the 'accuracy' and 'regularity' now demanded of the constitution, though the process of fully realizing this, both in theory and practice, was not complete until the Revolution, by means of which 'a uniform edifice was at last erected [the final version has "more uniform"]: the monstrous inconsistence, so visible between the ancient Gothic parts of the fabric and the recent plans of liberty, was fully corrected: and to their mutual felicity, king and people were finally taught to know their proper boundaries' (IX, 422, cf. VI, 556). It was this demand for uniformity and regularity in government which constituted the innovation on the part of the commons. It was this, for instance, which made the Petition of Right not a restoration or return to first principles, but 'such a change in the government as was almost equivalent to a revolution' (VII, 135): 'the great charter and the old statutes were sufficiently clear in favour of liberty' ('personal liberty' in the final edition), but as all kings of England had been accustomed in cases of necessity or expediency to elude them, 'the commons judged it requisite to enact a new law, which might not be eluded or violated, by any interpretation, construction or contrary precedent', and Charles' promise to return to the way of his predecessors did not satisfy them precisely because they thought that his predecessors had enjoyed too much discretionary power (VII, 129). To make the 'new plan of liberty...quite uniform and systematical' it was necessary to abolish all legislative power except that of parliament (VII, 296). The result was a retrenchment of the royal prerogative so great as to constitute a new type of government: a mixed monarchy in which the powers of king and commons were strictly defined, and the rule of law made absolute to a degree not found in any other government, something quite new in the history of political ideas not only in England,[1] but in any government, ancient or modern.[2]

What is acceptable and necessary in rude ages ceases to be so with the progress of civilization and political knowledge, 'nor will the same maxims of government suit...a rude people, that may be proper in a more advanced stage of society. The establishment of the Star Chamber, or the enlargement of its power in the reign of Henry VII might have been as wise as the abolition of it in that of Charles I' (x, 52). By the beginning of the seventeenth century, an economic, social and intellectual revolution had set the scene for great political changes. 'About this period the minds of men throughout Europe, especially in England, seem to have undergone a general, but insensible revolution.' Letters, revived in the preceding age, now began to spread among men of the world.

Arts, both mechanical and liberal, were every day receiving great improvements...Travelling was secure and agreeable. And the general system of politics in Europe was become more enlarged and comprehensive.

In consequence of this universal fermentation, the ideas of men enlarged themselves on all sides; and the several constituent parts of the Gothic governments, which seem to have lain long inactive, began, everywhere, to operate and encroach on each other. On the continent, where the necessity of discipline had begotten standing armies, the princes commonly established an unlimited authority, and overpowered by force or intrigue, the liberties of the people. In England, the love of freedom, which, unless checked, flourishes extremely in all liberal natures, acquired new force, and was regulated by more enlarged views, suitable to that cultivated understanding which became, every day, more common among men of birth and education. A familiar acquaintance with the precious remains of antiquity excited, in every generous breast, a passion for a limited constitution, and begat an emulation of those manly virtues which the Greek and Roman authors...recommend to us. The severe though popular government of Elizabeth had confined

---

[1] 'It would seem...that the idea of a *hereditary, limited* monarchy, though implicitly supposed in many public transactions, had scarcely ever, as yet, been expressly formed by any English lawyer or politician' (VI, 515).

[2] 'The noble and free genius of the ancients which made the government of a single person be always regarded as a species of tyranny and usurpation, and kept them from forming any conception of a legal and regular monarchy...' (II, 189). Cf. x, 184 (*Pelican classics*, 505n): 'Perhaps the English is the first mixed government where the authority of every part has been very accurately defined...'

this spirit within very narrow bounds: But when a new and foreign family succeeded to the throne, and a prince less dreaded and less beloved, symptoms immediately appeared of a more free and independent genius in the nation (vi, 486–7).

At the same time the middling rank of men had emerged as a potential new support of law and order. Hitherto the king, 'who in effect was the same with the law' (vi, 455), had supported law and order single-handed. 'In the feudal governments, men were more anxious to secure their private property than to share in the public administration; and provided no innovations were attempted on their rights and possessions, the care of executing the laws and ensuring general safety was without jealousy entrusted to the sovereign' (ix, 416–17). 'The name, the authority of the king alone appeared in the common course of government; in extraordinary emergencies he assumed, with still better reason, the sole direction; the imperfect and unformed laws left in everything a latitude of interpretation; and when the ends pursued by the monarch were in general agreeable to his subjects, little scruple or jealousy was entertained with regard to the regularity of the means' (x, 152, *Pelican classics*, 169–70). The check on the royal authority was provided by the power of the church (ii, 323), and the still more dangerous military power of the barons. '...on the whole, though the royal authority was confined within bounds and often within very narrow ones, yet the check was irregular, and frequently the scene of great disorders; nor was it derived from the liberty of the people, but from the military power of many petty tyrants, who were equally dangerous to the prince, and oppressive to the subject' (ii, 322). 'The sword...was not properly speaking in the hands of the people' (ii, 397). 'Thus all was confusion and disorder; no regular idea of a constitution; force and violence decided everything' (ii, 112, cf. i, 243).

But 'after the power of alienations, as well as the increase of commerce, had thrown the balance of property into the hands of the commons, the situation of affairs, and the dispositions of men, became susceptible of a more regular plan of liberty; and the laws were not supported singly by the authority of the sovereign'. The commons were 'resolved to secure liberty by firmer barriers than their ancestors had hitherto provided for it' (vi, 523).

The progress of 'commerce and the arts' which had contributed to scatter the immense wealth of the barons, that had rendered them so formidable both to king and people, had in its further progress, begun to ruin 'the small proprietors of land'; and by both events 'the gentry, or that rank which composed the house of commons', enlarged their power and authority. Residing on their estates and thereby husbanding their resources and acquiring independence and at the same time formidable local influence by their hospitality, 'they would not be led by the court: they could not be driven: and thus the system of the English government received a total and a sudden alteration in the course of less than forty years' (VII, 19). The leading members of the commons, 'men of an independent genius and large views, began to regulate their opinions more by the future consequences which they foresaw, than by the former precedents which were set before them; and they less aspired at maintaining the ancient constitution, than at establishing a new one, and a freer, and a better' (VI, 526–7).

Hume emphasizes more than once not only the wealth but the foresight and intelligence and ability of the leaders of the House of Commons. 'The house of commons, we may observe, [in 1625] was almost entirely governed by a set of men of the most uncommon capacity, and the largest views: men who were now formed into a regular party and united...by fixed aims and projects' (VII, 65. cf. also VI, 488–9, VII, 113, 115). These 'generous patriots' realized the need for regular government, they understood the spirit of the age and so were able to see that the choice would have to be between regular absolute monarchy on the continental model, as established in France by Richelieu,[1] which meant entirely abandoning the privileges of the people, because 'it would be impossible, they thought, when all these pretensions were methodized, and prosecuted by the increasing knowledge of the age, to maintain any shadow of popular government', or regular liberty (VII, 66). They saw Charles making a regular system of the royal prerogatives (VII, 102–3). 'In this dilemma, men of such aspiring genius and such independent fortune could not long deliberate: they boldly embraced the side of freedom...' (VII, 66).

And for this they deserve praise, and they get it from Hume, all the more because they were a pioneering minority[2] and especially because political liberty is not one of those immediate interests

[1] 'That confused and inaccurate genius of government of which France partook in common with other European kingdoms, he changed into a simple monarchy; at the very time when the incapacity of Buckingham encouraged the free spirit of the commons to establish in England a regular system of liberty' (VII, 105).

[2] 'At that time [1604] men of genius and enlarged minds had adopted the principles of liberty, which were as yet pretty much unknown to the generality of the people' (X, 140).

which strike most forcefully on the senses and the imagination and commonly move men to action at the expense of more remote interests; 'the people are always most affected by what is external and exposed to the senses' (VII, 229). Hume's praise of the 'generous patriots' can be linked to his psychology, to his description of the condition of England on the eve of the Civil War, happy in everything except the enjoyment of political liberty, and to the final sentence of the essay on *Government*, which makes the point that political liberty (the perfection of civil society) is apt to be neglected by men's indolence or overlooked by their ignorance, and therefore, it can be plausibly argued, needs to be guarded with more jealousy than authority, in so far as that is essential to the very existence of society, and 'supports itself'.

So Hampden 'has merited great renown with posterity, for the bold stand which he made in defence of the laws and liberties of his country' (VII, 213), and the merits of the Long Parliament, in its first, reforming phase, 'so much outweigh their mistakes, as to entitle them to praise from all lovers of liberty', and 'if the means by which they obtained such advantages savour often of artifice, sometimes of violence; it is to be considered, that revolutions of government cannot be effected by the mere force of argument and reasoning' (VII, 361–2). Nor does Hume say that the 'plan of liberty' necessarily led to the excesses which resulted eventually in 'slavery': what he has to say about the too 'fond' (later 'eager') pursuit of liberty leading to 'slavery' (VIII, 71, cf. 240), and the people seldom gaining anything 'by revolutions in government' (VIII, 102), is not an indictment of the 'new plan of liberty'. The excesses which had this unfortunate outcome were due to contingent factors, apart from which moderation might have prevailed; especially religious fanaticism, the 'infusion of theological hatred' (VII, 314–15), that 'great tang of enthusiasm in the conduct of the parliamentary leaders, which, though it might render their conduct sincere, will not much enhance their character with posterity' (X, 187). The commons' encroachments on the royal authority in 1641, which led to the War, would not have been 'in the power, scarcely in the intention of the popular leaders...had it not been for the passion which seized the nation for presbyterian discipline, and the wild enthusiasm which at the time accompanied it' (VII, 393).

On the other hand, Hume insisted that an establishment history cannot praise the patriots who stood for liberty unreservedly. Many constitutions, 'and none more than the British', have been improved by violent innovations, but 'the praise bestowed on those patriots to whom the nation has been indebted for its privileges, ought to be given with some reserve, and surely without the least rancour against those who adhered to the ancient constitution' (VI, 404). In so far as by the beginning of Charles I's reign, at least, they had formed a party and a plan whose object was to reduce their prince to subjection (VII, 149), they were the aggressors. Hume's account of Charles' first parliament is streamlined to make this point clear. From this point of view it was the commons who encroached and innovated.[1] And the new plan of liberty involved an experiment, a regular limited monarchy, shorn of all discretionary power, hitherto unheard of in the history of government and wholly untried. 'It must, however, be confessed, that the experiment here made by the parliament, was not a little rash and adventurous. No government at that time appeared in the world, nor is perhaps to be found in the records of any history, which subsisted without the mixture of some arbitrary authority, committed to some magistrate; and it might reasonably, beforehand, appear doubtful, whether human society could ever reach that state of perfection, as to support itself with no other control than the general and rigid maxims of law and equity.' In the event, in spite of some 'sensible inconveniences' it has been found to work (VII, 360), but to take the side of those who stood for liberty against authority without any reservations, to throw all the blame on those who resisted the 'patriots' in defence of the ancient constitution, would be tantamount to giving *carte blanche* to the most violent innovations and the most visionary schemes of perfection, because the plan of liberty was wholly new and untried, even now unique, and therefore an exceedingly hazardous venture when it first emerged.[2] And Hume took the occasion of

[1] 'Charles in the former part of his reign, had endeavoured to overcome the intractable and encroaching spirit of the commons...' (VII, 320). The Triennial Bill, however necessary to complete the 'regular plan of law and liberty' was a 'great... innovation in the constitution' (VII, 323). In 1621 'the wise and moderate in the nation' saw that it was 'not sufficient for liberty to remain on the defensive...it was become necessary to carry on an offensive war, and to circumscribe, within more narrow, as well as more exact bounds, the authority of the sovereign' (VII, 618).

[2] Cf. the *Original Contract* essay (464). Hume says that the violent innovations in the reign of Charles I 'were derived from faction and fanaticism', as those in the reign of Henry VIII from the will of an imperious monarch, and 'both of them have proved happy in the issue. But even the former were long the source of many disorders... and if the measures of allegiance were to be taken from the latter, a total anarchy must have place in human society, and a final period at once be put to every government.' This was part of a passage added in the last revised edition and appeared for

the execution of Charles I to repeat his teaching about the dangers of the doctrine of resistance to government, using the technique of imaginary contemporaries considering the question in general (VIII, 143-4, *Pelican classics*, 685-6). What has been justified by success was not necessarily justified at the time; and an establishment history therefore demands a bifocal view of the commons' plan of liberty.

The 'wise and moderate in the nation' who endeavoured, in 1621, 'to preserve...an equitable neutrality',[1] who found the rights and wrongs on each side equally balanced and foresaw an inevitable conflict, 'where no party or both parties would justly bear the blame', in which they would not know 'what vows to form; were it not that liberty, so necessary to the perfection of human society, would be sufficient to bias their affections towards the side of its defenders' (VI, 618-19), must represent the philosopher looking back from the standpoint of established and regular liberty. If this was the opinion of wise and moderate men at the time it would clash with Hume's own principles: according to them a wise, neutral contemporary who could not foresee the successful outcome of the struggle should have sided with authority and the established government against so novel and dangerous an experiment.

What the 'wise and moderate' saw in 1621 was that it was not either of the parties, but the constitution, that was to blame. Hume's analysis in *Parties of Great Britain* which traced the rise of the parties to the constitution, is given new meaning: the conduct of Charles I did not proceed 'from ambition and an unjust desire of encroaching on the ancient liberties of the people', but 'was derived in a great measure from necessity, and from a natural desire of defending that prerogative which was transmitted to him

---

the first time in 1777. In a letter to Catherine Macaulay, of 1764, Hume says that he differs from her 'in some original principles...For as I look upon all kinds of subdivision of power, from the monarchy of France to the freest democracy of some Swiss Cantons to be equally legal, if established by custom and authority; I cannot but think, that the mixed monarchy of England, such as it was left by Queen Elizabeth, was a lawful form of government, and carried obligations to obedience and allegiance; at least it must be acknowledged, that the princes and ministers who supported that form, tho' somewhat arbitrarily, could not incur much blame on that account; and that there is more reason to make an apology for their antagonists than for them.' He goes on to say that the partisans of the noble cause of liberty disgraced it by their violence and cant and bigotry, 'which more than the principles of civil liberty, seem to have been the motive of all their actions', *New Letters*, 81.

[1] Rapin's 'wisest part of the nation' were those who 'had long since perceived the king's and the court's policy and their artifices to pave the way to arbitrary power'. Rapin's *History of England*, XI, 62.

from his ancestors, and which his parliaments were visibly encroaching on' (x, 186–7). This encroaching by the commons was natural too, given the motive of self-importance,[1] and 'the natural appetite for rule', which 'made the commons lend a willing ear to every doctrine which tended to augment their own power and influence' (vi, 516). If James I and Charles I clung to the prerogative power they had inherited and even stretched it further, it was not because they had formed a plan to establish absolute government, but because they were forced to act as they did by the necessities of the situation in which they found themselves. This is the lesson of moderation of the essay *That Politics may be reduced to a Science*, designed originally for the party strife engendered by the opposition to Walpole's administration, and now seen in the historiographical phase of Hume's campaign in aid of the establishment: it is unphilosophical to blame statesmen for actions which are largely the necessary result of the prevailing form of government and state of society. As Hume said in the *History*: "Tis the situation which decides entirely of the fortunes and characters of men' (the edition of 1763 has 'chiefly' instead of 'entirely'). The King, tenacious of his prerogative, 'found that he could not preserve the old claims of the crown without assuming new ones: a principle similar to that which many of his subjects seem to have formed with regard to the liberties of the people' (*Pelican classics*, 381. This paragraph is omitted in the final version.) 'The philosophy of government, accompanying a narration of its revolutions, may render history more intelligible as well as instructive. And nothing will tend more to abate the acrimony of party disputes, than to show men, that those events, which they impute to their adversaries as the deepest crimes, were the natural, if not the necessary result of the situation, in which the nation was placed during any period' (*Pelican classics*, 391. This later became part of a note, but the sentences quoted were omitted in the final version.)

This particular lesson in moderation, joined to the idea of the progress of society, takes one to the heart of Hume's philosophical account of the conflict of King and Commons in the first half of the seventeenth century, and provides a built-in impartiality which the critics, hunting for 'Tory' hares, are liable to overlook altogether. The scientific or 'philosophical' historian relates the behaviour of rulers and statesmen to the nature of the constitution and the laws, or to the absence or imperfection of these restraints.

---

[1] vii, 78: '...men needed but little instruction or rhetoric to recommend to them practices which increased their own importance and consideration'.

Therefore he must have a knowledge of the progress of civilization and of the degree of knowledge and improvement of the particular epoch or society whose politics he is studying. 'The rise, progress, perfection and decline of art and science are curious objects of contemplation, and intimately connected with a narration of civil transactions. The events of no particular period can be fully accounted for, but by considering the degrees of advancement which men have reached in those particulars' (IV, 43). The actions of rulers in an irregular constitution in a rude state of society and at a low level of political civilization, in which there is little respect for law or realization of the advantages of an equal administration of justice, and in which power and authority are not strictly and accurately defined, cannot be judged by the criterion of the well-regulated freedom of the modern constitution which we enjoy. This is presumably the relativism which Comte found and admired in Hume's *History*,[1] and which C. J. Fox condemned. Thus in medieval England, during the 'Gothic' or feudal constitution, when law was in such a rudimentary condition and respect for it so lacking, what appear to historians of 'the popular party' to be tyrannical actions on the part of rulers can be largely explained by the imperfections of the constitution and weak hands on a defective steering wheel. In the medieval volumes of the *History*, this theme often recurs. Thus the Norman kings were faced by barons who were 'totally ignorant of the nature of limited monarchy and...ill-qualified to conduct, in conjunction with their sovereign, the machine of government'; the Normans who domineered in England may be pronounced incapable of any true or regular liberty, which requires improvement in knowledge and morals and 'several ages' of settled and established government. So 'the prince, finding that greater opposition was often made to him when he enforced the laws than when he violated them, was apt to render his own will and pleasure the sole rule of government', and 'to consider more the power of the persons whom he might offend, than the rights of those whom he might injure' (I, 425). In medieval England, when 'the form of the constitution' was 'unstable', and as a result the dispositions of the people were 'turbulent' (III, 2),[2] it was weak, not arbitrary government that led to disorder.

---

[1] See H. Gouhier, *La Jeunesse d'Auguste Comte*, Vol. I, (1933), 218–20, Vol. III, (1941), 270–1.

[2] Cf. III, 214: Edward III's foreign adventures gave the nobles no leisure to 'breed the disturbances to which they were naturally so much inclined, and which the frame of the government seemed so much to authorise'.

And men, instead of regretting the manners of their age and the form of their constitution...imputed all errors to the person who had the misfortune to be entrusted with the reins of empire.

But though such mistakes are natural and almost unavoidable while the events are recent, it is a shameful delusion in modern historians, to imagine that all the ancient princes who were unfortunate in their government, were also tyrannical in their conduct, and that the seditions of the people always proceeded from some invasion of their privileges by the monarch.... It is easy to see that a constitution which depended so much on the character of the prince, must necessarily, in many of its parts, be a government of will, not of laws. But always to throw, without distinction, the blame of all disorders upon the sovereign would introduce a fatal error in politics and serve as a perpetual apology for treason and rebellion' (III, 47-8).

Under Edward III, there were 'several vices in the constitution, the bad consequences of which, all the power and vigilance of the king could not prevent' (III, 226). Again, the secret execution, or rather murder, of Gloucester by Richard II 'really proceeded from a defect of power in the king rather than from his ambition, and proves that instead of being dangerous to the constitution, he possessed not even the authority necessary for the execution of the laws' (III, 292). The large discretionary prerogatives of the Crown were essential in those times of disorder, when the laws had been so feebly executed even during the vigilant reign of Edward III; too great limitation of them would have been dangerous. 'If the king had possessed no arbitrary powers, while all the nobles assumed and exercised them, there must have ensued an absolute anarchy in the state'(III, 315). Again: the people complained of the arbitrary measures of Henry VI, 'which were in some degree, a necessary consequence of the irregular power then possessed by the prince, but which the least disaffection easily magnified into tyranny' (III, 483).[1]

Applying this principle to the conflict of Crown and people in the seventeenth century, the political scientist can see that the Stuarts were bound to exercise their prerogative to the full, especially as their maxims of government were challenged by 'opposite doctrines which *began* to be promulgated by the puritanical party' (VII, 7), and which later '*began* to prevail' (VII, 170, 197 – the italics are not in the first edition). If lack of discretionary

---

[1] An interesting example of this sort of determinism is to be seen in Hume's account of the Reformation in Scotland, where he says that in the circumstances in which the Church of Rome found itself, 'persecution is less the result of bigotry in the priests, than of a necessary policy' (V, 336-7).

powers is not an unmixed blessing even in the present constitution and advanced state of civilization, it would have been much more dangerous – if not so fatal as in the feudal constitution – at a time when the laws still lacked a sufficient degree of accuracy and refinement. Thus we are told that James I ignored the complaint of the commons in 1610 about the proceedings of the high commission court – 'it required no great penetration to see the extreme danger to liberty arising in a regal government, from such large discretionary powers as were exercised by that court' – because 'he was probably sensible that besides the diminution of his authority, many inconveniences must necessarily result from the abolishing of all discretionary power in every magistrate; and that the laws, were they ever so carefully framed and digested, could not possibly provide against every contingency; much less, where they had not, as yet attained a sufficient degree of accuracy and refinement' (VI, 530). Even at the time of the Habeas Corpus act in 1679: 'it may...be doubted whether the low state of the public revenue in this period, and of the military power, did not still render some discretionary authority in the crown necessary to the support of government' (IX, 232).[1] The authority of the first two Stuarts rested solely on 'the opinion of the people influenced by ancient precedent and example. It was not supported either by money or force of arms. And, for this reason, we need not wonder that the princes of that line were so extremely jealous of their prerogative; being sensible that, when their claims were ravished

[1] This remark was added to the last edition. Cf. VII, 126: Hume stages a debate (anno 1628) in which the court party present arguments for the power of imprisonment. 'Impartial reasoners will confess, that this subject is not, on both sides, without its difficulties. Where a general and rigid law is enacted against arbitrary imprisonment, it would appear, that government cannot, in times of sedition and faction, be conducted but by temporary suspensions of the law; and such an expedient was never thought of during the age of Charles.' It was not then conceived that the king did not, of himself, possess sufficient power for the security and protection of his people, or that the authority of the commons would become so absolute that the prince must always conform himself to it and could never have any occasion to guard against their practices, as well as against those of his other subjects. In his notes on Hume's History in the National Library of Scotland (MS. 9376), Sir James Steuart says that proper security against imprisonment is the best characteristic of civil liberty, but that there is no country in Europe in which any such privilege is actually enjoyed by the subjects, notwithstanding the great variety of what we call free governments. 'In every state I am acquainted with, there resides an arbitrary power in some person to imprison at will.' Even in England, in spite of Habeas Corpus, the king has this power, and it is only due to the spirit of the times and of the people, that liberty from short imprisonment is so commonly enjoyed. 'The unlimited power of imprisoning the subjects at pleasure still appears to be inherent in the royal prerogative of an English King; though the unlimited exercise of it be circumscribed by the Habeas Corpus statute' (84–5).

from them, they possessed no influence by which they could maintain their dignity, or support the laws' (VII, 8–9).

Their skill in government was not sufficient to cope with 'the extreme delicacy of their situation' (X, 177–8, *Pelican classics*, 390, and cf. 381), it is true, but they had to function as kings of England when it was harder to do so than at any other time: at the end of a period, which, coming between the downfall of the old nobility and the rise of the commons, was exceptionally favourable to monarchy, and before the emergence of the modern system of controlling and 'managing' parliament. And a stage had been reached in the progress of society when there was bound to be conflict between those who regarded the constitution as irregular and potentially dangerous, and those in authority whose duty it was to govern and make the constitution work. This is what the 'wise and moderate' saw in 1621: that liberty could no longer remain on the defensive; the king's authority must be more narrowly and exactly circumscribed, and any king, however just and moderate, would endeavour to repress his opponents and in the process almost certainly overstep the bounds 'hastily and unknowingly' (VI, 618).

There was bound to be conflict because in reality the king was weak. As a result of the discovery and conquest of the West Indies, gold and silver became more plentiful in England, prices rose as never before since the decline of the Roman empire, but the revenue of the crown did not rise in proportion. The increase of wealth and luxury weakened the king in relation to his subjects, and made his need for money greater, just when the same cause bred in them a spirit of freedom and independence (VI, 522–3). At the same time, 'the majesty of the crown, derived from ancient powers and prerogatives... begat in the king so high an idea of his own rank and station, as made him incapable of stooping to popular courses, or submitting in any degree to the control of parliament' (X, 177, *Pelican classics*, 390). It has been seen already that in the English mixed government parliament must have certain privileges which cannot, in their very nature, be defined and bounded by law, and, given human nature and ambition, are almost certain to be abused, and that certain 'irregular checks' have at different periods, supplied what the laws cannot. Before the beginning of the seventeenth century, the king possessed an independent source of revenue in his large demesnes, the expense of government was comparatively small, the meetings of parliament precarious and infrequent, and in consequence its members were unable to combine in factions or become acquainted with public business. In the present constitution all this has changed, but the king now has sufficient revenue from new sources to be able to maintain the balance. 'It was the fate of the house of Stuart to govern England at a period when the former source of authority was already much diminished, and before the latter had begun to flow in any tolerable abundance. Without a regular and fixed foundation, the throne perpetually tottered; and the prince sat upon it anxiously and precariously' (x, 175-7, *Pelican classics*, 388-91).[1] If Charles I had been born an absolute prince, his humanity and good sense would have made his reign happy; in an accurately limited monarchy, his integrity would have made him regard as sacred the boundaries of the constitution. As it was, he was involved in an 'inextricable labyrinth' in which he was forced to raise his claims, or else cease to be a king, as he understood kingship in the ancient constitution, altogether (VII, 153-4).

It was a wrongheaded and superficial interpretation, therefore, which threw all the blame on the Stuarts. 'The inconveniences suffered by the people under the first two reigns of that family (for in the main they were fortunate) proceeded in a great measure from the unavoidable situation of affairs; and scarcely anything could have prevented those events but such vigour of genius in the sovereign, attended with such good fortune, as might have enabled him entirely to overpower the liberties of his people' (IX, 520). And in so far as it showed that the Revolution was not simply a restoration of ancient liberties but the achievement of something wholly new in the history of government (though for that very reason not without dangers and disadvantages) Hume could claim that his *History* did it more honour and was more Whiggish than that of the Whigs. 'To decry with such violence, as is affected by some, the whole line of Stuart;[2] to maintain that

[1] Cf. VII, 24: 'The same advantage...over the people which the crown formerly reaped from that interval between the fall of the peers and the rise of the commons, was now possessed by the people against the crown, during the continuance of a like interval. The sovereign had already lost that independent revenue by which he could subsist without regular supplies from parliament; and he had not yet acquired the means of influencing those assemblies.'

[2] That is, to make no distinction between the first two and the last two Stuarts. Hume thought that the second volume of his *History* would be less offensive to the Whigs, because Charles II and James II were less excusable; the constitution was no longer so ambiguous. 'Charles II knew, that he had succeeded to a very limited monarchy...' (*Letters*, I, 217). But even if Charles II was the aggressor in 1672, and his conduct cannot be justified, the fact that so indolent a king could attempt such hazard enterprises shows that there was still something seriously wrong with the constitution (IX, 521, and see below, p. 295).

their administration was one continued encroachment on the *incontestable* rights of the people; is not giving due honour to that great event, which not only put a period to their hereditary succession, but made a new settlement of the whole constitution' (IX, 520).

However this was not the sort of honour that appealed to Whigs who believed in the ancient constitution, nor was Hume's claim that his *History* was genuinely impartial in doing justice to both sides generally accepted in England. Contemporary opinion seems to have concluded either that a *History* which was not obviously Whig could only be Tory or Jacobite, or else that it was inconsistent.[1] Hume's programme was self-defeating. His bi-focal vision of the conflict of king and commons was too subtle for his critics, and there is some irony in the fact that Hume's very desire to be impartial in the interests of political moderation rendered that impartiality suspect, especially in the eyes of later critics like Macaulay, in so far as Hume was especially anxious to deploy it, so to speak, on the rather narrow legal front of constitutional controversy, or constitutional controversy carried on in a narrow legal way, and thereby laid himself open to the charge of neglecting or by-passing facts which told against the Stuarts.[2] Hume himself when he refers to the impartiality of his *History* gives the impression that he thinks of it as a matter of holding the scales, of doing both parties justice (*Letters*, I, 210), of dispensing praise and blame equally;[3] that it is guaranteed by his independence, financial and political, his good intentions (*Letters*, I, 226), and honesty of purpose, and proved by the disagreement of his critics as to his political principles.[4] In so far as Hume seems to believe that a

---

[1] This was the opinion of Daniel McQueen in his review of Hume's first volume: *Letters on Mr Hume's History of Great Britain* (Edinburgh, 1756), 236-49, and of Joseph Towers, *Observations on Mr Hume's History of England* (1778), 150-1: there are passages in the History highly favourable to the general interests of liberty and the common right of mankind, but counterbalanced by so many more of a contrary nature that we have little reason to applaud [Hume] for his consistency. Hume's *History* appeared to Hurd as that of a partisan of the house of Stuart: because the nation put up with the arbitrary government of one family [the Tudors], for certain temporary and political ends, does it mean that it should suffer another family to confirm and perpetuate that tyranny? *Dialogues*, 313.

[2] See my Introduction to the *Pelican classics* edition of Hume's History, 47-9.

[3] E.g.: 'This narrowness of mind, if we would be impartial, we must either blame or excuse equally on both sides' (VII, 246). In a letter of June 1753, Hume wrote to James Oswald: 'The truth is, there is so much reason to blame and praise alternately King and Parliament, that I am afraid the mixture of both in my composition, being so equal, may pass sometimes for an affectation...' (*Letters*, I, 179).

[4] 'Whether am I Whig or Tory? Protestant or Papist? Scotch or English? I hope you do not all agree on this head; and that there [are] disputes among you about

'philosopher above party' is bound *ipso facto* to be neutral, he plays into the hands of the more sophisticated critics who produce him as a prime example of the nemesis that awaits any historian who is too unselfcritically confident of his sincerity and objectivity.

In a letter to the Abbé Le Blanc of 1754 Hume wrote that in the first volume of his *History*, 'the philosophical Spirit, which I have so much indulg'd in all my Writings, finds here ample Materials to work upon' (*Letters*, I, 193). In the light of this remark, his better known saying as to 'his view of *things*' being 'more conformable to Whig principles', his 'representations of persons to Tory prejudices' (*Letters*, I, 237), is superficial, and begs too many questions to be very helpful. The 'philosophical spirit' goes beyond Whig principles and Tory prejudices, beyond right and wrong, good and evil, and discovers a guarantee of impartiality which is inherent in the structure of the story itself and not dependent on the expertise and honesty of the historian; the 'philosopher' is not content 'to throw the blame equally on both parties', but 'enlarges his view', and remarks on 'the necessary progress of human affairs, and the operation of those principles which are inherent in human nature' (v, 336–7). This is the nearest Hume comes (the context of the last quotation is the Reformation in Scotland), to explicitly professing an impartiality which, or something of which, Bentham grasped as characteristic of the *History of England*,[1] and which is the result of the application of the idea of the progress of society and the lesson of moderation of the essay on *Politics reduced to a science*. This allows one to see the conflict of king and commons as the result of political inexperience and ignorance on both sides: the progress of society created new conditions and new needs and demands, which rendered the irregular 'Gothic' governments unworkable, and which at first nobody properly understood.

In itself, the ignorance of James I was fortunate, and provided a great opportunity. James misread the situation. All his experience encouraged the 'speculative system of absolute government' in

my principles' (*Letters*, I, 196). Cf. the Letter of 1760 to the Comtesse de Boufflers in which Hume regards the anger of both parties 'as the surest warrant of my impartiality' (*Letters*, I, 344). James Hampton in *Reflections on Ancient and Modern History* (1746) had said that any English writer who had the courage to displease the zealots of both parties, will 'bid fairest for that character of truth, which constitutes the soul of history' (29).

[1] See Bentham's *Theory of Legislation* (ed. C. K. Ogden) 12. 'When Hume, in his History, wished to calm the spirit of party, and to treat the passions like a chemist who analyzes poisons, the mob of readers rose up against him; they did not like to see it proved that men were rather ignorant than wicked, and that past ages, always extolled to depreciate the present, had been far more fertile in misfortunes and crimes.'

which he believed: he thought of himself as equally entitled to the authority of the other hereditary sovereigns of Europe, without understanding the innovations they had introduced or the military power which made them possible and supported their authority. He did not realize that the opinion which was the sole support of his authority was changing, nor that the almost despotic powers which he inherited from the Tudor sovereigns were due to the special circumstances of the age; he ascribed them to royal birth and title. This opinion might have proved dangerous, if not fatal, to liberty, had not the king been so firmly persuaded of his right that he made no provision 'either of force or politics' to support it (VI, 487-8). While James was 'vaunting his divine vicegerency', he possessed 'not so much as a single regiment of guards to maintain his extensive claims; a sufficient proof that he sincerely believed his pretensions to be well-grounded, and a strong presumption that they were at least built on what were then deemed plausible arguments' (VII, 29). And his policy of forbidding the gentry to live in London, because if congregated together they might realize their strength and become inquisitive about matters of government, a policy exactly opposite to the common arts of arbitrary government, had precisely the contrary effect of what he aimed at, making them less submissive and more independent and powerful (VII, 18-19). The king did not realize, for nobody realized, just how powerful the commons had become. All previous history pointed the other way: nothing less than fatal experience could make the kings of England pay a due regard to that formidable assembly (VII, 83-4). And the art of managing parliaments, so necessary in the English limited monarchy, was still unknown.[1]

But if James I's ignorance was fortunate, that of the commons was not: it was their misreading of the situation and lack of experience which ensured that the transition to regular limited monarchy would not be peaceful. On the continent the transition from the Gothic or feudal constitutions to simple monarchy was comparatively smooth, except where religious fanaticism produced opposition, because, apart from the irresistible force of standing armies, it did not appear to involve the imposition of a new form

---

[1] '...the art of managing parliaments, by private interest or cabal, being found hitherto of little use or necessity, had not, as yet, become a part of English politics' (VI, 513). Circa 1614, a seat in the Commons began to be regarded as an honour, and country gentlemen competed for it. 'It was not till long after, when liberty was thoroughly established...that the members began to join profit to honour, and the crown found it necessary to distribute among them all the considerable offices of the kingdom' (VI, 554).

of government; the European princes did not change the form, but they changed the substance, and continuing the same appellations of magistrates, the same appearance of civil government, and restraining themselves by all the forms of legal administration insensibly imposed the yoke on their unguarded subjects (VI, 591). But in England it was the commons who wanted to change the form of government, and this meant an experiment hitherto untried: 'the plan, as yet new and unformed, of regular and rigid liberty' (VII, 277). The continental princes knew where they stood *vis-à-vis* the people; they knew their power and they knew what they wanted: simply an extension of the authority which they had inherited. But the commons in England did not know where they stood in relation to the king, and they could not know precisely what they wanted. A monarchy limited by law was new and unheard of: 'The jealousy of liberty, though roused was not yet thoroughly enlightened' (X, 140), the commons were as yet 'novices...in the principles of liberty' (X, 139), 'as liberty was yet new, those maxims which guard and regulate it were unknown and unpractised' (X, 145); whereas 'the king's despotism was more speculative than practical, so the independency of the commons was, at this time, the reverse; and though strongly supported by their present situation, as well as disposition, was too new and recent to be as yet founded on systematical principles and opinions' (VI, 533). Men had no experience of it and they misinterpreted the signs and symptoms. For example: the 'undertakers' who in the elections to the Parliament of 1614 had used their interest to secure a majority for the court: 'so ignorant were the commons, that they knew not this incident to be the first infallible symptom of any regular or established liberty' (VI, 553). In Charles II's reign the Commons still did not realize that the influence of the Crown in the disposal of places, honours and preferments is an engine of power vital to regular authority (IX, 230–1). And only the 'wise and moderate', reflecting on the situation in 1621, 'regarded the very rise of parties as a happy prognostic of the establishment of liberty', realizing that parties divided on principle were a necessary product of a mixed government, 'nor could they ever expect to enjoy in a mixed government, so invaluable a blessing without suffering that inconvenience, which, in such governments, has ever attended it' (VI, 618).

But it was the inexperience of the Commons in the financial aspects of limited monarchy that was crucial and fatal. Because at this time the burden of government lay so lightly on the people, they failed to understand the king's need for money: 'they were not as yet accustomed to open their purses in so liberal a manner as their successors in order to supply the wants of their sovereign, and the smallest demand, however requisite, appeared in their eyes unreasonable and exorbitant' (VI, 493). 'Habits, more than reason, we find in every thing to be the governing principle of mankind.' The nation was very little accustomed to the burden of taxes, and 'had never opened their purses in any degree for supporting their sovereign' (VII, 63–4). The king was at their mercy, but instead of using their financial power to bargain with him, and turn his necessities to good account – they could 'have bribed him to depart peaceably from the more dangerous articles of his prerogative' (VI, 524) – they continued in their customary parsimonious policy. The king's natural reaction made the more extreme measures of his opponents more plausible, and Charles I was driven to adopt expedients which would be regarded as irregular in the most absolute governments (VII, 94).

The situation was repeated after the Restoration. The Crown now relied entirely on the voluntary grants of the people, but the commons, not yet used to the new situation and ignoring the growing needs and expenditure of all European governments, continued to imitate 'too strictly the example of their predecessors in a rigid frugality of public money'.[1] The poverty of the Crown produced a feeble, wavering foreign policy, and continual uncertainty in domestic administration. 'No one could answer with any tolerable assurance for the measures of the house of commons', because few of its members were attached to the court by any other band than that of inclination. The attempt to win them over by offices and bribes and pensions caused alarm on account of its novelty, nor did the Crown possess sufficient means to be able to do it thoroughly (IX, 1–3). The crown still possessed considerable power of opposing parliaments: and had not as yet acquired the means of influencing them. Hence a continual jealousy between these parts of the legislature; hence the inclination mutually to take advantage of each others necessities; hence the impossibility, under which the king lay, of finding ministers who could at once be serviceable and faithful to him. Because parliament was not yet all-powerful, if the king neglected parliamentary interest in his choice of ministers, 'a refractory session was instantly to be

---

[1] Charles II's revenue, as settled by the Long Parliament, 'was put upon a very bad footing'; too small, if they intended to make him independent in the common course of administration; too large if they wanted to keep him in entire dependence. (See IX, 525.)

expected', but ministers chosen from the leaders of the commons could be expected to work in its interest and against that of the king (IX, 521-2).

'Indeed, could the parliaments in the reign of Charles I have been induced to relinquish so far their old habits, as to grant that prince the same revenue which was voted to his successor, or had those in the reign of Charles II conferred on him as large a revenue as was enjoyed by his brother, all the disorders in both reigns might easily have been prevented, and probably all reasonable concessions to liberty might peaceably have been obtained from both monarchs. But these assemblies, unacquainted with public business and often actuated by faction and fanaticism, could never be made sensible, but too late and by fatal experience, of the incessant change of times and stituations' (IX, 526-7).

Debate as to whether Hume's *History* is an essentially political history or whether it has serious claims to be regarded as something more, viz: a history of civilization,[1] is liable to miss the vital sense in which it is both at the same time. 'Civilization' for Hume is, anyway, essentially a political or legal concept: the progress of 'civility' is the development of 'law and liberty', of that 'salutary yoke of law and justice', (III, 532)[2] without which liberty is merely licentiousness, the realization in history of that 'justice' which is the object of government in Hume's political philosophy. But this theme of the development of law and liberty is unintelligible if divorced from the rise of commerce and arts and that middling rank of men, who in the essay on *Luxury* (later *Refinement in the*

[1] See, for example, W. Davidson's criticism in *Philological Quarterly*, XXI, (1942), of Mossner's article, 'An Apology for David Hume, Historian' in *Proceedings of the Modern Languages Association*, LVI, (September 1941).
[2] The context is Scotland. Cf. VII, 367. 'The English were, at that time, [1603] a civilized people, and obedient to the laws'. The Scots were not. A minor inheriting the Duchy of Normandy in the tenth century is 'a sure proof that the Normans were already somewhat advanced in civility, and that their government could now rest secure in its laws and civil institutions, and was not wholly sustained by the abilities of the sovereign' (I, 186). Cf. in Appendix I (I, 287-8) the 'steps' taken by the German nations 'towards completing the political or civil union' involve law and an attitude to law; '...when the German nations had been settled some time in the...Roman empire, they made still another step towards a more cultivated life, and their criminal justice gradually improved and refined itself'. King Edmund's laws against feuds 'were contrary to the ancient spirit of the northern barbarians, and were a step towards a more regular administration of justice' (I, 291). Note also the large place given to the discovery and diffusion of Roman law in Hume's concluding summary in Vol. IV: 'so complete an art, which was also so necessary for giving security to all other arts, and which, by refining, and still more by bestowing solidity on the judgement, served as a model to farther improvements', (IV, 47).

Arts) were said to be 'the best and firmest basis of public liberty', and to 'covet equal laws, which may secure their property and preserve them from monarchical as well as aristocratical tyranny'. The essay on *Luxury* or *Refinement in the Arts* is an abridged version of this aspect of the *History*. Progress in the arts 'has a natural tendency to preserve, if not produce, a free government': a predominantly agricultural society is divided into two classes: the landowners and their vassals or tenants; the latter, not possessing wealth or knowledge being in a servile condition; the former, either in a state of anarchical independence or else governed despotically by an absolute master (283–4).

This is the unobtrusive central theme or frame of reference of the *History*. Critics like Leslie Stephen, for whom eighteenth-century historical thought is 'atomistic', could not see it. 'It is no wonder if history presented itself as a mere undecipherable maze to the 18th century thinkers, of whom Hume is the most complete representative...they saw nothing but a meaningless collection of facts, through which ran no connecting principle' (*English Thought in the 18th Century*, II, 184–5). And in order to see it one must not only put aside the once common view of Hume's philosophy and psychology as 'atomistic' and 'mechanical'; one must adopt a European, and not exclusively English stance, because 'civilization' is not an exclusively English possession: the realization of 'liberty' is not an exclusively English, but a European theme.

In the retrospective survey at the conclusion of the reign of Richard III, Hume explains why the progress of the arts, which among the Greeks and Romans 'daily increased the number of slaves', should 'in later times have proved so general a source of liberty'; showing how 'villenage went gradually into disuse throughout the more civilized parts of Europe'; and goes on, 'Thus *personal* freedom became almost general in Europe; an advantage which paved the way for the increase of *political* or *civil* liberty, and which, even where it was not attended with this salutary effect, served to give the members of the community some of the most considerable advantages of it' (IV, 50–2). Elsewhere in the *History* he says that as a result of the progress of arts and commerce and decline of the feudal magnates: 'in all places the condition of the people...received great improvement, and they acquired, if not entire liberty, at least the most considerable advantages of it' (IV, 188). The development of the rule of law is a theme of modern European history, in the light of which England is seen to pursue her own peculiar destiny in the seventeenth century, achieving that 'entire liberty' which is exclusive to England. And liberty in the wider sense is a uniquely European achievement. Because in spite of what is said in the essay on the *Rise and Progress of the Arts and Sciences* about the ancient republics infallibly giving rise to law, in the essay on the *Populousness of Ancient Nations*, he says that although the ancients were extremely fond of liberty, they 'seem not to have understood it very well'; that 'property was rendered very precarious by the maxims of ancient government', that 'In those days there was no medium between a severe jealous aristocracy ruling over discontented subjects; and a turbulent, factious, tyrannical democracy'; that as a result, commerce, industry and police were in a rudimentary condition. 'The barbarity of the ancient tyrants, together with the extreme love of liberty, which animated those ages, must have banished every merchant and manufacturer, and have quite depopulated the state, had it subsisted upon industry and commerce'. In other words conditions were such as to make impossible the development of that middling rank of men who are the basis of public liberty (*Essays*, 406, 408, 413, 416).

Hume was not concerned with English civilization as such; he himself was a 'North Briton': he did not know the English law and constitution from the inside. It was as foreign to him as it was to Rapin. His *History* is not a history of the English people, or of English civilization: it is a history of civilization in England, just as his history of English literature (Mossner says that Hume's sections on this joined together make up the first history of English literature) is better described as the history of the progress of literary taste in England. Hume presents a new-style history of liberty: the history of liberty is the history of civilization: the result of economic and social progress. The question as to what sort of a *History* Hume was trying to write, whether a political tract or something much broader, can be answered by saying that Hume's immediate political purpose demanded a non-partisan approach to the conflict in the seventeenth century, which in turn demanded a history of civilization: an explanation of that conflict, and a resolution of the controversies concerning earlier events in English constitutional history which that conflict had given rise to, in terms of the progress of society, the hall-mark and organizing principle of Scottish 'philosophical' history. It is because it is a political history that it is also something more (though there is of course a great deal of enrichment and decoration which is that and no more). As has been seen, the crux of the whole history as a lesson in political moderation is the emergence of a new attitude to law and government due to the progress of society, which made it possible to give an account of the conflict of king and commons which goes beyond the rights and wrongs of the protagonists. But once again philosophical history is sceptical Whiggism and involves the destruction of cherished Whig idols and beliefs: Hume was fiercely criticized for describing the Whig scriptures as 'compositions, the most despicable, both for style and matter' – the footnote says 'Such as Rapin, Locke, Sidney, Hoadly etc' (IX, 524).[1] In particular, philosophical history made nonsense of ancient constitutionalism: 'the epoch of true liberty' was the Petition of Right (X, 40): the 'dawn of liberty' coincides with a new attitude to law and the constitution.

If real liberty is a matter of progress, if there can be no real liberty without respect for law and without the conditions which make that possible, it is just the rhetoric or high political rant of vulgar Whiggism to talk of England alone maintaining, and the great nations of the continent losing, their original Gothic liberty. All the civilized monarchies have outgrown the 'liberty' of the Gothic constitutions, which was really only the liberty of the nobles to oppress the people and defy the king, and anything earlier is more primitive still, and even less worthy of imitation. The 'pretended liberty' of the Saxons was 'only an incapacity of submitting to government' (IV, 48, 54). Hume himself seems to succumb to the gravitational pull of vulgar Whiggism when he sees modern European liberty as the legacy of 'the generous barbarians', and talks of the nations on the continent enjoying, in the seventeenth century, some 'remains' of liberty (VI, 555), or the 'spirit of civil liberty' gradually reviving 'from its lethargy' in England at the same time (X, 156). He does not however say that the European nations have lost this pristine liberty and the English retrieved or restored it. He says: 'The free constitutions then established [when the German invaders destroyed the 'military despotism' of Rome, and Europe 'as from a new epoch, rekindled her ancient spirit'], however impaired by the encroachments of succeeding princes, still preserve an air of independence and legal administration which distinguish the European nations, and if that part of the globe maintain sentiments of liberty, honour, equity and valour,

---

[1] Horace Walpole, in 1781, called this 'a saucy, blockheadly note'. *Correspondence*, Vol. 29, 105. The Scotch would annihilate our patriots, martyrs, heroes and geniuses etc, etc.

superior to the rest of mankind, it owes these advantages chiefly to the seeds implanted by those generous barbarians' (I, 262).

'The government of the Germans... was always extremely free' (I, 261), and so too was that of the Saxons in England: 'one of the freest nations of which there remains any account in the records of history' (IV, 53). (In this they resembled the ancient Britons, whose 'governments, though monarchical, were free', I, 4.) The independence of men was secured by the great equality of possessions, originally at least, but this was not however real liberty: it was an extreme love of liberty not balanced by an equal respect for authority. The Anglo-Saxons were 'a rude uncultivated people... untamed to submission under law and government, addicted to intemperance, riot, and disorder' (I, 305). There was little industry or trade; consequently a 'total want of a middling rank of men', so that the two ranks of nobility and commons remained distinct and apart (I, 277, 285). The central government did not have the power and authority necessary to protect its subjects, who were obliged to put themselves under the protection of the local magnates, so that a client-lord relationship developed, and 'the Anglo-Saxon government became at last extremely aristocratical'. And even if the administration of justice by the local courts was 'well calculated to defend general liberty, and to restrain the power of the nobles', the judicial power in a primitive people being so much more important than the legislative, and the nation less governed by laws than by custom, there is 'another power still more important than either the judicial or legislative; to wit the power of injuring or serving by immediate force and violence', which in all extensive governments where the execution of the laws is feeble, naturally falls into the hands of the principal nobility. Hume with his typical Lowland view of the Scottish Highlanders would find it easier to reject the myth of the 'free' Anglo-Saxon constitution. 'The Highlands of Scotland have long been entitled by law to every privilege of British subjects; but it was not till very lately, that the common people could in fact enjoy these privileges' (I, 282–5).

'On the whole, notwithstanding the seeming liberty, or rather licentiousness, of the Anglo-Saxons, the great body even of the free citizens in those ages, really enjoyed much less true liberty than where the execution of the laws is the most severe, and where subjects are reduced to the strictest subordination and dependence on the civil magistrate. The reason is derived from the excess itself of that liberty. Men must guard themselves at any price against insults and injuries; and where they receive not protection from the laws and magistrate, they will seek it by submission to superiors and by herding in some private confederacy which acts under the direction of a powerful leader. And thus all anarchy is the immediate cause of tyranny, if not over the state, at least over many of the individuals' (I, 275-6).[1]

Two problems connected with the Saxon government of England, difficult enough in themselves owing to our imperfect knowledge of Anglo-Saxon history and antiquities, and made even more difficult by party conflict (I, 265, 267), could be decided by the philosophical historian: the question of the succession of the kings, and the composition of the Witan. To settle the first, Hume applies the principle of the progress of society and the psychological principles which he had used in *Treatise* III to explain the rules of succession to private property and government. The idea of hereditary succession in authority is so natural to men and so strongly fortified by the usual rule in transmitting private possessions, that it must be very influential in every society, unless expressly excluded by the 'refinements of a republican constitution'. But as there is a material difference between government and private property, and everyone is not so much qualified for exercising the former as for enjoying the latter, 'a people who are not sensible of the general advantages attending a fixed rule', are apt to make 'great leaps' in the succession, and frequently pass over the person who, had he possessed the requisite age and abilities, would have been thought entitled to the sovereignty. This is the psychological force and counterforce argument that one finds in the *Treatise*. The imaginative power and naturalness of the idea of hereditary succession is countered by the failure in a primitive society to recognize the advantage of an inflexible rule. Thus these monarchies are not strictly speaking either elective or hereditary, and the quarrel between writers like Echard and Carte on one side and Tyrrel and Oldmixon on the other is otiose.[2] In 'an independent people so little restrained by law and cultivated by

---

[1] For Hurd, the Saxons were inspired by the spirit of liberty because that implied the rule of law (*Dialogues*, 244-5). 'Our Saxon ancestors conceived so little of government by the will of the magistrate, without fixed laws...' They were not primitive in Hume's sense.

[2] See Carte's *General History of England*, Vol. IV, (1755), 2-3, refuting Bolingbroke's assertion that James I was the 'first broacher' of the idea of divine right and hereditary succession. Oldmixon attacked Echard's account of the succession of the Saxon kings and quoted Tyrrel to the effect that only two of them up to the reign of King Edgar had not been elected, (*Critical History*, 19-22).

science', one could not expect to find either a strict hereditary or a regular elective principle (1, 263–5).

The primitive state of society also settles, or at least illuminates, the vexed question of the composition of the Witan (1, 265–70). The 'popular faction' claim that representatives of the boroughs sat there; but given the 'low state of commerce... we must exclude the burgesses or commons'. On the other hand, since the king was not absolute, and given the total absence of a middling rank, the more considerable landed proprietors must have sat there, because the churchmen and royal officials did not constitute a check to his power; and they would not have been very numerous, because the landed property of England was probably in few hands during the latter part, at any rate, of the Saxon period. But whether they did or not, it is certain that the Anglo-Saxon government had become 'extremely aristocratical' on the eve of the Norman conquest and the royal authority correspondingly limited.

The next great controversial issue in English historiography was the conquest itself, and in this Hume makes no concessions to vulgar Whiggism. William I's government may at first have 'borne the semblance' of a legal administration and not that of a conqueror, so that the English flattered themselves that they had changed not the form of their government, but only the succession of the crown (1, 317), but he soon found it necessary, in order to secure an unstable government and satisfy his rapacious followers, to adopt a 'concealed policy', provoking the English into insurrection to give him the pretext to exert his right of conquest to the full (1, 321–2), and from the first his military, as opposed to his civil institutions, were those of a tyrant and master (1, 318).[1] To argue that William's right was not one of conquest was to quibble about words: the dispute was in any case absurd: it could not affect the rights of Englishmen now (1, 377–9).[2] Indeed, and this is

[1] Hume seems to follow Brady pretty closely. Brady argued that the fact that William did not show his hand from the beginning does not mean that he did not intend to make an absolute conquest of the whole kingdom. His civil, as opposed to his military, rule was at first so much 'artifice to make the English secure'. See Brady's *Full Answer etc* (1684), 235, *et seq.*

[2] This argument that William conquered Harold and not the nation etc had extraordinary tenacity. Even the tough-minded and philosophical John Millar comes up with it, Joseph Towers (in 1778) did so also and quoted Lyttleton against Hume (*op. cit.*, 16–17, 23). Owen Ruffhead, reviewing Hume's first medieval volume in the *Monthly Review* (Vol. 25, 1761) regarded Hume's sentiments with respect to William's right to the title as 'singular and repugnant to the most respectable authorities'. There is a material difference between a conquest over a king and over a kingdom. William could make no pretence to the latter (407–9). This was Blackstone's teaching, *Commentaries*, 1, 192. In its review of De Lolme in 1775, the

the contribution of the philosophical historian, because the Normans were so far advanced in arts as to need and appreciate the value of large landed estates, as the invaders of the Roman empire, 'being accustomed to a rude uncultivated life', did not, they 'pushed the rights of conquest... to the utmost extremity', so that 'it would be difficult to find in all history a revolution more destructive, or attended with a more complete subjection of the ancient inhabitants' (I, 378). William made himself universal sole proprietor (I, 369), brought about 'almost a total revolution in the landed property of the kingdom' (I, 337), and introduced the feudal law, 'of a sudden' (II, 250). The feudal government which he established in England was essentially a military system, suited to an age of perpetual hostilities between the great lords, and in which war was the general passion (I, 396-7). There was little liberty in any real sense, even after Magna Carta. Nevertheless Magna Carta constituted an epoch in the history of law and liberty and civilization.

Hume uses expressions in connection with Magna Carta that appear to be in the key of ancient constitutionalism and vulgar Whiggism. He talks of the 'nation... vindicating its liberties' (II, 241); of the 'generous barons' (II, 255) 'seized with the national passion for laws and liberty' (II, 246) adopting a 'plan of liberty'. Magna Carta 'laid the foundations of the English constitution' (II, 353) and was 'a kind of original contract' between the king and his subjects (II, 334-5). But a philosophical account of Magna Carta distinguishes what it was at the time from what it became in retrospect. Magna Carta was an epoch in the feudal constitution and also, retrospectively, an epoch in the development of political civilization. At the time, the barons' 'plan of liberty' was the result of their emergence from the peculiar fortress conditions which accompanied the introduction of feudalism into England by the Conqueror, and, against its natural aristocratic bias, raised the power of the crown to a quasi-despotism (II, 240-1). When the Normans 'struck deep root' in England and were entirely 'incorporated with the people whom at first they oppressed and despised', they no longer needed the protection of the crown for the

Edinburgh Magazine and Review came out with all the old arguments: William was the legal heir and conquered Harold, not England etc, and criticized Hume for 'inadvertently' giving a sanction to Brady's assertion that the Norman Conquest is the real foundation of the English constitution (Vol. IV, 597). Kames in his *Essays on British Antiquities* was reluctant to think of William as a Conqueror. In his Appendix on 'the hereditary and indefeasible right of kings', he writes: 'supposing him to have conquered England, which will not readily be granted...' Cf. 16. 'a conqueror, at least one who treated his subjects as a conquered people'.

enjoyment and security of their possessions, and 'aspired to the same liberty and independence which they saw enjoyed by their brethren on the continent'. Their object now was to restrain the 'exorbitant prerogatives and arbitrary practices which the necessities of war and the violence of conquest had at first obliged them to indulge in their monarch'. The memory also of a more equal government under the Saxon kings, 'which remained with the English, diffused still further the spirit of liberty, and made the barons both desirous of more independence to themselves, and willing to indulge it to the people' (I, 129). Together with 'this secret revolution in the sentiments of men', went the threat to the barons' property caused by innovations in the military system begun by Henry II, who found the hire of mercenaries more efficient than the feudal levy. The barons saw the king's consequent need for money as a threat of endless exactions: this resulted in a contest which took place in all the countries of Europe, in which the king either lost or acquired authority (II, 133-4). At the time, therefore, Magna Carta was primarily concerned with the privileges of the feudal magnates. 'These were the principal articles, calculated for the interest of the barons; and had the charter contained nothing farther, national happiness and liberty had been very little promoted by it, as it would only have tended to increase the power and independence of an order of men who were already too powerful, and whose yoke might have become more heavy on the people than even that of an absolute monarch' (II, 252). But the barons had to take into account the interests of the inferior ranks of men who had supported them against John, so that Magna Carta is not exclusively concerned with the feudal law and the rights of tenants-in-chief, but contains articles designed 'to ensure the free and equitable administration of justice', which 'involve all the chief outlines of a legal government, and provide for the equal distribution of justice and free enjoyment of property; the great objects for which political society was at first founded by men, which the people have a perpetual and unalienable right to recal, and which no time, nor precedent, nor statute, nor positive institution, ought to deter them from keeping ever uppermost in their thoughts and attention' (II, 255). Hume conjectures that these latter articles were the famous laws of King Edward which the English so obstinately wished to see restored. They concern all free men, but Hume is careful to distinguish these from the villeins, who he says probably constituted the majority of the nation (II, 254).

Retrospectively, therefore, Magna Carta is an epoch in the constitution, but not in the sense of Coke and the parliamentary lawyers of the seventeenth century. Hume says that Magna Carta laid the *foundations* of the constitution, and was a kind of original contract. In Hume the original contract is the act by which government is instituted for the better security of the basic rules of society: 'justice', or the personal liberty and security of individuals under the rule of law. Magna Carta is a stage in the development of civilization in this sense, not a peculiarly English palladium of parliamentary rights and privileges.[1] There is no question, for example, of no taxation without general consent, because only party zeal could imagine that the commons are referred to in this connexion (II, 296–7). 'It introduced no new distribution of the powers of the commonwealth, and no innovation in the political or public law of the kingdom. It only guarded...against such tyrannical practices as are incompatible with civilized government, and, if they become very frequent, are incompatible with all government. The barbarous licence of the kings, and perhaps of the nobles, was henceforth somewhat more restrained: men acquired some more security for their properties and their liberties; and government approached a little nearer to that end for which it was originally instituted, the distribution of justice, and the equal protection of the citizens...And thus the establishment of the Great Charter, without seeming anywise to innovate in the distribution of political power became a kind of epoch in the constitution' (II, 226–7).[2] And in spite of his reference to the memory of the greater liberties of the old Saxon government, Hume insists that 'it was probably the example of the French barons which first emboldened the English to require greater independence from their sovereign' (II, 297). The immediate context and the broader perspective are both European, not exclusively English.

---

[1] As used by Coke and the commons. Cf. Faith Thompson, *Magna Carta: Its role in the Making of the English Constitution 1300–1629* (1948), 296, 297, 309, 366. Hume's view of Magna Carta in general seems to be fairly close to that of modern scholarship: somewhere between 'the extravagant eulogy of the old time historian and the extreme depreciation of the 'myth of Magna Carta' school (373). His 'generous barons' are not Brady's 'seditious and dissolute barons' who never intended Magna Carta to be of much advantage to ordinary free-men or free-holders (*A Complete History of England*, 1685, xxx, xxxiv). Cf. J. C. Holt, *Magna Carta* (1965): lawyers reinstated it as a document of political importance in the seventeenth century (8).

[2] One of Hume's revisions of his *History* brings out the point. In the 1754 volume the sentence: 'The truth is, the great charter and the old statutes were sufficiently clear in favour of liberty' (*Pelican classics*, 300), was changed in later editions to 'personal liberty'.

As to the origin of the House of Commons – the crucial issue in the seventeenth-century debate to which all the others on the historiographical front were subordinate – it had been settled by general consent in favour of the royalist thesis: even the 'ruling party', the Whigs, agreed that the commons were no part of the great council, till some ages after the Conquest (II, 292). What remained for the philosophical historian was to use the idea of the progress of society to set the seal on this conclusion, for 'even if history were silent on the head, we have reason to conclude, from the known situation of society during those ages, that the commons were never admitted as members of the legislative body' (II, 298) until general causes had prepared the way and made it first expedient and then necessary, and to tell the story, for the first time, in a comprehensive, coherent and at the same time economical manner. This is Hume's contribution. The crucial date for Hume was not the famous and much fought over 49 Henry III, but Edward I's parliament of 1295: 'the real and true epoch of the house of commons, and the faint dawn of popular government in England' (II, 503). Leicester had summoned knights and burgesses, but Leicester was a usurper, and the crucial thing was that his experiment would certainly not have been repeated and regularized by Edward I if there had not been general causes at work which made it inevitable. Leicester's policy 'only forwarded by some years an institution for which the general state of things had already prepared the nation' (II, 421). This 'general state of things' included alterations in the state of landed property since the Conquest, producing a division between greater and lesser tenants-in-chief and a greater diffusion of wealth, the increasing wealth and importance of the towns and burgesses, the decay of the feudal military system.[1] Given the king's need for money, to hire troops, and for allies against the greater barons, the political

[1] For the economic causes of the rise of the commons, see II, 493 *et seq*, 509–11. Rapin and Guthrie do not mention them, Carte does so only very briefly and indirectly. Guthrie accepts Leicester's parliament as 'the first plain and evident outlines of an English representation as it is now modelled', but suggests that nevertheless the commons before then had a 'deliberative voice in parliament', though not summoned by their representatives in the same manner (I, 802–3). John Dalrymple in his *Essay towards a general history of Feudal Property in Great Britain* (1757), had insisted that the key to the problem of the origin of the Commons was the gradual evolution of the feudal system. To make de Montfort or Edward I responsible 'arises from attending too much to political and too little to natural and to feudal views. The feudal system, slow and regular in its movements, was not to be whirled about, in subserviency to ministers or even to exigencies' (4th edition, 1759, 319, 33–4). The book is dedicated to Kames, and in the dedication Montesquieu is described as the greatest genius of our age.

outcome was inevitable. '...the commencement of the house of burgesses, who are the true commons, was not an affair of chance, but arose from the necessities of the present situation...' (II, 511).

9
The limits of philosophical history

The social science or even the 'philosophical history' of eighteenth-century Scottish thinkers is not so homogeneous as some commentators seem to think; Hume, in particular differs from the others in some important respects. Something of this has been seen already: in so far, for example as Hume still found a use for the original contract as an explanation of the origin of government, or is not concerned with the corruption of 'manners' and morals as a principle of sociological explanation, or such problems as the deleterious effects of the division of labour: it would be difficult to unearth anything like a theory of 'alienation' in Hume. And there is a greater emphasis on the causal agency of forms of government and legislators, and the play of 'chance' and historical contingency. In fact Hume did not consistently and systematically do the sort of philosophical history of which Adam Smith seems to have been the seminal mind in Scotland. One is tempted to exaggerate the difference between Hume's social and political theory and that of Smith and his 'school'. The history of ideas would be easier to write about, more dramatic, if what looked like chiaroscuro did not nearly always on closer inspection cease to be so. The colours always run, and the picture becomes complex and messy. There is in the social and historical theory of Smith and Millar a large element of historical accident and contingency, nor is there, in their thinking, any necessary connection between 'natural improvement' and liberty (as has been argued). In fact they are basically in agreement with Hume that the achievement of political liberty in England was an exceptional affair, due to exceptional circumstances, and even the development of civil liberty they see as something uniquely European, derived from certain historical contingencies in the transition from the late classical to the medieval world producing 'unnatural' conditions. Hume and Smith have more in common in the whole range of the science of politics than is generally realized.[1] The fact remains that it was

[1] As I have tried to show in *Essays on Adam Smith*, ed. A. S. Skinner and T. Wilson. Oxford 1975.

not Hume, but Smith who was described by Millar as the Newton of the history of civil society. From the point of view of Smith and Millar, Hume's philosophical history has gaps and inconsistencies and hesitancies which from another point of view might be said to be philosophical in a more truly historical, because more sceptical sense. The historian looking back at the progress of civilization in Europe and tracing the 'general causes' at work in the story of liberty is observing unique events, not illustrations of or exceptions to some 'law' or principle of 'natural' improvement which can be deduced quite independently of history from the facts of human nature. There is no such 'law' in Hume's science of man.

It will be remembered that Hume wrote his *History* backwards, so that his valedictory remarks come at the end of the medieval volumes. The final paragraph summarizes the message of the historiographical phase of Hume's programme of providing the post-revolutionary establishment with philosophically respectable intellectual foundations. Hume asks, in effect, what is the point of studying these remote periods of the constitution? First, to reveal the illusion of the appeal to a primeval perfection which never existed, and to instruct men to cherish their present constitution, 'from a comparison or contrast with the condition of those distant times'. And secondly, to instruct them 'in the great mixture of accident, which commonly concurs with a small ingredient of wisdom and foresight, in erecting the complicated fabric of the most perfect government' (IV, 54–5). In this valedictory conclusion of the *History* (as in the first edition it was), the progress of civilization is stripped to its barest political function of destroying the myth of the ancient constitution, which has so often cloaked the 'turbulent spirit and...private ambition' of those who have appealed to it, and of promoting moderation and the acceptance of the government as it is; for, in all the alterations of the constitution which have been followed, the only intelligible rule of government is the established practice of the age. The fact that there was nothing inevitable about the achievement in Britain of 'the most perfect and most accurate system of liberty that was ever found compatible with government', should teach men to value it all the more. That political civilization is a precarious thing is Hume's most general and most useful and lasting lesson of moderation. As has been suggested already, there is a special reason why this should be so in England, where civil liberty or the rule of law is supported and guaranteed by a political liberty which is not an object of immediate interest to the great majority of men. In

Hume's psychology what is contiguous strikes more forcibly on the imagination than what is remote, and political liberty is a remote interest for most men. They do not see the connection between their personal security and freedom, and public liberty. 'The people' are 'more attentive to present advantages, than jealous of general laws' (I, 466–7). The middling rank 'covet' equal laws which guarantee their personal security and liberty, but political liberty or 'free government' is a more remote interest, and demands an intelligent vigilance and ability to foresee remote consequences which is confined to a minority like the leaders of the Commons in the reigns of James I and Charles I. It has been seen how Hume emphasizes the exceptional quality of these men, and also the fact that Charles I dreaded no opposition from the people, 'who are not commonly much affected with consequences'. Presumably Hume had these events in mind when in the essay on *Luxury* he said that progress in the arts has a 'natural tendency to preserve, if not produce, a free government' (283). A 'natural tendency' is not an automatic guarantee. And in the *History* (IV, 52) Hume says that the progress of arts gave rise to personal liberty which 'paved the way' for the achievement of political liberty in England. The actual achievement of political liberty was due to accident together with some 'wisdom and foresight'.

In the 'production' of the modern English constitution the 'ingredient of wisdom and foresight' is represented most notably by the leaders of the Commons, the 'mixture of accident', by the passions without which their 'plan of liberty' could never have succeeded, passions which are utterly unpredictable and unreliable, because they are of the furious sort which quickly burn themselves out: love of novelty, religious enthusiasm, and that 'natural love of liberty' akin to anarchy, tamed, but not permanently, by submission to law, an excess which quickly generates its opposite. Hume has been given credit for saying that the English owed their constitution and their liberty to the religious zeal of the Puritans: the rational emerging out of the wholly irrational. It is seen by Meinecke in his chapter on Hume in *Die Entstehung des Historismus* (I, 217–18) as an intimation of a more historical way of thinking than the rationalistic 'pragmatic individualism' alleged to be typical of the age. It is not a wholly convincing example of what Meinecke is looking for, however, because civil liberty is not seen as the unlooked-for by-product of a struggle for more immediate objectives, not even religious ones; the 'plan of liberty' is present, or the gist of it, from the beginning as an objective of the political

Puritans, even if they did not realize precisely all its implications, and even if the passions of the religious Puritans supplied the driving force to carry it to success. But the leaders of the commons knew what they wanted and adapted means (control of supplies) to this end. In their political thinking they are shown as forward looking; which is more than they deserve, even if they lagged far behind in their attitude to government finance.

The importance of general causes in fixing the late origin of the Commons has been seen already. Commerce and manufactures and the growth of the towns are crucial, but these factors themselves did not have the sort of spontaneous origin which one might expect from Hume's description, in the essay on *Civil Liberty*, of the natural force of avarice: 'Avarice, the spur of industry, is so obstinate a passion and works its way through so many real dangers and difficulties...' (94). In the *History*, Hume says that the feudal system effectively prevented the growth of towns and commerce, and held the people in abject slavery. 'The languishing state of commerce kept the inhabitants [of the towns] poor and contemptible; and the political institutions were calculated to render that poverty perpetual' (II, 285). There was a vicious circle: no commerce because no liberty and security for the great majority; no liberty and security because no commerce. The introduction and progress of commerce and the arts resulted in the progress of freedom, and the vicious circle which prevented this was broken by the practice, begun in Italy and imitated in France, of erecting communities and corporations endowed with privileges and a separate municipal government, which gave them protection against the tyranny of the barons (IV, 49). The first edition of 1762 reads: 'the practice begun in France' (443), and this corresponds with what Hume says elsewhere in the *History*, when we are told that 'the erecting of these communities was an invention of Lewis the Gross, in order to free the people from slavery under the lords and to give them protection...' (II, 294), a policy copied by the kings of England,[1] so that English liberty owes a great deal to France. 'It may therefore be proposed as no unlikely conjecture,

---

[1] Cf. II, 504: 'During the course of several years the kings of England, in imitation of other European princes, had embraced the salutary policy of encouraging and protecting the lower and more industrious orders of the state: whom they found well disposed to obey the laws and civil magistrate...' In Carte (*General History of England*, II, 255), there is no question of imitation, but a contrast between royal policy in England, the king's desire to encourage trade and prevent oppression, which was gradual, with the 'more sudden' policy of Louis le Gros in France, due to political views (Louis' need for money to raise forces), 'rather than the ease of the people'.

that both the chief privileges of the peers in England [this refers to the feudal clauses in Magna Carta] and the liberty of the commons [because the 'boroughs and corporations of England were established in imitation of those of France'] were originally the growth of that foreign country' (II, 297) – another shot at the chauvinistic Francophobes. Thus the original cause of the great chain of events that resulted in personal and civil, and in England civil and political, liberty, was a political 'invention'.

But the Commons only achieved real weight in the constitution as a result of the shift in the balance of property in the sixteenth century: this was, as Hume pointed out in the essay on *Luxury*, a commonplace: 'all the world' acknowledges it (284). Hume's account of this development in the *History* is poised between the classical view of English historians that it was due to the policy of Henry VII, more or less conscious and designing, depending on the writer, and the famous account in *The Wealth of Nations* (Book III, Chap. IV). Rapin's account of Henry VII is eccentric, in that he sees him as wholly self-centred, with only two aims: to make himself absolute and to hoard money (VI, 451). According to the usual interpretation, following Bacon and Harrington, Henry VII 'politickly took care to put gradual stops to the power of the nobility', and passed laws designed to diminish their exorbitant power and encourage 'the middle sort' – especially the statute of alienations – 'by all which, the balance of the nation was gradually altered, and the commons obtained a greater power and figure than ever before' (Echard, *History of England* (1707), 593, 620–1). The account in the government journals of the 1730s is more sophisticated in that Henry VII is seen taking advantage of 'accidents' such as the discovery of America and the revival of arts, which 'put the barons on an expensive way of living'. 'This provident King [he is described as a wise and cautious prince looking back and forwards, like Janus] took hold of these occasions'...to get several acts passed, to encourage trade, and make it possible for the lords to alienate their estates: the result was that the people acquired by industry and frugality what the lords squandered in an extravagant way of living made possible by greater plenty of money (*London Journal*, 20 November 1731). Bolingbroke says that by pulling down the power of the nobility Henry VII became the instrument of raising another power, that of the commons, but that neither they, nor he, were able to 'discern these consequences in their full extent' (*Remarks on the History of England*, 109, 136). Guthrie has a dissertation (*General History of England*, III, 1393)

THE LIMITS OF PHILOSOPHICAL HISTORY

'Concerning the Alienation and Accession of Property, with the great Effects they have had upon our Constitution since the Reign of Henry VII', in which 'that wise prince made use of the circumstances of the times he reigned in, to encourage commerce and agriculture, and to raise the middling state of the subjects, as the only balance against the dangerous power of the barons'. In this, he was greatly assisted by the state in which the barons found themselves: they wanted to enjoy the sweets of peace, but were in debt. By the statute of alienations he was able 'to put the industrious and trading part of the nation into a method of becoming proprietors in the soil', thus fixing their wealth in England. 'The pale was now broken down between the commons and the nobles in matters of property. The trading part of the nation called their money home to England.' Hurd says that Henry VII's policy 'was much assisted by the genius of the time' (*Dialogues*, 336-7). Mrs Macaulay called Henry's law 'the Magna Carta of the Commons of England' (*History of England*, v, (1771), 381-2).

In his discussion of the character and laws of Henry VII, Hume, with reference to the practice of the nobility of keeping armies of retainers, says in Smithian style that 'the increase of the arts, more effectually than all the severities of law put an end to the pernicious practice' (IV, 181: this is unchanged from the first edition of 1759, as are all the quotations on this subject which follow). But he immediately goes on to say that 'the most important law in its consequences' of Henry VII's reign was that by which the nobility and gentry acquired a power to alienate their estates. 'By means of this law,[1] joined to the beginning luxury and refinement of the age, the great fortunes of the barons were gradually dissipated and the property of the commons increased in England.' Hume adds: 'It is probable, that Henry foresaw and intended this consequence' (IV, 182). A few pages later, describing the results of the Great Discoveries, the tenor of his remarks becomes more typically Smithian once more. 'The enlargement of commerce and navigation increased industry and the arts everywhere: the nobles dis-

---

[1] Hume inserted a footnote later which meets the objections of the lawyers who pointed out that Henry's law did not first give the barons the power to break entails, as Bolingbroke and other writers asserted. See D. Barrington, *Observations upon the Statutes*, (2nd ed), 354, 366. Hume says that Henry's statute indirectly gave a sanction to the practice begun in the reign of Edward IV: till then, it was not properly speaking law (IV, 182n). The gist of this note was in fact in Hume's text further on in the 1759 edition, in what later became Appendix III. In fact Kames had explained the meaning of Henry's law and the business of fine and recovery to Hume before August 1757: Hume told Gilbert Elliot all about it in a letter (*Letters* I, 262).

sipated their fortunes in expensive pleasures: men of an inferior rank both acquired a share in the landed property, and created to themselves a considerable property of a new kind...' In some nations this increased the privileges of the commons; in most nations the kings established standing armies and 'subdued the liberties of their kingdoms'; but everywhere the condition of the people improved and they acquired if not complete liberty, at least 'the most considerable advantages of it. And as the general course of events thus tended to depress the nobles and exalt the people, Henry VII, who also embraced that system of policy, has acquired more praise than his institutions, strictly speaking, seem of themselves to deserve on account of any profound wisdom attending them' (IV, 187-8). And in Appendix III, Hume's survey of the whole development is entirely Smithian. 'Whatever may be commonly imagined, from the authority of Lord Bacon, and from that of Harrington, and later authors, the laws of Henry VII contributed very little towards the great revolution which happened about this period in the English constitution...the change of manners was the chief cause of the secret revolution of government, and subverted the power of the barons' (VI, 455-6). The 'manners of the age were a general cause which operated during the whole period' to diminish the wealth and still more the influence of the aristocracy (IV, 454).[1]

[1] 'The habits of luxury dissipated the immense fortunes of the ancient barons; and as the new methods of expence gave subsistence to mechanics and merchants, who lived in an independent manner on the fruits of their own industry, a nobleman, instead of that unlimited ascendant which he was wont to assume over those who were maintained at his board, or subsisted by salaries conferred on them, retained only that moderate influence which customers have over tradesmen, and which can never be dangerous to civil government.' The landed proprietors now farmed for profit and dismissed 'those useless hands which formerly were always at their call in every attempt to subvert the government...' This is the example of a 'general cause' which Hume gave in his discussion of the rules distinguishing 'chance' from 'causes' at the beginning of *The Rise and Progress of the Arts and Sciences* (1742). 'The depression of the lords and rise of the commons in England, after the statutes of alienation and the increase of trade and industry, are more easily accounted for by general principles, than the depression of the Spanish and rise of the French monarchy' (after the death of Charles V). The reviewer of Hume's *History of England under the House of Tudor* in the *Monthly Review* (Vol. 20, 1759) did not think that Hume had done justice to Henry VII's institutions. Quoting the passage about the increase of the arts more than the severity of laws, he says Hume mistakes an effect for a cause. The reviewer agrees with Harrington that Henry did not foresee all the consequences of his policy, but that however selfish and limited his motives, the institutions were wise in themselves and extensive in their consequences. Hume's opinion to the contrary appears to be singular and erroneous (351). The reviewer of Ruffhead's *Statutes at Large*, in 1765, says that it was Henry's ruling policy to raise the commons by depressing the nobility (Vol. 32, 56). John Dalrymple in his *Considerations upon the Policy of*

On the other hand, 'general causes' and the progress of society are not used to explain the revival of Roman law which is so important in Hume's account of the progress of civilization and which, as in Blackstone, Giannone and most writers, is ascribed to the accidental discovery of a copy of the Pandects at Amalfi in 1130 or thereabout: an explanation which Millar regarded as unsatisfactory.[1] And to account for the Renaissance, Hume, in his panoramic survey at the end of the medieval volumes, falls back on the swinging pendulum of the classical historians and Machiavelli which suggests a cyclical view of history that cannot be squared, among other things, with the progress of commerce and the arts and the rise of the middling rank and growth of liberty in modern Europe. This well-known description of 'the general revolutions of society' in which 'almost all the improvements of the human mind had reached nearly to their state of perfection about the age of Augustus' (IV, 44) to be followed by a downward movement to 'a point of depression...from which human affairs naturally return in a contrary direction and beyond which they seldom pass either in their advancement or decline', which nadir Hume fixes 'about the age of William the Conqueror', from which the sun of science beginning to reascend threw out many gleams of light which preceded the full morning when letters were revived in the fifteenth century: all this is, from the point of view of Hume's conception of the progress of society, an aberration. The assertion that almost all the improvements of the human mind had nearly reached their state of perfection at the time of Augustus can only apply to literature and the fine arts, and makes nonsense of Hume's whole notion of civil liberty and the progress of political experience and knowledge. So far as there is an explanation of the revival of letters in the fifteenth century, Hume subscribes to the Flight of the Scholars in 1453 (IV, 189-90), and it is the political

Entails in Great Britain (1764), says that Henry VII wished to deliver England from the condition of an extensive nation without trade, or something like it, when, as we are told by Lord Bacon, he 'laid his scheme' for the dissolution of the great families. But in his *Essay towards a general history of Feudal Property in Great Britain* (1759 – the first edition was 1757), he says that the 'politic prince' who freed the lawyers from the trouble of inventing future devices against entails was helped by the 'genius of the times' which 'was bent against the feudal system'. In the end commerce and luxury undermined the great families (164-6).

[1] *Historical View of the English Government*, II, 321: 'we may be allowed to entertain some doubt, whether an event of that magnitude could have proceeded from a circumstance apparently so frivolous'. Kames in *Essays upon several subjects concerning British antiquities* (1747), wrote that 'All the world knows that the Roman Law, after being buried in oblivion for ages, came to be restored in Italy by an accident' (15-16).

effects of the revival of letters in which he is chiefly interested in the *History*.[1]

Nor does he view the Reformation in terms of economic and social progress; according to Hume, it began in backward regions. 'The theological disputes, first started in the north of Germany, next in Switzerland, countries at that time wholly illiterate...' (v, 363).

This is a far cry from Millar, whose 'economic interpretation of history' is, largely owing to Marxist or Marxist-inspired historians, one of the best-known features of the Scottish Enlightenment. Nor did the leading Scottish social theorists have much use for the Legislators and Founders of States, saluted by Hume in the classical style at the beginning of the essay on *Parties in General*. 'Of all men that distinguish themselves by memorable achievements, the first place of honour seems due to Legislators and founders of states, who transmit a system of laws and institutions to secure the peace, happiness, and liberty of future generations.'[2] Not that Hume's idea of law in the making was crudely unhistorical. For one thing, Hale's *History of the Common Law* was a standard work which Hume knew and refers to. Hume knows that the making of law is a slow process, the work of time and accumulating experience, in large states, at least. 'To balance a large state or society, whether monarchical or republican, on general laws, is a work of so great difficulty, that no human genius, however comprehensive, is able by the mere dint of reason and reflection, to effect it. The judgements of many must unite in this work: Experience must guide their labour: Time must bring it to perfection: And the feeling of inconveniences must correct the mistakes, which they inevitably fall into, in their first trials and experiments' (*Rise and Progress of Arts and Sciences*, 125). The perfecting of law and government presupposes a certain degree of advancement in the 'more vulgar arts at least of commerce and manufacture'. We cannot expect a government to be well-modelled by a people who do not know how to make a spinning-wheel (*Luxury* or *Refinement in the Arts*, 280). Thus the appearance of the legislator presupposes a certain level of civilization, and is not altogether due to chance, because as Hume says, the rise and progress of the arts and sciences is not wholly 'a question concerning the taste, genius and spirit of a

---

[1] For another example of the pendulum, cf. VIII, 382 (1660). The passion for liberty carried to extremes began 'by a natural movement' to give place to a spirit of loyalty and obedience.

[2] This seems to be an echo of the opening sentence of Chapter 10 of Book I of Machiavelli's *Discourses on Livy*.

few, but concerning those of a whole people and may, therefore, be accounted for, in some measure, by general causes and principles' (*Rise of Arts and Sciences*, 115). On the other hand, applying the rule suggested by Hume in the essay on the *Rise and Progress of the Arts and Sciences* (113) to distinguish chance from general causes, there must be a large element of chance in the appearance of the political genius with the 'very accurate *reason* or *judgement*... often requisite to give the true determination amidst such intricate doubts arising from obscure or opposite utilities' (Appendix I in the *Enquiry concerning Morals*, 286). And Alfred the Great, 'that great legislator' (1, 293), is a notable example of the sort of 'sage or wise man' which philosophers imagine rather than ever expect to see in flesh and blood, emerging in a state of barbarism and gross superstition. 'That he might render the execution of justice strict and regular, he divided all England into counties' and hundreds and tithings, and framed a body of laws, even if the similarity of these to the customs and practice of other northern nations 'prevents us from regarding Alfred as the sole author of this plan of government and leads us rather to think that like a wise man he contented himself with reforming, extending and executing the institutions which he found previously established'. Alfred did not invent the laws: nevertheless the spotlight falls on him and his laws and not, as in Millar and other Scottish social theorists, on the fact that they are typical of a certain stage of civilization, and that institutions similar to the tything can be found in all nations at a similar stage of development. 'Fortune alone', Hume says, threw him 'into that barbarous age' (1, 120-8).

And whereas other Scottish social theorists were anxious to explain the laws of Lycurgus and the institutions of Sparta as typical of a certain stage of social evolution, the point Hume is anxious to make is that they were unnatural. 'It is well known with what peculiar laws Sparta was governed, and what a prodigy that republic is justly esteemed by every one who has considered human nature, as it has displayed itself in other nations, and other ages. Were the testimony of history less positive and circumstantial, such a government would appear a mere philosophical whim or fiction, and impossible ever to be reduced to practice' (*Of Commerce*, 264). According to the philosophical history of Millar, Hume's point that lack of commerce and manufactures does not strengthen, but weakens a state, could have been made more powerfully by insisting on the naturalness of the Spartan government.

And there seems to be a gap in Hume's general theory of the historical origin of law. In the *Treatise* III, Part II, Section 8, the first governments are said to be simple monarchies: the civil government which succeeds the military is monarchical, and republics arise only from the abuses of monarchy and despotic power. In the essay on *The Rise of Arts and Sciences* it is said that law can only arise in republics – a republic, no matter how barbarous, gives rise to law 'by an infallible operation' (119); the form of government makes it inevitable. A barbarous monarch, on the other hand, 'unrestrained and uninstructed', can never become a legislator (116–18). A republic without laws cannot last: in a monarchy, law does not arise from the form of government: on the contrary there is in monarchy, as such, something repugnant to law. But Hume does not explain how the primitive republics, which infallibly give rise to law, do in fact emerge in the first place. He says, famously, in the *Original Contract* essay, that the origin of 'amost all' of the governments of recorded history is violence. But this violence is not here seen as a positive, state-building agency: its role is exclusively anti-contractarian. Between the 'force' of the *Original Contract* essay, and the 'barbarous republics' of the essay on the *Rise of Arts and Sciences* there is a logical gap: without the Legislators and founders of states it is difficult to see how the process of civilization could begin.[1]

Mandeville's theory of social evolution does not seem to have impressed Hume so deeply as it did Adam Smith. The only obvious reference to it is in the *Dialogues on Natural Religion* (p. 167 of Kemp Smith's edition) where it is pressed into service against the design argument.[2] How much Mandeville, if any, there is behind the conjectural history of society in Book III of the *Treatise* can only be guessed at. There the basic social rules or 'natural laws' are seen emerging spontaneously to meet the growing needs of society, the work of an 'inventive species', of the self-interest and passions of men. 'Whatever restraint they may impose on the passions of men, they are the real offspring of those passions...Nothing is more vigilant and inventive than our passions...' (*Treatise* III, Part II, Section 6).

But this line of thinking is abandoned when it comes to the actual progress of civilization in recorded history. Nor is there an analogy between that and the 'natural history of religion', where a natural

---

[1] See the essay *The Stoic*. 'The great end of all human industry is the attainment of happiness. For this were arts invented, sciences cultivated, laws ordained, and societies modelled, by the most profound wisdom of patriots and legislators' (149).
[2] See G. Carabelli: *Hume e la retorica dell'ideologia*, 255.

progress can be deduced from the religious psychology of the crowd and confirmed by history; for the natural history of religion is an enquiry into or pathology of popular religious belief, or what Hume calls 'false' religion. Unlike 'true' or 'philosophical' religion this does not advance – a natural progress is not necessarily progressive – but is necessarily subject to a perpetual flux and reflux. The progress of civilization, on the other hand, accidents apart, is the result of the intelligent adaptation of means to preconceived ends by legislators and creative minorities, whose progressive enlightenment and growing experience and the diffusion of that, such as it is, corresponds to the progress of 'true' religion.

The historical role of the people, as such, is uncreative and passive. They receive their 'manners' and morals and 'national character' from the 'people in authority', the 'governing part of a state' (Essay on *National Characters*, 212). The legislators are a powerful influence in the fashioning of a people's character and 'manners', both directly, through their personal example in the infancy of society, and indirectly through the laws and institutions they establish. An enthusiast for liberty like Brutus, placed in authority on the first establishment of a republic, will 'naturally have an effect on the whole society, and kindle the same passion in every bosom. Whatever it be that forms the manners of one generation, the next must imbibe a deeper tincture of the same dye: men being more susceptible of all impressions during infancy, and retaining these impressions as long as they remain in the world...all national characters where they depend not on fixed *moral* causes, proceed from such accidents as these...' (*id.*, 208–9). These remarks about the influence of rulers on a nation's 'manners' occur in a paragraph which begins by stressing the imitative nature of the human mind and the power of sympathy in forming the ethos of a society. Sympathy, which is so suggestive when expounded in the *Treatise*, is now seen to be the channel by which influences spread downward through a society from the government and those in authority, or else it becomes the 'contagion' which Hume is so fond of as an explanatory sociological principle: a popular disease which it is the task of the political scientist to obviate.[1]

---

[1] See, e.g. the *Idea of a Perfect Commonwealth*; all numerous assemblies are mere mob. 'This we find confirmed by daily experience. When an absurdity strikes a member he conveys it to his neighbour, and so on, till the whole body be infected. Separate this great body...influence and example being removed, good sense will always get the better of bad among a number of people' (509). Cf. *Principles of Government*: 'For though the people, collected in a body like the Roman tribes, be quite unfit

The role of society is to provide the 'opinion' on which all governments are said to be founded. But this 'opinion' is a negative check on government: not a positive social force. The people in the last resort can unmake a government: they cannot make one. As Hume says in the *Original Contract* essay, in any real revolution, it 'never comes to the body of the people'. The revolution of 1688 was not a real revolution, only the succession in the regal part of the government was changed; even so, 1688 was the work of a tiny minority only. The wishes of the people may be 'consulted' in a settled constitution; they have never governed themselves: Athens, 'the most extensive democracy that we read of in history', was governed by a minority of the people ('that establishment was not, at first, made, nor any law ever voted, by a tenth part of those who were bound to pay obedience to it'), and in a notoriously disorderly and licentious fashion (458–9). The majority of the people are always found either in a state of political inertia, owing to the enormous power of habit and habitual deference to authority, so that, in addition to inspired leadership, external factors, like religious enthusiasm or a special conjunction of circumstances are required to translate opinion into action: 'such is the influence of established government' that even James II might have been successful in his rash and ill-concerted projects, 'had not an attack been made from abroad' (IX, 457); or else, owing to the power of new ideas to excite the imagination, and the force of sympathy or popular contagion, they are swept by violent winds of change like a cornfield in a gale – and the more violent the wind, the more complete the apathy that inevitably follows.

So for Hume *qua* historian, laws and political institutions do not arise out of customs or 'folkways', or the movements and conflicts of society as a whole, and it could be argued that he is more stimulating and suggestive from a sociological point of view, in his abstract theory of government and society as seen in the *Treatise*, and more 'materialistic', than in his *History*. While his account of political obligation has been seen as too narrowly and exclusively economic, as a historian he has been criticized for neglecting economic factors and the 'materialist' foundation. This criticism of the *History*, is in general misguided, if one remembers Hume's main theme, but contains an element of truth. His account

for government, yet, when, dispersed in small bodies, they are more susceptible both of reason and order; the force of popular currents and tides, is in a great measure, broken; and the public interest may be pursued with some method and constancy' (33, 'some' was added in 1753). The *History* is full of examples of popular 'contagion'.

of how the Civil War divided the nation, for instance, is brief and general. 'The nobility, and more considerable gentry, dreading a total confusion of rank from the fury of the populace, inlisted themselves in defence of the monarch from whom they received, and to whom they communicated, their lustre' (VII, 459). This is the sort of 'philosophical' deduction which the genuine historian distrusts; it contrasts unfavourably with Carte's examination of the state of the Lords in the fourth volume of his *History* (1755). (Carte argues that the Lords were no longer the 'buckler of the crown', standing between the Crown and the people; James I had filled the peerage with moneyed men and favourites, of whom only a quarter fought for the royal cause in his son's reign [301–2].) The City of London and most of the great corporations adopted 'the democratical principles' of the parliamentary side because 'the government of cities...even under absolute monarchies, is commonly republican'. And he mentions, quoting Clarendon, those 'families...lately...enriched by commerce' who aspired to the level of the ancient gentry (VII, 460). But later, Hume says that when the zeal for liberty and presbyterian discipline had aroused an equal ardour for monarchy and episcopacy, 'each county, each town, each family almost, was divided within itself' (VII, 484). This corresponds to the purely ideological interpretation of the essay on the *Parties of Great Britain*, in which there is no hint of the economic and social causes of the conflict: 'In this question, so delicate and uncertain, men naturally fell to the side which was most conformable to their usual principles; and the more passionate favourers of monarchy declared for the king, as the zealous friends of liberty sided with the parliament. The hopes of success being nearly equal on both sides, *interest* had no general influence in this contest: so that Roundhead and Cavalier were merely parties of principle...' It can be seen from this what Hume means by 'interest': simply the political ambition of individuals; as he said at the beginning of the same essay, the leaders of parties are most governed by 'interest', the rank-and-file by 'principle'. Hume's political science does not know class-interest, apparently, or the social and economic aspect of parties.

It was his history of the seventeenth century that was most immediately geared to the political needs of his age, as Hume saw them: the need to heal a division that was essentially a question of political theory and morals. The economic interpretation, such as it was, was not controversial and divisive: it was a generally accepted commonplace. In so far as Hume's practical purpose is brought to bear on the story, the social and economic background recedes, the spotlight falls on the clash of parties and principles.

And Hume's emphasis on the fundamental importance of law and government, and a proper attitude to law and government, in the development and continuance of civilization, is as conspicuous in the *Treatise* as anywhere else in Hume's writings, perhaps even more so. There is a passage in the section on Liberty and Necessity in Book II of the *Treatise*, describing how the kaleidoscopic pattern of manners and customs, the variety of history, is owing to government, which rises to a kind of breathless crescendo unusual in Hume's writings. 'The different stations of life influence the whole fabric, external and internal; and these different stations arise necessarily, because uniformly, from the necessary and uniform principles of human nature. Men cannot live without society, and cannot be associated without government. Government makes a distinction of property, and establishes the different ranks of men. This produces industry, traffic, manufactures, law-suits, war, leagues, alliances, voyages, travels, cities, fleets, ports, and all those other actions and objects, which cause such a diversity, and at the same time maintain such an uniformity in human life' (*Treatise*, 402).

Not only is government absolutely essential to the progress of civilization, it is an active agent in the process. The beneficial influence of government extends beyond the administration of justice and the provision of security. With the invention of Government 'men acquire a security against each other's weakness and passion, as well as against their own, and under the shelter of their governors, begin to taste at ease the sweets of society and mutual assistance. But government extends still further its beneficial influence; and not contented to protect men in those conventions they make for their mutual interest, it often obliges them to make such conventions, and forces them to seek their own advantage by a concurrence in some common end or purpose' (*Treatise*, 538).

Society without the need for government is so primitive as to be barely society at all: in this sense it has universally in fact taken place (*Original Contract*, 453). And seen in the context of the actual progress of civilization the state of nature becomes something more than a useful fiction, as France experienced in the fourteenth century: the dissolution of the civil authority led to the dissolution of society: 'here the wild state of nature seemed to be renewed: Every man was thrown loose and independent of his fellows: And

THE LIMITS OF PHILOSOPHICAL HISTORY

the populousness of the country, derived from the preceding police of civil society, served only to increase the horror and confusion of the scene' (III, 185). 'Renewed' in the context of Hume's political theory is loose language: if the phrase is not to be taken as simply rhetorical, the non-social state of nature ('men thrown loose and independent of their fellows') is the alternative, in the history of civilized societies, to government, and the greater the degree of civilization, the more real and horrible the state of nature.

It is the necessity of submission to positive law and government – 'the salutary restraint of law and government' (*History*, I, 124) – which tames and civilizes men. With government, 'men acquire a security against each others' weakness and passion, as well as against their own...' (*Treatise*, 538). In the essay on *Polygamy and Divorces*, Hume argues that the marriage laws of modern Europe are more useful to society than polygamy and divorce, because, among other reasons, the 'necessity' of the married state changes the violent passion of love, which thrives on liberty, into the calm passion of friendship, a 'sober affection' which 'thrives under constraint'. If it is true that 'the heart of man naturally delights in liberty...it is also true...that the heart of man naturally submits to necessity, and soon loses an inclination, when there appears an absolute impossibility of gratifying it' (193). The psychological equilibrium of civilized behaviour is achieved in society as the result of the necessity of submitting to law and government. Remove the pressure of the necessity, and the spring of the violent passions flies out: hence the need for the general rule of strict obedience to established government, and the danger of the doctrine of resistance. A political theory which makes a fetish of the right of resistance is like a theory of matrimony which makes a general rule of divorce: it is necessary, perhaps, but only in exceptional circumstances.

It is this sort of political orientation and emphasis which, more fundamentally perhaps than anything else apart from his scepticism distinguishes Hume's philosophical history from that of thinkers like Ferguson and Smith and Millar who fill so much more space than he does in the general histories of sociology and social theory. But such considerations take one beyond the scope of this study of Hume's philosophical politics.

Appendix

Hume's History, and the revisions

There are a great many editions of Hume's *History of England*, and no standard one. The edition I have used and referred to is that of 1808-10 (London) in ten volumes, the last volume being one of Notes and Index, because this is the edition I happen to possess. One cannot ignore the versions that were revised and corrected by Hume himself: the changes are very numerous. I had to make sure that I was not missing any significant developments in Hume's thinking over a period of twenty years or so, and perhaps falsifying the picture by presenting as a static thesis what was essentially a development, making *AB* out of what really is *A* followed by *B*. I had to find out what sort of effect these revisions of the text of the *History* had on the gist of Hume's philosophical politics in general and his interpretation of English history. The variations in the medieval volumes, up to 1485, are not of great significance: having discovered this by comparing my edition with Hume's first edition of the medieval volumes (1762), I left it at that. But having noted significant changes as between the first Stuarts (1754 and 1757) and Tudors (1759) and my edition, it became necessary to find out when these had been made. To do this I looked at the 2nd edition of the Stuarts (1759), and the complete histories of 1763, '73 and '78 (which has the final corrections and is presumably the same text as mine: there was no harm in checking on that anyway). The edition of '67 is the same as that of '63. I was able to use the edition of '70 for the Tudors, but not for the Stuarts: there is thus a gap there, but my list of these variants suggests that this does not matter, since most of the changes seem to have been made either in '59 or in the last version. This collating was done before I suggested to Penguin Books that they should reprint the 1754 *History of Great Britain in the reigns of James I and Charles I* for their Pelican Classics series (1970). Since this is now more readily available to most readers than the actual 1754 volume, I have referred to it where necessary: it deals with by far the most important period in the whole *History*. I have not given the page references to any other editions, though I have them. I cannot claim to have carried out a complete and thorough collation such as one would make for a variorum edition: it is sufficient, I hope, to allow me to argue (1) that in essentials Hume's interpretation is there from the beginning; perhaps I ought to say, my interpretation of that, or the 'philosophical' core of it, and (2) that to expound and follow this through every change and

APPENDIX

every detail would almost call for a book in itself. This is owing to the difficulty of deciding into what categories one is to put all these changes, and the need to explain most of them at some length. To illustrate the difficulties, or at least the need for fairly lengthy discussion, and also my contention that in the last resort Hume does not radically alter his main thesis in spite of all the changes: there are, for example, revisions which appear to be politically significant which turn out on closer inspection, or rather, in casting about more widely, to be stylistic, to avoid repetition, for greater euphony etc; or to make more clearly a point made earlier, or to get rid of rhetorical exaggeration in the interest of greater precision (this is a conspicuous item in the changes Hume made in the *Essays* also), or for greater economy. (One must also always remember, and keep a check on the fact that Hume withdrew things from the text in order to put them into notes – they have not necessarily disappeared.) Thus, the 'exorbitant' of James I's 'exorbitant prerogative' on p. 106 of the 1754 (*Pelican Classics*) edition was later withdrawn: in itself this may be considered a 'Tory' revision, but the 'exorbitant' on p. 108 (the context is the same) was not. What looks like a 'Tory' amendment, if one does not turn over the page, is not, as soon as one does. After 'But James' in 1754 (*Pelican Classics* 229, line 21) there is in the latest edition, and in no other previous one, a remark: 'besides that he had certainly laid no plan for extending his power' (in my edition, VII, 18) which appears to be a straightforward 'Tory' addition: in fact, it is merely drawing the conclusion from what (in 1754) is said on pp. 235–6. Hume could have inserted his addition there without any straining whatever. (Let the reader test the matter for himself.) In *Pelican Classics,* 278, the remark that in 1626 'the nation was thus treated like a conquered province' was later withdrawn: it is an imprecise exaggeration: the nation was *not* treated like a 'conquered province', but anyone who knows all the editions of the *History* reasonably well knows that Hume's judgement as to Charles I's treatment of the nation was and remained harsh. Again, on p. 352 (*Pelican Classics*), Hampden 'deservedly' acquired popularity for his stand on the ship-money issue: 'deservedly' was later withdrawn, but 'and has merited great renown with posterity' remains. This, it seems to me, is due to Hume's realization of the implications of what I have called his 'bifocal' view of the conflict of king and commons: he deserved his popularity retrospectively, in the eyes of 'posterity', but not at the time. Such a slip is perfectly understandable in anyone putting forward a new and subtle interpretation in place of the generally accepted one, especially if one has subscribed to the latter for quite a long time oneself. On p. 417, 'had the King abstained from all invasion of national privileges', becomes in 1759 had the King 'been able to abstain', and in the final edition: 'been able to support government and at the same time to abstain...' This is a progressive clarification of Hume's initial 'philosophical' thesis about the position in which Charles I found himself and

APPENDIX

which obliged him to act in a certain way, which he says in 1754 is a lesson in moderation (390–1). Why he later withdrew this remark about the lesson of moderation (391), when the lesson itself remained, I just do not know. A similar verbal cleaning up operation is seen on p. 79. Elizabeth, in spite of fulsome praise on p. 2 is described as 'that arbitrary princess'. 'Arbitrary' was withdrawn in 1759. Hume's point was that Elizabeth was not acting arbitrarily: her quasi-despotic rule was perfectly constitutional, given the nature of the constitution as generally accepted at that time (though the matter is not quite as simple as this). As Hume came to collect more examples of the exercise of royal prerogative from the Tudor reigns and earlier, he made the necessary changes in the Stuart volumes, for example, regarding the rights and wrongs of the king's use of tonnage and poundage, but the germ of his later views is already present in 1754 (*Pelican Classics*, 109, 221). Then 'the men' of 1754 (*id*, 260) becomes 'generous patriots' of 1763. If this has political significance, it works against the Hume-becoming-more-conservative thesis, unless one is going to get really subtle and say that he is being ironical, as possibly elsewhere he was, when 'the leaders' of 1754 (*id*, 417) becomes 'the patriots of this age' in the latest edition, that is, some time after 1773. The context of the remark does suggest irony: but 'generous patriots' is, I think, sincere, here as elsewhere. Again, in 1754 (*id.*, 103, line 3), the Commons are given credit for their 'careful attention towards public good and national liberty' (in November, 1606). Hume later withdrew 'public good and': it is there in '73, gone in '78. Is this because their concern for 'national liberty' militated against 'public good' as an 'old-Hume-the-reactionary-Tory' interpretation would no doubt have it? But then why does Hume continue to allow compliments on nearby pages with respect to the Commons' concern for trade, to remain? He gives no further details to suggest that the Commons had not earned the compliments paid them, and allow the reader to judge for himself. Is it just stylistic? dislike of a pleonasm? A sudden fit of spleen on coming to the phrase when revising? Sometimes there seems no reason at all for an addition like that summary remark on the reign of James I. 'In all history it would be difficult to find a reign less illustrious, yet more unspotted and unblemished than that of James in both kingdoms.' That went in in the last edition, but might have been in any earlier one. It seems therefore that one cannot label these changes without a great deal of further consideration, and that this is not going to have any serious effect on my interpretation.

Bibliography

This is a short working bibliography for reference. It merely lists the editions of works used fairly extensively and/or in such a way as to make *op. cit.* and its equivalents possibly bothersome. For editions of works by Hume see list of abbreviations and Appendix (for the *History*), and add (1) *Hume's Early Memoranda*. The complete text (ed. E. C. Mossner) in *Journal of the History of Ideas*, Vol. 9, 1948; (2) *A Letter from a Gentleman to his friend in Edinburgh* (1745), Edinburgh University Press, 1967.

Blackstone, W.	*Commentaries on the Laws of England*, 4 vols, Oxford, 1765–9.
Bolingbroke, Henry St John	*A Dissertation upon Parties*, 8th edition, London, 1754.
	Remarks on the History of England, London, no date.
	The Works, London, 1844.
Carte, T.	*A General History of England*, 4 Vols, London, 1747–55.
Cumberland, R.	*A Treatise of the Laws of Nature*, London, 1727.
The Craftsman	14 Vols, London, 1731–7.
Dalrymple, J.	*An Essay towards a General History of Feudal Property in Great Britain*, 4th edition, London, 1759.
Echard, L.	*The History of England*, London, 1707.
Grotius, H.	*The Rights of War and Peace*, with Barbeyrac's notes, London, 1738.
	Prolegomena to the Law of War and Peace, Library of Liberal Arts, 1957.
Guthrie, W.	*A General History of England*, 3 Vols, London, 1744–51.
Heineccius, J. G.	*A Methodical System of Universal Law, translated and illustrated with notes by G. Turnbull*, 2 Vols, London, 1763.
Hurd, R.	*Moral and Political Dialogues*, 2nd edition, London, 1760.
Hutcheson, F.	*A Short Introduction to Moral Philosophy*, 2nd edition, Glasgow, 1753.
	A System of Moral Philosophy, 2 Vols, London, 1755.

BIBLIOGRAPHY

McCosh, J.	*The Scottish Philosophy*, London, 1875.
Mossner, E. C.	*The Life of David Hume*, Nelson, 1954.
Oldmixon, J.	*The Critical History of England*, 3rd edition, London, 1728.
Pufendorf, S.	*Of the Law of Nature and of Nations*, Oxford, 1703.
	Whole Duty of Man according to the Law of Nature, London, 1716.
Rapin-Thoyras	*The History of England*, trs: N. Tindal, 15 Vols, London, 1726–31.
Rutherforth, T.	*Institutes of Natural Law*, 2 Vols, Cambridge, 1754–6.
Shaftesbury, Anthony, Earl of	*Characteristics of Men, Manners, Opinions, Times*, 6th edition, 3 Vols, 1737.
Stewart, D.	*Collected Works*, ed. Sir W. Hamilton, 11 Vols, Edinburgh, 1854–60.
Towers, J.	*Observations on Mr. Hume's History of England*, London, 1778.
Turnbull, G.	*A Discourse upon the Nature and Origin of Moral and Civil Laws* in Heineccius *Methodical System, op. cit.* Vol. II.
	The Principles of Moral Philosophy, London, 1740.
	The Principles of Moral and Christian Philosophy, London, 1741.

Index of Persons

Where a reference is made to a note as well as a page, only the page is indicated. References to Hume's writings are in Index of Subjects.

Aarsleff, Hans, 7n, 74n
Addison, Joseph, 141n, 145, 155
Albissin, N. G. d', 233n
Alfred the Great, 317
Allen, John, 182n
Anne, Queen, 193, 203, 233
Ardal, P. S., 8
Aristotle, 5, 29, 107
Arnall or Arnold, William ('Walsingham'), 148n, 214n, 234n, 243, 249
Atterbury, Francis, 241

Bacon, Francis, 8, 312, 314, 315n
Balcarres, Earl of, 137
Balfour of Pilrig, James, 62
Barbentane, Marquise de, 187
Barbeyrac, Jean, 6, 27, 31f, 42f, 45, 51n, 74n
Barre, Chevalier de la, 187n
Barré, Isaac, 133
Barrington, Daines, 149, 313n
Bayle, Pierre, 9n, 57, 61n
Becker, Carl, 113n
Beckett, Archbishop, 216n
Beckford, Alderman, 176
Bedford, 4th Duke of, 133
Bennett, G. V., 241n
Bentham, Jeremy, 57, 161n, 292
Berkeley, George, 9n, 58, 65
Black, J. B., 102-3
Blackstone, Sir William, 27, 74, 101n, 143n, 149f, 156n, 178n, 207n, 251ff, 270, 302n, 315
Blackstone, W. T., 32n, 56
Blackwell, T., 158n, 161n, 178n
Blair, Hugh, 133n, 187
Blanc, Abbé le, 150n, 189n, 253n, 262n, 292
Blanchard, Rae, 97n, 145
Bodin, Jean, 32
Bolingbroke, Henry St John, Viscount, 147f, 152, 161, 174, 177, 194-202, 205-10, 213, 214n, 216, 219, 222ff, 226, 233, 240-7, 255, 263, 267f, 270, 276, 312
Boufflers, Mme de, 133, 138f
Boulainvilliers, Henri, comte de, 153
Boswell, James, 207n, 253n
Boyle, Robert, 16
Brady, Robert, 238, 242, 243n, 244, 254, 302n, 303n, 315n
Brown, John (*Estimate*), 224
Buckingham, 1st Duke of, 241, 281n
Burke, Edmund, 133, 213
Burnet, Gilbert, 259
Burton, J. H., 141n
Bute, 3rd Earl of, 126ff, 130-3
Butler, Joseph, 8, 33n, 48, 57
Butterfield, Sir Herbert, viii
Bynkershoek, 32

Campbell, A. H., 41n
Campbell of Cawdor, 206
Carabelli, G., 81n, 318n
Carlsson, P. A., 57n
Carmichael, Gershom, 30f, 40
Carneades, 6
Carte, Thomas, 225, 253n, 265n, 301, 306n, 311n, 321
Castignone, S., 89n
Charles I, 208n, 234ff, 236n, 237f, 246, 248f, 255n, 256ff
  Hume and, 260ff, 264n, 267, 270-5, 278f, 281, 283ff, 290, 295f, 310, 325
Charles II, 198, 290n, 294, 295n, 296
Chesterfield, 4th Earl of, 153n
Cheyne, George, 9, 59
Church, R. W., 9n
Christie, I. R., 191n
Cibber, Colley, 183n
Cicero, 4, 16, 32, 44, 48f, 51n, 54, 109
Clarendon, Edward Hyde, Earl of, 235, 256, 321
Clarke, Samuel, 9, 16, 66

INDEX OF PERSONS

Cleghorn, William, 44
Clovis, 197
Cobban, A., 103n
Cocceius, Samuel, 51ff
Cohen, I. B., 61
Coke, Sir Edward, 305
Collingwood, R. G., ixn, 103f
Comte, Auguste, 286
Conway, Henry Seymour, General, 131f, 133n, 138
Cotes, Roger, 3
Coxe, William, 138n
Cragg, G. R., 140n
Craig, John, 167
Cromwell, Oliver, 272n
Cudworth, Ralph, 9, 16, 66
Cumberland, Richard, 18–26, 29, 32, 42f, 45, 49, 51n, 53f, 75n, 79n
Cyrus, 14

Dalrymple, Sir John, 161n, 179n, 306n, 314–15n
Davenant, Charles, 144
David, King of Scots, 253n
Davidson, W., 296n
Davies, R. M., 250n
De Lolme, J. L., 161n, 302–3n
Descartes, 9, 194
Dickson, P. G. M., 175n
Diogenes, 107
Dionysius, the tyrant, 92
Dobrée, Bonamy, 140n
Domat, Jean, 5
Dudgeon, William, 80–3
Duncan, William, 15n, 16n
Dunn, J., 65n

Echard, Laurence, 178n, 235, 239, 301, 312
Edgar, King, 301n
Edward the Confessor, 239, 244, 250, 304
Edward I, 239, 247, 251, 265n, 306
Edward II, 226
Edward III, 268, 276, 278, 286n, 287
Edward VI, 240
Elizabeth I, 160n, 171, 178, 180n, 218n, 219, 236, 245f, 248, 255, 258, 259n, 264n, 265n
  in Hume, 269f, 271f, 274, 279, 284, 326
Elliot of Minto, Sir Gilbert, 127, 129f, 132f, 136f, 188n, 191, 313n
Elrington, Thomas, 142

Fagerstrom, D., 134n
Ferguson, Adam, 85, 128, 133, 229, 323

Ferguson, W., 134n
Filmer, Sir Robert, 34, 75n, 144
Fletcher of Saltoun, Andrew, 144–5
Foord, A. S., 136n
Forbes of Culloden, Duncan, 179n
Fox, C. J., 133f, 286
Fox, Henry, 137
Franklin, Benjamin, 134n, 189n
Fraser, J., 253

Galileo, 16
Garioch, Robert, 84n
George III, 126, 128, 130, 135, 190
Giannone, Pietro, 315
Giarrizzo, G., xi, 126n, 135n, 136n, 174n
Gibbon, Edward, 189n
Gough, J. W., 105
Grafton, 3rd Duke of, 132
Gray, Thomas, 253n
Greene, D. J., 254n
Grenville, George, 133, 270n
Grotius, Hugo, xi, 4, 6, 16–19, 21ff, 25, 27f, 30, 32, 34, 41ff, 49, 51, 54f, 68, 86n, 95, 97, 99n, 162, 164
Guthrie, William, 176n, 178n, 225, 253–8, 306n, 312f

Haig, R. L., 148n
Hale, Sir Matthew, 244, 316
Halifax, George Savile, Marquis of, 144
Hampden, John, 262n, 282, 325
Hardwicke, Philip Yorke, 1st Earl of, 177, 179, 206–7n
Harie, Dr, 253n, 254n
Harold, King, 252, 257, 302–3n
Harrington, James, 5, 32, 180n, 195, 197n, 211, 229, 312, 314
Hartley, David, 119n
Hegel, G. W. F., 105, 107
Heineccius, J. G., 3ff, 27, 31f, 38n, 43f, 47, 51–4, 72n
Hendel, C. W., 9n, 61n, 106
Henry I, 239, 250–1
Henry II, 239, 251, 304
Henry III, 160, 239, 241n, 243, 251, 306
Henry IV, 240n
Henry VI, 287
Henry VII, 178n, 207, 268, 312ff, 314–15n
Henry VIII, 245, 259, 268–9, 279, 283n
Hertford, Francis Seymour Conway, 1st Earl of, 127, 130–33, 138
Hervey, John, Lord, 148, 217, 247ff
Hoadly, Benjamin, 75n, 145, 299
Hobbes, Thomas, 8, 20ff, 29, 32, 38, 52f, 68, 71n, 72f, 74n, 80, 85

330

INDEX OF PERSONS

Hody, Humphrey, 240, 244
Hooke, Nathaniel, 148f
Hooker, Richard, 195f
Horace, 68
Hunt (*Argumentum anti-Normanicum*), 244
Hurd, Richard, 180n, 258ff, 270n, 291n, 301n, 313
Hurlbutt, R. H., 64n
Hutcheson, Francis, 8, 16, 27, 32–42, 44–8, 50f, 55–61, 63f, 66, 68f, 72, 83ff, 89, 92, 93n, 99n, 156n, 161f, 165

James I, 171, 200, 226, 234–7, 237f, 240f, 245f, 248f, 250n, 255ff, 321
   Hume and, 260ff, 264n, 267, 271–4, 285, 288, 292f, 310, 325f
James II, 96, 99, 100f, 254, 290n, 320
Jeffner, A., 62n
Jessop, T. E., 193n
John, King, 239, 247, 258, 304
Johnson, Samuel, 206n, 207n, 253n
Justinian, 12

Kames, Henry Home, Lord, 11, 12n, 14f, 63, 87, 94n, 189n, 234n, 303n, 306n, 313n
Kelsey, F. H., 6n
Kemp, Betty, 136n
Kennett, White, 241
Kenyon, J. P., 144
Kliger, S., 238n
Kluckhohn, C., 112n
Knapp, L. M., 253n
Koyré, A., 61
Kramnick, I., 174n, 195
Kuypers, M. S., 64n
Kydd, R. M., 18n

Laing, B. M., 116n
Laird, John, 83n, 87n, 105
Laprade, W. T., 148n
Larkin, P., 88n, 89–90n
Laslett, P., 7n, 142
Lechmere, Nicholas, 145
Leechman, William, 32, 45f, 61
Leibniz, G. W., 54, 83n
Leicester, *see* Montfort
Lehmann, W. C., 94n
Leroy, A., 83n
Lévi-Strauss, C., 76n
Locke, John, 7f, 9n, 27, 32, 65n, 66n, 68, 71n, 73f, 75n, 77f, 80, 84, 86, 93, 142, 149, 164, 166, 194f, 214n, 299
Loftis, John, 183n
Longinus, 155

Louis le Gros, 311
Lycurgus, 317
Lyttleton, George, Lord, 180, 244n, 249–50n, 250f, 302

McCosh, James, 4, 80f
Macaulay, Catherine, 284n, 313
Macaulay, Thomas Babington, 291
Machiavelli, 160, 195, 224, 229, 248, 315, 316n
Mack, M. P., 161n
Maclaurin, Colin, 63, 104
MacNabb, D. G. C., 83n
McQueen, Daniel, 291
Marshall, Dorothy, 176
Malebranche, Nicolas de, 8f, 10n, 18, 107, 130
Mallet, David, 128
Mandeville, Bernard, 8, 85, 318
Marx, Karl, 108
Maynard, Sir John, 259
Medick, Hans, 52n, 53n
Meinecke, Friedrich, 103, 106, 310
Menary, G., 179n
Mercer, P., 106n
Methuen, Sir Paul, 149n
Millar, Andrew, 129
Millar, John, 167, 182, 302n, 308f, 315ff, 323
Millar, W. G., 33n
Molesworth, Robert, 143–4
Monboddo, James Burnett, Lord, 80
Montesquieu, 16, 138, 149f, 157n, 160, 165f, 179f, 185n, 189, 224, 240n, 306n
Montfort, Simon de, 239, 251, 306
Morrow, G. R., 106n
Mossner, E. C., 65n, 94n, 193n, 220, 221n, 253n, 296n, 298
Mure of Caldwell, William, 127, 130, 133, 213

Nero, 92, 96, 100f, 159, 272
Newcastle, Duke of, 128, 137, 207n, 254
Newton, 5, 16, 33, 60f, 83, 104, 194, 309
North, Lord, 132n, 191
North, Sir Dudley, 150

Oldmixon, John, 143, 234f, 244, 301
'Osborne, Francis' (James Pitt), 148, 195, 214f, 218, 248f
Oswald of Dunnikier, James, 127, 133, 136, 189n, 291n

Pascal, 107
Passmore, J., 119n, 120n

331

INDEX OF PERSONS

Pelham, Henry, 149n, 253-4
Perceval, John, 2nd Earl of Egmont, 209n
Perry, T. W., 193n
Petyt, William, 240, 244
Philip II of Spain, 92
Phillipson, N. T., 134n
Pitt, William (Earl of Chatham), 127f, 130ff, 137, 206
Pitt, William (the Younger), 167
Plato, 9n
Pocock, J. G. A., 238n, 241n
Polin, R., 65n, 77n
Polybius, 5
Price, H. H., 10
Pufendorf, Samuel, xi, 4, 6f, 16f, 21f, 27-31, 33f, 38, 40, 42, 45, 50ff, 54f, 60, 68ff, 72f, 74n, 76-9, 85
Pulteney, William, Earl of Bath, 138

Quintillian, 27n

Ramsay of Ochtertyre, John, 253n
Raphael, D. D., 32n
Rapin-Thoyras, Paul de, 233-40, 241, 243, 245, 251, 254f, 284n, 312
  Hume and, 261ff, 268, 273, 298f
Rex, W., 57n
Richard II, 236, 240, 287
Richelieu, 281
Robbins, C., 134n
Robertson, William, 18, 129, 269
Robinson, Sir Thomas, 218n
Rotwein, E., xi, 87n, 104n, 178n
Ross, I. S., 9n, 94
Rouet, W., 127n
Rousseau, J. J., 80, 189
Rudé, G., 188n, 191n
Ruffhead, Owen, 302n, 314n
Rutherforth, T., 75n, 98n, 99n, 156n, 162-5
Rycaut, Sir Paul, 150n

St Amand, George, 238, 244
Scaevola, Mucius, 116
Schütt, Marie, 257n
Schochet, G. S., 74n
Scotus, Duns, 126
Selden, J., 244
Seliger, M., 73n
Seneca, 43
Shaftesbury, 3rd Earl of, 8, 32, 48, 62, 74-5n, 91, 146, 155, 218n, 219
Shebbeare, John, 206n
Shelburne, 2nd Earl of, 133, 207
Shippen, William, 140n

Sidney, Algernon, 97, 144, 244, 299
Smith, Adam, 65n, 76, 87, 130, 133n, 136, 138, 172, 189n, 216n, 250, 308f, 318, 323
Smith, Norman Kemp, 17, 62n, 318
Smith, T. B., 140n
Smollet, Tobias, 131, 206, 253n
Socrates, 8
Somers, Lord, 259n
Somerset, Lord, 218n
Spink, J. S., 57n
Stair, Viscount, 7n, 90n, 140n
Stanhope, James, 1st Earl, 97
Steele, Richard, 97, 145
Stein, Peter, 41n, 90n
Stephen, King, 239, 251
Stephen, Leslie, 297
Sterne, Lawrence, 74n
Steuart, Sir James, 158n, 288n
Stewart, Dugald, 8n, 9, 16f, 72, 157n, 166f
Stewart, J. B., 264n
Strahan, William, 133n, 152, 178
Strato, 61n
Suard, Jean Baptiste Antoine, 184n
Sutherland, Lucy, 134n, 176

Tacitus, 64, 121, 143n, 196, 220, 257
Temple, Sir William, 72n, 75
Thales, 8
Thompson, Faith, 305n
Thucydides, 25
Tindal, N., 233n, 238, 240
Towers, Joseph, 291n, 302n
Turgot, 177n, 184n, 187f
Turnbull, George, 3-6, 9n, 27n, 38n, 42, 44, 47f, 52, 80n, 85
Tyrell, James, 240, 244, 254, 301

Vico, 80
Vlachos, G., 114f
Voltaire, 102, 253n

Wake, William, 241
Wallace, Robert, 157-8n, 234n
Walpole, Horace, 132, 139, 206, 253n, 299n
Walpole, Sir Robert (Earl of Orford), 127n, 138, 193ff, 199f, 220ff, 225, 240, 249
'Walsingham', *see* Arnall
Warburton, William, 65, 86n, 148
Ward, Addison, 149n
Watkins, F., 88n
Wedderburn, Alexander, 129, 133
Wellek, R., 102n, 155n
Welzel, Hans, 77n

332

INDEX OF PERSONS

Westfall, R. S., 64n
Wilkes, John, 128f, 130, 133, 189f
William I, 238f, 241, 249f, 252, 257, 259, 263n, 302f, 315

Wollaston, W., 16, 66
Wyndham, W., 149n

Yolton, J. Y., 7n, 65n, 74n

Index of Subjects

Alienations, Statute of, 312f
Amalfi, 315
American colonies, Hume's attitude to, 133–4, 190n
Association of ideas, x, 8f, 10, 15, 63, 106
Athenian republic, 228
Augustus, age of, 315

Bill of Rights, 248

Cato's Letters, 79n, 146–7
chance, 120, 316f
checks, natural, to growth, 190
China, 227
Chinese government, 169, 212, 250n
Church and State, 214ff
Church of England, 215
Christianity, 57n, 61, 233n
'civilization' in Hume, 296; see also progress of civilization
'civilized monarchies', 141, 152–60, 167, 181, 187, 272n
Civil War, the English, 235; Hume and, 261, 272, 287ff, 321; bifocal view of in Hume's *History*, 265, 285, 291
Commons, House of, 177, 230, 271f, 273; able leaders of, in Guthrie, 256; in Hume, 281, 310f; financial inexperience of, 294f; origin of, in Rapin, 239; Bolingbroke, 241; Ministerialist writers, 243; Lyttleton, 252; Hurd, 260; Hume, 306f, 311; on the defensive in Hume's *History*, 274; on the offensive, 275, 282f, 285
Common Sense, or *The Englishman's Journal*, 148, 158n, 197n, 220
Conduct of the Opposition (1734), 217n
Constitution
  Ancient Constitution, controversy over in 1730s, 218, 241 *et seq.*; in Rapin etc, 233 *et seq.*; continuity of, 244ff; attacked by Ministerialist writers, 246; in Hume, 267, 272, 278, 309

British Constitution, Addison on, 145–6; Bolingbroke on, 195 *et seq.*; Montesquieu on, 165; Rapin on, 235 *et seq.*; Hume and, 93, 186, 222 its disadvantages, 70 *et seq.*; 181 *et seq.*; 189f; its fluctuations, 267 *et seq.*; irregularity of the medieval, 226, 278, 280, 286–7; improved by violent innovations, 282f; right and fact in historical, 276f; singularity of, 143, 152, 168, 186
  Saxon Constitution, 197, 226, 238n, 239ff, 245, 250n, 257; Hume and, 267, 300f, 305
  Anglo-Norman Constitution, 251, 267f, 303f; see also Norman Yoke
conservatism, problem of Hume's, x, 135, 139, 168, 174f, 187, 191f, 326
Contract theory of government, Hume's critique, 66f, 83f, 92f, 141
corruption, parliamentary, Bolingbroke on, 198, 216; see also dependence. Machiavellian, 199, 209, 217f, 225f, 228f; see also Machiavellian moralism
Craftsman, 147, 194, 198f, 200n, 207, 211, 214n, 217n, 218n, 223, 234n, 243ff, 249, 267
Critical Review, 206n
criticism, 64n
cyclical history, 315

Daily Gazetteer, 148, 195, 215f, 218n, 220, 234n, 243, 248
dependence, system of parliamentary, 135, 136n, 181f, 207, 211, 216f, 295f
despotism, usage of, 156ff; Turkish, 142, 144f, 150, 156f, 175, 197n, 269
Detector detected, The, 208n, 209n
discretionary powers, in absolute monarchies, 157; in republics, 170; lack of in England, 167f, 172f, 181, 283, 287f

English, excessive liberty of the, 187, 189; 'foolish prejudices' of, 141;

INDEX OF SUBJECTS

barbarism of, 189; prone to extremism, 223; snobbery, 188f
economic basis of Hume's political philosophy, 86–9; economic interpretation of history in Hume, 280f, 320f
economy, Newtonian principle of, 76, 83–6
Edinburgh Magazine and Review, 161n
Edinburgh Review (1825), 182n
Eleven Years Tyranny, 275
Esprit des Lois, 165f, 233

Faction detected (1743), 208n, 209n, 213n
family the, Hume and, 70f, 75, 80
feudalism, feudal government, 238f (Rapin), 250 (Lyttleton), 252, 259f (Hurd), 306 (Dalrymple); Hume and, 267f, 276, 280, 286f, 303f
Five Knights Case (1626), 277
Fog's Journal, 195
forfeiture of the Crown, lineal succession and, 99
France, Hume's love for, 140
Francophobes, Hume and, 312
Free Briton, 211f
French and English government compared by Hume, 172f, 187
French hegemony, Hume on danger of, 150–1n
French monarchy, Bolingbroke and, 196f
French 'slavery', 143 *et seq.*; Hume and, 152f, 161; *see also* vulgar Whiggism

General Warrants, 129, 132, 190f
Genoa, Bank of St George, 228
Gentleman's Magazine, 215n, 218, 253n
gentry, rise of, 177, 281, 293
German invaders of the Roman Empire. 257, 296, 299, 300, 303
Goodwin's case (1604), 274
'Gothic' government, 278, 292, 299
government, crucial role in Hume's political science, 224 *et seq.*; 308, 322f; benefits of, 322f; free government defined by Hume, 153f; origin of, 28–31 (Pufendorf), 31f (Heineccius), 38–41 (Hutcheson), 74–5 (Shaftesbury), 74 (Blackstone); 74 (Locke), 75f, 84ff (Hume); parental, 29, 75
Granville-Broadbottom crisis (1744–6), 138
'Greek loves', 109ff, 113n

Habeas Corpus Act, 170, 288

Hanover, Treaty of, 193
Hanoverian establishment, x, 91, 129, 262
Harringtonian maxim, balance of property and power, 5, 199, 207–10, 241, 250; disputed by Hume, 208f, 211, 229f, 242n; in Hume's history, 177, 280, 312
heritable jurisdictions, abolition of, 179
Highlands of Scotland, 87, 300
Historismus, 106, 114
Holland, 170, 171n, 183, 193n
Hume, David, separate works of,
  Abstract, 60f
  A Dialogue, xi, 107, 109, 111f, 114, 118
  Dialogues concerning Natural Religion, 62, 67, 318
  Dissertation on the Passions, 107
  Enquiry concerning Human Understanding, 67, 103, 105, 113f, 115, 117, 224
  Enquiry concerning the Principles of Morals, 6n, 8, 15f, 26, 28, 65n, 68f, 73n, 78, 80, 83, 85, 107–10, 112, 153, 225f, 317
  Essays
    Balance of Power, 151n, 223n
    Balance of Trade, 151n, 159n, 190
    Civil Liberty, 113, 115, 154, 156–60, 173ff, 311
    Character of Sir Robert Walpole, 184, 193, 220f
    Coalition of Parties, 128, 205f, 208, 265ff, 268n
    Commerce, 88, 108, 125, 159n, 317
    Eloquence, 120, 219
    First Principles of Government, 91, 182, 210, 213, 230, 242, 319–20n
    Independency of Parliament, 181f, 211, 217, 219f, 227
    Jealousy of Trade, 183
    Liberty of the Press, 156n, 169f, 183f, 219, 229
    Luxury (or *Refinement in the Arts*), 87f, 176f, 228, 296f, 310, 316
    Middle Station of Life, 176f
    National Characters, 65, 106, 111, 115n, 177, 223n, 226f, 319
    Natural History of Religion, 62n, 69, 233n
    Original Contract, 29, 65n, 73n, 76–7n, 89n, 92f, 100f, 141f, 261, 283n, 318, 320, 322
    Origin of Government, x, 75n, 76–7n, 153f, 190, 192, 282
    Parties in General, 177, 185n, 202, 216n, 233n, 316
    Parties of Great Britain, 94, 169n,

335

INDEX OF SUBJECTS

Hume,—*contd.*
   176, 185, 201ff, 206, 221, 261, 262f, 284, 321
   Passive Obedience, 92f, 100f, 262
   Perfect Commonwealth, 168f, 172, 181n, 183, 186, 212n, 319n
   Politics reduced to a Science, 114, 156n, 159f, 168, 194, 219, 221–4, 227ff, 263, 285, 292
   Populousness of Ancient Nations, ixn, 150n, 182, 184n, 228, 233n, 298
   Polygamy and Divorces, 323
   Protestant Succession, 95, 97, 151, 183, 207n, 212n, 261f, 272n
   Public Credit, 120, 127, 151n, 170n, 174f, 177f, 180, 207n, 212n
   Rise and Progress of the Arts and Sciences, 71, 120, 150n, 155ff, 159, 169, 212, 298, 314n, 316ff
   Some Remarkable Customs, 168n, 262n
   Simplicity and Refinement, 225
   Standard of Taste, 227
   Stoic, The, 318n
   Superstition and Enthusiasm, 152, 214ff
   Taxes, 159n
   Whether the British Government inclines etc, 65, 151, 152n, 180f, 193n, 208–12, 222, 230
   Essays, moral and political (1741), 114n, 193n
   History of England (general), x, 102, 120f; publication of, 260–1n; an establishment history, 263 *et seq.*; in what sense a tract for the times, 264; relativism of, 286; impartiality of, 291 *et seq.*; as a history of civilization, 296ff
   Letter from a Gentleman, 63f, 78
   Memoranda, early, 113n, 159n, 171n
   Memoranda for my History of England, 263n
   Treatise of Human Nature, x, 3, 16, 32, 64f, 67, 76, Introduction, 8, 62, 64, 80, 83, 104, Book II, 8, 73n, 105f, 117, 322, Book III, 8–15, 16n, 24, 60, 67, 70f, 73ff, 79, 84–7, 91n, 93–98, 105, 153, 301, 318, 322f
Hyp Doctor, 243n
hypothesis, 3, 61f; 'religious hypothesis', 62, 66, 68

imagination (Humean), 9–15, 95, 98f, 101, 203, 310; and the rules determining property, 9–12, 95; and political obligation, 12f, 95, 301; and allegiance to particular governments, 13ff, 95f
independence, Hume's desire for political, 125
Independents in Civil War, 238; independents in eighteenth-century politics, 126, 136f
individualism of Hume's political thought, 105
instructions to MP's, 210, 213, 240n
'is–ought' passage in *Treatise*, 60

Jacobites, 93–6, 100, 128, 140, 179, 185, 204ff, 206–7n, 214, 218n, 234n, 249, 253, 254n, 269, 291
Jansenists, 152
Junius, Letters of, 150n, 191n
Justice, in Hume, 54, 60, 68ff, 78f, 85f, 89; as 'peace and liberty', 96; as 'peace and order', 153, 175; a matter of social progress in Hume, 79f, 296; origin of in Hume and Cumberland, 26; Dudgeon and 81ff; *see also* Natural Law

'King's Friends', 126, 130ff, 134f, 191

Lancastrian kings, Hume and, 268f
Law, absolute in England, 167f, 170, 186f, 191, 277, 279, 283; making of, 316, 320; origin of in republics, 155, 318; rule of in absolute monarchies, 156f, 159
Legislators, 229, 308, 316f, 319
Letter from a By-Stander (1741-2), 207, 212
Letter from a Gentleman in Worcestershire (1727), 212
liberty, 'civil' and 'political', not distinguished in vulgar Whiggism, 143; in Hutcheson, 161f; Rutherforth, 162–5; Montesquieu, 165f; Dugald Stewart, 166f; Hume, 153 *et seq.*, 160f, 297f, 309f
liberty and authority, 190ff, 282
and progress of society, 297 *et seq*
new plan of, 276ff, 282f
an untried experiment, 283, 294
European context in Hume, 140f, 158n, 297f, 305
and faction (Bolingbroke), 199
of the press, 185f, 188, 213
liberty and necessity, 115f
Long Parliament, 275n, 282
London, City of, 321

INDEX OF SUBJECTS

London Journal, 148, 208n, 211, 213n, 214n, 215, 218, 233, 243, 246f, 249
London Magazine, 162
Lowland outlook, Hume's, 87, 110n, 300

Machiavellian moralism, 224f; *see also* corruption
Magna Carta, 239f, 242f, 248ff, 252, 258, 270; Hume and, 266, 268, 276ff, 303ff, 312
malcontents, 266; *see also* Jacobites
method, *a posteriori* and *a priori*, 18f, 21; inductive in morals, Hutcheson, 32 *et seq.*; Hume, 3, 8f, 16, 59 *et seq.*, 63f
middling rank, 94, 176-9, 257, 276, 280, 296, 300, 310, 315
militia, 211-12
moderation, political, 91, 194, 219 *et seq.*, 309, lessons in, 181, 221, 265, 285, 326; political science and, 221ff.; progress of society and, 292, 299 *et seq.*, 309
monarchy, absolute, 166, 187, 197n, similarity to republics, 169f; Hutcheson and, 161f; tendency in England towards, 180f, 211; *see also* 'vulgar Whiggism' and 'civilized monarchies'; mixed monarchy, 170f, 287; and parties, 185f; resistance in, 93, 97–101, 153
Monthly Review, 302n, 314n
morality, ground of, 15, 109f
Mortmain Act, 177n

National Debt, 126f, 173ff, 179f, 187, 210
Natural Law, Modern School of, 3 *et seq.*; theological ground of, 41 *et seq.*; 'empirical' derivation of in Turnbull, 3-6; Grotius, 6, 18; Pufendorf, 6f, 21f; Cumberland, 18-23, 42; Hutcheson, 32 *et seq.*; social evolution and, 28f; obligation, problem of, 42 *et seq.*; human nature as a 'system', 48, 60, 63, 85; the Great Society, 48 *et seq.*; Society and Justice, two levels of meaning, 51-5, 77; sociability, principle of, 50ff; state of nature a social state, 72f; laws absolute and hypothetical, 55
Hume's empirical and secular version, 68 *et seq.*, 91
Natural Law used by Ministerialist writers and attacked by Opposition journalists, 195

natural religion, Hume and, 62
necessity, Hume on, 115f
Newcastle Journal, 221n
Norman Conquest, 225f, 238f, 242, 252, 259; Hume and, 267f, 302f, 306
Norman Yoke, 241, 246, 252 (Blackstone), 257 (Guthrie)
novelty, force of, 210, 310
'Newtonian', 'Newtonians', 3, 5, 8f, 16f, 59, 63f, 83, 84n, 86, 104, 106, 140

Oceana, 183, 241
opinion, 91f, 320
opposition, parliamentary, 128, 191, 214n
Old Whig, 214-15 n
original contract, in Hume, 76; *see also* contract

Pandects, 315
passive obedience, 92, 98, 214
Parliamentary History, 218n
Parties, political, as necessary evil, 135, 184ff, 294; court and country 'natural', 135, 185f, 202; 214, Hume's analysis of Whig and Tory parties, 201 *et seq.*, of behaviour of party men, 219f; and coalition of parties, 205f, 265ff; and extinction of Whig and Tory parties, 128f; 'personal' and 'real' parties, 185; Rapin and, 234 *et seq.*; origin of Whig and Tory parties in Rapin, 237, Bolingbroke, 200f, Hume, 261f, 284
Peasants Revolt (1381), 189n
pendulum, historical, 315f
people, the, 178, 243, 310; historical role of in Hume, 319f
pessimism, Hume's, 135f, 225
Petition of Right, 256, 278, 299
piety, in Hutcheson, 56f, 69
politics, Hume's three phases, as seen in his Letters, 127–34; his friends and connections, 132ff; Westminster politics a 'whirl', 137; Hume's detachment, 138f
political obligation, 12f, 95, 100; Hume's theory applied to English Civil War, 271 *et seq.*
Porteous riots, 94
prerogative, royal, problem of, 214; of Stuart kings in Hume, 269f, 272, 278, 281, 285, 287, 325f
Presbyterians, 235, 237
Presbyterian Whigs in Scotland, 94

INDEX OF SUBJECTS

prescription, Kames on, 14, 244n
prime ministers and civilized monarchy, 160
Principia (Newton's), 3
progress of civilization, Hume's belief in, 87f, 187, 279, 286; role of government, 322
progress of society, in Hume's *History*, 297 *et seq.*, 301f, 306, 309, 313ff, 318f; in ministerialist writers, 217f
promise, institution of, 26f, 54f, 78, 86f
Proper Answer to the By-Stander (1742), 208n
property, Kames and, 14f, Grotius, 23, 27, 55; Cumberland, 24ff, 49f; Pufendorf, 27f; Hutcheson, 34–7; Hume, 24, 26f, 86; rules determining, 9–12, 95
Puritans, 235, 237, 246; and liberty, 264f, 269, 310; Hume and 'political' puritans, 275f

republican government, Hume and, 168, 182f
republics, origin of, in Hume, 318; infallibly give rise to law, 155
Reformation in Scotland, Hume on, 287n, 292
Reformation, Hume and the, 316
Renaissance, Hume and the, 315–16
Revival of Letters, 279–80
religion, Hume and, 59, 61ff, 134; in England, Hume on, 65, 92, 223n; absence of in Hume's political philosophy, 65 *et seq.*; effect on contract theory, 66f; natural history of, 318f
resistance, right of, 12f, 92ff, 96–101; Hutcheson and, 92; in ministerialist writers, 217; Hume's two doctrines, 100f; applied in the *History*, 271 *etseq.*
Restoration (1660), 244, 247, 295
Revolution of 1688, Hume and, 96ff, 100f, 139, 141f, 168, 203f, 278, 290f, 320; Bolingbroke and, 198f, 200, 207, 242, 244
rights, Hume and, 88f; natural and adventitious, 84; Hutcheson and, 34 *et seq.*
Rockingham ministry, 131; party, 131ff, 138
Roman commonwealth, Bolingbroke and, 196f

Roman law, 11f, 17n, 140, 296, 315
Roman republic, downfall of, 228
Roundhead and Cavalier parties, 321

Sacheverell Trial, 97, 145
science of man, Hume's, two phases of, 104, 119
Scots Magazine, 162n, 179n, 221n
selfish system (of ethics), 80
self-preservation, 49f, 86
self-value or 'pride', 107
Septennial Act, debate to repeal (1734), 218n
ship money, 274
society, Hume's exclusively sociological idea of, 78ff
sociological realism in Hume, 71f, 75
sociological relativism in Hume, 115, 117
Sparta, 317
Spectator, 145, 219
Stage Licensing Act (1737), 183n
Stamp Act, repeal of, 130f
standing army, 127n, 129, 159n, 172, 211f
Star Chamber, 279
states, 'natural' and 'adventitious', 33
state of nature, 53, 72, Hume and, 70, 73, 78, 322f
stockjobbing, Hume and, 126f, 174
Stoics, 48
superstition and enthusiasm, 202, 214f
sympathy, 15, 105f, 319
Swiss cantons, 284n

Triennial Bill, 127n, 213, 278, 283n
Tudor monarchy, 172, 258, 260, 267, 268ff, 277, 293, 326

United Provinces, *see* Holland
utility and moral judgements, 107, 110f
Utrecht, Peace of, 193

Vicar of Wakefield, 178n

Walpole's administration, 193, 285,
Wareham election, 127
Wealth of Nations, 312
Witan, 241, 301f
Whiggism, vulgar, 143 *et seq.*; in Hume, 150 *et seq.*, 303; 'plaguy prejudices of', 129f

338

Printed in Great Britain
by Amazon